The Arkansas Delta

The Arkansas Delta

LAND OF PARADOX

Edited by
JEANNIE WHAYNE
and
WILLARD B. GATEWOOD

THE UNIVERSITY OF ARKANSAS PRESS
FAYETTEVILLE   1993

Copyright 1993 by Jeannie Whayne and Willard B. Gatewood

All rights reserved
Manufactured in the United States of America

00 99 98 97 96   5 4 3 2 1   .

First paperback printing 1996

Designed by Alice Gail Carter

⊛ The paper used in this publication meets the minimum
requirements of the American National Standard for Perma-
nence of Paper for Printed Library Materials   Z39.48-1984.

Library of Congress Cataloging-in-Publication Data

The Arkansas Delta: land of paradox / edited by Jeannie Whayne
    and Willard B. Gatewood.
        p.   cm.
    Includes bibliographical references and index.
    ISBN 1-55728-287-0 (alk. paper)
    ISBN 1-55728-465-2 (pbk.: alk. paper)
        1. Arkansas Delta (Ark.)—History.   I. Whayne, Jeannie M.
II. Gatewood, Willard B.
F417.A67A75   1993
976.7'8—dc20   92-43140
                                          CIP

Contents

Contributors

MORRIS S. ARNOLD, United States Circuit Judge for the Eighth Circuit, holds engineering and law degrees from the University of Arkansas, Fayetteville, and graduate degrees in legal history from Harvard University. He is the author of eight books and numerous articles, including *Colonial Arkansas 1686–1804: A Social and Cultural History* (1991).

THOMAS FOTI is chief of Research and Plant Community Ecology of the Arkansas Natural Heritage Commission. The author of numerous scientific and technical papers, he has also published popular articles in newspapers and magazines. His *Arkansas and the Land* appeared in 1992.

WILLARD B. GATEWOOD, Alumni Distinguished Professor of History at the University of Arkansas, Fayetteville, is the author and editor of ten books, including *The Governors of Arkansas*. He is currently engaged in research on a wealthy slaveowner and planter in the Arkansas Delta.

BYRD GIBBENS, associate professor of English at the University of Arkansas at Little Rock, is the author of *This is a Strange Country: Letters of a Westering Family 1880–1906* (1988) and co-author of *Far From Home: Families of the Westward Journey* (1989).

FON LOUISE GORDON, assistant professor of history at the University of Kentucky, is the author of articles and papers dealing with various aspects of African-American life and history. She is currently preparing a book-length study of black Arkansans between 1880 and 1920.

DONALD HOLLEY, professor of history at the University of Arkansas at Monticello, is the author of *Uncle Sam's Farmers:*

The New Deal Communities in the Lower Mississippi Valley. A specialist in agricultural history, he is currently engaged in research on the transformation from sharecropping to mechanization in cotton culture and its impact on Arkansas.

KENNETH R. HUBBELL was the first director of the Delta Cultural Center in Helena, Arkansas, and currently directs the Delta Center Foundation. He was the coordinator of and a major contributor to *Persistence of the Spirit: The Black Experience* and *The Arkansas Delta: A Historical Look at Our Land and Our People* (1990).

CARL MONEYHON, professor of history at the University of Arkansas at Little Rock, is the author and editor of numerous works, including *A Documentary History of Arkansas* (1984). His forthcoming book focuses on the impact of the Civil War and Reconstruction on Arkansas from 1850 to 1874.

ELIZABETH ANNE PAYNE, associate professor of history at the University of Arkansas, Fayetteville, is the author of *Reform, Labor and Feminism: Margaret Dreier Robbins and the Trade Union League* (1988). She is currently engaged in research on the Southern Tenant Farmers' Union.

BOBBY ROBERTS, historian and director of the Central Arkansas Library System, is the author of several historical articles and the co-author of three books on the Civil War, including one on the Civil War in Arkansas. He is currently engaged in research on the Civil War in the Confederate states.

JEANNIE WHAYNE, assistant professor of history at the University of Arkansas, Fayetteville, and editor of the *Arkansas Historical Quarterly*, has written extensively on the Arkansas Delta, including articles in *Agricultural History* and *Forest and Conservation History*. She is currently completing a book-length study on the evolution of the plantation system in Poinsett County (Arkansas) between 1900 and 1970 and editing a volume on the history of an Arkansas plantation between 1830 and 1950.

Preface

JEANNIE WHAYNE

Historians of the South have, with few exceptions, subjected the state of Arkansas to little systematic analysis and have generally neglected to integrate the history of the Arkansas Delta in particular into the context of Southern history. Too often when historians think of the Mississippi Delta, they think of it in terms of the states of Mississippi and Louisiana only. No doubt the problem rests not so much with professional historians themselves as with the place Arkansas occupies in the historical process. Late arriving on the stage of Southern history, its role has been obscured by the pre-eminence of the older South and subordinated to the dramatic and highly visible character of other frontier states such as Mississippi, Louisiana, and even Texas. This failure to incorporate Arkansas into the study of the Southern frontier, however, distorts the history of the region and prevents a more complete understanding of the forces that helped to define the South.

As Willard Gatewood asserts in his introduction, the Arkansas Delta is a microcosm of the Southern experience. It epitomizes the tensions "between man and the physical environment, between blacks and whites, between rich and poor." By the time of the outbreak of the Civil War, Arkansas "already mirrored those traits associated with a distinctive South." Historians still debate what makes the South distinctive, but they usually include in their analyses a compendium of conditions and ideas, conditions and ideas that were particularly prevalent in the Arkansas Delta.

At the same time, however, Gatewood defines the Arkansas Delta as "a land of paradox," a characterization echoed by several of the contributors to this volume. Thomas Foti outlines the "gifts and curses" of the state's rivers and depicts the capriciousness of life in the Arkansas Delta is dramatically depicted. While the rivers helped to create some of the richest soil in the nation and provided the waterways necessary to commerce, they also brought flood, disaster, and devastation. Morris S. Arnold, meanwhile, demonstrates that although the Arkansas Delta promised boundless opportunity in the colonial era, the legacy of that era was one of chronic poverty and unrealized dreams. As Bobby Roberts suggests in his treatment of the Civil War, Arkansas's experience then conjoined with that of the rest of the South as "desolation itself" visited the entire region.

The Civil War experience illustrates that paradox was not something unique to Arkansas, and the contribution by Fon Gordon brings to the fore the theme initiated by Arnold, that of unrealized dreams. Blacks in the Arkansas Delta during the antebellum era experienced greater difficulties than elsewhere since "slavery was harsher in the Arkansas Delta than in the older states because of its rural isolation and frontier conditions." After the Civil War, blacks mistakenly considered Arkansas a "land of opportunity," but were soon disappointed as disfranchisement and segregation took hold there as it did in the entire region.

Just as blacks learned that Arkansas was not the "promised land" in the post–Civil War era, women learned the harsh reality of life in a frontier state. Perhaps nothing more poignantly epitomizes the "juxtaposition of joy and dread" that was a woman's lot in the Arkansas Delta, especially in the antebellum era, than the experience Elizabeth Anne Payne writes about in her contribution to this volume. Payne writes movingly of Mary Edmondson's encounter with both life and death on the same day. The birth of one child was accompanied by the death of another. While women everywhere faced the same juxtaposition, it was almost certainly more frequently encountered in the disease-ridden Delta, where malaria, swamp fever, and other ailments were especially common.

But blacks and women did not always retreat from the challenges of the Arkansas Delta. When disfranchisement and segregation threatened them, blacks banded together in self-help groups and created their own clubs and organizations that gave them sustenance and provided them with a bulwark against an unfriendly environment. While middle-class blacks relied on these more conservative responses to the challenges they faced, poorer blacks organized themselves in more radical ways, and, as in the case of the Farmers and Laborers Household Union of Phillips County in 1919, paid an enormous price for doing so. Significantly, however, by the time of the New Deal, poor blacks organized alongside poor whites to confront federal programs that threatened to displace them. Poor women, both black and white, played an important role in the functioning of this latter organization. Middle-class women, meanwhile, like middle-class blacks, responded to their environment in a more conservative manner, forming organizations that bettered the conditions of their communities at the same time that they provided a means of expression for the women involved.

Foreign settlers to Arkansas faced the same problems that all newcomers encountered, but like women and blacks, these "strangers in the Arkansas Delta" had special problems associated with their peculiar nationalities and ethnic origins. Byrd Gibbens demonstrates that "their stories illustrate ingenuity, resilience, determination, anguish, hope, and humor." Jews and Catholics sometimes encountered religious intolerence in this predominantly Protestant culture. Some nationalities, however, assimilated or found acceptance more readily than others. German and Irish settlers, for example, adapted and were more easily integrated than were eastern Europeans, the Chinese, and Italians, who were often considered a "third race." Gibbens demonstrates, however, that whether they found acceptance or intolerance, foreign settlers often exercised an influence in the Arkansas Delta disproportionate to their numbers.

One of the ways that these ethnic groups and nationalities stood out was in their social customs. Dancing and drinking were far more accepted among the Irish and Italians than among the evangelical Protestants surrounding them. But social life in the Arkansas Delta among the dominant culture was not without its own attractions. Here again, we find the theme of paradox emerging almost full force. As Ken Hubbell asserts in his contribution, this "sportsman's paradise" was "characterized by both abundance and limitation." And people found many ways to cope with the harshness of their environment. Wild meats, fish, and vegetables supplemented their diets, and local plants and foods often promoted healing. Folk medicine developed into an art. While they used the existing environment on the one hand to cope, they created clubs and organizations and enjoyed outside attractions such as circuses and traveling theater troupes. National holidays were occasions that bound together the family and the community, and religious services not only cemented their relationship to God, but also provided a social space within which they could relate. Hubbell concludes with the observation that the inhabitants of the Arkansas Delta had a "sharpened appreciation of fate and chance because of dependence on the land and rivers," and this contributed to their appreciation, on the part of some at least, for games of chance; games of chance were often accompanied by an abundant supply of moonshine whiskey, brewed and bottled in the Arkansas Delta.

Some Delta towns became notorious for both liquor and gambling, and all Delta towns served as focal points for the country people who flocked to them on Saturdays to trade or seek entertainment. Carl Moneyhon underscores the pivotal role that Delta towns played until the transformation of agriculture that took place after World War II brought decline and stagnation to many of these formerly dynamic and thriving towns. Donald Holley, in his treatment of the plantation heritage, details this transformation at the same time that he drives home the paradoxical nature of the Arkansas Delta. Perhaps nothing more clearly and unequivocally proves the Arkansas Delta's intimate connection to the rest of the South than its agricultural history. According to Holley, "the Delta has always meant rich land and poor people." Holley concludes that Arkansas's "agricultural legacy of wealth and poverty, of privilege and exploitation, still hangs over the region's future." This observation of Holley's is as true of much of the rest of South as it is of Arkansas.

This work does not purport to be a comprehensive treatment of the Arkansas Delta, but rather focuses on special topics, special topics that match the particular research interests of the contributors, many of whom are at work on larger studies that deal more intensely with the topics under discussion. We hope that their insights will stimulate interest and additional research and prompt more historians of the South to integrate the Arkansas Delta into the larger picture of the region.

A number of individuals and institutions have contributed significantly to the creation of this volume. The editors and authors would like to thank Andrea Cantrell and the staff of the Special Collections Division of Mullins Library at the University of Arkansas for their tireless efforts in retrieving documents and locating suitable photographs. Russell Baker and the staff of the History Commission performed similar and equally valuable services. Robert Pugh, a native of the Arkansas Delta, provided rich insights into the contemporary Delta. Kenneth Hubbell, beyond his essay and at least partly through the auspices of the Delta Cultural Center in Helena and the National Endowment for the Humanities, supported the effort in many important ways. Certain individuals in Mississippi County contributed interviews and photographs: Dr. Eldon Fairley, mayor Dickie Kennemore of Osceola, and attorney Oscar Fendler. Judge Steve Ryan of Harrisburg, in Poinsett County, was generously forthcoming and helpful, and Mary Ann Ritter Arnold of E. Ritter and Company in Marked Tree provided both insights and photographs. Gary Shepherd, of the University of Arkansas's Media Services, skillfully turned those photographs and negatives into suitable form for this volume. While Johnthy Williams and Fletcher Smith provided essential research assistance, Mary Kirkpatrick, secretary in the department of history at the University of Arkansas, worked endlessly on typing the manuscript. Finally, Pete Daniel, one of the few historians of the South to treat the Arkansas Delta seriously, has advised and assisted us in innumerable ways.

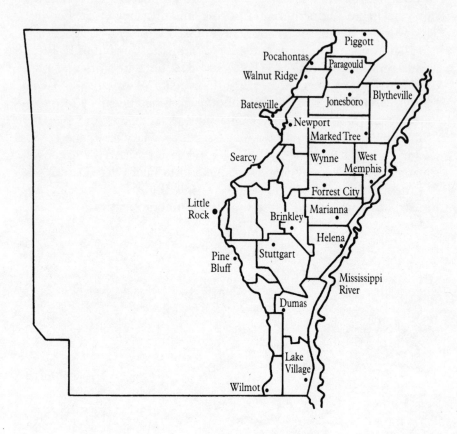

Piggott

Pocahontas

Paragould

Walnut Ridge

Batesville

Jonesboro

Blytheville

Newport

Marked Tree

Searcy

Wynne

West Memphis

Little Rock

Forrest City

Brinkley

Marianna

Helena

Pine Bluff

Stuttgart

Mississippi River

Dumas

Lake Village

Wilmot

The Arkansas Delta

The Arkansas Delta:
The Deepest of the Deep South

WILLARD B. GATEWOOD

Visitors to the Arkansas Delta, especially the area closest to the Mississippi River, are likely to be impressed by its "horizontalness." Bereft of its once dense forests, the land has been cleared and drained to such an extent, according to one observer, "that the horizon is just an ambiguous seam along which the earth and ether meld."[1] This flat, stark land of pushed-back horizons is crisscrossed by drainage ditches and dotted with small towns and communities that often exhibit abundant evidence of decline. The horizontalness of the landscape is interrupted only by rows of utility poles, occasional towering grain and rice elevators, and the scattered remains of the region's once magnificent forests. Shacks that formerly housed tenants and sharecroppers have either disappeared or have been abandoned. Few laborers remain in the vast cotton, soybean, and rice fields except those who operate costly, complicated farm machinery. The most ubiquitous symbol of machine labor that has replaced human labor is the large tractor, whose operator, having consulted computer printouts, climbs into an air-conditioned cab replete with stereophonic equipment. The cost of a single tractor in 1993 may well exceed the net worth of a wealthy Delta planter of a half-century earlier, but it plants, plows, chops, and harvests faster and more efficiently than the hand labor of dozens of farm workers.

The portion of the Mississippi Alluvial Plain in Arkansas, universally known as the Delta, encompasses ten million acres of land and a third of the seventy-five counties in the state. One of six natural subregions in Arkansas as defined by topography, climate, and vegetation,[2] the alluvial plain stretches from Eudora in the south to Blytheville in the north and as far west as Little Rock. Often stereotyped as flat and monotonous, despite considerable topographical diversity, the Delta is a land of fickle rivers meandering southward, notably the Mississippi, the Arkansas, the White, and the St. Francis, that have shaped both the physical environment and the culture of the area. Over time the rivers have created a mosaic of basins, prairies, lowlands, and ridges and have bestowed upon the region oxbow lakes, bayous, and swamps as well as some of the richest soil in the world. This soil, coupled with a benign climate, has nurtured lush natural vegetation, majestic forests, and bountiful harvests of cotton, corn, rice, and soybeans. But the area, similar in some respects to alluvial plains in other parts of the world, remains a land of paradox—a land that harbors human misery and poverty in an environment richly endowed by nature.

The first Europeans to enter the Arkansas Delta encountered the original Americans, the Indians, who, over thousands of years, had evolved a complex society in the region. They organized towns, domesticated native plants, engaged in agriculture, created extensive trade networks, and established fishing and hunting patterns that persisted long after the demise of Indian civilization. Europeans profited by the Indians' experience, settlement patterns, trails, and hospitality as they explored and colonized the area. That so little remained of the once-thriving Indian societies by the early nineteenth century was graphic testimony of the degree to which the Delta's earliest inhabitants fell victim to forces from another civilization.[3]

The first European settlement in the Arkansas Delta and indeed west of the Mississippi was Arkansas Post, established in 1686 by the Frenchman Henri de Tonty and located near the mouth of the Arkansas River. During the next 117 years, sovereignty over the area passed from France, briefly to Spain, and back again to France. Throughout, Arkansas Post remained a remote, imperial outpost, an *entrepôt* for travelers on the Mississippi. Plagued by floods and hostile Indians, the settlement failed to establish a stable agricultural community and never contained more than a minuscule European population, which consisted largely of "*voyageurs* and *coureurs de bois*" whose attachment to European civilization was "extremely tenuous at best." Not surprising, then, a rapid and "total substitution of cultures" followed the purchase by the United States in 1803 of the vast Louisiana territory of which Arkansas was a part.[4]

The Arkansas Delta, though still a frontier society at the outbreak of the Civil War, already mirrored those traits associated with a distinctive South, an idea as enduring as it is elusive. Although there have been and are "many Souths," the concept of "one South," of a region sharply differentiated from the rest of the nation, has tenaciously persisted. Some have located the source of Southern exceptionalism in the region's "climate, soil and productions," and others are no less certain that it is found in the South's ruralism, race relations, folk culture, evangelical Protestantism, penchant for violence, collective historical experience, or a combination of these. Still others suggest that the South is "pure America" and what is taken for distinctiveness is nothing more than the degree to which the region exhibits, in exaggerated form, national flaws such as racism, xenophobia, and violence. To an extraordinary degree, the Arkansas Delta represents in microcosm the distinctive environment, behavior, and historical experience of the South. In few other areas have the tensions characteristic of southern society been more obvious than in the Arkansas Delta. These tensions have manifested themselves in various ways—between man and the physical environment, between whites and blacks, between rich and poor.[5]

The peculiar physical environment of the Delta shaped a society, economy, and culture easily distinguishable from those in other sections of Arkansas. The same waterways that enriched the land and served as the principal arteries of commerce and travel prior to railroads and motor transportation also inhibited settlement, produced isolation and disease, and regularly wreaked devastation. Riverfront towns routinely experienced cave-ins that swallowed up streets and buildings; in certain instances entire towns disappeared into the water.

The rivers and streams were never far from the center of Delta consciousness. The departure and arrival of boats, often laden with bales of cotton or crowded with travelers bound for Memphis, New Orleans, Arkansas City, or Pine Bluff, were newsworthy events. But if the ubiquitous streams served as the umbilical cords of the region, their presence possessed a "patina of terror" for residents who were only too well aware of the destruction that floods and overflows could create. Delta residents wrote at length about rising waters, levee breaks, and floods that periodically destroyed their crops, damaged their homes, drowned neighbors or relatives, and cut off all connection with the outside world. Rampaging floods that inundated entire counties, causing staggering economic losses, numerous deaths, and indescribable human suffering, occurred with sufficient regularity to remind Delta people how quickly their beneficent rivers could be transformed into sources of torment and affliction. Few public issues attracted so much attention or generated so much controversy as the efforts either to reclaim old land or to claim new land from the omnipresent streams, swamps, and bayous. Fully aware that their livelihood and even their lives were at the mercy of the rivers' vagaries, Delta residents devoted much time and energy to drainage and levee construction.[6]

The same rivers and bottomlands that nourished the Delta's economy jeopardized public health. Malaria was a constant threat to inhabitants, while contaminated water supplies, worsened by frequent floods, accelerated the spread of cholera and dysentery. In 1862, a writer characterized the Delta as a "vile" place where even the snakes had chills. As late as the twentieth century, an official of the Rockefeller-sponsored Sanitary Commission referred to malaria and hookworm as "the twin sisters of wretchedness" in the area.[7] Throughout the year Delta inhabitants consumed large quantities of folk remedies and patent medicines for ailments that they variously referred to as "the chills," ague, and swamp fever.[8]

In addition to the fertile soil traversed by numerous rivers and small streams, the Arkansas Delta possessed a climate that shaped its economy as well as the mores and behavior of its inhabitants. In few other respects did the Delta conform more precisely to the stereotyped view of the South, a region traditionally known as "sunny" and more recently as the "sunbelt." Studies demonstrate that heat and cold have direct physiological and psychological effects on human beings that can increase or decrease their energy, efficiency, alertness, appetite, and assertiveness. Endowed with a relatively warm, humid climate, the Delta possesses a long growing season that has simultaneously contributed to high agricultural production and to the growth of microbes, insects, and parasites that either cause or transmit diseases.[9] Delta author Alice French detected a direct link between the climate and the personal qualities of Delta people, whom she described as hot-headed but hospitable, not particularly ambitious but careful to "enjoy small pleasures" and "do small courtesies," and honest and kindly but "unhasty." Such qualities, French noted, "seem to harmonize with the climate."[10]

The climate, along with the constant threat of disease, the frequent visit of death, especially upon children, and the isolation that characterized rural life in the Delta, conspired to make the area especially forbidding to women. Few women in the Arkansas Delta conformed to the later stereotype of the "Southern lady"—a magnolia madonna noted for her delicacy, leisure, and frilly femininity. By 1850 a few wealthy planters' wives undoubtedly did resemble the image; Mrs. Isaac Hilliard of Chicot County, for example, fretted over the damage done by dampness to her "books, piano, furniture [and] silks" and visited New Orleans to shop and attend a succession of balls and parties.[11]

Most Delta women, however, possessed no piano or fine furniture, and their worries over dampness were more likely to concern family health. Even fewer traveled to New Orleans or anywhere else outside the immediate vicinity of their isolated homes. For women, life in the Delta was a life of work. Giving birth every two or three years themselves, women also served as midwives, tended the sick and dying, and mourned the frequent loss of their own children and those of friends. A Delta resident, in commenting on the life of women there in the 1890s, observed: "They age early and die when under happier chances, they would be in their prime." Despite the toll taken by hard work, frequent childbirth, and disease, Delta women managed to enjoy "the small pleasures" and to perform "the small courtesies," especially with other women with whom they exchanged visits and to whom they looked for support and nurture.[12]

While the home remained the focus of women's lives even after the Delta wilderness gave way to a network of villages and a series of bustling towns, their domestic concerns inspired and shaped their civic efforts. In the post–Civil War decades, Delta women, both white and black, formed organizations that promoted self-culture, temperance, community beautification, and hospital, school, and library construction. Typical of such organizations among white women were the Marianna Self-Culture Club and the Mothers' Half Hour Club in Pine Bluff. Described as the "banner club town" in 1900, Helena was the home of Pacaha Club, a women's organization that sponsored a wide variety of civic and child-oriented activities. The Ladies' Aid Society in Osceola, organized in 1882, raised sufficient funds to construct a "hall" that functioned as a community center.[13] In the 1930s the wives of sharecroppers, of both races, joined their husbands in launching the Southern Tenant Farmers' Union, an organization dedicated to advancing the economic welfare and protecting the legal rights of the Delta's most disadvantaged citizens.[14] Individual women, on occasion, mounted campaigns that brought about changes. Among these was a female resident of

Osceola who, concerned about dogs urinating on fresh vegetables displayed in front of stores in the town, succeeded in having grocers place such wares "above the high water mark."[15]

In ethnic composition, no less than in climate, the Arkansas Delta serves as an exaggerated version of an exceptional South. In comparison to the rest of the nation, the South historically has been classified as the most homogeneous in population. Arkansas exhibited even more ethnic homogeneity than other states in the South. Although the state attracted relatively few of the so-called "New Immigrants" from southern and southeastern Europe in the late nineteenth and early twentieth centuries, its population was not without ethnic diversity. Dominated by those of British and African ancestry, Arkansas and especially its Delta counties also included French, German, Swiss, Italian, Slovak, Russian, and Chinese citizens, whose contributions to the economy and culture were disproportionate to their numbers. Beginning in the late nineteenth century, county immigration societies organized to attract industrious settlers to take advantage of the Delta's fertile but cheap land, abundant water, and "inexhaustible" hardwood timber.[16] "We cordially invite immigration to our section," the *Arkansas City Journal* editorialized in 1895.[17] In spite of all the immigration publicity generated principally by railroads and chambers of commerce, the cordial invitation was extended only to those considered of the "right kind," especially those who were "prosperous, frugal, thrifty and sturdy." Those from southern and eastern Europe were unwelcome because they were viewed as constituting the "criminal pauper immigration" whose numbers included many "antagonistic to every principle sacred to American citizenship."[18]

Contrary to the image of the Arkansas Delta as a land devoted to cotton culture from the demise of Indian civilization on, its earliest European and American inhabitants were primarily hunters, fishermen, and trappers rather than farmers. To borrow a concept from Walter Webb,[19] these early white settlers were recipients of the "primary windfalls," the first easy pickings that required relatively little investment of either time or energy. The trans-Mississippi frontier abounded in wild game and fur-bearing animals. Its numerous streams yielded a plentiful supply of fish and water fowl. Convinced that these "primary windfalls" were inexhaustible, the early Delta inhabitants saw little need for restraint in exploiting and consuming the natural abundance of their environment. Even more damaging to the land than this initial waste was the encroachment of those concerned with the "secondary windfalls": the lumber and agricultural interests cut the virgin forests and cleared and drained the land for cotton culture. Deforestation and the emergence of a single-crop economy following the Civil War meant the gradual disappearance of "the paradise terrestrial"[20] of the Arkansas Delta and with it the way of life it afforded.

When in 1836, the year of Arkansas's admission to the Union, Albert Pike observed that the new state "bore but a poor character abroad,"[21] he was referring primarily to a reputation that emphasized Arkansans' inclination for violence and lawlessness. A substantial portion of the state's reputation for banditry and brutality emanated from the Delta, suggesting, again, how closely that region conformed to the stereotypical view of the South as the most violent region of the country. An early foreign visitor to Arkansas obviously exaggerated when he claimed that the state had more violence "than ten other states put together." But as late as 1880, a resident of Pine Bluff lamented that so little was being done "to put a stop to the frequent murders we hear of in this section now almost daily."[22] The common practice of "pistol-toting" ultimately aroused sufficient opposition to have it outlawed. Alice French, who on occasion defended Arkansas against what she interpreted as an unjustified reputation for lawlessness and crime, nonetheless admitted that the state unfortunately was a "refuge for human failures of all kinds," and criminals often escaped trial "due largely to the costliness of convictions and the poverty of the state."[23] The number of well-publicized duels, lynchings, peonage investigations, prison and chain gang exposés, and incidents of nightriding and whitecapping, as well as homicide statistics during the century after the Civil War, only embellished the Delta's reputation for lawlessness, crime, and violence.

Notwithstanding its reputation for violence and bloodshed, the Arkansas Delta, according to many if not most observers, was inhabited by "social souls" who were "kindly affectioned one to another" and none more so than those "with black skins."[24] "We are a sociable, hospitable and congenial people," a Delta resident boasted in 1890.[25] Visiting was a significant part of their social lives; whole families, including their several dogs, regularly descended upon one another. Sometimes, especially on Sundays, such visits lasted an entire day. Gathering at the store or post office was a ritual for those who lived in or near towns and villages; men in particular congregated at taverns for lengthy sessions of "conversing and expectorating with slow zest" and for satisfying their thirst for strong drink. Their broad, rich, and gentle humor, occasionally colored by a penchant for the grotesque that one observer explained as the "product of the fervid sun," prompted frequent outbursts of laughter.[26]

The Delta's biracial and hierarchial society shaped its organized social life in the post–Civil War era. Racial mores precluded the social mingling of blacks and whites; therefore, each race had its own churches, entertainments, clubs, and fraternal orders. Organized social activities, of course, were more numerous and variegated in towns than in rural areas. Universally popular among town and rural residents alike were picnics, barbecues, fish frys, baseball games, and bicycle races. By the end of the nineteenth century, several baseball leagues existed in the Delta. Rivalry between them was intense, and local newspapers provided extensive coverage of games.[27]

Accompanying the growth of towns in the Delta was a proliferation of social organizations composed of what local editors referred to as "our best people." Such organizations defined the class hierarchy in the Delta. Among the annual social events organized by the Delta's white elite were the Mardi Gras celebrations begun in the late nineteenth century and patterned after the one in New Orleans that traditionally had attracted sizable contingents of Delta planters and their families. Little Rock sponsored its first Mardi Gras in 1875; it was followed several years later by Pine Bluff, Osceola, and other Delta towns. While a town's "most prominent ladies and gentlemen" were present at the round of parties and balls held in connection with Mardi Gras, less-affluent residents held their own separate celebrations, usually in local saloons.[28]

Hunting and fishing have persisted as principal forms of recreation in the Delta. Hunting, in particular, has been and remains largely the preserve of men. Historically, learning to hunt constituted an important part of the initiation of boys into manhood. Sportsmen of all ages attached significance to the quantity of game and fish they shot, trapped, and caught. Blacks and whites often hunted together, but whether blacks served as guides or merely as companions, their place in the field with whites was rarely any more one of equality than their place in society. Because of its bountiful supply of wild animals, fish, and game, the Delta acquired an enviable reputation among sportsmen throughout the nation. In time the region became dotted with hunting and fishing camps where men, freed from the constraints of "female-centered evangelical family life," not only engaged in shooting and fishing, but also indulged their appetites for good food, strong drink, and language considered inappropriate for mixed company.[29] In 1879 a six-man hunting party left Pine Bluff accompanied by a large pack of dogs, two wagons, and two buggies. "We presume," an observer noted, "that they were well supplied as we noticed two circular receptacles that certainly never held molasses."[30]

The same society that boasted a reputation for violence and a varied, sometimes bawdy folk culture also manifested a revivalistic, evangelical Protestantism. The Arkansas Delta was even more monolithically Protestant than the South in general. In 1900 Baptists and Methodists were dominant, followed by Presbyterians, Episcopalians, and various other Protestant groups. In eleven Delta counties Baptists of different varieties claimed one-half or more of the church members. Among non-Protestants in the Delta, Roman Catholics were most numerous, especially in places that attracted immigrants. The organization of separate, all-black Baptist and Methodist denominations after the Civil War not only reinforced the evangelical Protestant emphasis of the Delta, but also played an important role in the development of its African-American culture. As in the past, the black church remains a multifunctional institution that continues to serve as a center of social, political, and often economic activities.[31]

While census statistics provide clues about church membership in the Arkansas Delta, they reveal little about the religious values that informed its culture. Delta residents embraced the same or similar theological assumptions as most other southerners—that is, they tended to believe in a Bible-centered faith focusing on human imperfectability and sinfulness, on a God that was "concrete and virile," and on revivalism as the means of achieving individual regeneration. Many undoubtedly equated consensual attitudes with a divinely ordained scheme of things. But if their religion was more adept at fulfilling a social- and cultural-conserving function than a prophetic one—notwithstanding the fact that it could and did on occasion exhibit a prophetic quality—it served its adherents in affirming personal worth, in ordering a chaotic world, and in providing an explanation of social reality.[32]

Life in the Delta, especially in the nineteenth and early twentieth centuries, conformed to the notion advanced by Ted Ownby that two cultures existed side by side in the South: one, an evangelical culture

dominated by women and centered in the home and church, emphasized piety, harmony, and self-control; the other, a masculine culture
of self-indulgence, bravado, and physical competitiveness, manifested
itself in drinking, fighting, gambling, and other forms of male recreation.[33] Private disciplinary actions by churches and pressure applied
by "the best people" managed to curb the most public excesses of
male culture (for a time) and to separate the moral from the immoral.
Ultimately, evangelicals and their allies succeeded in securing legislation that imposed their values on all of society. The result was a proliferation of laws against alcoholic beverages, gambling, "binge"
hunting, and other male pleasures.

The most intense and persistent moral campaign to visit the
Delta was the crusade to ban alcoholic beverages. Supported by
both rural and urban elites, the prohibition movement in the Delta
came to involve questions of public order, social control, morality,
regional racial mores, efficient labor, and election "reform." Until the
twentieth century all forms of alcoholic beverages were readily available to Delta residents at drug and grocery stores as well as at saloons
and grog shops. Prohibitionists emphasized the link between the
"whiskey traffic" and a host of "kindred evils," including rowdyism,
the alarming number of homicides, gambling, disregard for Sabbath
observance, and the fraternization of blacks and poor whites in
saloons.[34] A resident of Frenchman's Bayou in Mississippi County
complained in 1885 that the local saloon was "dealing out its liquid
fire, by the wholesale, about equally and extravagantly patronized by
the whites and sons of Ham" who made "the night hideous with their
howls."[35] The goal of the campaign, spearheaded by the Women's
Christian Temperance Union and a host of other temperance organizations and law-and-order leagues, proved to be difficult to achieve
in the Delta. Under local option arrangements, the numerically superior working classes, both black and white, voted to retain saloons
that were a principal place of recreation—working-class "clubs." As
a result, early in the twentieth century, temperance forces shifted
their strategy from local option to statewide prohibition. Their effort
to impose a legal ban on alcoholic beverages ultimately succeeded,
only to be followed by a proliferation of bootleggers and unlicensed
saloons known as "blind tigers" in the Delta. Throughout the long
campaign against "demon rum," the Delta remained the stronghold
of opposition to temperance and prohibition. Into the 1990s "wet"
counties in Arkansas are concentrated in the region.[36]

In education, no less than in religion, the Arkansas Delta closely resembled the rest of the South. Virtually all statistical indices relating to education have persistently pointed to the Delta's educational deficiencies. Despite the enactment of the Common School Law of 1842, Arkansas lacked a statewide public school system until Reconstruction when the Republican-dominated legislature created a racially segregated, dual system of tax-supported schools. The concept of public education was slow to win the support of Delta whites. In a letter to the *Osceola Times* in 1883, a Delta resident attempted to explain the lack of support for "common schools" when he wrote: "Some of us have regarded it [public school] as a charitable institution imposed upon the taxpayers for the benefit of the poor we always have with us; others because colored people, who lately were listed with our horses and cows as property, share the benefit with the free born; others because the teachers who drift down here are rarely properly trained for the work; and others because no special system of theology is taught. . . ."[37] The meager tax support for public schools in the Delta counties reflected these objections with the result that school terms were brief and schoolhouses grossly inadequate. For example, most of the public schools in Mississippi County closed in mid-November 1889 because "the houses cannot be made comfortable in winter."[38] By 1900 the situation had changed little; in that year official statistics for the amount spent per school-age child in five Delta counties bordering on the Mississippi River ranged from $2.14 in Chicot County to $5.99 in Mississippi County.[39]

The tradition of private education that predominated among antebellum Delta planters persisted well into the twentieth century and contributed significantly to the slow progress of public schools. In 1886 a Chicot County resident observed that whites paid the annual five mill school tax "but never think of it going to educate their own children." Instead, affluent whites built "a little school house in their yard" and employed "a teacher to instruct their children."[40] Reliable statistics about private schools apparently do not exist, but Delta newspapers regularly referred to such institutions. Larger towns often had several private academies or institutes that catered to the more affluent element of the population. Nor was it unusual for villages such as Wynne and Bardstown to have at least one private school.[41] Although the tradition of private education declined as the twentieth century progressed, it was easily revitalized in the wake of the *Brown* decision of 1954. This tradition, coupled with the Delta's racial and class arrangements, insured the perpetuation of high illiteracy rates and a wide educational gulf between the highest and lowest strata within its hierarchial society.

In no way did the Arkansas Delta exhibit characteristics associated with the South more than in matters relating to race. Notwithstanding the significance of other ethnic and racial groups in the Delta, the most numerous and important were white and black Americans, one free and the other slave, both drawn largely from the older southern states. In the soil-rich, swampy frontier of the Arkansas Delta, white masters and black slaves established a plantation system similar, but not identical, to that east of the Mississippi. By the outbreak of the Civil War, much of the primeval wilderness along the Mississippi, Arkansas, White, and St. Francis rivers had been transformed into productive cotton plantations that made the cotton counties among the wealthiest in Arkansas.

From the early nineteenth century on, African Americans, first as slaves and later as free people, were involved in most of the significant concerns of the Arkansas Delta. Understanding the society and culture of the area is impossible without appreciating the interaction between blacks and whites. Despite the fact that the Delta possessed racially separate societies, nowhere else in the nation has there been a more intimate fusion of the European and the African, a mingling that shaped much of the Delta's culture from vocabulary and accent in speech, through foods and cooking, to economy, politics, and music.[42] Referring to the South in general, Wilbur J. Cash remarked that "The Negro entered into the white man as profoundly as the white man entered into the Negro—influencing every gesture, every word, every emotion and idea, every attitude."[43] Cash's observation is peculiarly applicable to the Arkansas Delta, where blacks and whites have lived together, albeit on unequal terms, for almost two centuries. Whatever whites taught blacks, blacks lost something and added something, which they in turn fed back to whites. The result was that "white culture became progressively blacker and black culture progressively whiter."[44]

Slavery in the Arkansas Delta expanded dramatically in the decade immediately prior to the Civil War as land was cleared and cotton farming expanded. By the outbreak of the war, the population of some Delta counties included substantially more blacks than whites. While the number of free blacks in the area was minuscule, there was always a sizeable population of poor, non-slave-owning whites. But the destiny of the Delta lay in the hands of large planters whose land holdings, slaves, and cotton production continually increased, especially in the 1850s. In this dynamic, growth-oriented economy, the relationships between white masters and black slaves were infinitely varied. Although whites considered blacks to be an inferior, childlike people, whites' treatment of their slaves ranged from an affectionate, paternalistic indulgence to outright brutality. Many slaves bore the marks of the dreaded whip for life, and if some expressed affection for "old master" or "old mistress," their recollections of hired overseers were almost universally negative. Among Delta whites of all classes, the notion that productive labor by blacks required at least the threat of physical coercion persisted even after Emancipation.[45] A common complaint by whites in the immediate postwar era was that the legal prohibition against the use of the whip left them without effective means to force freedmen to work.[46]

Within the tightly restricted world of slavery, blacks in the Delta, as elsewhere in the South, underwent acculturation, managed to control important aspects of their lives, and created a subculture that became an important ingredient in the life of the region and the nation. They not only resisted the slave system but also learned to manipulate it, often to the utter frustration of their white masters. In Chicot County in the summer of 1850, the wife of an affluent planter recorded in her diary: "Deplorable state of things here. Negroes are nothing but a tax and annoyance to their owners." So exasperated did a few planters become that they sold out and sought their fortunes in nonslave areas of the country.[47]

In the rush of events that led to the South's departure from the Union, political spokesmen for the Arkansas Delta displayed less ambivalence and uncertainty regarding secession than those from the hill country. The Delta politicians represented those Arkansans whose primary sources of wealth rested on a slave-labor system. Although few planters in the Arkansas Delta displayed their wealth by constructing elaborate mansions as their counterparts did in Louisiana and Mississippi, Arkansans nonetheless shared their values and attached considerable social prestige to slave ownership. In certain Delta counties such as Chicot and Phillips the lifestyles of the wealthiest planters came as near as any in Arkansas to conforming to the romantic images of the Old South. In such counties white planters were among the most vocal in embracing the cause of the Confederacy.[48]

In few areas of the South did residents know the death and destruction of the Civil War more intimately than those in the Arkansas Delta. Its proximity to the Mississippi River, whose control was considered essential by both armies, ensured that the struggle in the area would be bloody and intense. In virtually all parts of the Delta, on rivers as well as on land, the Union and Confederate armies fought battles and skirmishes and staged raids. Foraging parties and plundering expeditions destroyed crops, homes, and civilian lives and confiscated food supplies. A visitor who returned to Chicot County shortly after the war discovered that the plantations around Old River Lake that he remembered as "a continuous garden . . . with elegant houses" were abandoned and grown up in weeds.[49] Confederate soldiers who survived to return to their homes in the Delta found levees broken, bridges destroyed, fields overgrown, family members in abject poverty, and slaves freed.

For many whites in the Arkansas Delta, as for other white southerners, the war and its aftermath constituted a distinctly un-American experience;[50] among a people wedded to invincibility and unending success, they had suffered a resounding defeat. Secession, aborted independence, and military defeat constituted a historical experience that, diverging sharply from that of the rest of the nation, reinforced the region's position as the nation's "largest and oldest counterculture."[51] After the collapse of the Confederacy, those in the Arkansas Delta who had clamored loudest for secession and independent nationhood became active in this counterculture, sharing in and contributing to a regional mythology that served as a mechanism for ordering and making intelligible a world turned upside down. The mythology conjured up images of an idyllic, antebellum past in sharp contrast to the shabby present. For some "unreconstructed" Delta residents, especially those with aristocratic pretensions, references to almost anything in the postwar era prompted them automatically to allude to the idealized period "before the war." When a visitor to the Delta in the 1890s commented on the beauty of the moonlight, her hostess replied: " . . . oh, you should have seen our moonlight before the war."[52]

During the war more than five thousand bondsmen, primarily from the Arkansas Delta, joined the Union army to participate in what, for them, was a war of self-liberation. As soldiers, many secured the rudiments of education in regimental schools, and through travels and experiences denied them as slaves, acquired a new self-confidence. The appearance of the black veteran in the Arkansas Delta at the close of the Civil War symbolized as nothing else the defeat of the old order in the area and the emergence of a new one that for a moment held high the hope of fulfilling black aspirations for equality, justice, and first-class citizenship.[53]

Following Emancipation, the immediate concern of blacks in the Arkansas Delta was the acquisition of education and land. For four years beginning in 1865, the federal government sponsored the Freedmen's Bureau to assist blacks in the transition from slavery to freedom. Bureau officers appeared in all Delta counties where they supervised the making of labor contracts, supplied food, shelter, clothing, and medical care to the destitute, established schools, and enabled some freedmen to settle on abandoned lands. With the inauguration of Radical Reconstruction in 1867, newly freed slaves in the Delta, joined by "black carpetbaggers" from elsewhere, participated in politics under the banner of the Republican Party—the party of Lincoln and Emancipation. They voted, served on juries, were elected to public office, and assisted in drafting a new constitution for the state. Some acquired education and property, and a few even carved out and held on to niches in the economy that insured a relative degree of prosperity. But the masses remained trapped in poverty and illiteracy.[54]

The return of the Democrats to power and the ratification of a new state constitution in 1874 marked the beginning of the political decline of Delta blacks, but that decline was gradual. Blacks in the Delta counties managed for some years to hold on to a substantial measure of political power. As late as 1886, for example, blacks in Chicot County held every elective office except that of county treasurer.[55] Between 1868 and 1893 at least sixty-four black men from Delta counties served in the state legislature, including seven in the senate. As late as 1891 the general assembly had twelve black members: eleven in the house, one in the senate, and all from the Delta.[56] But the emergence of a virulent racism in Arkansas and throughout the South, especially in the closing decade of the nineteenth century, accompanied by a succession of Jim Crow stratagems, virtually eliminated blacks from politics.

Having survived the degradation of slavery and briefly tasted the joys of liberation, Delta blacks by the turn of the century were a poor, politically powerless people with few influential friends. After the war, they continued to constitute the principal labor force in an agricultural economy. Those who participated in organized efforts to escape the economic shadow of slavery encountered swift and often violent white resistance. Both the cotton pickers who staged a strike in 1891 and the sharecroppers who organized the Farmers and Laborers Household Union in 1919 were brutally suppressed. The Elaine race riot, allegedly linked to the formation of a sharecroppers' union, left little doubt about the dire consequences likely to result from any organized effort by blacks that challenged the economic interests and racial mores of Delta whites.[57]

The "have-nots" of the post–Civil War Delta did not, however, consist exclusively of blacks. The war decimated the ranks of poorer whites and left the remainder more impoverished than ever. The antebellum planter elite in the Delta, despite losses suffered during the conflict, not only survived but also continued to exercise significant influence over the region's destiny. In time these planters came to share status and power with merchants, businessmen, and professionals whose emergence accompanied the growth of towns and whose economic base also rested, to a considerable degree, on cotton, timber, and related industries.

After the war, planters quickly shifted from a slave to a free labor system. This new system, known as sharecropping, evolved in the cash-poor economy of Arkansas in the postwar period. Shares of the crop rather than monthly wages increasingly became the norm of the new labor system inaugurated by the Freedmen's Bureau. In many Delta counties, agents of the Bureau reported favorably on the receptivity of the "better class" of planters to the new arrangement and on their willingness to treat blacks "fairly." Both agents and planters were cognizant that such treatment was in the planters' self-interest. According to some Bureau officials, those most prejudiced against blacks and most inclined to engage in "Ku Klux activities" were "poor, ignorant white men." No less evident from Bureau reports was the presence of tensions between these "poor, ignorant white men" and the large planters.[58] The latter, intent on maintaining and controlling their black labor force and aware of the unreliability of poor white support, participated in a racist campaign that bound the poor whites to planters, a sometimes uneasy alliance predicated on race that divided the "have nots" and perpetuated the planters' hegemony. Beginning with the Freedmen's Bureau, planter elites in the Delta attempted with varying degrees of success to co-opt or manipulate outside agencies and forces that intruded upon their domain.

After the Civil War, planters, in conjunction with merchants, businessmen, bankers, and professionals, not only wielded economic power in the Delta, they also exerted impressive statewide political influence. For many years, the Delta counties exercised a significant, if not preponderant, power in the state government. From the beginning of statehood in 1836 until the outbreak of the Civil War, the Delta-oriented organization, known as the "Dynasty" or the "Family," composed of members of the Conway, Sevier, and Johnson families, was the most influential political force in Arkansas. Following the end of Reconstruction, Democrats in the Delta, called "Swamp Democrats," constituted a powerful factor in state politics and were often locked in fierce combat with the party's hill country faction. This rivalry between the Delta and the hill country, prompted by differences in the economies and societies of the two sections, existed from the beginning of statehood. Such differences first surfaced in the struggle over the apportionment of delegates to the constitutional convention in 1836. The Delta, with a majority of the state's slaves, insisted on apportionment based on total population, while the hill country demanded that it be based on the free white male population. Although the Delta counties contained a substantially smaller white population than that of other counties, they managed to secure compromises that gave them "reasonable equality." In view of the sparse free population of many Delta counties, these compromises meant that their vote "counted for more in the legislative halls than the same vote" from other counties. Economic differences between the two sections, coupled with the Delta's distrust of "the more equalitarian political thought of the hill country," have influenced the course of Arkansas politics for more than a century and a half.[59] Changes in population patterns, along with federal legislation and court decisions, have reduced the political clout of the Delta counties, but even in the 1990s it is not insignificant. Perhaps the most dramatic evidence of political changes that have occurred since the 1960s is the increasing number of blacks holding elective office in the Delta.[60]

After the Civil War, the Arkansas Delta remained essentially a rural, agricultural society tied to the land, to the rivers, and to the blessings and curses of the physical environment. During the century and a half following Arkansas's admission to the Union, the landscape, economy, and demographic contours of the Delta counties underwent dramatic changes. The frontier character of the region receded in the wake of manmade "progress." Towns grew in number and size, especially in the decades between the 1870s and 1940s, but declined thereafter. In addition to more successful efforts at flood control, the growth of towns owed much to changes in the financing and marketing of cotton crops and especially to improvements in transportation. Although river transportation in the post–Civil War era became less irregular, faster, and more dependable, it was the construction of railroads that figured far more significantly in town growth. For example, the completion of the Mississippi River, Hamburg and Western Railroad from Luna Landing to Crossett in 1902 not only marked the beginning of the demise of river transportation and hastened the development of the lumber industry, but also ended the isolation of people in the rural, southeastern corner of the Delta. No less important than being able to travel to the state capital in a single day was the fact that residents of Ashley County could go anywhere in the nation on "Jay Gould's black horse."[61] Railroads crisscrossed the Delta in the early twentieth century, creating new towns and linking old ones to one another and to the outside world.

The towns throughout the Arkansas Delta participated fully in the boosterism and ballyhoo associated with the concept of an industrialized "New South." Proud of its riverport, timber-related industries, and railroad terminal, the town of Helena, for example, crusaded for a more diversified industrial economy. "The smokestack habit," declared the *Helena World* in 1899, "is a splendid habit. If we could double the number we have, we would be a city of fifteen thousand people inside of three or four years."[62] When the long campaign to "bring cotton mills to the cotton fields" resulted in the opening of the Premier Cotton Mill in nearby Barton three years later, the operation was immediately pronounced an "immense success."[63] No less than New South boosters elsewhere, those in the Delta tended to exaggerate the significance of the industries that they secured. With the aid of rhetorical alchemy, they easily transformed their plans for industrial development into claims of the existence of a real industrial economy.

Responding to demands by Helena's "pushing businessmen's league," John I. Moore, a candidate for the legislature from Phillips County in 1900, promised if elected to introduce a bill to establish a textile school in the town "for the proper training of that vast army of men who will soon be called upon to man the cotton manufacturing plants with which Arkansas will ere long be dotted." Like many New South enthusiasts, Moore embraced a vision of an industrialized region without abandoning his nostalgic commitment to a mythical past encompassed in the Lost Cause. But his first act as a legislator was to secure an appropriation for a Confederate memorial, rather than to seek a textile school for Helena.[64] The school was never established, and Moore's part of the state was never dotted with cotton mills.

Despite the presence of grist and roller mills and a few foundries and pearl button and brick factories, Delta towns remained inextricably tied to cotton culture, lumbering, and transportation. The ever-increasing emphasis on cotton production during the post-Reconstruction decades resulted in a proliferation of gins, compresses, and cottonseed oil mills. Other industries that flourished for a time in these towns were timber- and lumber-related enterprises such as logging, sawmills, and manufacturers of wagons, staves, boxes, cooperage, shingles, and other finished lumber products. If cotton-related industries rested on a crop bountifully produced in the rich Delta soil, the Delta's lumber industry was no less directly linked to the presence of thousands of acres of forests. As elsewhere in a nation not yet attuned to conservation and environmental concerns, Delta people recklessly exploited and depleted their timber supply. Not only did railroads play a critical role in transporting cotton and lumber products to markets, but they also generated industries and employment in the Delta towns, especially in machine shops and iron foundries.[65] But like much of the South, the industrial economy represented by these towns was, to a considerable extent, a "colonial economy," often owned by corporations and individuals outside the state and almost always functioning as a tributary of a new industrial order emerging beyond the ex-Confederate states.

Despite the exaggerated claims of industrialization in the Delta by New South advocates, the region in the post–Civil War era remained a land of cotton. The recovery of the cotton culture after the war was remarkably swift, and by 1880 all Delta counties, save one, had exceeded prewar production levels.[66] Joining lumber interests, planters engaged in extensive land reclamation projects so that by 1930 Arkansas possessed numerous levees and almost five thousand miles of drainage ditches. These projects resulted in more land for cotton production. For a time after the Civil War, cotton was even more solidly enthroned as king, especially in the lower Arkansas Delta, than it had been in the antebellum era.

The plantation system that existed in the Arkansas Delta in the postwar era rested on credit and cheap labor and included numerous absentee landlords. Because cotton was the money crop, planters focused on cotton production to the exclusion of corn and food crops. The Delta succumbed to a one-crop economy that rested on an ever-expanding labor force of debt-ridden sharecroppers. By the 1930s more than half of the Delta counties had tenancy rates of 80 percent or above. The wretchedness of the sharecroppers' existence ultimately led many to migrate elsewhere in search of a better life and led those who remained to organize the biracial Southern Tenant Farmers' Union in the 1930s in an attempt to reclaim a portion of what they considered their birthright.[67]

Between the world wars, a convergence of developments produced dramatic changes in the Delta's cotton economy. Among these were a steady out-migration of labor, the infestation of the boll weevil, agricultural diversification, and an acceleration of mechanization. Leading the onslaught against king cotton was rice, which in time became the principal crop on the Grand Prairie. The great flood of 1927 and the drought of the early 1930s, followed by the full impact of the Great Depression, set in motion radical alterations in Delta agriculture that culminated during and after World War II in the demise of the old plantation system.

The New Deal farm programs, despite their resettlement efforts and the farm tenant act, basically sought to raise agricultural prices through crop reduction, a procedure that temporarily rescued the Delta's planter class, bequeathed a legacy of crop price support, and dispossessed sharecroppers. The increased flight of inexpensive labor, especially during the Second World War, deprived the old plantation system of its means of survival. Unlike during the post–Civil War era when the plantation system had been able to flourish because sharecropping replaced slave labor, the post–World War II era left the traditional plantation system without an alternative labor supply.[68]

In the half-century since the end of World War II, the Arkansas Delta, while still tied to the land and the physical environment, has pursued a radically new course that not only has influenced its economy, but also the contours of its society as well. In the process of modernization, the Delta has acquired a few industries, but of more importance is the fact that its agriculture has been transformed into agribusiness, attuned not merely to yields and profits but also to market analysis, scientific research, cost efficiency, and centralized management. The new agriculture embraced technology and mechanization, crop diversification that dethroned cotton, conservation measures, and a variety of strategies to control pests, diseases, and weeds and to produce new crop varieties. More Delta timberlands disappeared, a half a million acres in the 1950s alone, to make way for this large-scale agriculture. Everything from public policy and legislation to tax formulas and the design of farm machinery conspired to promote bigness in Delta agriculture.[69] Delta farmers used elaborate irrigation systems to compensate for the lack of rainfall and introduced climate control in their homes, farm offices, and tractor cabs through the use of air-conditioning. But for all its modernization, Delta agriculture has not succeeded in solving the persistent problems common to all American agriculture, namely over-production and market fluctuations that breed instability and uncertainty. And those Delta rivers, despite the valiant efforts at constructing levees, periodically prove, as they did in 1990, that they can still be unruly and destructive.

Like the industrial revolution experienced by other parts of the nation in the late nineteenth and early twentieth centuries, the agricultural revolution in the Arkansas Delta did not occur without substantial costs to the landscape, environment, and human condition. The relentless draining and clearing of land for agriculture drastically reduced ecologically important forests, wetlands, and wilderness areas. Perhaps the ultimate irony is that portions of the Delta—an area in which water has been and remains an essential resource for a flourishing agriculture—have experienced a serious decline in ground-water levels.[70] The heavy applications of chemical fertilizers, pesticides, and herbicides have contributed to widespread water pollution.

No less significant is the deterioration of the human condition in the Delta. Virtually all the usual indices, from per capita income, unemployment, and housing to health, teenage pregnancies, and school dropouts, provide a statistical portrait of a people in distress. The once-flourishing towns, with few exceptions, bear all the earmarks of places that have seen better times. Accompanying their decline has been the steady shrinkage of the small middle class. The result is a socioeconomic class structure in the Delta that perhaps more than ever resembles a pyramid: a few large agribusiness people at the top and an ever-expanding number of low-income groups at the base. Poverty among Delta blacks is omnipresent. In an era in which agricultural units steadily increased in size, the number of black landowners plummeted during the agricultural revolution. Among blacks it is primarily the elderly who remain in the Delta, while the young seek a better life elsewhere.[71] Throughout the Delta, black residents have initiated a wide variety of self-help movements and organizations in an effort to address the crisis that confronts them.

In the 1940s Arkansas's premier man of letters, John Gould Fletcher, wrote movingly of the Delta and its people—the "back-bowed figures dragging their long sacks and picking [cotton] ceaselessly" in the relentless heat and humidity. Capturing the ambience of the Delta, he spoke of the "monotonous flatness of the land" where "one could almost smell the cotton growing" and where "the stark, ugly cabins" of sharecroppers and the black cypress swamp combined to give the area a sinister appearance. Of those features that Fletcher described, only the flatness of the land can be observed fifty years later: cotton pickers dragging their long sacks are extraordinarily rare; their shacks have disappeared, and even the cypress swamp has probably been drained and its trees cut. And one may well smell soybeans, rather than cotton, growing.[72]

The Arkansas Delta remains a place in which nature has done so much even though it presents a vastly different landscape from that first glimpsed by settlers in the eighteenth and nineteenth centuries. For better or worse, the transformation of this once watery, wilderness frontier over the last century and a half represents a staggering investment of human effort and emotion. If the Delta has undergone visible and easily quantifiable changes, it also exhibits important social and cultural continuities. Natives and long-time residents of the region are self-consciously Delta people. They possess what a native of Desha County describes as a "southern sensibility." This mindscape, as distinctive as the area's topography, persists long after natives have left the Delta, and it is apparent in the ways in which it shapes one's view of the world, behavior, and use of language. Delta people obviously attach especial significance to place in both the physical and social sense. It is important, for them, to know where someone is from, not in a general way, but with great specificity, and to know the intricacies of kinship, even to distant cousins. While the phrase, "in their place," has most frequently been used (and is generally thought of) in a racist context, the fact is that Delta people insist upon everyone being in his or her place. Regardless of their place, Delta people are likely to emphasize manners and exhibit "the small courtesies" in personal relations that may appear quaint or insincere to outsiders. Their talk and conversation differs from that of hill people both in the softness of their accent and in their penchant for circumspection. Their invoking of metaphor and telling of stories, in lieu of directness, prompts some outside the Delta to conclude that they are saying one thing and meaning another.[73]

In fact, the Delta is a dramatic example of what John Shelton Reed, in referring to the South in general, has described as the region's "subcultural persistence in a mass society."[74] In many respects, continuity, rather than change, characterizes the values, attitudes, and habits that, as products of the Delta's past, inform its life today. The persistent struggle to exploit its abundant resources and control its unpredictable streams influences contemporary Delta attitudes toward environmental concerns as surely as the long interaction between blacks and whites figures in the area's culture and race relations of today. The repeated dissolving of optimistic expectations into disappointment and defeat in the past has scarcely bequeathed an enthusiasm for utopian schemes or a strong belief in human perfectibility. Furthermore, Delta people, even those trapped in an exploitive economic system, possess a life of rootedness and a personalism in human relations that has persisted in the face of a new agricultural system that more nearly resembles the modern corporation than the family farm. These cultural and social continuities are significant ingredients in the quality of Delta life that is sometimes confused with the more measurable standard of living.

If, as Robert Coles claims, no other part of the nation "struggles as hard as the South to survive its ruinous contradictions,"[75] in few if any other portions of the region has the struggle been more intense than in the Arkansas Delta. The Delta has witnessed plenty of change, to be sure, but as a resident across the Mississippi River has explained: ". . . it's the same as it always was, but it's different too."[76] The Delta today still presents the basic paradox of human want amidst abundance, of some of the nation's poorest people living on some of the nation's richest land.

"Mustered out" colored volunteers at Little Rock, Arkansas.
Courtesy University of Central Arkansas Archives.

Battle at Fort St. Charles on the White River in Arkansas.
Courtesy of the Library of Congress.

Delta wetlands, around 1940.
Courtesy Jesse Laurence Charlton Collection, Special Collections Division, University of Arkansas Libraries, Fayetteville.

Scott Bond's store.
Courtesy of Special Collections Division, University of Arkansas Libraries, Fayetteville.

In town in Osceola, Arkansas, circa 1910.
Courtesy city of Osceola, mayor's office.

Equipment used in creating drainage ditches.
From Eliott B. Sartain, It Didn't Just Happen (Osceola, Ark.: Drainage District No. 9, 1975), 31.
Courtesy Grassy Lake and Tyronza Drainage District No. 9.

The River's Gifts and Curses

THOMAS FOTI

The Mississippi River Delta is a land of rivers, built by the rivers, and defined by the rivers. The Mississippi River and its major tributaries, including the Ohio, St. Francis, White, Arkansas, Yazoo, and Red rivers, have carved away older rocks and deposited hundreds of feet of rich topsoil. The Delta extends from the mouth of the Ohio 600 miles to the Gulf. At its widest, from Little Rock to near Memphis, it is 150 miles wide.

The true delta of the Mississippi—that is, the area where it fans out through distributaries on its final plunge into the sea—is only the southern tip of this huge area. The rest, including all of the Arkansas Delta, is properly termed the Mississippi Alluvial Plain. However, the whole area was long ago dubbed the Delta (with a capital "D"), and Delta it will remain. The Arkansas Delta is that part of the Mississippi River Delta in Arkansas.

The rivers created this land, and they dominate the landscape today. The creatures of the Delta, including the people, are adapted to the rivers and attuned to their flows and moods. To understand the land and people of the Delta, one must begin with the rivers.

A river is constantly changing. A wise person realizes that one cannot step in the same river twice; the sage understands that one cannot step in the same river once. No matter how fine one splits the instant, there is motion, albeit often slow. Motion where? Downstream. Downstream are other towns, other states, and eventually the sea. And the sea leads to other rivers. Up those other rivers are other lands, other nations, everywhere. By their very nature, rivers connect everywhere to everywhere else.

The kid growing up on the banks of the Arkansas or White or Mississippi knows that, without being able to say it. *Here* there may be no prospects for change, but *there* is the river. The river is a way out, if only in the imagination. No river kid can grow up truly parochial; he or she is too clearly linked to everyone else or at least every place else.

In the mind's eye we see the whole cycle of the river: In the distant seas the drops of water evaporate, to enter the atmosphere and do the seemingly impossible: flow uphill. Moisture of the Appalachians (down the Ohio), from the east slopes of the Rockies (down the Missouri and Arkansas), from the Ozarks (down the White) and within the Delta itself gathers into streams and rivers. Eventually, from a thousand miles away or from right in the Delta, the water flows together to feed the Mississippi.

Delta rivers flow gently, seldom having a fall of more than a few feet in a mile. It is 350 miles from Helena to the Gulf as the crow flies, but rivers do not follow the paths of crows. Rivers meander. By the path the Mississippi takes, it is 650 miles from Helena to the Gulf, with a fall of only a foot every four miles, and the length of the Mississippi is nearly twice as long as the straight-line distance.

Straighten out a lowland river and it immediately starts forming new meanders. Each meander grows broader and broader until eventually the river cuts across it to shorten its route to the sea.

In looking at the cutoffs formed by this process, Mark Twain noted that in 176 years the Lower Mississippi had shortened itself 242 miles. Therefore, he deduced, with tongue firmly in cheek, ". . . any person can see that seven hundred and forty years from now the Lower Mississippi will be only a mile and three quarters long, and Cairo and New Orleans will have joined their streets together, and be plodding comfortably along under a single mayor and a mutual board of aldermen."[1]

Why does the river meander? Geologists say that meandering is a way for rivers to rid themselves of excess energy as their slopes get ever gentler closer to the sea. In essence, the water at any given point is being pushed by faster-moving water from above *into* slower-moving water below. Where's the water to go except sideways? How, then, does the river spend that excess energy? In caving and carving the bank on the outsides of bends, and in depositing new land on the "point bar" on the insides of bends. As the river gives, it takes.

Always the river gives and takes.

The changes that characterize the Delta and its rivers today are just the continuation of a dynamic history that extends over millions of years. Many of these changes have left their marks for us to see on the surface of the land today. The "marks" may be subtle features that only a geologist or an ecologist would notice, but other changes have left regional landforms that dominate the landscape. The most striking landform is not truly a part of the Delta at all. It is, however, completely surrounded by the Delta and is small enough that in many ways it is overwhelmed by its sprawling neighbor. It is known as Crowley's Ridge. Understanding a bit about the geological history of Crowley's Ridge will help place the adjacent Delta, and the long history of river changes, into a better perspective.

Whereas most geological history requires the ability to think back millions or even hundreds of millions of years, the important part of the Delta history, that is, the part that shows at the surface and affects us today, occurred only within the past several thousand years. Crowley's Ridge is a major exception to that rule. In a deep creek bed at the base of the Ridge, say along Crow's Creek near Forrest City, one can find shark teeth and other fossils. They settled to the bottom when a huge bay of the Gulf of Mexico extended all the way up to what is now southern Missouri. This shallow bay existed about fifty million years ago. It extended from today's Arkadelphia, up past present-day Little Rock and Pocahontas, to the mouth of the Ohio and down through Tennessee east of Jackson. Near Arkadelphia on the west and Tuscaloosa, Alabama, on the east, the bay widened out to the full expanse of the Gulf.[2]

As the Gulf gradually withdrew to its present limits, it left behind rolling deposits of sand, gravel, and clay that had made up its bottom and shores. As it withdrew, the rivers that would reshape the landscape flowed into the abandoned bay. The Mississippi, the Ohio, and the other rivers gradually removed ocean-bottom material and laid down flat deposits of deep soil that characterize the Delta today.

These rivers did not always flow where they flow today, though, or look like the rivers we know. Within the last twenty thousand years, the Mississippi has flowed down the west side of Crowley's Ridge, instead of the east side where it flows today. It rejoined its present course about where the White River now flows into the Mississippi. While the Mississippi flowed west of the ridge, the Ohio was flowing east of Crowley's Ridge. The Arkansas took the route now occupied by Bayou Bartholomew along the western edge of the

Delta. Those three rivers did not get together until they had reached midway through today's Louisiana.[3]

As the Ohio and the Mississippi followed their separate paths through the northern Delta, they carved away the old marine deposits, lowering and leveling the landscape. They meandered widely across the landscape, but never quite across its full breadth. They left between them a low ridge of ocean-bottom material. This ridge became the backbone of Crowley's Ridge.

The character of the rivers also has changed over time. As the glaciers advanced to near St. Louis, they locked up huge amounts of water as glacial ice. The "mighty Mississippi" and Ohio rivers became just trickles. Sea level dropped dozens of feet. The rivers downcut into their valleys. Then as the glaciers waned, the rivers swelled to unimaginable proportions. Floods swept the full width of the Delta and even over parts of the adjacent uplands. Features of the former landscape were swept away.

At times when the flow was high, floods deposited inches or even feet of glacier-ground rock from the north. During dry intervals, this silt was picked up by the winds in enormous dust storms. The dust was piled high against any barrier that obstructed it, and the budding Crowley's Ridge was such a barrier. Up to fifty feet were added to its height, and it became the notable landscape feature it is today, the site of Helena, Forrest City, Jonesboro, and many other cities. Dust was also piled along the eastern side of the Delta, forming the Chickasaw Bluffs from Osceola to Memphis, as well as the bluffs at Vicksburg and Natchez. In the northern Delta, from Newport to Paragould, the sandbars of the Mississippi were swept by these winds into sand dunes that still exist but have been so rounded by time that they were only recognized as dunes in the 1970s.

At the height of glacial advance, the forest of the Delta was a boreal forest of spruce, changing only much later to the familiar bottomland hardwood forest we know today.

Then as now the rivers continually changed their courses a mile here or a few feet there. Occasionally, though, the changes were more dramatic, as one river "captured" another. At the northern end of the Delta, the Ohio eventually captured the Mississippi. The Ohio was a clearer stream (as it is today), and because of that it had scoured its bed deeper than that of the Big Muddy. Tributaries of the Ohio eroded headward toward the channel of the Mississippi, and when they reached the higher channel, the flow of the

Mississippi was diverted down the former course of the Ohio—the Mississippi was captured.

The Black River took over part of the former channel of the Mississippi, as did the White, the Cache, and the L'Anguille. This latter stream cuts *through* Crowley's Ridge in a cut originally made by the Mississippi. The Arkansas took a shortcut more or less straight across the Delta to the Mississippi, and Bayou Bartholomew occupied the old Arkansas channel.

The constant change of the rivers creates a varied landscape. Ask an outsider about the Delta and you may hear "The Delta is the Delta is the Delta." Point out the differences in the landscape and the response may be, "Well, that's not the *real* Delta." A person may develop a stereotype of the Delta and then consider the *rest* of the landscape mosaic as atypical. The unity of this land is that rivers have played the dominant role in its shaping; any variation on that theme is fair. The variation can be thought of at two scales: the topographic diversity that enlivens any small area, and the geographical diversity that makes whole regions distinctive.

The visitor often perceives the Delta as flat and monotonous. On a macro scale it may indeed be flatter than a tabletop, with only a few feet of relief within a square mile. However, in the Delta, a few feet may mean the difference between dry and wet. On an outing in the White River Refuge, a birdwatcher was told the Swainson's Warbler he was looking for was in a canebrake "over that high ridge." The group found the bird, but after returning the visitor asked: "Where was the ridge?" The refuge manager responded that they had crossed it twice. They walked back to the top, a full three feet high. When the floods come, those three feet make the difference between dying and living to animals, plants, and even people. In a year with a normal springtime flood, the turkeys that nest on that ridge will hatch many chicks. Let the flood be two feet higher, and the refuge will not produce turkeys that year.

Residents recognize the importance of these subtle differences in elevation. They can describe not only bottomlands, terraces, and uplands, but also "first bottoms" and "second bottoms," which may distinguish areas with an elevation difference of only a foot or two. Being able to recognize and adjust to these differences is vital to survival in the Delta. The Delta influences outlook, behavior, language.

The first bottoms are the lowest lands in the floodplain. They flood almost every year for long periods. The forest in these bottoms is dark and damp and infested with mosquitoes and water moccasins. Ground cover is often lacking because it is killed by the floods; the ground is often bare mineral soil because leaves and mulch are swept away by flowing waters. Cypresses and tupelos may grow in the bottoms, but typically these bottoms are dry enough for a variety of water-tolerant oaks, like overcup oak, named because the cup, usually only at the base of the acorn, almost covers it. Nuttall oak, named for the British botanist Thomas Nuttall who was the first to list it in the Arkansas (Territory) Delta in 1819,[4] is here, too. Throughout the forests, a water line can be seen on the trees: below that line moss and lichens do not grow on the trunks; they are killed by floods. One reason the trees themselves are not killed is that they remain dormant late in the spring, so they need little oxygen while their roots are flooded. In the fertile, moist bottoms, they can afford to wait a bit before putting on their new leaves.

Because of the nearly ideal growing conditions, the trees can reach huge proportions, and in a mature forest with closed canopy that allows little penetration of light and maintains high humidity, the bottomland forest has a primeval character approaching that of the jungle. With its snakes, mosquitoes, and dank gloom, the forest achieves an impersonal grandeur that is many people's emotional concept of wilderness. Here is none of the easily romanticized, sentimental beauty of less powerful places, but it *is* a place where visitors realize that they are a part, and only a small part, of a world beyond their comprehension.

According to Nuttall, the scenery at the mouth of the White River was ". . . almost destitute of every thing which is agreeable to human nature . . . one vast trackless wilderness of trees, a dead solemnity, where human voice is never heard to echo. . . . All is rude nature as it sprang into existence, still preserving its primeval type, its unreclaimed exuberance."[5]

These bottoms were not friendly places then, nor are they now. Friedrich Gerstäcker, a German sportsman who lived in the Arkansas Delta in the late 1830s, hunted deer, turkey, bear, bison, panthers, and wolves and was repeatedly incapacitated by bouts of malaria. After he moved west to the Ouachitas and Ozarks, saying, ". . . another attack of ague—I decided on bidding adieu to the unhealthy swamps, and trying the hills . . . ," his malaria attacks almost ended.[6] Nevertheless, the adventure of the bottoms was a great temptation. He returned, alone and in the middle of winter, to hunt along the Cache River. For several days he killed no game and had to subsist on a little corn he carried. "Suffering from raging hunger," he felt it growing colder every moment. "I made haste to light a good fire, and threw myself before it completely exhausted." As the cold deepened, snow began falling, but Gerstäcker professed to be comfortable by his fire. However, he was awakened in the night "by the frightful howling of wolves, which probably had no better sport than myself, and I consoled myself that perhaps they were only half as hungry." After continuing his hunt, he was forced to swim the river in spite of the cold and suffered a recurrence of malaria.[7]

It is not so much different today: the bottoms should be approached with considerable care. Even within the last twenty years there have been reports of the White River Monster, a scaly beast that has reportedly overturned boats and frightened fisherpeople. However, fear of the river and its bottoms has inspired many to destroy the wildness—perhaps as the curse that accompanies the many gifts the river provides—rather than to accept it as a part of our heritage. Even the wildness, at the right moment, is magically transformed into a gift: the prettiest and most benign time to explore the bottoms is in the fall. Snakes and "skeeters" have gone wherever those creatures go, the water is low and has been so for months, so even the swamps are dry; leaves begin to drop, so the woods are brighter than in July, and the remaining leaves show the reds and yellows that mark their forthcoming abscission. At that time, a bayou can be as pretty as any upland stream around.

Second bottoms are a little higher than first bottoms. As the land rises gently from stream level, the change may be gradual, but eventually the difference is apparent. Ground cover is denser, and dead leaves and other litter often cover the ground: the floods are not as frequent nor as long-lasting here. The forest changes: water oak and willow oak become more common. Cherrybark oak, whose English name refers to its resemblance to the wild cherry tree but whose beautiful scientific name *pagodifolia* refers to its pagoda-shaped leaves, is here, too.

All of the floodplain, first bottoms and second bottoms, is a sometime extension of the main channel of the river. What we recognize as the channel is the area that the river flows through every year, most of the year. The "normal high water" level is set by the depth at which the river flows often enough to kill typical land plants such as oak trees and cane. Willows, cattails, and cypresses may occur below normal high water. Much of the channel goes dry in the driest part of the year, leaving sand or mud bars. This is the land originally referred to by the French as the "batture." Today that term has come to refer to all the land on the river side of the levee.

Just back from the channel is often a natural levee, frequently marked today by the presence of a flood-control levee that adds to the height and effect of the natural feature. The natural levee is formed by silt deposited by the stream during floods. As long as the river is within its channel, higher flows equate to some extent with faster flow. However, as soon as the river tops its banks, it can spread out over the whole floodplain. When it does so, it slows down. Silt that has been maintained in suspension by the rapid flow falls out. Most silt falls out adjacent to the channel when the water first slows down. As it accumulates, this "levee" becomes higher and more distinct. High-ground trees, like sycamore and swamp chestnut oak, may thrive here. In many cases, so do people. On the largest rivers, particularly the Mississippi, the natural levees are hundreds or thousands of feet wide, and higher than many floods. Here the earliest French and Spanish settlers chose to establish their plantations. This settlement pattern was made practical by the ease of river travel and transport compared to overland. It was, in fact, a river-centered society. The early land grants were described from a given river mile to another river mile, running back . . . to where? To the swamp that usually was on the back side of the natural levee, appropriately called the backswamp.

The backswamp is created by water impounded behind the natural levee. If the land in the first bottoms slopes upward gradually from the river and if a high natural levee is deposited right along the channel, how is floodwater to drain back to the river? In many cases, it does not. It gets trapped behind the levee where a permanent or semipermanent body of water is formed. This backswamp is the domain of cypress and tupelo. Cypresses up to twelve feet across the buttresses and a thousand or more years old still can be found in a few of these swamps. When Hernando de Soto's party crossed the Mississippi in 1541, they found themselves in such a swamp: Immediately after crossing the "Rio Grande" or Mississippi, de Soto marched a short distance to the town of Aquixo, which he looted. Traveling from there to Casqui, he crossed a small river. All that day, until sunset, he marched through water, in places coming to the knees. Elsewhere it was waist deep. According to one account, "They rejoiced greatly on reaching the dry land because it appeared to them that they would travel about, lost, all night in the water."[8]

The meandering of a river causes constant changes in topographic features. As the meander cuts away the outer bank, it forms a point bar on the inside of the bend. This new ground begins as a low and often-inundated sandbar that is unvegetated. During low water, Least Terns and Killdeer may nest on the bar. As the bar grows higher with the deposition of more material, it becomes high enough for colonization by terrestrial plants. Often willow is the first species to invade; alternatively, cocklebur may be first (this may be the natural habitat of cocklebur). On higher and drier ground further back, these are replaced by cottonwood, whose feathery "cotton" fills the air in the summer. Sugarberry may follow, particularly in the lower areas in the swell and swale topography that typically forms on the point. On sandy soils that are fairly well drained, pecan trees grow. This may be the most valuable tree of southern bottomlands. Its wood is as valuable as walnut for furniture, its nut is a favorite food, and the shape of the tree is pleasing enough to be a favored shade tree. In these bottoms, pecan trees often reach 100 feet tall, and the tallest recorded tree is 160 feet.[9] Originally, locals rode the railroad into the woods and dispersed for a day or more to collect wild nuts. As the woods were cut, though, orchards of pecans, selected for their thin shells and large, tasty nuts, were established to satisfy the market.

For sheer dollar value of wood, none can match that of another occupant of these forests, the persimmon. Although it may be looked down upon by those people who have had the misfortune to taste the fruit of the persimmon tree before it was ripe (it causes a semi-permanent pucker), persimmon wood can bring more than twelve dollars a cubic foot at the sawmill. Persimmon is related to ebony and is very hard—it makes great golf club heads. It can be valuable enough to cause special cuts where every persimmon larger than six inches in diameter is cut from the forest over thousands of acres.

Once a meander bend has been formed, it grows into an ever-larger loop with the neck becoming smaller and smaller until at some point the river cuts across the neck and leaves the bulk of the loop cut off as an "oxbow lake." Historian Pete Daniel described the process this way: "Because the banks of soft earth often crumbled into the stream, the river channel was tentative, fickle, snaking through bends and horseshoes, detouring for miles to arrive a hundred feet from where it began, and later, tiring of circumambulation, eating through the narrow strip of land to abbreviate itself.

Too restless to sleep in one bed, the river for centuries had carved and re-carved the valley with its channels."[10]

Oxbow lakes were virtually the only natural lakes in Arkansas at the time of settlement. Occasionally a sinkhole in the Ozarks would plug up and hold water, forming a lake that was really little more than a pond, but the bottomlands were dotted with oxbow lakes, ranging from tiny to huge. Lake Chicot, at sixteen miles long and three-fourths mile wide, is one of the largest oxbow lakes anywhere along the Mississippi. The oxbow lake is intimately related to the river system. Often rising and falling with the river, it clears and warms faster than the river in the spring and consequently frequently provides a more productive fishery.

Like everything else about the bottomlands, the oxbow lake is ephemeral. Each flood brings in a new load of silt, continuing the inexorable process of filling and eradicating the lake. Cypresses and tupelos become established in the shallows on the edge, and gradually they march toward the center of the lake. The trees are joined in these open shallows by smaller plants that are shaded out when the dominant trees form a continuous canopy. Cattails and southern wild rice may become abundant, giving rise to the many lakes named "Grassy." Buttonbush, named after its spherical fruits, may grow so thickly that it makes large areas impenetrable to boats. It is often called "buckbrush" by locals. Water elm may form an inconspicuous virgin forest of trees only forty feet high with trunks only eighteen inches in diameter for the few feet below their first forks.

Wading birds sometimes form huge nesting colonies in these brushy swamps. Little Blue Herons and their white immature offspring were the most common birds in these heronries. They have lately been outnumbered by the alien cattle egrets that are smaller and are white even as adults. Patches of buffy on head and back during the breeding season make them among the prettiest of wading birds. Native to the plains of Africa, they suddenly appeared in South America in the mid-twentieth century and began migrating north in ever-increasing numbers. Unlike other wading birds, they glean insects from pastures, strolling virtually under the feet of grazing cattle as their ancestors did with the vast herds of ungulates on the Serengheti. The larger Great Blue Herons and Great Egrets prefer nest sites in the highest cypresses, rather than in low shrubs. Hunted almost to extinction for their plumes and then decimated by pesticides, the wading birds had all but disappeared from the Delta by the 1960s, but the change to nonpersistent pesticides has allowed them to begin recovering their numbers, even to the point of sometimes becoming pests at minnow farms.

As the process of filling the lake continues, "water lilies" or "yancopins" (lotus) become established across it in water several feet deep. Eventually no open water is left at all. Cypresses and tupelos cover the lake, which may be reduced to a fraction of its original width. When the lake is reduced to a narrow channel, it has become a "slough."

All of these changes are occurring at a rapid rate, not just on a geological scale, but also on a human scale. In the mid-1980s, boaters on the lower Arkansas noticed something sticking out of a caving outer bank. Closer inspection showed it to be a flat-bottomed barge of heavy wood timber, fastened with hand-crafted iron spikes. It was covered with eight feet of sand and silt, on which was growing a forest of sizeable trees. The story revealed by the river was that this barge had sunk and had been covered with eight feet of soil; the river had moved away and allowed a forest to become established over the burial, and then the river had returned to exhume the corpse, all in only a century.

As Nuttall noted nearby, "We nowhere see such enormous trees as those which so frequently occur along the banks of the Ohio; this, however, may in part be occasioned by the instability of the soil, from whence they are occasionally swept at no very distant intervals."[11]

Above all else the Delta is changing; the rivers are constantly giving, always taking.

As individual rivers have impressed their characters on particular parts of the Delta, they have created regions distinct from one another that provide a different level of diversity to the overall landscape: a geographic mosaic. The microtopographic variations described above are repeated in changing combinations through all the regions, indeed throughout all alluvial bottomlands. The regions, however, possess characteristics that distinguish them from the others. For purposes of understanding the diversity of the Arkansas Delta, it is useful to recognize five distinct regions: the St. Francis Basin, Crowley's Ridge, the White River Lowlands, the Grand Prairie, and the Arkansas River Lowlands.

However, the description of the geography of the Arkansas Delta should begin with its overall boundaries. Its northern boundary is totally arbitrary, a huge bite having been taken out of Arkansas

Territory because the residents preferred to remain in Missouri. The southern boundary roughly coincides with a natural one, though. In 1804 William Dunbar, leading the earliest United States government expedition into this part of the Louisiana Purchase, noted that Spanish moss found its northern limit almost precisely at what is now the southern boundary of Arkansas. Dunbar wrote, ". . . we saw no long moss /Tillandsia/ above Latitude 33 degrees . . . it would appear, that Nature herself has marked with a feature of distinction the line which Congress has thought proper to draw between the Territories of Orleans and of Louisiana."[12] Indeed, Spanish moss occurs only very slightly into southern Arkansas.

The western boundary of the Arkansas Delta is a distinct one in most cases. From the Missouri state line to Little Rock, the Ozark and Ouachita mountains rise abruptly from the river bottoms of the Delta, often hundreds of feet. From Little Rock to the Louisiana state line, the boundary is less imposing but no less clear. There, the marine deposits of the Coastal Plain often rise only thirty to fifty feet from the alluvial bottoms, but the slightness of the topographic change only emphasizes the distinctness of the two regions: the alluvial Delta soils, with bottomland hardwood forest or flat fields of cotton and soybeans, give way at the first sign of a slope to the rolling piney woods of the Coastal Plain where timber, not cotton, is king.

The Arkansas Delta has often been ignored by folks on the other side of the Mississippi, who equate "Mississippi River Delta" with "State of Mississippi Delta." For instance, William Alexander Percy defined the Delta this way: "My country is the Mississippi Delta, the river country. It lies flat, like a badly drawn half oval, with Memphis at its northern and Vicksburg at its southern tip. Its western boundary is the Mississippi River, which coils and returns on itself in great loops and crescents, though from the map you would think it ran in a straight line from north to south."[13]

Therefore it would be only appropriate to reciprocate by defining the eastern limit of the Arkansas Delta to be the Mississippi River. However, as the River continually changes course, some land that *was* Arkansas finds itself on the east side, and some land that was Mississippi is cut off on the west side. Truly there is no substantial difference between the east and west sides; they are all "the river country."

The first of the five regions of the Arkansas Delta described here is the St. Francis Basin. This region extends from Crowley's

Ridge eastward to the Mississippi, and from Helena northward to Blytheville (or on to Cape Girardeau, if the state line is ignored). It may well be considered the "archetypal" Delta, in that it is flat, flat, flat, and almost featureless. There is seldom over five feet of local relief in any given square mile. In fact, the only notable features are *below* normal ground level rather than above: The St. Francis Sunk Lands and Big Lake, reputedly formed by the action of the New Madrid Earthquake, and Wapannoca swamp, a Mississippi River backswamp.

Le Page du Pratz, a resident of Natchez in the 1720s, visited the St. Francis and remarked, "It is on this river of St. Francis that the hunters of New Orleans go every winter to make salt provisions, tallow and bears oil, for the supply of the capital. The lands adjoining to it are always covered with herds of buffaloes, notwithstanding they are hunted every winter in those parts. . . ."[14]

Because of the level topography, farmers have been able to impose maximum control over the landscape. Thomas Jefferson might have been proud to see his survey system physically present on the land: almost every square mile (or section) is bounded on all sides by a drainage ditch. Right Hand Chute of Little River and its floodwaters were enclosed within paired levees, but eventually the stream was ditched so the land within the floodway could itself be cleared and farmed. Clearing is so complete that in all of Mississippi County only a few scattered tracts of forest remain except on the river side of the levees. The most exciting scenery in the county is the view of the Chickasaw Bluffs across the river in Tennessee.

Yet the water-control projects have left major segments of the river in a relatively natural state. The St. Francis Sunk Lands were leveed to serve as a floodway, and much of the forested bottoms have been acquired by the Arkansas Game and Fish Commission. A similar development has protected Big Lake, with four huge ditches carrying into it the runoff of the Missouri Bootheel. A very different development downstream at Marked Tree has protected a reach of the St. Francis: the river channel was too inefficient for the drainage interests so they directed the major flow *away* from the river through a floodway and ditch, leaving the old channel of the river intact, and along with it, one of the last populations of the endangered fat pocketbook pearly mussel.

At the mouth of the St. Francis, come hell or (particularly) high water, the flow of the river is *pumped* into the Mississippi. The St. Francis Basin represents both the archetypal Delta landscape and the archetypal response to the river's curses: drain, ditch, levee, and control.

The next important region to consider is Crowley's Ridge. Strictly speaking, as already explained, Crowley's Ridge is *in* the Delta but not *of* the Delta. It is the one piece of ground in the vicinity that was *untouched* by the rivers. That in itself tells us a lot about what the rivers *did* by seeing what they *did not do*. Crowley's Ridge is made up of hills that are often over a hundred feet from base to crest. The soils are wind-blown loess. In a sense these hills are products of the rivers in that rivers brought the glacier-ground rock flour down and spread it out conveniently for the wind to pick up and pile on Crowley's Ridge. The forests of Crowley's Ridge are unlike the forests of the Delta: they are composed of species that thrive on well-drained uplands. Therefore, they are more similar in composition to the forests of the Ozarks than to those of the Delta. When looked at in more detail, though, it can be seen that there are several species that are typically found only east of the Mississippi, like the tulip tree and the white walnut. Therefore, the forests of the ridge are in many ways unique in Arkansas.

Crowley's Ridge has been of paramount importance to the Delta folk as a place to live. Gerstäcker lived for an extended period on the ridge, which was settled at that time, whereas the Cache River and Bayou DeView bottoms to the west were still wilderness. (Gerstäcker originally stayed on the ridge because "After supper, to our no small horror we learnt that unless we could swim twenty-eight miles, further progress was not to be thought of, as the whole swamp between this and White river was under water."[15]) In time, both rich planters and the business people who were not tied down to the Delta plantations often chose to live on or at the foot of the ridge. Towns grew there, and today Helena, Forrest City, Wynne, Jonesboro, and others usually thought of as "Delta" towns actually owe their locations (though not their economies) to Crowley's Ridge. A telling point is that the county seat and largest city of every county that straddles Crowley's Ridge is located on the ridge.

The wildest of the Delta regions is the White River Lowlands. This region stretches from Piggott and the Missouri Ozarks past Helena down the western side of Crowley's Ridge, lying between the ridge and either the Ozark Mountains or the Grand Prairie. This is a "new" land, Delta in its rivers and its economy, but with significant differences that result from its having been isolated from the

Mississippi and having been extremely flood prone, even by Delta standards. The Cache River and Bayou DeView, L'Anguille River, and the Black and White rivers all turn this region annually into an inland sea that was often, as Gerstäcker found, uncrossable and inaccessible. Control of the sort exercised by people over the St. Francis River Basin was never possible here.

The lower White River is a special place. It was virtually a trackless wilderness until very recently, and it is still the wildest region of the Delta. It got that way because the White flows for a major part of its length through the Ozarks and is consequently a clearer stream than most waters of the Delta. Clearer streams scour deeper, and as a result the White is lower than the nearby Mississippi and Arkansas. Therefore, when the Mississippi floods, the White is subjected to "backwater flooding" for up to forty miles of its length. As a result, the lower White has stayed wild, with a National Wildlife Refuge and state Wildlife Management Area being among the more important developments in the area. It also hosts the only indigenous black bear population in Arkansas, the only productive eagle nest in the state, its own "White River Monster," and a few remaining denizens of the tribe known as "river rats."[16]

The region never really was developed until the twentieth century, when sufficient levees and ditches were put in place to allow some semblance of control over the rivers. It was actually the 1970s before the relaxation in acreage restrictions on rice allowed the area to become an agricultural force. There are few plantations, few truly old families, and a lower proportion of blacks than in much of the Delta.

The fact that water resources development was so late in coming caused the job to be incomplete in the 1970s at the blooming of the environmental movement. Therefore, the proposed channelization of Cache River and Bayou DeView became one of the major environmental controversies of that decade. The result was that the proposal to channel the rivers was abandoned and a new National Wildlife Refuge was established.

The most distinctive Delta region is the Grand Prairie. Southwest of the White River Lowlands, lying between them and the Arkansas River lowlands, is the highest and flattest terrace of the Arkansas Delta, known as the Grand Prairie Terrace. On its higher, eastern side it is often fifty feet higher than the adjacent White River Bottoms. As the White River has cut into this terrace, it has carved bluffs that have encouraged settlement at such places as Des Arc,

De Valls Bluff, Crockett's Bluff, and St. Charles. As they have cut down to the White River, streams of the terrace have carved out rolling hills in the otherwise flat landscape. Up on the terrace is one of the flattest parts of the Delta: it has been tens of thousands of years since any river has meandered over this land, so the microtopographic features that characterize the more recent bottoms have melted into a flat, featureless plain, which is crossed at infrequent intervals by streams such as Bayou La Grue, Little Bayou La Grue, and Mill Bayou. Each of these has incised deeply down into the terrace.

What this terrace lacks in topographic diversity, however, it makes up for in startlingly different vegetation. The Grand Prairie, at the time of settlement, was the largest prairie, or natural grassland, in Arkansas, containing almost a half-million acres.

John Treat, director of the United States Factory at Arkansas Post, said of the Grand Prairie in 1805, "Those prairies . . . commencing with two and a half miles of this village affords (when in Yellow Plume) a scene as perhaps not to be excelled in Nature. . . ."[17]

What makes the prairie so unusual here is that prairie grasses are adapted to dry climates, just as the grasses are in today's Oklahoma and Kansas. However, the Delta is abundantly watered by rivers and high rainfall. In the Delta, trees should be, and typically are, the dominant vegetation. Conditions are different on the prairie terrace, however. The rivers that formed this terrace deposited clay for thousands of years. As a result, the prairie terrace is underlain by a hundred feet of tight clay. That clay will not allow rainwater to penetrate far and will not give up much water to plants, so the site is a drouthy one for plants. Therefore, grasses have a bit of an edge over trees here.

At the time of settlement, grasses had an edge over trees in another way as well: wildfires frequently swept the land. These do little damage to grasses but may kill woody plants. In addition to lightning-set "natural" fires, Le Page du Pratz, who lived in Natchez from 1720 to 1728, affirmed that Indians burned large areas every September to facilitate hunting and travel.[18] The combination of fire and a drouthy site apparently kept the Grand Prairie a prairie.

Grand Prairie probably became a prairie during one of the many climate changes that have occurred during and since the advances of the glaciers. We know that over the last twenty thousand years the climate has changed from cool-moist through warm-dry to today's warm-moist. A warm-dry interval of hundreds or thousands of years could have allowed the western prairies to shift their range to eastern Arkansas. Fire and a drouthy site allowed the prairie to remain in some places even after the climate made its transition to warm-moist.

In the twentieth century, farmers discovered that rice (appropriately a grass) would grow well on the Grand Prairie. The same deep clay that made the terrace drouthy and allowed native grasses to dominate there also provided a waterproof bottom for a rice field that would allow the field to remain flooded through the growing season with a minimum of infiltration into the soil. Today, most of the original vegetation has been removed, but a grass still dominates the Grand Prairie landscape.

The Arkansas River Lowlands region extends in a fairly narrow belt from Little Rock to Pine Bluff, bounded by the pine-covered hills of the Coastal Plain on the right descending side of the Arkansas River and by the Grand Prairie on the left. East of Pine Bluff, the lowlands widen out and bend southward, paralleling the Mississippi into Louisiana. Today, much of this area is not even in the watershed of the Arkansas River, but the river has meandered through this whole area and is responsible for the soils and much of the character of these lowlands. Bayou Bartholomew flows through an old channel of the Arkansas with piney woods on its right and bottomlands on its left, much like the Arkansas upstream of Pine Bluff. Bayou Bartholomew meets Spanish moss at Wilmot and soon enters Louisiana and the Deep South.

The Arkansas River Lowlands are a reflection of the character of the Arkansas: the river is monumentally long and can only be compared with its equally long neighbors, the Red and the Missouri. It crashes grandly through the Royal Gorge in Colorado only to be sucked dry in Kansas by arid winds and thirsty crops. Therefore, even though it is *long*, it is not *large* compared to the much shorter, home-grown White River. Each is fed by the same moist landward breezes of the Gulf. However, the Arkansas carries an enormous load of sand. Its bars, now mostly inundated by the McClellan-Kerr Navigation System, were a vast Sahara-like playground for the growing river brat. The soil along the river is consequently sandy. This is not rice country; there is often not enough clay to make a watertight bottom. In much of these lowlands, cotton is still king.

The landscape of the Arkansas River Lowlands is quite flat; few high terraces add diversity. Most streams have been ditched, and few trees remain. One notable exception is Macon Ridge (often

pronounced "Mason" in Louisiana) near Eudora. It is like a minia-
ture Crowley's Ridge in geology and shape. However, its lower and
flatter shape have allowed it to be cleared and farmed.

These regions, the St. Francis Basin, Crowley's Ridge, the White
River Lowlands, the Grand Prairie, and the Arkansas River
Lowlands, show clear links to rivers and resulting similarities, but
they reflect different rivers with different characters, providing
regional distinctiveness.

If thus far the rivers have sounded somewhat like the natural
equivalent of Rousseau's Noble Savage or perhaps like a benign and
somewhat sensitive sculptor of the land, it must be made clear that
they are sometimes more savage than noble. Those times come after
the rains have pelted the earth for weeks or even months on end, as
happened in 1927.

Not all floods are disastrous, and the blessings provided by flood
control may be mixed. As William Alexander Percy of Greenville
wrote, the levee of 1893 ". . . was about four feet high, had been built
by Irishmen with wheelbarrows and paid for by local taxation; it
always broke. The levee of today is forty feet high, has been built by
caterpillars and drag lines and paid for by the United States
Government; it sometimes breaks." He pointed out that the 1893 levees, ineffectual as they were to keep the Mississippi off the cotton
fields, had certain real advantages: "When they broke, the water
trickled in gradually, stood quietly over the land two or three weeks,
deposited a fine nutritious layer of sediment, and withdrew without
having drowned anybody or wrecked any buildings or prevented a
late planting of the crop. You called that an overflow." However, the
". . . great dikes of today, when once breached, hurl a roaring wall
of water over the country, so swift, so deep, so long-lasting, it scours
the top soil from the fields, destroys everything in its path, prevents
crop-planting that year, and scatters death among the humble . . ."[19]

He described his first overflow as "a jolly affair." Like Percy, folks
on the Arkansas side tended to take the "overflow" in stride. The
diary of James Millinder Hanks of Helena reflects the same attitude:

Mar. 5, 1867 . . . All further exertion is useless and that the levee
must break. We are to have an overflow and it will be a most terrible calamity. I intended to prop up our field fence, but the
weather was so inclement I did not venture out.

Mar. 6, 1867. Sure enough the levee broke last night and this morning the water is flooding the whole country . . . I propped up our fence as best I could this morning . . . I am afraid we will lose it all. But after all perhaps 'tis for the best and all will yet end well.

Mar. 7, 1867. I was engaged for some time this morning in catching and fastening our fences. The larger part of it is gone forever. Had some sport shooting snipe. Went to town. Had some fun.[20]

The major floods, though, like those of 1927 and 1937, were terrifying fights for survival. These floods were caused by protracted periods of unceasing rains and were aggravated, as Percy pointed out, by the tall levees that confined the river, giving it no small and gentle ways of reducing pressure. They were also augmented by the clearing of millions of acres of forest and prairie that once slowed the water and transpired a significant part of the rainfall back into the atmosphere.

According to Percy:

The 1927 flood was a torrent ten feet deep the size of Rhode Island; it was thirty-six hours coming and four months going; it was deep enough to drown a man, swift enough to upset a boat, and lasting enough to cancel a crop year. The only islands in it were eight or ten tiny Indian mounds and the narrow spoil-banks of a few drainage canals. Between the torrent and the river ran the levee, dry on the land side and on the top. The south Delta became seventy-five hundred miles of mill-race in which one hundred and twenty thousand human beings and one hundred thousand animals squirmed and bobbed.[21]

As the rivers swept over the land, the first reaction was a panicky attempt to escape by any means possible, often over flooded roads and rails. At the same time people poured into the towns from the countryside, and ". . . for thirty-six hours the Delta was in turmoil, in movement, in terror. Then the waters covered everything, the turmoil ceased, and a great quiet settled down. . . . Over everything was silence, deadlier because of the strange cold sound of the currents gnawing at the foundations, hissing against the walls, creaming and clawing over obstructions."[22]

Those who experienced it were deeply affected by the sound of the flood. Percy described "walking the levee," which was done to protect the levee from those who might dynamite it to relieve the pressure on another levee and to discover weak spots, particularly "boils" or leaks in the levee: "During these times the river is a savage clawing thing, right at the top of the levee and sounding at night like the swish of a sword, or the snarl of a beast. It puts ice in your heart when you're trudging the darkness on the slippery berm and hoping not to step on a snake."[23]

According to Pete Daniel, "For the next two months the river tore through the lower valley with the fury of a wild animal . . . people who heard it compared the sound to a tornado, a strong wind, Niagara Falls, a deep animal growl."[24]

Not all the change in the Delta has been wrought by the rivers. Huge areas were transformed by the New Madrid earthquakes of 1811 and 1812. Not just one, but several of these quakes were the largest ever recorded in the country, greater than the earthquakes in San Francisco or Charleston. The greatest earthquake did damage as far away as St. Louis, was heard in Ohio, and felt in Boston. It caused large areas to sink and others to rise, creating extensive "sunk lands." Sandblows and fissures were formed over much of northeast Arkansas and the bootheel of Missouri. Few people were killed on the land because of the lack of large buildings (and the sturdiness of well-mortised log walls), but the loss of life on the Mississippi River was high because of caving banks, uprooted trees, and wild currents caused by sinking of the bottom that apparently caused temporary waterfalls and even caused the river to flow backwards at places for a while.

The first shocks occurred about two o'clock on the morning of December 16, 1811, when ". . . inhabitants of the region were suddenly awakened by the groaning, creaking, and cracking of the timbers of the houses or cabins in which they were sleeping, by the rattle of furniture thrown down, and by the crash of falling chimneys."[25] The ground rose and fell as waves passed across its surface, opening deep cracks in the soil as the surface was bent. Landslides swept down the bluffs and hillsides; areas were uplifted, and still larger areas sank and became covered with water. "On the Mississippi great waves were created, which overwhelmed many boats and washed others high upon the shore, the return current breaking off thousands of trees and carrying them out into the river. High banks caved and were precipitated into the river, sand bars and points of islands gave way, and whole islands disappeared."

One contemporary account reported: ". . . the house danced about and seemed as if it would fall on our heads. I . . . cried out it was an Earthquake, and for the family to leave the house; which we found very difficult to do, owing to its rolling and jostling about. The shock was soon over, and no injury was sustained, except the loss of the chimney. . . ." According to this witness, ". . . a vapor [rose] which seemed to impregnate the atmosphere, and had a disagreeable smell, and produced a difficulty of respiration." After venturing forth, another shock occurred, and ". . . the earth seemed convulsed—the houses shook very much—chimneys falling in every direction. The loud, hoarse roaring which attended the earthquake, together with the cries, screams and yells of the people, seems still ringing in my ears."[26]

Other great shocks occurred on January 23 and February 7, 1812. One authority concluded that for a year from these dates small shocks "occurred at intervals of a few days, but as there were no other destructive shocks the people gradually became accustomed to the vibrations and gave little or no further attention to them."[27]

Congress, in a magnanimous gesture, decided to provide reparations to the earthquake victims by authorizing certificates allowing them to take up land elsewhere in the territory. Then, as now, though, Congress was slow to act, and the authorization did not pass until 1815. Before victims knew of the act, speculators had purchased much of the land for very low prices in order to obtain the certificates and to lay claim to higher-value land. These "New Madrid Certificates" surfaced several times in the possession of a group among whom was the not-yet-notable Stephen F. Austin. This group tried to claim the site of the new territorial capital at Little Rock, and later claims were made on the hot springs. Rebuffed in these attempts, Austin moved away to hatch grander schemes elsewhere.[28]

The landscape of the Arkansas Delta changes constantly in space and time. Microtopographical changes of a foot can dramatically alter the natural system and the uses to which the land can be put. Regions of the Delta are distinct to the point that some people would not even include them all under the term "Delta," yet they are all united by rivers and riverine processes. On any temporal scale from instants to eons, the Delta changes, sometimes in increments as tiny as grains of sand or molecules of clay, or as large as millions of acres of material deposited or removed. Sometimes it seems that only the people resist change and value what *was* instead of the eternal change. Maybe that's good; of all earth's creatures, only *Homo sapiens*, the "self-aware" one, has the ability to value the past, conceive of the future, and change behavior accordingly. In our relationship with the natural processes of the Delta, we may need to treasure some remaining bits of the past in order to alter our behavior and attitudes, to build a new, more appreciative relationship with the land.

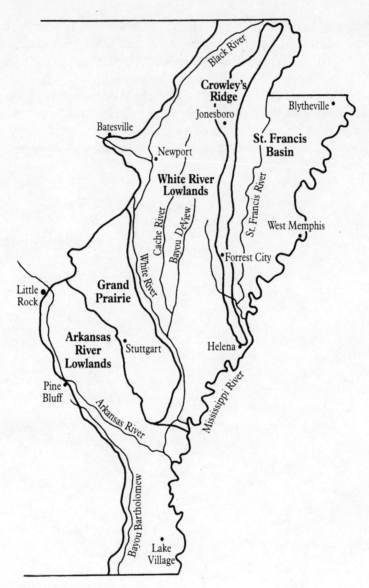

Rivers and Regions of the Delta.
Courtesy of Tom Foti.

A logger from the Bluff City Lumber Company selecting
hardwoods in Jefferson County, 1909.
From American Lumberman *magazine. Courtesy Library of Congress.*

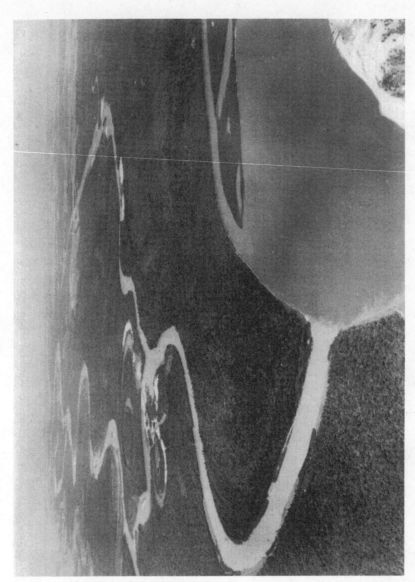

Arkansas River. *Courtesy Arkansas History Commission.*

A "cross-walker" used in the construction of drainage districts.
From Elliott B. Sartain, It Didn't Just Happen (Osceola, Ark.: Drainage District No. 9, 1975), 37. Courtesy Grassy Lake and Tyronza Drainage District No. 9.

Protecting the levee.
From Elliott B. Sartain, It Didn't Just Happen *(Osceola, Ark.: Drainage District No. 9, 1975), 36. Courtesy Grassy Lake and Tyronza Drainage District No. 9.*

Protecting the levee.
From Elliott B. Sartain, It Didn't Just Happen *(Osceola, Ark.: Drainage District No. 9, 1975), 37. Courtesy Grassy Lake and Tyronza Drainage District No. 9.*

Levee break.
From Elliot B. Sartain, It Didn't Just Happen *(Osceola, Ark.: Drainage District No. 9, 1975), 35. Courtesy Grassy Lake and Tyronza Drainage District No. 9.*

Survey crew and a snake.
From Elliott B. Sartain, It Didn't Just Happen *(Osceola, Ark.: Drainage District No. 9, 1975), 10. Courtesy Grassy Lake and Tyronza Drainage District No. 9.*

The Delta's Colonial Heritage

MORRIS S. ARNOLD

The expanding French fur-trading empire came very early to the Delta region of Arkansas—earlier, in fact, than to any other part of that vast country that would, in time, become Jefferson's Louisiana. René-Robert Cavelier de La Salle had arrived at the Arkansas River in 1682, six months before William Penn set foot on the New World to found Philadelphia, in an effort to attract the trade of the Quapaw Indians and to effect a military alliance with them. After some initial nervousness, the Quapaws received LaSalle and his men with numerous displays of public and private affection.[1] Even at this distance, the Quapaws' motives for offering their allegiance are not difficult to divine: they needed the trade goods that the French could provide and no doubt particularly coveted European firearms. (Firearms, though not superior to bows and arrows in terms of penetrating power, had the advantage of producing a long and flat trajectory for a cheap and expendable projectile.) Then, too, the Quapaws had been long-time enemies of the Chickasaws, who were probably already allied with the English, so it is possible that the Quapaws had no use for Great Britain by the time La Salle arrived.

Four years later, in the summer of 1686, Henri de Tonty, a close associate of La Salle's who had accompanied him on his 1682 voyage, established six Frenchmen on the Arkansas River near the present-day Arkansas County community of Nady. Hard by were the Quapaw inhabitants of a village called Osotouy with whom Tonty hoped to establish a trade for furs and skins, chiefly beaver and deer. This little French establishment, generally called the first Arkansas Post, evidently did not actually have a name; Tonty simply referred to his "commercial house" or "fort" in the Arkansas during the fourteen years or so of its existence. (In 1687, some French travelers stumbled into this trading post and commented on a "French-looking" house there made of horizontal logs; but whether anything that we should term a fort was ever built there may be doubted.) Tonty made a few land grants at and near this post, including two to the Jesuits on condition that they establish a chapel; but the Jesuits, though hardy and intrepid as could be, because of their small numbers, were never able to take up Tonty's invitation.

Jean Couture, a carpenter from Rouen who was in charge of Tonty's Arkansas enterprise, seems to have defected to the English interest about 1694 on account of unfavorable colonial trade laws, for in that year he is reported in Savannah Town, spinning tales of gold beyond the Appalachians. It is not likely that Tonty's post, at least as a year-round presence, would long have survived Couture's defection. In any case, it seems that the French had abandoned the place by 1699.[2]

The illegal fur traders and hunters that the Canadian French deprecatingly called *coureurs de bois* (forest runners) operated sporadically in the Arkansas region following the failure of Tonty's post, and there is evidence even of horse trading with the Osages on the Arkansas River in the early eighteenth century. The French government occasionally projected forts on the Arkansas, though these plans were not realized in the two decades following the demise of the first post. Permanent European settlement did not return to the Grand Prairie region of the Delta until the summer of 1721, when some *engagés* (workmen) of the financier John Law arrived to clear land, build houses, and otherwise prepare the way for a grand colonizing scheme. Law's plan was to import large numbers of German peasants from the Palatinate to people a huge grant of ten miles square that he had secured for himself from the Company of the Indies, which he, not incidentally, also headed. In 1720, some German colonists did indeed arrive at Biloxi, a staging area from which they were planning to make the transition to Arkansas; but Law's bankruptcy intervened, and in 1721 his colonists settled a few miles above New Orleans at what came to be called the German Coast. Many, perhaps all, of Law's *engagés* were released from service by the company, and some remained in the Post area to hunt and engage sporadically in some desultory efforts at agriculture. A small military post, established in 1721 near the French settlement, was abandoned in 1725. In 1726, the census taker said that the

French at the Arkansas were "poor and lived only by the hunting of wild animals." Father Du Poisson, a Jesuit missionary, said the next year that there were, all told, only thirty Frenchmen at and around his Arkansas station.[3]

In 1731, because of the bellicose activities of the pro-English Chickasaw nation, the French felt the need to buttress their alliance with the Quapaws and therefore re-established a military garrison at their remote *Poste des Arkansas*. The new commandant was able to establish a swift rapport with the Quapaws, and soon they were sending war parties against the Chickasaws and torturing prisoners to death in their village. They took part, moreover, in two elaborate but ultimately disastrous general wars against the Chickasaws in 1734 and 1738, both of which involved considerable military activity near the site of present-day Memphis; the 1738 war even required the building of a fort at the mouth of the St. Francis River and the transportation of cannon, animals, and other matériel through the Delta to what is now West Memphis. The Chickasaws, however, emerged victorious in both encounters.[4]

Despite these dismal military failures, the Quapaws remained firm friends of the French in their neighborhood and, in the 1740s, continued their raids on the Chickasaws in aid of a colonial war that coincided with, and was in a measure absorbed by, a more general contest between the French and the English. In 1749, the Chickasaws, infuriated by the constant attacks on them by the Quapaws and other Indians allied with the French, struck the Arkansas Post, captured a number of settlers, and attacked the fort there. The garrison, safely barricaded inside its redoubt, fired cannon and guns at its attackers, and a lucky grapeshot struck the Chickasaw Chief Payah Matahah, whereupon the attackers felt obliged to retreat. Unfortunately, the male captives were killed in retaliation for the wounds inflicted on the chief; the women and children were later ransomed at Charleston and New Orleans.[5]

One of the reasons that this attack had been so successful was that the Quapaws, probably on account of a great flood in 1748, had removed themselves from their old venue near Nady to the higher ground a few miles upriver that the French called *Écores Rouges* (Red Bluffs). When the Chickasaws arrived at the Post, therefore, they did not encounter the stiff opposition that they expected. The ensuing disaster to French arms might well have been averted had the Quapaws been available to help defend the tiny garrison; the simple truth is that, if for no other reason than military necessity, the French of Arkansas had to treat the Indians as equals and consult them with respect to important decisions. But in fact their cultural connection went much deeper than mere necessity, for many of the hunters and trappers, and even some of the merchants of the Post, were married to Quapaws and to Indians of various other tribes. Interestingly, a nineteenth-century visitor reported that the white denizens of Arkansas spoke a language that was a mixture of French and Quapaw. Other writers opined that the continued existence of the Post depended on the mixed-blood character of the population which created a mutual and literally symbiotic bond between Indian and European.[6]

After the 1749 raid, and probably in the same year, the Post was moved to *Écores Rouges* in order to take more effective advantage of the essential Quapaw alliance. But because of the Seven Years' War, French and Quapaw alike abandoned this new outpost in 1756 and relocated downriver only about eight or nine miles from the Mississippi so that they could be more useful to the convoys that plied the great river between New Orleans and St. Louis. There the Post remained until 1779 when, discouraged by the continual floods that made agriculture impossible in the Delta, its population removed yet again, but this time finally, back to *Écores Rouges* on the edge of the Grand Prairie.[7]

The chief occupations of the Europeans of Arkansas Post, who never, even by the late colonial period, could have much exceeded 350 in number, were hunting and trading with the Indians of the region. Only a few of Arkansas's eighteenth-century residents engaged in agriculture, and even well into the nineteenth century the Post found it necessary to import flour from the Illinois country and elsewhere. In 1768, it is true, the commandant of the Post sent a *sac de pecannes* (a sack of pecans) to the governor with his compliments and a note explaining that they were from a tree growing on the St. Francis River; but there is no record of the exportation of agricultural products from the Post in serious amounts. The chief exports of the Arkansas country were furs, skins, salted buffalo meat, bears' oil, and tallow. In 1770, for instance, one François Ménard, who in time would become Arkansas Post's richest citizen, secured a contract from the Spanish government to supply 10,000 pounds of tallow for its arsenals in Havana.[8] Bears' oil was put to a wide variety of uses, including salad dressing, cooking oil, mosquito repellant, and even hair oil. It was also burned in lamps, and it is a good bet that a number of Arkansas bears were consumed in the lighting system installed late in the eighteenth century by Governor Carondolet in what is now called the New Orleans French Quarter. Salted buffalo tongues from Arkansas were also much in demand as a delicacy in New Orleans and even in Madrid.[9]

Despite there being very little sustained agriculture at and around the little Louisiana outpost on the Arkansas, there were black slaves there as early as 1721 when Law's abortive settlement effort got underway. By the end of the eighteenth century, the Post census reported about sixty slaves residing there in a population of almost four hundred.[10] No doubt some of these slaves were field hands; many of the larger French farms had a few slaves, up to six or eight, and it is a good guess that some of these blacks were engaged in agriculture. (The industrious German farmers, on the other hand, of whom there were four or five in the late eighteenth century, had no slaves at all, a probable indication that they were conscientiously opposed to slavery.) Blacks also worked in the houses of the commandants and, presumably, of the other gentry of the Post as servants and kitchen workers. Others labored by dressing and packing skins and loading and unloading boats for the merchants. For instance, in 1798, Françoise Ménard, widow of François Ménard, was listed in the census as a *marchande* (merchant) and had nine slaves in her household.[11] Still other blacks were skilled artisans. For example, when Pedro Rousseau put his Spanish war galiot in at the Post in 1793, he secured the help of an old black man, an experienced blacksmith, for repairs to his rudder.[12] There were also a few, a very few, free blacks at the Arkansas, some of whom evidently engaged in farming on a small scale. And in 1790, the census reveals the presence of two female mulattoes, both of them listed as seamstresses.[13]

One of the many police duties of the commandant on the Arkansas River was the capture of runaway slaves for return to their masters. In 1783, for instance, Captain Jacobo Dubreuil, who commanded at the Post from 1783 to 1787, drafted a notice that read as follows:

Notice of a Black Runaway Held in the
Fort of Carlos III of Arkansas.

Cezar, a creole [i.e., native] of Virginia, age twenty years more or less, with large eyes, well-shaped nostrils, long chin, and no beard, five feet and six inches tall, lean body, and suffering greatly from back [or kidney] pain. Arkansas, 1 August, 1783.

Jacobo Dubreuil

This notice was presumably sent to the governor in New Orleans for circulation to the other towns and posts of Louisiana, and perhaps also to some of the constituent republics of that new country called the United States.[14]

An extremely interesting incident that occurred in 1783 involved some slaves who had run away from their St. Louis owners and had found their way to one of the Quapaw villages. The Quapaws first asserted that they were *cadeaux*, a word that ordinarily means "presents" in French; but in Arkansas it was also used as a spelling for Caddos, the name of an Indian tribe allied with the Quapaws that lived on the Red River. (Perhaps, then, the Quapaws were trying to pass the runaways off as dark-skinned Indians!) Whatever the meaning of the excuse originally proffered, the Quapaws soon switched to the argument that "a man of the slaves' color is born to freedom as soon as he enters the house of a chief."[15] The appearance of this interesting legal theory in eighteenth-century Arkansas demonstrates, probably, a social intercourse with other tribes who engaged in "free-soil" practices; moreover, it reminds us how very easy it is to overemphasize the remoteness, insularity, and isolation of the Quapaws and their French colleagues. Arkansas Post, it is true, was out in the middle of nowhere; but that is precisely what gave it strategic importance and assured it a continuing and sustained contact with the outside world.

One indication that the Post was by no means altogether a cultural backwater is that, by the late colonial period at least, the architecture of the houses there was in the style of those in the sophisticated precincts of New Orleans. The typical colonial Louisiana plantation house, many aspects of which were transplanted from the French West Indies very early in the eighteenth century, had several distinctive features, all of which, the records reveal, were incorporated into the houses at the Post. These houses had hip roofs, galleries all around, numerous doors and windows opening onto the gallery, interior chimneys, glazed casement windows, and wood shutters, and were raised six feet or so from the ground to provide storage space. They were built of upright posts either stuck in the ground (called *poteaux en terre*) or fitted to wooden sills (called *poteaux sur solle*).

The interstices of the posts were filled with *bousillage*, a mixture of mud, moss, and animal hair. In other places in Louisiana, bricks were used as nogging material, but there is no indication at all in the records of any bricks being employed in eighteenth-century Arkansas. Nor were there any building stones available in the Arkansas Delta region, so fireplaces and chimneys were necessarily constructed of sticks, branches, and mud. Some houses had their kitchens in separate buildings to reduce the destruction that an accidental fire there would cause.

Most of the houses at the Arkansas Post were very modest, two-room affairs built on the so-called medieval model: one general, all-purpose living room, dining room, and kitchen (the *salle*), the other a bedroom (the *chambre*). The size of an average dwelling was probably around six hundred square feet, a small house indeed. But some houses were a good deal larger, and the wrap-around gallery sometimes contained more sheltered space than was available even inside. The gallery was used as a place for gathering with family and friends and for sleeping when weather (and insects) permitted.[16]

The government of the Post and the Arkansas region, which included the Arkansas, White, and St. Francis rivers, was given over wholly to one man, the commandant of the Post. He was frequently styled "Judge Civil and Military" of his district, emphasizing the totality of his control over local affairs. The judicial duties of the commandant have been rather exhaustively explored elsewhere,[17] but it may be instructive to visit briefly some episodes of local legislative activity on his part. It seems to have been assumed, in the Spanish period at least, that the Post commandant possessed considerable latitude to fashion regulations that touched on matters of local concern. For instance, in 1783 Captain Jacobo Dubreuil published the following document:

Copy of an Order Published in the Post of
Arkansas on the 26th day of December, 1783.

Don Jacobo Dubreuil, Captain of Infantry and Commandant of the Post and District of Arkansas: In order to avoid the accidents that occur frequently on account of unexpected fires at this place, and on account of the dangers that drunken Indians or evil-intentioned persons who commit criminal acts create, I order that there cannot be in any house of this place more than six pounds of powder. And in order to effect this order, persons who have a quantity of powder that exceeds the aforesaid six pounds shall take it all to the king's warehouse today, and the owner of it shall put a tag with his name [on his barrel] along with the weight of the barrel and its contents, and second corporal Lucas Perez will receive it after verifying the said weight. It is to be understood that every time that the said owner wants to dispense his powder to hunters . he can present himself [to the warehouse] at convenient times. In order to have this order observed by travelers as well as those who reside at this post, travelers must take their munitions to the aforesaid warehouse immediately upon arrival.

Arkansas, 26 December, 1783
Signed: Jacobo Dubreuil[18]

Because the Post was in the main a trading and hunting village, the regulations promulgated there, like the one just noted, naturally tended to deal with the skin and fur trade. In 1778 and 1798, what the French of the Post referred to as ordinances were passed that worked out priorities between merchants who supplied hunters and the hunters' employees, and created appropriate liens to enforce these obligations.[19] An interesting feature of the 1798 ordinance is that it was worked out by the commandant in consultation with two persons each from the hunter and merchant classes. It included some fines for its violation. The governor approved it with some changes that he ordered. These kinds of business regulations are not merely intrinsically interesting, though they are certainly that: they are revealing for the light they shed on the suppositions that gave shape to colonial Louisiana government and society. There was never a specific grant of legislative authority to Post commandants so far as we know, but such was the hierarchial character of Spanish society that it was simply assumed that the patriarchal commandant had the power, indeed the duty, to create an efficient and moral arrangement for his inhabitants. In addition to his legislative duties, the commandant was expected to use his military personnel to execute the judgments of his own court and of the governor's court in New Orleans. He was the very embodiment of the colonial government. It is difficult to imagine a view of a proper political order more different from the republican postulates of equality, limited government, and the separation of powers that gave life to the new American nation that acquired Louisiana, and therefore Arkansas, in 1803.

The only other person in eighteenth-century Arkansas whose power and authority could have even approached that of the commandant was the priest. But the church had very little influence in Arkansas because of the nature and small size of the Post population. Although there was a priest resident among the Quapaws as early as 1700, he was soon martyred, and for most of the eighteenth century the French of the Arkansas region had to be content with episodic visits from peripatetic missionaries. There were to this general picture of neglect two main exceptions of significance. About 1752, first of all, Father Louis Carette came to the Post as resident missionary and was given a position of prominence, for a large building built there in about the same year contained a chapel and living quarters for the priest and the commandant. This arrangement could only have created an impression of a certain equality between church and state, though the priest lived in only one room while the commandant had two. When the Post moved downriver in 1756, however, no chapel was provided, and the priest was segregated in a separate one-room building which doubled as his chamber and chapel. This annoyed Father Carette greatly, but he persevered in the Delta for two more years when an event that he considered seriously sacrilegious precipitated his departure.[20] In 1796, Father Pierre Janin, who had made the mistake of telling the bishop that he did not like big cities, found himself assigned to the remote post of *Los Arcos*, as the Spanish called Arkansas Post, with the job of establishing the first canonical parish ever erected there. He called it the parish of St. Stephen, because that was the name of the fort erected at the Post in 1792; the commandant had given the fort that name to flatter the governor, Esteban (i.e., Stephen) Miró. Unfortunately for the small cadre of the devout at the Post, in 1799 Father Janin was called away to the more populous and prestigious parish in St. Louis, and the Louisiana church was never able to find a replacement to tend the Arkansas flock.[21] Of course, with the change of sovereignty in 1803 came the end of the established church, and preachers and priests alike were slow to come to the wilds of Arkansas in the nineteenth century.

When the American era dawned in Arkansas, it revealed a very small, mostly uneducated population of approximately four hundred Frenchmen and a Quapaw tribe so decimated by disease, alcohol, and warfare that it probably numbered no more than five hundred itself. After five generations of intermarriage and cultural symbiosis, a certain homogeneity of Indian and white had been achieved in such diverse matters as dress, food, moral habits, and language.

There were always a few families of gentry at the Post who clung to their European traditions of religion, law, and even literary culture; but their number was so small that they could in no way provide a bulwark against assimilation by the American immigrant tide of the nineteenth century. Unlike New Orleans and southern Louisiana—with their much larger European population of probably twenty thousand who had rather well-developed ties with the Continent and had as well created a strong local colonial culture, including a press, an opera, professional law courts, and impressive governmental and religious buildings—the weakly established European culture on the Arkansas River had virtually no adhesive power. For one thing, the population was extremely small, and, for another, its demography, skewed toward the lower classes, tended to have less influence on the establishment of political and economic orders. The class structure of the Arkansas was, simply put, that of a banana republic, except that the gentry were less numerous than one could expect even for that sort of social arrangement, and they were inclined not to stay for long in the Arkansas region.

The coming of the Americans meant a great deal more to the French *habitants* of Arkansas's Delta than a merely formal substitution of sovereigns. The ancient residents found themselves in a numerical minority and their new neighbors regarded them with suspicion and hostility. Some of the newcomers ridiculed the French for their "superstitious" religion[22] and their patriarchal political and legal system. They sneered at their lack of medical science,[23] though American medicine was hardly, if at all, more advanced. They even spoke deprecatingly of the style and construction of their houses.[24] And they repeatedly criticized what they considered French "indolence" and especially disliked their diversions like gambling and dancing. Segregated on account of their language and manners, the French were effectively excluded from participation in government: they only very rarely served on juries and almost never sought political office.

Standard Arkansas histories have not ordinarily devoted much space to the colonial epoch or allowed it much significance, if any. The truth is, however, that we are only just beginning to understand the ways in which our present is connected to our colonial past, and a few quite important links are becoming rather clear. For one thing, Arkansas's persistent and chronic poverty, though frequently traced to the territorial period, was in fact already being noted and remarked on by the census taker in 1727, who, as we saw, wrote that the Arkansas population was "all poor and lived only by the hunting of wild beasts." Indeed, as we also saw, the larger part of Arkansas's colonial European population consisted of hunters, many of whom were fugitives, and the reputation of Arkansas as an asylum for outlaws and a haven for the feckless was a prominent feature of the antebellum literature about the place. Of course, stable agricultural settlements, a prerequisite for civilized life, were impossible in most regions of the Delta because of the dangers of floods, and settlements in the interior ran the risk of attack from Indians, principally the Osages. The Spanish government never made a significant investment in Louisiana, and certainly not in Arkansas. Public improvements in Louisiana, such as roads and levees, were supposed to be made by the landowners on which the improvements were located, but this never happened in Arkansas because of the minute size and poverty of the populace. There were no significant taxes in Louisiana to support public works, for the lack of taxes was a device that the Spanish employed to encourage immigration. As a result, agriculture of an appreciable character was not feasible in Arkansas. Then, too, the commercial possibilities of the Arkansas region were never allowed to be properly exploited because the French government for most of the eighteenth century insisted that the Osage trade belonged exclusively to the small oligopoly gathered in St. Louis, and the St. Louis merchants on the whole succeeded in their efforts to stifle economic growth at the Arkansas.[25] As a result of all these impediments and more, Arkansas became part of the United States in an impoverished and underdeveloped state and has struggled ever since to become part of the nation's cultural mainstream.

Men cross the river.
From David Dale Owen, Second Report of a Geological Reconnaissance of the Middle and Southern Counties of Arkansas *(Philadelphia: C. Sherman & Son, Printers, 1860).*

Early travelers in the Delta.
Courtesy Library of Congress.

"Desolation Itself":
The Impact of Civil War

BOBBY ROBERTS

Tuesday, February 5, 1861, was a raw, wintry day in Little Rock, and the few townspeople who ventured outside were surprised to see armed militia entering their city. The first of these companies came mainly from the Delta counties of Phillips, Monroe, and Arkansas. Men from other counties arrived that evening, and by Wednesday the "streets were alive with the stir and commotion of armed soldiery."[1] They came because of a false rumor that Federal troops were being sent to reinforce the small garrison occupying the arsenal in the capital city, and the men meant to seize the facility before that happened. The secessionist-minded governor, Henry M. Rector, had previously denied that he had the authority to take such action, but he equivocated enough to convince some hotheads that the issue could and should be forced. On Friday the Union garrison surrendered peacefully. The authorities allowed the troops led by Capt. James Totten to embark on a steamer for St. Louis, but before the captain left, the ladies of Little Rock presented him with a fine ceremonial sword.[2]

Totten's action undoubtedly avoided bloodshed, but the seizure of the arsenal was the first overt act of defiance of Federal authorities in Arkansas. Similar scenes had already happened throughout many of the Southern states, and they were harbingers of the terrible civil war that would soon engulf the nation.

The capitulation of the Little Rock Arsenal did not, as some had hoped, immediately push Arkansas closer to secession. The state remained in the Union until after the attack on Fort Sumter on April 12, 1861, and President Abraham Lincoln's subsequent call for troops to suppress the insurrection. However, the seizure of the arsenal did show that the southern disunionists were willing to take extreme measures to further their cause. The heavy participation of men from the Delta counties clearly demonstrated the widespread support for secession in the region.

The immediate concern of the disunionists was the election of Abraham Lincoln, an election that implied that the North would now try to contain slavery within its present boundaries. Southern apologists then and now believed that the root of the conflict rested in such diverse factors as states' rights issues, sectionalism, economic differences, and cultural incompatibility between North and South. Most also believed that these differences were exacerbated and given focus both by the abolitionists, who were determined to abolish slavery, and the southern fire-eaters, who were equally determined to protect their "peculiar institution." These arguments add to our understanding of the dynamics that ultimately led to war, but the fundamental issue that underpinned them all and indeed caused those differences to develop was the persistence of slavery in the southern states. And it was the existence of slavery and the South's willingness to use force to defend that institution that eventually led to disunion and war.

Throughout the South, the search for cheap land had drawn both yeoman farmers and slaveholders westward. By the early nineteenth century, a trickle of settlers was entering Arkansas in search of farm land, and within thirty years 25,812 whites and 4,576 slaves had migrated into the territory.[3] Most of the slaves and their masters were inextricably tied to the cultivation of cotton, which flourished near the river bottoms of eastern and southern Arkansas. By the mid-1850s that trickle of slaveholders had grown into a steady stream as liberalized land laws and the draining of swampland dramatically increased the available land.

On the eve of the Civil War, the number of slaves in several of the Delta counties already exceeded 50 percent of the population, and the major sources of wealth and social prestige in the Delta rested on cotton production and the ownership of slaves. The region was not yet a plantation society, but the aspiring gentry aped the ways of more-established planters in eastern slaveholding states and shared many of their values. Most slaveholders in the Arkansas Delta now accepted slavery as an economically viable labor system that bestowed wealth and social status on the master. These men saw little that was oppressive about the "peculiar institution," and many believed in the moral superiority of a society that rested on slavery. Across the South these slaveholders and the nonslaveholding whites, who often followed their lead, formed the core of the movement that was now driving the nation toward civil war.

The movement toward disunion had been gathering momentum throughout the Deep South since the late 1850s, but even after the secession of seven slaveholding states, Arkansas remained committed to the Union. Thus, after the capture of the Little Rock Arsenal, the convention that opened on March 4, 1861, to consider secession refused to be stampeded into taking such drastic action and adjourned to await further developments.

The final drama in Arkansas's agonizing decision to secede began nine hundred miles to the east on April 12, 1861, when Confederate gunners opened fire on Fort Sumter in South Carolina. Three days later President Lincoln asked for seventy-five thousand troops to put down the rebellion. These two actions finally tilted Arkansas toward the Confederacy, and on May 6, 1861, the reassembled convention quickly voted to secede. Immediately after the vote, Thomas C. Hindman, a congressman from Helena and one of the leading fire-eaters in Arkansas, happily telegraphed President Jefferson Davis that the convention passed an "ordinance of secession at 4 P.M. by a unanimous vote."[4]

Once the nagging question of secession had been resolved, the war fever swept across the state. English-born Henry M. Stanley was working in a store at Cypress Bend when he heard the news, and he almost immediately joined the 6th Arkansas Infantry. His reaction was typical of many young men who suddenly felt a compelling urge to fight. "The fever of military enthusiasm was at its height, in man, woman, and child," he later remembered, "and we who were to represent them in war received far more adulation than was good for us. The popular praise turned our young heads giddy, and anyone who doubted that we were the sanest, bravest, and most gallant boys in the world would have been in personal danger."[5] Throughout the Delta enthusiastic volunteers like young Stanley, who later became famous for his exploration of Africa, joined companies with such exotic names as "Clan McGregor," "Jackson Guards," "Crockett Rifles," and "Augusta Guards."

When the soldiers marched off to war, the citizens usually gathered to present battle flags to these self-proclaimed heroes. In Mound City, Arkansas, for example, the people watched Miss Lillian Rozelle present the company banner to Capt. C. H. Carlton of the

Jefferson Guards. Miss Rozelle, who came with a group of ladies from Pine Bluff, gave the flag to the Jefferson County company, proclaiming that "with souls ripe in loyal patriotism we strive with happy willingness sparing no toil or labor in endeavoring to make the offering, this flag, to wave o'er the glorious and gifted sons of Jefferson, and that with every breeze may be wafted endless chimes of your honor, valor, and glory. Our hands made it," she declared. "Your hearts must defend it." Miss Rozelle then handed the blue silk banner to Captain Carlton, who, according to an observer, was a "gallant soldier and true gentleman as ever flashed a sword," before turning the flag over to his regimental commander, Col. Patrick Cleburne of Helena.[6] Such was the romanticized view of the looming conflict in those early days, but the men such as those who heard the brave words of Miss Rozelle and Captain Carlton would soon cease to be strangers to war. In Arkansas alone, more than sixty thousand men eventually served in the southern armies. Thousands died from wounds and disease. Many more were disabled, and most soon learned that war brought not glory but suffering and death. Almost all would be poorly clothed and ill fed while they served their new country. But those realities lay in the future, and now Arkansans, like the majority of white southerners, were enthusiastically preparing to meet the enemy.

Throughout the early months of the war, the organization of regiments continued. No exact figures exist on the number of enlistments from the Delta counties, but at least seven infantry regiments including the 1st, 2d, 8th, 9th, 15th, 19th, and 23d were predominantly from that area. Other muster rolls also contained companies from the Delta counties and indicate that they were scattered among many of the thirty-nine infantry regiments, nineteen cavalry units, and thirteen artillery batteries that served from the state.[7]

These same counties also sent a number of important military leaders into the Confederate armies. Phillips County alone furnished seven generals for the South, including Thomas C. Hindman, who became the ranking general from Arkansas, and Patrick R. Cleburne, who was generally recognized by his fellow officers as one of the best divisional commanders in the Army of Tennessee. Equally respected was Daniel H. Reynolds from Lake Village. Reynolds eventually became a brigadier general in the Army of Tennessee and received repeated praise from his superiors. He led his brigade until the waning days of the war when he lost a leg at Bentonville, North Carolina.

Early in the conflict many of the regiments first raised in Arkansas were transferred east of the Mississippi River, where most served throughout the war. The last major transfer of Arkansas troops occurred shortly after the Confederate defeat at Pea Ridge in northwest Arkansas on March 6–7, 1862. The decision appeared to leave the state at the mercy of Union forces in Missouri, which were now preparing to advance into the heart of Arkansas, and the state's citizens were about to face the grim reality of war. By the middle of April 1862, thirteen thousand Union troops under the command of Maj. Gen. Samuel Ryan Curtis were advancing southward, and even though spring rains had delayed the march, by May 4 the Union army occupied Batesville.

To most observers, Curtis's forces appeared overwhelming, and the capture of Little Rock seemed a certainty. However, the commanding general was at the end of a tenuous supply line that ran northward to Missouri through some of the most difficult terrain imaginable. Curtis knew that he could not continue to depend on that route for supplies and that he must capture the capital city before shortages forced him to retire. Still, given the heretofore token Confederate resistance, his advance seemed relentless and only desperate measures would stop him. Those measures were about to be taken by Maj. Gen. Thomas Hindman of Phillips County, who assumed command of the district on May 31, 1862. That day he issued a proclamation to the soldiers and citizens of the district stating that he had "come here to drive out the invaders or perish in the attempt." "To achieve such success," he added, "it is essential that the soldier and the citizen each shall do his duty."[8]

When Hindman issued his statement, the vanguard of Curtis's army was a scant thirty-four miles from Little Rock. Most officials of the state government had already fled the capital, and throughout much of Arkansas, courts were suspended. The remaining military authorities had done little to recruit, train, and equip a force to defend the state. Furthermore, marauding bands of Confederate soldiers were terrorizing certain sections of Arkansas; recruitment for the Union army was widespread; and many were openly trading with the invaders.[9]

Hindman, acting with almost dictatorial powers, immediately took drastic steps to deal with these problems. In the following weeks he declared martial law, rigorously enforced conscription, and seized anything that he needed to prosecute the war. Hindman, realizing the seriousness of Curtis's logistical problems, began systematically to eliminate all local sources of supplies and hastily organized guerrilla units to harass federal wagon trains, foraging parties, and patrols. He told Brig. Gen. Albert Rust: "Resist the enemy to the last extremity, blockading roads, burning bridges, destroying all supplies, growing crops included, and polluting the water by killing cattle, ripping the carcasses, and throwing them in."[10] These extreme tactics earned him the hatred of many Arkansans who suffered as much from Hindman's actions as from those of the enemy, but it had a telling effect on Curtis's army. "We suffered terribly for want of water," wrote Iowa cavalryman Charles D. Field, "as the rebels filled the wells up. We could not find any forage for everything had been destroyed for many miles in front by the retreating army."[11]

The difficulty of supplying the army from its bases in Missouri and the growing Rebel resistance now forced Curtis to abandon temporarily his drive to Little Rock and to appeal to his superiors for assistance. The Federal command responded by sending a naval expedition up the White River to meet Curtis, who then began moving down the east bank of the stream in the hope of establishing a new line of communication somewhere on the river. However, Confederate resistance at St. Charles and a rapidly falling river forced the expedition to turn back before it could reach the beleaguered army. Curtis now had to think about the very survival of his men, and he needed to find a secure logistical base immediately. By June 24, 1862, Curtis's army was in motion toward Helena.

On July 7, 1862, a Confederate force led by Rust tried unsuccessfully to bring the retreating army to bay at Hills Plantation near Cotton Plant. The Confederates attempted no other major attack on the retreating Union army, but throughout the long march Curtis's men were engaged in almost daily skirmishes with Confederate detachments. Everywhere the Federal soldiers marched, they saw deserted houses, ruined orchards, burning cotton, and destroyed forage and foodstuffs.[12]

By July 13, 1862, Curtis's entire army was concentrated in Helena. At the time of its occupation, the town was an established community and steamboat landing of about 1,500 people. Although most of the homes were frame, there was a smattering of brick structures, and a general air of prosperity was evident. On the outskirts of town several stately plantation houses surrounded by fields of cotton and corn attested to the wealth of the area.[13]

However, when Curtis's weary soldiers began crowding into Helena they were not impressed by what they encountered. "It is a low muddy place," wrote one soldier, "with numerous ponds of filthy green looking water."[14] Another noted that when it rained the streets became impassable even on foot. One soldier's fanciful tale included the remark that he had seen mules sink so deep in the mud that all that was left showing were the animals' ears. Indeed, many soldiers' memories of Helena centered mainly around the omnipresent floods, mud, heat, and malaria. Many surely agreed with some of the men of the 33d Iowa Infantry who called it "Hell-in-Arkansas."[15]

If the Union soldiers were unhappy about being in Helena, it is certainly true that the majority of Helenians were equally unhappy to have them there. When Curtis's soldiers began crowding into the town, they immediately appropriated buildings, homes, lumber, and anything else that they needed to establish quarters. Soon, the town appeared to be a city of small huts and dingy log cabins as the garrison settled into its routine. In the ensuing months, citizens and soldiers learned to tolerate one another. In some cases they became friends and collaborators in the illicit cotton trade that was quickly becoming the most lucrative business in the South. Undoubtedly the presence of the garrison eventually helped the economy, and the Union sympathizers, such as H. P. Coolidge, who owned a local store, saw little reason to worry about the presence of Federal troops in Helena.[16]

For the next year the war in the Delta was little more than a stalemate, but Helena soon proved to be an important base for the Union army. The very presence of such a large garrison in Arkansas forced Confederate authorities to keep troops in the state that could have been more profitably employed elsewhere. Furthermore, the town quickly became a major steamboat landing and depot for the use of Union troops employed in the extensive operations against Vicksburg, Mississippi. Lastly, the soldiers' presence in Helena insured Union control of trade along the waterways of the Arkansas Delta and the enlistment of contrabands as soldiers in the Union armies.

Once Curtis's men had been resupplied, they began throwing together a series of breastworks on the high ground around Helena and sending out patrols into the surrounding countryside. There, Confederate cavalry and guerrillas waited to pounce on any weak, isolated detachment of men. The fights were usually short and vicious. A typical engagement occurred on October 11, 1862: three companies of the 4th Iowa Cavalry were returning from a routine patrol when they were surprised near Lick Creek by the 21st Texas Cavalry. The men of the 4th Iowa had seen no Confederates all day and were almost within sight of their camp when the attack began. The troopers, "marching at ease, stretched out and in bad order, careless of danger," were thrown into disorder by the sudden assault. Within a few minutes three Federal soldiers were dead, two were wounded, and fifteen were captured. One of the Iowans, after surrendering, was killed by the Confederates when he refused to run to the rear with the other prisoners. Additional Union troops arrived on the field and saved the remainder of the detachment before it could be destroyed by the Confederates.[17] Similar scenes happened almost daily as Union detachments moved through the Delta counties. For the men who had to fight under such conditions, it was a nasty, brutish business with little glory for either side.

In addition to the hardship imposed by active campaigning, most soldiers had to endure endemic illnesses that often crippled whole regiments. Reports from various Union hospitals in Arkansas established the state as the most unhealthy command in the army. During the period from July 1, 1863, to June 30, 1865, for example, the average monthly strength of the Union army was 28,462 soldiers, but at least one-half were absent at any one time due primarily to illness. During that same two-year period, Union hospitals accepted 178,194 admissions for illness.[18]

Statistics for illness among Confederate soldiers are more difficult to obtain, but since the South suffered from shortages of doctors, medical supplies, and food, it is likely that their conditions were even worse. And, along the marshy areas of eastern Arkansas, soldiers were often victims of malaria, yellow fever, diarrhea, and various lung infections. Assistant Surgeon Junius Bragg remarked that Arkansas Post was such a "vile place" that only mosquitoes could live there and that jaundice was so bad among Confederate soldiers that they looked like Indians. "I am credibly informed by the oldest inhabitant," he jokingly wrote his wife, "that the snakes have chills."[19]

Conditions were no better in Helena, where the hospitals were soon filled with sick soldiers. Because the hospitals themselves were so unhealthy, many men loathed going on sick call. Sgt. Leander Stillwell of the 61st Illinois Infantry later remembered his fear because he "had a superstitious dread of an army hospital. I had seen so many of the boys loaded into ambulances, and hauled off to such a place— who never returned, that I was determined never to go to one if it could be avoided in any honorable way." Stillwell eventually did have to be taken to the hospital where he lay for eight days. He and others were cared for by soldiers who were themselves too weak for fatigue duty. At night the only light came from small candles inserted in bayonet sockets, and when they burned out, the sick remained in darkness until morning. If they were still alive the next day, those who could eat were usually given a thin soup and hardtack.[20]

Faced with such primitive conditions, hundreds of soldiers died and were buried in the hills that surrounded the town. Unfortunately, conditions in Helena never improved significantly, and even as late as 1864, officials reported that the town appeared to be the "most deadly place on the river."[21]

When Union forces established themselves along the banks of the White River in the fall of 1863, they encountered similar difficulties. Federal authorities constructed a number of large hospitals at their major garrison at De Valls Bluff. Illness sometimes so weakened the garrison that, as Brig. Gen. Christopher Columbus Andrews explained on July 17, 1864, it was impossible to assemble the necessary labor to complete the town's defenses. He added that it was "no small job either to dig the graves that are now required."[22] South of the garrison, the little village of Clarendon was so unhealthy that the soldiers began to refer to any bad fever as the "Clarendon Shake," which they noted "is to ordinary chills and fever about as a bulldog is to a pet poodle."[23] By the end of the war, the graves of thousands of Union and Confederate soldiers littered the Arkansas Delta. Most had died from disease rather than from enemy bullets.

The civilians who found themselves in the paths of the warring armies also felt the impact of the total war that was beginning to emerge throughout the South. Capt. Edward S. Redington of the 28th Wisconsin Infantry sat down in Helena shortly after a patrol and wrote his wife, Mary, describing what he had just seen of the countryside:

> The country we passed was desolation itself. The road ran through one continued series of plantations of the best land in the world, all deserted, not an acre under cultivation. The houses were almost all empty, and when anyone was to be seen, it was the wife and children of some poor white trash (as they call them here) who wither voluntarily or involuntarily were in the Rebel army, and were obliged to stay from sheer necessity. The poor things looked frightened to death, and well they might be, for many of the troops, especially the kansas regit. was composed of men who had their homes spoiled by the raids of the Rebels and have about as much feeling for a Secesh as a wolf had for a lamb.[24]

The conditions that Redington described were in the immediate vicinity of Helena, but soldiers found that the same desolation was prevalent throughout the Arkansas Delta. In the fall of 1862, Sylvester C. Bishop of the 11th Indiana Infantry found the same situation at Napoleon, Arkansas. "The people of napoleon are the most poverty stricken of any I've seen yet," he wrote his mother. "One poor woman," he added, "is literally starving to death."[25] Nine months later, Joseph R. Edwards of the 12th Michigan Infantry traveled by boat from Helena to Des Arc, and he too was shocked by what he saw. Along the rivers he encountered abandoned plantations and numerous burned-out houses with nothing left standing but chimneys.[26] A. F. Sperry of the 33d Iowa Infantry found similar conditions in Clarendon, which had been burned in 1862 by the Union Army. However, such drastic measures did not always intimidate the local population for, as Sperry noted, "a secesh gentleman burned his own house to prevent its being used as a hospital for our sick soldiers."[27]

Such devastation eventually reduced many people in the Delta to starvation. Mary Edmondson, for example, lived near Helena, and by the fall of 1863 she and her family were running out of food. "All our efforts to procure salt have failed thus far," she recorded in her diary. "Our hogs are eating up our small supply of corn fast. What shall we do?" Union authorities responded to worsening conditions by opening to southerners occupied towns which contained desperately needed foodstuffs, but only on condition that they take the oath of allegiance. The Edmondsons faced such a choice. "We were almost overcome by the apparent necessity of our case, and went so far as to make out our bills and prepare to go to town last night." The next morning her husband "concluded to wait and skimp a little longer in the hope of being saved from so repugnant and perhaps sinful an alternative . . ."[28] The Edmondsons managed to remain on their farm until the war ended, but many persons simply had no choice except to take the oath. In Helena, "There are a great many women and some men, coming in all the time," wrote Captain Redington. "Poor, lean, hungry looking creatures we could not help feeling sorry for them . . ." Redington than noted prophetically that "there is an awful future in store for them, no matter whether the North or the South succeed in this war. It will take years to get to comfortable living and a generation for things to be in as good a state as they were . . ."[29]

Civilians in the Arkansas Delta not only had to contend with the deprivation caused by both Union and Confederate troops, but they were also often victims of official government policy that sought to gain military advantages from either the seizure or destruction of cotton. Prior to the Civil War, cotton had been the main cash crop of the South, and the new Confederacy hoped to use it as a source of revenue for its war effort. Federal authorities were equally determined to deny that resource to the Confederacy. Early in the war Union authorities decided to treat cotton as a contraband of war so that it could be seized and sold by the government. Confederate authorities responded on March 17, 1862, by allowing local commanders to seize or burn cotton if it was in danger of falling into Union hands. Hindman immediately began ruthlessly enforcing the policy, and even though "many planters complained," he remained adamant.[30] Despite the efforts of Hindman and his successors, substantial amounts of cotton remained within reach of the Federal government.

In towns such as Helena, the Union forces were routinely employed in cotton-raiding expeditions that netted thousands of bales of the valuable commodity. The most vulnerable targets lay along the Mississippi, St. Francis, White, and Arkansas rivers, where Union authorities could use their control of the waterways to quickly swoop down on large caches of cotton. One of the most successful vessels employed in the trade was the gunboat *Eastport* that helped capture thousands of bales of Confederate cotton.

Many honest Delta families were trapped between the conflicting policies of the two governments and lost everything they owned. Others quickly recognized that huge profits could be made by smuggling cotton between the lines. And almost immediately, as one soldier noted, cotton speculators began crowding into occupied Helena. As prices soared from prewar levels of ten cents a pound to as high as one dollar, the lure of riches began to attract unscrupulous persons to the illicit trade. Throughout the South, numerous speculators, corrupt officers, cotton producers, and government officials on both sides were busily engaged in the lucrative business of cotton trading across the lines.

By the fall of 1862, illegal cotton trading had become such a scandal that the Federal government established a series of custom houses to attempt to control those activities. One of these agencies opened in Helena, and even though it did make smuggling more difficult, it was beyond the power of either government to control the human greed that motivated the trade. Some officers, who were more interested in lining their own pockets than in pursuing the Confederates, sometimes used soldiers under their command to conduct cotton raids into the interior. "Had we used half the force and industry to put the rebels down in Arkansas that were employed to steal cotton," wrote a soldier of the 4th Iowa Infantry, "it would have been better for the nation and the Army."[31] Throughout most of the war, Helena remained the center for cotton smuggling in the Arkansas Delta.

Union forays into the interior of the Arkansas Delta netted not only cotton but also thousands of slaves. Sometimes the slaves were forcefully seized by the army, but in most cases they willingly left the plantations. Indeed, wherever the Union army went, blacks flocked toward the blue columns and followed them back to their camps. On Curtis's march to Helena in the summer of 1862, an Illinois Cavalry trooper remembered that "the negroes had fairly swarmed around us, coming from every mansion, log cabin, and habital [sic] place in the whole region. . . . So excited a body of humanity never was seen before; here was the realization of the hopes of liberty which they had kept alive for years."[32] By 1863 an estimated thirty-six hundred freedmen had crowded into Helena. The influx of blacks into towns such as Helena usually caught officials by surprise, and they were not equipped to handle such large numbers of people who had to be fed and clothed.

A partial solution to the problem was initiated in 1863 when the Military Division of the Mississippi under the direction of Adj. Gen. Lorenzo Thomas began organizing black regiments to serve in the Union army. In Arkansas alone more than five thousand ex-slaves enlisted in the service before the war ended. Union authorities were often reluctant to use these black regiments in combat and preferred to employ them in garrison and fatigue duty. However, several black units did serve in combat, and organizations such as the 56th and 60th United Stated Colored Infantry proved that they were as dependable as white regiments. Undoubtedly they added strength to the Union war effort while simultaneously depriving the South of a major source of labor.

Thomas was also instrumental in developing programs to put black women, children, and men who were not fit for military service to work on the so-called abandoned plantations that surrounded Helena. Many of these deserted farms, in fact, belonged to men who were fighting for the Confederacy. Under the program, individuals leased the farms and employed the blacks to tend the land, thus producing staples such as cotton and relieving the Federal government of the necessity of supporting the freedmen. By 1864 there were at least thirty leased plantations in the vicinity of Helena, and though the system was not without its abuses, it did provide useful employment for many destitute freedmen.[33]

Military activities in Helena began increasing toward the end of 1862 as the Union army under Maj. Gen. Ulysses S. Grant stepped up the pressure against the great citadel at Vicksburg. Increasingly, Helena was being used as both a logistical base and a supplier of troops for the complex operations aimed at breaking the Confederate grip on the Mississippi River.

In January 1863, for example, several units from the Helena garrison joined Maj. Gen. John A. McClernand's forces in the assault on Arkansas Post. This little village lay about twenty-five miles above the mouth of the Arkansas River, and the Confederates were completing a square-bastioned fort on a nearby hill that dominated a bend in the stream. If the Confederates could retain control of the position then they could both protect the interior of the state from waterborne invasion and use it as a potential staging area to disrupt Union operations against Vicksburg. However, past military experiences at Fort Henry, Fort Donelson, and Island No. 10 had already proven that fixed fortifications could almost always be overcome by the more mobile riverine forces that the Union could deploy at will.

The Confederate officer who ultimately made the decision to commit his scarce troops to such a questionable defense was Maj. Gen. Theophilus Holmes, who had succeeded Hindman as commander in Arkansas. Holmes had earlier had an undistinguished career as a divisional commander under Gen. Robert E. Lee, who had prudently removed him from command after the Seven Days campaign in the spring of 1862. Holmes, who was too old for active field command and partially deaf, soon acquired the nickname of "granny." "Mental suffering, old age, and a life of great exposure," wrote a fellow officer, "had told heavily upon his physical development and correspondingly upon his intellectual faculties."[34] Such was the quality of leadership that the authorities in Richmond chose to command the defense of Arkansas.

Holmes, with no understanding of the odds against holding Arkansas Post against a determined Union attack, decided to commit approximately five thousand men to its defense. He later issued orders for his soldiers to hold the place until either reinforcements came or until every man died there. Undoubtedly many soldiers stationed at Arkansas Post did not share Holmes's enthusiasm for defending their position to the last man. "If 'Granny Holmes' were down here where he could smell a little gunpowder," wrote William W. Heartsill of Texas, "he would get better of the 'hold on' fit which has so recently seized him at LITTLE ROCK."[35]

On January 9, 1863 , McClernand's army of thirty-two thousand men accompanied by nine gunboats arrived near the fort. The next morning the fleet steamed forward to bombard the fortifications, and the Union army began deploying for battle. Had McClernand succeeded in coordinating the attack between the fleet and his infantry, the Confederates would have been overwhelmed. However, Union coordination was poor that day, and little was accomplished; on January 11 they were better organized and forced the surrender of the entire garrison. The fiasco had cost Holmes five thousand soldiers that he desperately needed to defend Arkansas, and the Federals could now move at will up the Arkansas River. Fortunately for Holmes, the Union operations against Vicksburg continued to divert the Federals' resources away from a general offensive aimed at the capture of Little Rock.

Soldiers from Helena also supported Grant's attempt to reach the northeastern approaches to Vicksburg by opening a levee that sealed the Yazoo Pass. Once the levee was opened, Union strategists believed that gunboats and transports could maneuver through the meandering bayous and streams until they reached high ground along the Yazoo River. A Union force of twenty-two boats and five thousand men managed to penetrate the pass, but when they reached the confluence of the Tallahatchie and Yazoo rivers the Federals found their way blocked by a hastily constructed earthen fortification known as Fort Pemberton. Between March 10 and 20, 1863, the Union flotilla tried to dislodge the stubborn defenders, but the Federals were unsuccessful. The flotilla eventually withdrew to Moon Lake where it linked up with reinforcements and again returned to attack Fort Pemberton. Between April 1 and 3, 1863, the flotilla conducted two more unsuccessful artillery duels against the fort. By the time the force withdrew, hundreds of troops aboard the transports were sick. Many of these ill soldiers were disembarked in Helena where the hospitals were already overflowing with sick men.[36]

Neither the Arkansas Post campaign nor the Yazoo Pass expedition contributed directly to the fall of Vicksburg. However, these and dozens of other probing attacks at the citadel did help disperse and weaken the limited resources that the Confederacy had available to protect Vicksburg. By mid-May 1863, Grant finally had the town isolated, and Confederate authorities were desperately looking for some way either to raise the siege or to re-establish control of the river at some other point.

In Richmond, Secretary of War James A. Seddon believed that both aims might be accomplished if forces in Arkansas could seize

Helena. On May 25, 1863, he suggested the idea to Gen. Joseph E. Johnston, who forwarded the recommendation to the commander of the Trans-Mississippi Department, Lt. Gen. E. Kirby Smith. Smith, lacking any solid information about the strength of the garrison at Helena, forwarded the suggestion to Holmes for his review. On June 15, 1863, Holmes telegraphed his superior the following message: "I believe we can take Helena. Please let me attack it." The next day Smith replied, "Most certainly do it."[37]

Neither Seddon, Smith, nor especially Holmes had any real idea about either the strength of the garrison or its defenses. Instead they acted out of a sense of desperation rather than from a careful analysis of military realities. Although the size of the Helena garrison had been reduced, the fortifications surrounding the town were immensely strong. Furthermore, the Union army was supported by several gunboats.

On June 18, 1863, Holmes ordered his infantry in Little Rock and Jacksonport to begin concentrating at Cotton Plant to prepare for the move on Helena. Eight days later, the Confederate army, which numbered about eight thousand men, moved toward Helena. Horses and men alike were plagued by millions of prairie flies and periodic rains as the columns sloshed through the swampy bottoms of the White and Cache rivers. Holmes finally got his weary army in front of Helena on the morning of July 3, 1863.[38]

Inside the garrison Maj. Gen. Benjamin Prentiss had been fully informed of Holmes's movements, and his five thousand soldiers were waiting for the attack. In contrast the Confederate commander had no real notion of Prentiss's strength nor of his dispositions. Furthermore, Holmes only at this point got his first glimpse of the series of fortified redoubts that protected Helena, and he later confessed that "the place was very much more difficult of access and the fortification much stronger than I had supposed before undertaking the expedition."[39] He decided to attack anyway, and at daybreak the next day three Confederate columns moved toward the forward redoubts on Rightor, Graveyard, and Hindman hills.

The assault against Hindman Hill, which protected the southern approaches to Helena, got under way first, and some of the Confederate infantry managed to penetrate the Federal rifle pits, but they were soon pinned down. About an hour after the first assault, two Confederate brigades under the command of Maj. Gen. Sterling Price fought their way into the Federal batteries atop Graveyard Hill in the center of the Union lines. However, Union artillery fire from both Fort Curtis and the gunboat *Tyler* contained the assault until a counterattack drove Price's men back. The fainthearted cavalry advance on Rightor Hill to the north fared no better. Around 10:30 A.M. Holmes called off the uncoordinated attack and began moving his army back toward Little Rock.

In about six hours of fighting the Confederates lost 173 killed, 645 wounded, and 772 missing. Union casualties amounted to 57 dead, 146 wounded, and 36 captured. When the Federal army advanced onto the battlefield, they saw a sickening sight. "The ridges & ravines were thickly strewn with ghastly corpses covered with gore—hands, arms, legs shot away—mutilated in almost every man by shot & shell—while the moans of the severely wounded could be heard on every side," wrote Capt. Thomas N. Stevens of the 28th Wisconsin Infantry.[40] Probably the worst carnage befell the men in Price's column, which had to endure hundreds of rounds of eight-inch shells fired by the gunboat *Tyler*. The day after the fight a Union officer visited the area where Price's men had been trapped by the gunfire. "The Rebbels was laying thick," he wrote his mother. "Some of them tore all to pieces with shell and some shot through with solid shot." He added that the men had been on the field twenty-four hours and had begun "to smell bad and look tuff."[41]

Clearly, as Secretary of War Seddon noted some five months after the battle, the failure did not lie with the performance of the Confederate infantry, which fought well, but rather with Holmes, for it was he who had failed to grasp the defensive power of the Federal positions and had consequently sent his men forward against almost impossible odds.[42] The price for such an error was evident in the mangled bodies that lay in the hills around Helena.

Thirty minutes before Holmes called off his July 4 attack, more momentous developments were taking place downriver at Vicksburg. There the Confederate garrison was surrendering to Grant's forces. The loss of Vicksburg was a catastrophe for the South because it split the Confederacy; the loss was particularly ominous for Arkansas because it freed thousands of Union troops who could now be redeployed for the conquest of the state.

By mid-July thousands of Union troops that had been released by the surrender of Vicksburg were now assembling for the long-awaited advance on Little Rock. When Union Maj. Gen. Frederick Steele assumed command at Helena, he had approximately thirteen thousand soldiers and five artillery batteries to deploy in the campaign. In Little Rock, Holmes, who was too ill to command the

District of Arkansas, had turned his duties over to Maj. Gen. Sterling Price. His fourteen-thousand-man army was scattered throughout Arkansas. The majority of the infantry available for the defense of Little Rock was stationed at Pine Bluff, Des Arc, and Searcy. Those forces numbered about eight thousand soldiers.

Price, knowing that the Union army was about to advance toward Little Rock, redeployed his infantry along Bayou Meto, twelve miles northeast of the city. He then began constructing a second line of defenses opposite Little Rock near the north bank of the Arkansas River. Finally, Price ordered his cavalry forward to delay the Union advance as long as possible.

On August 11, 1863, Steele ordered his own cavalry forward to clear the way for the Union infantry. Four days later the first skirmishes with the Confederate cavalry began, and they continued almost daily. However, the Confederates were far too weak to check the advance, and by September 7, 1863, Steele's infantry had reached Ashley Mill, a little south of Little Rock. Steele wisely declined to attack Price's entrenched positions and instead decided to outflank him by crossing the river below the city. On September 10, 1863, Union forces, in the face of only token resistance, threw a pontoon bridge across the Arkansas River a few miles below Little Rock. Before noon, the better part of a division was across the river, and Price, fearing that his army would be trapped, ordered a general retreat to Arkadelphia. Price had been badly outgeneraled by Steele, and at a cost of only 137 casualties the Union now controlled the state's largest city.[43]

After the capture of Little Rock, most of the fighting between regular Union and Confederate field armies shifted to the southern half of Arkansas. Operations in that part of the state ended in the defeat of Steele's Camden campaign during the spring of 1864. After the Camden expedition failed, the Union army lacked the resources to assume the offensive and withdrew into fortified positions in Little Rock, Fayetteville, Fort Smith, Helena, Pine Bluff, and De Valls Bluff. Outside these garrisons Confederate cavalry and guerrillas operated almost at will, while the Union forces seldom ventured out except to protect their lines of communications and to forage for supplies.

For the remainder of the war, the most hotly contested areas in the Arkansas Delta lay along the banks of the White River and the path of the railroad that ran from De Valls Bluff to Huntersville across the river from Little Rock. Along this tenuous route came most of the more than 140 tons of daily supplies that Steele needed to maintain his armies in Little Rock and Fort Smith.

One of the favorite tactics that the Confederates used against the steamers plying the river was to hide snipers or artillery in the thick foliage along the banks and suddenly fire rounds at almost point-blank range into the pilot houses. The steamboat captains often countered by mounting field artillery on their decks to return fire against their antagonists. Although the casualties from such tactics were remarkably small, the fear of such sudden random attacks kept the crews unnerved and often forced the steamers to travel in convoys protected by gunboats.

The Confederates seldom tried to match their firepower against that of the Union gunboats, but even these vessels were not completely immune from surprise attacks. On June 24, 1864, for example, Confederate cavalrymen found the *Queen City* at anchor near Clarendon and managed to capture her before the surprised crew could defend the vessel.[44] The harassing attacks against Federal boats caused the Union some problems, and the loss of the *Queen City* was a real embarrassment, but the Confederates had no chance of permanently disrupting Steele's line of communications along the river.

However, the fifty-mile stretch of railroad was far more vulnerable to Confederate raids, and it became the favorite target of the Confederates. Steele could not afford to have this vital link cut permanently because its loss would threaten the survival of his army. He therefore ordered a series of blockhouses built along the road and maintained constant patrols along the entire line. These patrols were tedious and dangerous operations, but they did keep the line open most of the time. Still, the Confederates managed to disrupt operations and to force the Union to tie down large numbers of troops to protect their supply line.

Elsewhere in the Delta, Confederate guerrillas, such as the notorious Doc Rayburn, who operated out of the bottoms on the Little Red River, continually harassed isolated detachments of Union forces. Similar activities were carried out near St. Charles by Dr. John A. Morgan. Along the lower portions of the Arkansas River, Brig. Gen. William Cabell's men, operating along Bayou Bartholomew and the Red Fork, carried out attacks against the Union patrols that ventured out of the garrison in Pine Bluff. In late May 1864, Cabell's men defeated a Federal force on Lake Chicot and began attacking Federal steamers on the Mississippi River.[45]

Perhaps the best indication of the ability of the Confederates to strike almost anywhere in the Arkansas Delta occurred in the summer of 1864 when Brig. Gen. Joseph O. Shelby decided to disrupt the operations of the leased plantations in the vicinity of Helena. Confederate authorities had been outraged by the very existence of the program, and in July 1864, Shelby sent Col. Archibald Dobbin at the head of two thousand men to swoop down on the plantations. Directed to "ravage and destroy" the leased plantations, he carried out his orders to the letter. At the first plantation Dobbin's men burned "cotton, houses, plows, harrows, dry goods, negro quarters, storehouses, and everything the eye could rest upon bearing any impress of the United States Government." Dobbin's troopers repeated the same scene again and again as they burned and pillaged their way through the plantations. "This kind of work went on uninterruptedly for ten miles," wrote one of his officers, "and every plantation laid as bare and black under the sunlight as a prairie after the fall fires sweep through it." By the end of the raid, Dobbin's men had beaten up schoolteachers who had been sent to help the freedmen, had shot several black soldiers, had stolen three hundred animals, and had captured about two hundred freedmen.[46] The raids on the leased plantations destroyed the system and dramatically demonstrated the ability of the Confederates to conduct successful attacks almost within sight of the Federal garrisons that now dotted the Delta. By the summer of 1864, the situation had so deteriorated in the state that one Arkansas commander privately wrote President Abraham Lincoln that the entire area "seems to have degenerated into bushwackers" and "it is hardly safe to go out of our lines a mile."[47]

The Union forces were, in fact, encountering a new kind of warfare that was based on speed and harassment, rather than on superior numbers and firepower. They could find no permanent solution, and the guerrilla warfare dragged on until the Union victories east of the Mississippi River destroyed the Confederacy. Fighting officially ended in the Arkansas Delta on May 11, 1865, when Brig. Gen. M. Jeff Thompson surrendered his men at Wittsburg and Jacksonport. Thompson's ragged force of 7,454 men had only 500 guns, several hundred canoes, no animals, and very little food. Lt. Col. C. W. Davis, who accepted their capitulation, noted that "they seemed highly pleased at the surrender, and said that all they wanted now was to be allowed to live at home."[48] Indeed, all through the South soldiers were going home. For civilians and soldiers alike, the long nightmare of war had ended, and now they had to begin to put their lives in order.

Throughout the Arkansas Delta, returning soldiers found widespread destruction, including burned towns, wrecked farms, large stretches of unattended land, and ruined businesses. The war itself had decimated the military-age population: Arkansas lost perhaps a quarter of the more than seventy-four thousand men who fought on both sides. Furthermore, the slave-labor force was now free, which meant that blacks and whites would have to establish a new relationship among themselves.[49]

Initially the Federal government tried to help blacks adjust to their new freedom through the Bureau of Refugees, Freedmen, and Abandoned Lands. The Bureau carried out limited programs to educate blacks and to relocate them on farms, but much of its time was absorbed in protecting the freedmen from efforts of whites to either intimidate blacks or to impose social control on them. Unfortunately, mismanagement, self-interest, corruption, the hostility of many whites, and the ultimate failure of will on the part of the federal government undermined much of the agency's effectiveness. Within a decade after the war, blacks were largely ignored by the federal government and thus were forced to survive in a hostile environment.[50]

The most immediate problem in the Delta was to re-establish the economy that the war had largely destroyed. However, economic recovery was slow, and the production of the area's major cash crop, cotton, did not reach prewar levels until the early 1870s. Throughout Arkansas the number of acres under cultivation lagged behind prewar levels, and the value of those lands had declined by 65 percent. But there were hopeful signs as manufacturing began to increase and the railroads opened more lands in the Delta to both farming and timber operations. By 1880, the economy in the Delta had largely recovered, and some diversification was underway.[51]

Concurrent with the recovering economy was the development of farm tenancy. Southern whites needed cheap labor, but their major source of labor, slaves, no longer existed, and they had little cash with which to hire workers. White farmers responded to this problem by parceling out land to freed blacks who farmed for shares of the produce. Blacks, lacking money to buy their own land, had little choice but to participate in this system, which had the net effect of condemning them to becoming tenant farmers with almost no chance of saving enough cash to buy their own land. "This was the beginning of the credit system in the South," wrote John C. Wright, an ex-soldier from Union County, "which made dependents and serfs of the white people who heretofore had been 'Masters' in every sense of the word, as well as in name and changed only in name and for the worse, the slavery of the negro."[52] Unfortunately, Wright and others like him used the farm tenancy system to keep blacks under white social control, thereby retarding their real integration into society.

Ex-Confederates who returned to the Delta also found that political control no longer rested in their hands. During the next decade, they battled for control of the government with the Reconstruction regime that dominated the state. During this period some blacks did enter the political arena and were elected to local and state offices. However, supporters of the Reconstruction government, even with the voting power of the newly enfranchised blacks, were never a majority in the state. In March 1873, their opponents succeeded in amending the constitution to restore full political rights to all ex-Confederates, thus paving the way for the rise of a resurgent Democratic Party dominated by those very men who had supported secession.

In the Arkansas Delta, cotton was still the measure of wealth and status, although the growing timber industry was beginning to make some inroads. And blacks, who had hoped to gain political, social, and economic freedom, were trapped in a system that denied all three.

White Southerners not only succeeded in regaining social, economic, and political control, but they also set out on the long process of legitimizing their actions in the war. Undoubtedly many returning soldiers shared the sense of despair of Brig. Gen. Daniel Harris Reynolds, who, after arriving at his home at Lake Village in the summer of 1865, wrote in his diary that "the war is over & we failed."[53] In the ensuing decades that psychology of failure gradually subsided as southerners succeeded in convincing themselves of the correctness of their actions in 1861 and in rationalizing the subsequent defeat on the battlefield. Out of struggle with these problems came the "Myth of the Lost Cause." The basis of the myth eventually came to rest on the conclusion that the South had fought not to protect slavery but to defend its constitutional rights. Thus, the cause had been righteous, and the superior military prowess of the Confederate soldier had simply been overwhelmed by the numerical superiority and wealth of the northern states.

The roots of explaining away the real cause of secession—the South's willingness to use force to protect slavery—had begun in the antebellum years, when the white southerners shifted the issue away from slavery and toward a defense of the rights of states to determine what constituted property. This argument was given further definition during the war and continued to be refined in the decades following the conflict. Writing in 1898, Dr. Charles E. Nash of Helena, for instance, explained President Andrew Johnson's conservative positions on Reconstruction as follows: "Johnson knew full well that nine-tenths of the southern army did not fight for the continuance of slavery, and that they would give them up and return to the union in good faith, if they could be guaranteed state's rights."[54] Such thinking was common among the vast majority of white southerners, and those persons living in the Arkansas Delta generally shared Nash's views on the issue. Within a few years after the war, slavery, the real issue that caused the conflict, had been replaced by the comfortable notion that the conflict was over the more acceptable idea of states' rights. Even today, no section of the nation continues to hold that concept in as high regard as does the South.

The second phase of the myth, that the southern armies were superior soldiers who were overwhelmed by the numerical superiority of the Union, began to emerge among veterans almost as soon as the war ended. Junius Bragg of the 33d Arkansas Infantry was in Marshall, Texas, when he learned of the impending death of the Confederacy. "I cannot talk about it. My feelings cannot find vent in language," he wrote his wife on April 23, 1865. "From a thousand hard won battlefields," he added, "the spirits of our martyrs have gone to reap the reward due to patriotism, and the suffering in a righteous cause."[55] Throughout the remainder of the nineteenth century, ex-Confederates would echo the same theme as they set about writing their memoirs. As Joe M. Scott, a soldier from northwest Arkansas, wrote, "When history becomes impartial the records will show the Confederate soldiers to be the best fighters on earth." "It is well known," he added, "that we fought a superior force from first to finish, yet we were victorious in many hard-fought battles."[56] The majority of ex-soldiers living in the Arkansas Delta surely shared Scott's views, and, as one old veteran living in Helena remarked, "God has the name of every Confederate soldier inscribed in the Book of Life," and when any dead Confederate reached heaven, St. Peter would say, "Walk in you had Hell enough in the 60's."[57]

Closely connected with the idea of the innate superiority of the southern soldier was the widely accepted belief that their Federal counterparts had needlessly plundered the South. Indeed, by 1864, the property of southern states was being targeted and systematically destroyed by the Union, but these acts, however horrible they may have appeared to be to the victims, were necessary if the war-making potential of the Confederacy was to be eliminated. However, the level of destruction was there for all to see, and a new generation of southerners soon accepted the ideas of their elders. On March 28, 1872, Lila Jabine, a young school child in Little Rock, undoubtedly echoed the sentiment of many of her friends when she wrote in her English grammar book the following poem.

> Mary had a little lamb
> She got it from her aunt
> It was so good at taking things
> She called it U.S. Grant[58]

The Myth of the Lost Cause was first transmitted to Lila and others like her by the writings of ex-Confederates, and it later was strengthened by the organization of various groups that helped perpetuate it. One of the most important of these organizations was the United Confederate Veterans, which formally organized in 1889. It grew out of the fondness of old soldiers to gather together for periodic meetings in local groups called camps. By 1904, at least one hundred camps were active in Arkansas, and many were in the Delta counties.[59] The UCV's publication, *The Confederate Veteran*, gave soldiers from throughout the South a mechanism for contributing to the myth. The articles, including many written by Arkansans, were replete with stories of the bravery, suffering, and military prowess of Confederate soldiers.

Southern women also found an outlet to develop the ideal of the "Lost Cause" through the United Daughters of the Confederacy, which organized its first chapter in Arkansas at Hope in 1896. Seven other chapters were active within a year, and one of the UDC's early presidents clearly stated its goal when she told the 1900 annual meeting at Helena that it was the organization's duty "to see that the truth shall be taught our children, so that when those of us who bear personal and correct memories of those trying years have passed away, they shall have been properly taught that their forefathers fell in a just and right cause . . ." She added that "it is not our object to set down aught with malice, but it is our sacred *duty* to perpetuate the truth of history, and by the grace of god we will endeavor to do it."[60]

Equally important efforts to remind later generations of the sacrifices of Confederates were made by the various memorial associations that sprang up in Arkansas after the war. Throughout the last quarter of the nineteenth century, these groups raised funds to preserve Confederate cemeteries, erect battlefield markers, and build public monuments commemorating the Confederacy. One of the earliest of these groups began in Helena in 1869. Its original purpose was to set aside a portion of the Maple Hill Cemetery to serve as a burial ground for Confederates. Later, the organization, known as the Phillips County Memorial Association, began raising funds to build a monument there. On May 25, 1892, a life-sized Confederate soldier standing atop a thirty-foot granite shaft was formally dedicated.[61] Judge James Hanks attended the ceremony, and even though he thought that the dedicatory speech was too long, there was a good crowd, and he remarked that "the monument is a fine one."[62] Other towns in the Arkansas Delta had similar organizations by the late nineteenth century, and the landscape slowly became dotted with memorials to Confederate soldiers.

Through the efforts of individuals and groups such as the UCV, the UDC, and the various memorial associations, the idea that the Civil War was a heroic but lost cause took root in the southern mind. However, the myth ignored the truth that the war had been fought to preserve slavery and obscured the grim reality that the conflict had wrecked the South's economy and practically destroyed a generation of young men.

Time and the work of later historians have weakened the Myth of the Lost Cause, but it is far from dead in the popular mind. Indeed, the war still holds a fascination that manifests itself both in the continuing stream of literature on the subject and in the various Civil War roundtables, in re-enactment organizations, and among relic hunters who spend much of their spare time studying the great conflict.

Today, no person can travel many miles in the Arkansas Delta without stumbling upon some monument, marker, museum, or site that still stands as mute testimony to the role that the war played in the region. Few southerners who grew up among such relics of the past have remained unaffected by them. This legacy of slavery, secession, war, and defeat still conspires to set the South apart from the rest of the country, which did not share in those experiences.

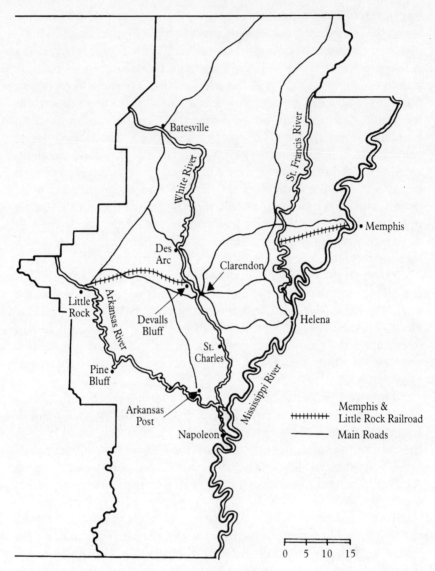

Batesville

White River

St. Francis River

Memphis

Des
Arc

Clarendon

Little
Rock

Arkansas River

Devalls
Bluff

Helena

St.
Charles

Pine
Bluff

Mississippi River

Arkansas
Post

Napoleon

+++++++ Memphis &
Little Rock Railroad

——— Main Roads

0   5   10   15

Map of the Delta region during the Civil War.
Courtesy of Bobby Roberts.

Helena, Arkansas, during the Civil War.
Courtesy of the Library of Congress.

The Capture of Arkansas Post.
Courtesy of the Library of Congress.

The bombardment of Fort Hindman at Arkansas Post.
Courtesy of the Library of Congress.

Battle at St. Charles on the White River in Arkansas.
Courtesy of the Library of Congress.

The Sam Corley Camp, United Confederate Veterans, at Helena.
Courtesy Phillips County Historical Museum.

From Slavery
to Uncertain Freedom:
Blacks in the Delta

FON LOUISE GORDON

From the introduction of slaves in the Louisiana Territory in the eighteenth century, the black experience in the Arkansas Delta has been characterized by rurality, poverty, economic exploitation, the cultivation of cotton, caste discrimination, and violence. During the antebellum period, slavery was harsher in the Delta region, the center of the institution in the state, than in older states because of the Delta's rural isolation and the persistence of frontier conditions. Not until the Civil War and the demise of slavery was there the possibility of real change in the quality of life for black Arkansans in the Delta.

For twenty years, from the beginning of Reconstruction and Republican state government in 1868, the perception of Arkansas was that of a "new El Dorado."[1] After the Civil War, the state attained a reputation as a land of opportunity for African Americans. During the Exodus of 1878–1880 and for almost another decade, many blacks in the Deep South sought refuge in Arkansas.[2]

One reason for this perception of Arkansas as a promised land was the state's historic and geographic location. The trans-Mississippi West was historically considered the natural limit of slavery expansion and a destination of hope. By being on the outer limits of the slave South, Arkansas was not considered a Deep South state but rather a border state.

A second reason for the postbellum reputation of Arkansas as more tolerant than its sister states was the ratio of black to white population. In Mississippi and Louisiana, both of which shared the Delta with Arkansas and were considered Deep South states, the black populations were significantly larger. In the forty years following Reconstruction, blacks averaged over 56 percent of the population of Mississippi and over 46 percent of the population of Louisiana. In contrast, during the same period, the black population of Arkansas averaged less than one-third of the population.[3]

A third reason for black immigration to Arkansas after Reconstruction was the encouragement of labor agents employed by Delta planters. William Pickens, a native of South Carolina, a graduate of Yale, and the field secretary for the NAACP after the First World War, moved to Arkansas with his family in 1888. His parents were persuaded to make the move because of the promise of more fertile soil and higher wages.[4]

But despite the high expectations for Arkansas after Reconstruction, the state did not become a promised land. During the period from 1880 to 1920, Jim Crow was legalized and institutionalized in the state, and the foundation was laid for race relations that has yet to be significantly altered. The Second World War and the introduction of the mechanical cotton picker transformed southern agriculture by eliminating the need for abundant black labor and resulting in the massive migration of millions of blacks from the Delta and the South. The civil rights movement invalidated segregation and disfranchisement and made possible voting rights and access to public accommodations. But the long presence of blacks in the plantation economy, their consequent inability to acquire income-producing property, and the continuing lack of sufficient industrial and alternative employment has made the black experience in the Delta still economically and occupationally disparate.[5]

From the early eighteenth century to the purchase of Louisiana Territory by the United States in 1803, blacks maintained a sparse but unbroken presence in the Arkansas Delta. For 80 years during French and Spanish domination, the number of slaves probably did not exceed 50 until the final census in 1803, when the population of 874 included 107 slaves and 2 free blacks. This sudden increase was related to the influx of settlers after the American Revolution and to United States control of Mississippi Territory, which included a population of 4,500 whites and 2,400 slaves, in 1798.[6]

The *Code Noir*, adopted by the French in 1724, was the legal codification of slavery in Louisiana during French and Spanish occupation. While restrictive and severe in punishing slaves, the code liberally provided for both the spiritual and physical welfare of the slave: it had provisions for the catechism in Roman Catholicism, adequate food and clothing, continued care in old age, and valid marriages. Regarding manumission, the code was particularly liberal, stipulating that freed slaves were to enjoy the same status as freeborn persons. While the *Code Noir* ameliorated the treatment of slaves in lower Louisiana, the harsh frontier conditions in the remote and isolated settlements of the Delta probably made its application less tolerant. The liberal provisions of the *Code Noir* that produced a large free black population in Louisiana did not survive in the territorial and state laws of Arkansas, which circumscribed both the numbers and privileges of free blacks.[7]

With the purchase of Louisiana Territory, slavery remained intact and the area of slavery in the United States expanded. Between cession and Arkansas statehood in 1836, the institution became firmly established in the state.[8] The legal statutes concerning slavery, as throughout the slave states, regarded slaves as both persons and as chattels personal (personal property). Territorial statutes in Arkansas recognized slaves as persons in allowing their emancipation; the statutes also permitted a slave as "a poor person" to sue for freedom, to charge persons with assault and battery, and to bring suits of false imprisonment against claimants. As chattels personal, slaves could not strike whites, carry weapons and ammunition without a license, or participate in riots, unlawful meetings, and seditious speeches. Capital offenses included the administration of medicine without permission or attempting to "consult, advise or conspire" in rebellion. In 1825 the Arkansas territorial legislature introduced the slave patrol. Slave patrols, organized in each township by the county court and composed of no more than eleven members, were responsible for the supervision of slave activities. Statutes pertaining to free blacks were identical to those for slaves (chattels personal) except that the former were exempt from the lash and required to possess free papers rather than written passes.[9]

With admission into the Union in 1836, Arkansas became the twenty-fourth state of the Union and the twelfth slave state. The state constitution adopted in the same year guaranteed slavery. It recognized slaves as persons in allowing emancipation, in urging slaveowners to treat their slaves with humanity, and in guaranteeing slaves the right to defense counsel and jury trial if arrested. The document also outlawed slave trading and the immigration of slaves guilty of high crimes in other states or territories. It subjected slaves to the same penalties as whites for capital crimes.[10]

The statutes permitted free blacks to own real and personal property and, beginning in 1838, prohibited interracial marriage. The statutes also proscribed free blacks from immigration into the state without posting bond and prohibited carrying weapons and ammunition without a license. Free blacks between the ages of seven and twenty-one could be bound out as apprentices or servants. As a class, in Arkansas as throughout the South, free blacks were regarded as a threat to the organic system in which "whites were free and Negroes were slaves." Thus, Arkansas laws were part of the general pressure of the last generation before Emancipation to force free blacks out of the South or to reduce them to *de facto* slavery and integrate them into the existing system of bondage. As a result of this growing pressure, the legislature barred free blacks from entry into the state in 1843; and in 1859 the legislature prohibited manumission and the residence of free blacks in the state after January 1, 1860. Despite the popularity of the latter law, its impracticability led to its suspension in January 1861 for two years.[11]

As a result of legislation, the free black population of the state had significantly declined by 1860. Between 1810 and 1850 the free black population rose from 2 to 608. But by 1860 the free black community had fallen to 144 persons. Of that number, only 51, or 35 percent, resided in the Delta.[12]

Throughout the antebellum period, slavery in Arkansas was a powerful and flourishing institution. From 1820 to 1850 the percentage of increase of the slave population was greater than that of any other slave state: 1820–30, 182 percent; 1830–40, 335 percent; 1840–50, 136 percent. From 1850 to 1860 the percentage of increase, 135 percent, was second only to Texas at 213 percent. The total percentage of increase of the slave population from 1820 to 1860 was 6,771 percent as compared to the total percentage of increase of the white population at 2,476 percent. The proportion of slaves in the total population also increased each census year, from 11 percent in 1820 to 26 percent in 1860. In total slave population among slaveholding states, Arkansas rose from fifteenth in 1820 to twelfth on the eve of the war.[13]

The Delta was the center of slavery in the state, and by 1860 nearly two-thirds of the slave population was located in this area. While only 35 percent of the white population and 46 percent of slaveholders lived in the Delta, 67,286, or 61 percent, of the slave population lived there.[14]

With the election of Abraham Lincoln in 1860, the South began talk of secession; and with the firing on Fort Sumter the following year, the Civil War began. Arkansas became the ninth Confederate state in May 1861. Approximately fifty thousand Arkansans enlisted in the Confederate service; fifteen thousand enlisted in Federal regiments.[15]

Memphis fell in April 1862, and by midsummer, Helena, in Phillips County, was under Union occupation and the federal government assumed responsibility for the freedmen in much of the Delta region. By midsummer 1863, all territory north and east of the Arkansas River was under Union control. Freedom, then, came to Delta blacks with the appearance of Union troops. Lucretia Alexander, a slave in Chicot County, remembered, "One time I saw the Yankees a long way off. They had on blue uniforms and was on coal black horses . . . I heard them tell the slaves they were free. A man named Captain Barkus who had his arm off at the elbow called for three near-by plantations to meet at our place. Then he got up on a platform with another man beside him and declared peace and freedom. He pointed to a colored man and yelled, 'You're free as I am!' Old colored folks . . . that was on sticks, throwed them sticks away and shouted."[16] Jeff Bailey, born in Drew County, recalled hearing of freedom in the Monticello Courthouse yard. "I remember what they said when they freed my father. They said, 'You're free. You[r] children are free. Go on back there and work and let your children work. Don't work them children too long. You'll get pay for your work.'"[17]

As black refugees fled behind Union lines, they were employed in various capacities as laborers and servants. In October 1863, Boston Blackwell, born on a Georgia plantation and sold at the age of thirteen to the Blackwell Plantation south of Pine Bluff, decided to run away with another boy to Union protection. "When we gets to the Yankee camp all our troubles was over. We get all the contraband we could eat . . . the Yankees . . . made me a driver of a team in the qua[r]te[r]masters department. I was always keerful to do everything they told me . . . iffen you could get to the Yankee's camp you was free right now."[18] Yet, freedom also meant uncertainty, deprivation, and ambivalence about the future. Lewis Chase, a slave in Prairie County remembered, "[Slaves] what I knowed didn't spec nothing an they sho didn't get nothin but freedom."[19]

In the spring of 1863, Union officers in Helena began organizing the freedmen into companies, and in May 1863 the First Arkansas Volunteers of African Descent was mustered into service. At the end of the year three more black regiments were organized with a total enlistment of 2,348. The black regiments, designated by numbers of the U.S. Volunteers (Colored), were the Forty-sixth, the Fifty-fourth, the Fifty-sixth, and the Fifty-seventh. At the end of the war, the Union army included 5,526 Arkansas freedmen.[20]

Prior to 1865 and the establishment of the Freedmen's Bureau, the employment and education of the freedmen fell to Freedmen's Home Colonies. In 1863 home colonies were established throughout the Delta in Helena, Pine Bluff, De Valls Bluff, and Little Rock. With the passage of the Freedmen's Bureau bill, this agency assumed responsibility for the freedmen and the home colony system already in place. During the tenure of the Bureau, monthly wages for freedmen ranged from 15 to 50 dollars. Where planters could not afford money wages, freedmen contracted for a share of the crop, an arrangement that in time evolved into the sharecropping system.[21] To provide education the Bureau established as many schools as possible. In 1868, the Bureau reported that in Arkansas there were 27 day and night schools, 24 Sabbath schools, and 2 high schools, all with a combined total of 285 teachers and 3,460 students.[22]

Reconstruction entered a new phase with the enactment of the Reconstruction Acts of March 1867. Arkansas became part of the Fourth Military District, and black males in the state registered to vote. The official registration of 66,805 identified 33,047 people as white and 21,969, or 33 percent, as black. At the November election for a constitutional convention and delegates, the question for the convention carried. Of the 75 delegates elected to the convention, 8 were black; of these, 6 represented the Delta counties of Phillips, Pulaski, Chicot, and Jefferson.[23] The constitutional convention meeting in Little Rock during early 1868 adopted a constitution that outlawed slavery and provided for both universal male suffrage and a system of free public schools. By midsummer 1868, Arkansas ratified the Fourteenth Amendment and was readmitted to the Union.[24]

During Reconstruction from 1868 to 1874, blacks in Arkansas participated in government, assumed the responsibilities of citizenship, and affiliated with the Republican Party. The Party drew its greatest numerical strength and loyalty from the black electorate. And the overwhelming majority of the black electorate lived in the Delta. Two blacks, William H. Grey and Joseph C. Corbin, held state office. Grey was commissioner of Immigration in 1871, and Corbin served as state superintendent of Public Instruction from

1873 to 1875. Both were "black carpetbaggers" who had taken up residence in the Delta and had come to exercise considerable political power. Powell Clayton was boss of the state Republican Party from his term as governor, 1868–1871, and as senator from Arkansas, 1873–1877, until his retirement in 1913. Part of Clayton's success in maintaining control of the state Republican organization was his commitment to the black electorate. Even after passage of the secret-ballot law in 1891 and the poll tax in 1892, black Republicans remained "a very important factor in the Republican organization of [the] state . . ."[25]

The return to power of the Democrats in 1874, which marked the end of Reconstruction in Arkansas, radically reduced the influence of black politicians such as Grey and Corbin, but it did not abruptly end office holding by blacks. During the remainder of the 1870s, after Redemption, the Democratic Party, under the leadership of such moderates as Augustus Hill Garland and William R. Miller, seemed to accept black suffrage as a political fact of life and campaigned for the black vote. Garland's administration was characterized by one black Republican as conservative but fair.[26] When Governor Miller assumed office in 1877, he pledged "to use the whole power of the state" in protecting blacks in their legal and constitutional rights.[27]

The moderation or conservatism of the Democratic Party that sought to appeal to the black electorate was demonstrated in the paternalistic, *noblesse oblige* attitudes manifested by Party leaders toward blacks. Conservatism was predicated on black inferiority but sought to preserve a place, albeit subordinate, for blacks in society. During the tenure of Little Rock's Redeemer mayor, John G. Fletcher, from 1875 to 1881, at least seven blacks served on the city police force.[28] Augustus Garland, as governor and senator, frequently extended his patronage to Arkansas blacks. Upon his election as governor in 1874, for example, he refused to remove W. Hines Furbush, the three-term black sheriff of Lee County, at the request of white Democrats. Later, Garland secured a federal clerkship in the United States Land Office in Washington, D.C., for the widow of James W. Mason, a former state senator and controversial black political "boss" of Chicot County.[29]

As a consequence of slavery, the majority of the black population was concentrated in the Delta counties. From 1870 to 1910, an average of 64 percent of the state's black population resided in the

Delta. By 1920, 70 percent of the black population lived there. During the same period, of the fifteen counties in which blacks made up the majority of the population, thirteen were in the Delta. Yet, the black proportion of the total population of the state during this period never exceeded 28 percent. Although complete black domination was unlikely, the prospect of shared power in eastern Arkansas was altogether unacceptable to whites. Rather, with a smaller black population than neighboring states and a belated tendency to fanatical racism, Arkansas exhibited in the post-Reconstruction era a slightly less virulent form of radical racism, but the effect was identical to the effect in the Deep South: political, legal, economic, and educational inequality and proscription. The black community concentrated in the Delta was overwhelmingly agricultural and rural: it was poor, debt-ridden, and undereducated. As a former Confederate state both culturally and geographically a part of the Deep South heartland, Arkansas inevitably succumbed to the post-Reconstruction phenomenon of Jim Crow with its usual ingredients of segregation, disfranchisement, and lynching.

The evolution of Jim Crow, however, was not initially evident to the black South or to black Arkansans. In the immediate post-Reconstruction era, Arkansas was perceived as a land of opportunity for black people. By 1891 the growth of the black rural electorate and the emergence of a vital urban black middle class were sufficient to create alarm among whites. Although the vast majority of the state's black population lived in rural areas, the number of blacks living in urban areas had substantially increased. Blacks were the majority in two of the most important Delta towns, Helena, where 64 percent of the population was black, and Pine Bluff, where 54 percent of the population was black.[30]

Black progress and political activism in eastern Arkansas were part of a regional response of blacks to their political reduction after Redemption. The black struggle to preserve political life generally took three forms: 1) continued activism in heavily black-populated areas; 2) an "echo" or second Reconstruction and second Redemption that occurred in the upper South and border states; and 3) blacks formed coalitions with agrarian challenges to the Democratic Party.[31] All three responses took place in eastern Arkansas. Despite Redemption, blacks in the Delta continued political activism because of the moderation of the Democratic Party and because of the Powell Clayton–controlled state Republican Party.

The Democratic Party could afford to accept and campaign for the black vote because there was no danger of blacks establishing predominance over state government, since they made up only a minority of the population. The real possibility of black rule existed at the county and municipal levels in the black majority counties of the Delta. With Redemption, many of the black Republican-controlled counties passed under Democratic rule. But in several other counties, such as Phillips, Desha, Chicot, and Jefferson, blacks remained in office. It was in these counties that Democrats and black Republicans entered into "fusion" arrangements. In Jefferson County, for example, the Democrats usually nominated the county judge, one clerk, the assessor, and the state senator. The Republicans usually named the sheriff, one clerk, and representatives to the lower house of the legislature.[32] Thus, Democrat-inspired fusion and moderation aided the prolonged political life of blacks in the Delta after Redemption.

The Republican Party controlled federal patronage in the state, and black Republicans were included in Party councils and in federal appointments. For example, Mifflin W. Gibbs of Little Rock, the state's most influential black Republican until his death in 1915, was appointed registrar of the United States Land Office in 1876 by President Rutherford B. Hayes and reappointed by President Chester A. Arthur in 1881. In 1889 President Benjamin Harrison appointed him receiver of Public Monies. From 1891 until 1897, Gibbs served as secretary of the state Republican Central Committee. The capstone of his career was his appointment as United States consul to Madagascar in 1897 by President William McKinley.[33] John E. Bush was appointed receiver of the United States Land Office at Little Rock in 1898, a post he held for fourteen years. The position made him the highest-ranking black federal office holder in the state and an important Clayton lieutenant.[34] Two other black Republicans, Aaron M. Middlebrooks, of Pine Bluff, and Jacob N. Donohoo, of Helena, were appointed deputy revenue collectors for the Eastern District of Arkansas in 1897.[35]

The Republican Party was also the base of black power at the local and state levels. Ferdinand Havis, of Pine Bluff, along with Gibbs and Bush, was the third member of the black Republican triumvirate. Jefferson County, a black-majority county, was a black Republican stronghold, and Havis, beginning in Reconstruction, became a powerful force in the city and county Republican organizations. He was elected alderman in every election from 1871 to

1889, elected circuit clerk for ten years from 1882 to 1892, and served as chairman of the Republican County Central Committee from 1886 to 1906.[36] S. W. Dawson, also of Jefferson County, served as secretary of the Republican County Central Committee for twenty-two years from 1886 to 1908 and was elected to the legislature for two terms in 1888 and in 1890.[37] J. Pennoyer Jones was the black Republican "boss" of Desha County. An attorney, he served variously as county sheriff, county clerk, and as county judge from 1874 to 1890.[38] H. A. Johnson of Chicot County was elected sheriff in 1884 and in 1886.[39]

Despite the loyalty of blacks to the Republican Party and their use of the Party as a base for prolonged activism, they also represented the Party's primary liability. As its largest bloc of voters, the black electorate burdened the Party with a constituency unacceptable to most whites. The lily-white movement within the Party was not only an effort to make the Party more palatable to whites and to broaden its base, but it also involved an attempt by dissident "outs" to wrest control of the Party from the regular Clayton black-and-tan organization. Dissension among black Republican leaders largely resulted from a desire for greater patronage recognition, the choice of more black Party officers, and the selection of more black candidates for public office as well as from their disparate responses to lily-whitism.

With the demise of Democratic conservatism and continued black discontent in the Republican Party, black Republicans, beginning in 1888, sought coalitions with agrarian parties. Because the majority of blacks were engaged in agriculture, there was an affinity between black and white farmers based on common grievances. Both black and white farmers suffered from increasing tenancy, low crop prices, the crop-lien system, discriminatory railroad rates, and state statutes that favored the mortgagor.

Black farmers in Prairie County organized a local alliance in 1882. By 1885, blacks in the Delta region had organized other local alliances known as the Sons of the Agricultural Star with headquarters in Monroe County. In 1886, at the state convention in Jackson County, the Agricultural Wheel eliminated its "whites only" eligibility clause and provided for separate black Wheels. With the revision of its membership rules, the Sons were absorbed into the Wheel as its first Negro locals. In 1888, there were two hundred black Wheels out of nearly two thousand locals. But admittance of black local Wheels into the white organization, revision of the membership rules, and common interests did not eliminate the racial antipathy of white farmers. As members of the state organization, black Wheels were required to pay dues. But at the state Wheel convention in July 1887, white Wheelers attempted to deny recognition to black delegates from St. Francis County. In reaction to this imposition of the color line, the black Wheels, while retaining membership in the white Wheel, organized the Colored State Agricultural Wheel the following year. In 1889, the national Wheel merged with the National Farmers Alliance and Cooperative Union of America to become the National Farmers Alliance and Industrial Union. The new organization excluded blacks, and the state Wheel, as part of the larger organization, again drew the color line.[40]

In 1888 and again in 1890 a coalition of Wheelers, black and white Republicans and dissident Democrats, combined to form the Union Labor Party in Arkansas. The Republican Party did not nominate a state ticket in these years and, instead, endorsed the Union Labor slate. As a result, the Union Labor-Republican coalition, in 1888, came closer to upsetting the Democratic Party than had any other Party since Redemption.[41]

The strategy used by the Democratic Party in the campaigns of 1888 and 1890 involved the use of race baiting and appeals to good Wheeler Democrats to remain loyal to the Party. Fraud and violence abounded in these campaigns. In an effort to inject the issue of "social equality," B. D. Cleveland, Union Labor candidate for state representative from Jackson County, was reported in the Democratic press to have said, "The time is not far distant when the [Negro] and the white man would eat side by side at the same table and sleep side by side in the same bed."[42] After the election, A. J. Streeter of Illinois, Union Labor candidate for president, bitterly criticized the outcome in the state. He said, "I was in the state a day or two before the election, and was plainly told by leading [D]emocrats that they were going to carry the state, fairly if they could, but violently and fraudulently if they had to resort to such measures to seat their candidate."[43] In the elections of 1890, the corruption and race baiting of 1888 were repeated.

The elections of 1888 and 1890 had significant political consequences for blacks. Each election demonstrated the political power of blacks in the state. In 1888, eight blacks were elected to the state legislature and in the next election, in 1890, twelve were elected, including one to the senate. As a result of black political participation and the Union Labor-Republican challenge, the coalition polled 46 percent of the vote in 1888 and slightly less, 44 percent, in 1890.[44]

By 1891 the growing political power of the black rural electorate, concentrated in the Delta region, and a growing urban black middle class, prompted white Democrats to demand a new election law and ratification of a poll tax amendment to the constitution.

The increasing black electorate and the gains of the black middle class produced a sizable number of black legislators during the 1880s. From 1880 to 1890, at least thirty black legislators served in the general assembly, and one served in the senate. With the exception of Pulaski County, which elected four black representatives and where blacks made up only 46 percent of the population, all of the representatives were from black majority counties of the Delta.

These facts were not lost on the white Democratic press, which by 1889 began to complain about the growing black migration into the state. One editorial predicted that "if Arkansas is not a safe Republican state within a few years it will not be the fault of the importers."[45] From the white perspective, a growing black population portended a stronger Republican Party or a Republican-supported agrarian coalition. Democrats would necessarily resort to election fraud to maintain their hegemony in the face of this perceived threat.

Ironically, the prevalence of corrupt elections was often attributed to blacks and/or Republicans when they were, in fact, more the province of white Democrats. Nevertheless, the clear existence of corrupt elections was widely heralded by white Democrats as a reason for reform and black disfranchisement. In 1889, in answer to a survey to legislative members circulated by the Little Rock *Arkansas Gazette*, improvement of the election laws by means of a poll tax to insure fair and accurate counts was considered to be the most important issue of the session.[46] Generally, throughout the South, it was claimed that black disfranchisement would not only purify elections, but would also eliminate the black vote as the balance of power in elections and put the Negro securely "in his place."[47] Black disfranchisement was also a function of radical racism. The radical view, which displaced conservatism and prevailed after 1889, held that blacks, no longer subject to the civilizing influences of slavery, were rapidly retrogressing to their natural state of bestiality. To support such a view, radical racists cited the increasing crime rate among blacks. And of all Negro crimes, the most heinous were those purportedly involving sexual assaults on white women by black males. To thwart this alleged threat to white civilization, whites embraced a multifaceted strategy to proscribe the rights and opportunities of blacks, to consign them legally to an inferior place in society, all in the name of reform. Black disfranchisement was the first part of that strategy.[48]

The Democratic Party began its crusade for a new election law in 1889, and by 1891 there was a general demand for reform of the election law. The result was the secret ballot in 1891 and the poll tax in 1892. Both had an immediate impact on voting activity in the state. The total vote count for governor in the three elections of 1890, 1892, and 1894 were 191,448, 156,186, and 126,986 respectively. In 1890 an estimated 75 percent of whites and 71 percent of the black electorate voted. In 1892, with the secret ballot law operating, only 58 percent of the white electorate and 24 percent of the black electorate voted. The poll tax reduced voter participation an additional 15 percent among blacks and 12 percent among whites.[49] The secret ballot and poll tax laws remained the state's means of disfranchisement until adoption of the third and final device, the white primary, in 1906.

In the years following Redemption in 1874, blacks in the Delta counties took advantage of several factors to continue political activism. The strong organization of the Republican Party in the region and the heavy concentration of blacks meant that while the Democrats successfully reclaimed the state, Redemption in the Delta counties was milder than in the Deep South and did not automatically eliminate black voting or the Republican Party. Rather, the move for disfranchisement in the early 1890s represented a second Redemption where the first one did not "take." The effort of blacks in the region to ally themselves with agrarian third parties, most notably the Union Labor Party, was an attempt to forestall the onslaught of radical racism, to prevent a second, more thorough Redemption, and to continue political participation. Yet, Democratic politicians, who invoked the rhetoric of reform and resorted to the use of overt racism, ultimately succeeded in eliminating Delta blacks' fragile grip on political power.

The federal Civil Rights Act of 1875 provided that all public accommodations, such as streetcars, trains, steamboats, restaurants, theaters, hotels, and parks, be open to all citizens regardless of color. Earlier, in 1873, the Reconstruction government in Arkansas passed a state civil rights law that forbade discrimination on the basis of race in all public accommodations, public carriers, hotels, inns, restaurants, saloons, and places of amusement.[50] Separate schools in the state were first mandated by this law, which provided for "equal and like accommodations" in the operation of the schools. The federal law of 1875 corresponded to what has been described as Conservative segregation. Conservative segregation insured the safety of black people and protected their dignity. Rather than attempting to degrade blacks, the Conservative Democrats sought to preserve and encourage black self-esteem and to protect blacks from abusive whites. The black community desired separate schools as a means of providing a degree of autonomy, leadership training, and employment for educated members of the community. Particularly in urban areas, teaching, in many instances, provided one of the few alternative employment opportunities to domestic service for educated black men and women. Finally, following Emancipation, education represented the third significant area of voluntary separation by blacks after agriculture and religion.

The Separate Coach Law of 1891 further threatened the civil and political rights of blacks. This law represented the first phase of the legal separation of the races as a result of radical racism that emerged in 1889. Legalized segregation was the other half of a two-pronged radical effort to manage and render powerless the black population. The radical motives in instituting separation were to depress black expectations, especially those of black men, and to make them less secure and less aggressive and to demonstrate white supremacy and its power. Hence, the emergence of segregation gave rise to a different type of color line. As practiced by white supremacists, segregation was designed to degrade and debase black people by strictly enforced laws of separation, a rigid racial etiquette, and relegation to inferior facilities.[51]

The response of the black middle class to the introduction of the Separate Coach law was immediate. The black middle-class community of Little Rock provided the most ardent and articulate opposition to the law. At two mass meetings held in the city in January 1891, approximately one thousand blacks gathered in protest and passed resolutions condemning the bill.[52]

Of the twelve black representatives in the Arkansas legislature of 1891, including one in the senate, none was more eloquent in opposing the Separate Coach bill than John Gray Lucas, representing Jefferson County. Said Lucas, "We read between the lines of the

Separate Coach bill. . . . The provisions as seen between its readings mean degradation, not elevation; obloquy, not civil citizenship; civil ostracism, not civil recognition, and lastly, it means inferior and insufficient accommodations for the colored man—the 'Jim Crow.' . . . The working of the bill, apparently intending to secure 'equal accommodations' is a delusion and a snare."[53]

The Separate Coach law in Arkansas and the white supremacist effort to eliminate race mixing primarily affected the middle-class black community. The majority of rural blacks did not have the means or wherewithal to travel the state's railways. Passage of the law and its legitimizing of other forms of segregation ended a period that had witnessed more fluid race relations.

The second Jim Crow law in the state was not enacted until twelve years later. The Separate Streetcar law, patterned after similar measures in Virginia and Georgia, became effective in 1903. The black communities in Little Rock and Pine Bluff responded with protest meetings and boycotts. On the day the law became effective, May 27, blacks in Little Rock began a boycott of the streetcars and formed a "We Walk" league. Members of the club agreed to voluntarily submit to fines for each time they rode the streetcars. Black patronage on the first day of the boycott was estimated at only 10 percent of the normal traffic and less than 5 percent on some routes. Prior to the boycott, black fares accounted for approximately 60 percent of the streetcar traffic. In Pine Bluff, the boycott ran from May 27 to June 17, 1903.[54]

Just as blacks had become degraded in politics and in their civil rights, they were also accorded a disparate status in the state's system of law enforcement and legal justice. Violence in the form of lynching was frequent. During the thirty years from 1889 to 1918, there were 214 lynchings in the state. Of this number, 182 victims, or 85 percent of the total, were black. Five of the 182 were black women. Ninety-three, or 43 percent, of the 214 victims were black residents of the Delta. Of the 10 states which had 100 or more lynchings during the period, Arkansas ranked sixth after Georgia, Mississippi, Texas, Louisiana, and Alabama. South Carolina ranked tenth with 120.[55]

The use of private and official violence by the white population of Arkansas against the black population culminated in the Elaine riots of 1919. The black unrest in Phillips County grew out of a sharecropping system that had degenerated into peonage. In 1920,

Phillips County had a total population of 44,530 with a black population of 32,929, or 74 percent.[56] The majority of the black population was engaged in agricultural labor. A typical sharecropper in the county in 1919 raised 14 bales of cotton or 7,000 pounds at 43 cents per pound. Each bale contained a half ton of seed valued at 70 dollars per ton. Therefore, the sharecropper's crop was worth about 3,500 dollars. During the year, the farmer bought or "took up" goods worth only $23.50. But in settling with the plantation owner, the value of goods "taken up" totaled the value of his crop. With the weight of the law and custom on the side of the plantation owner, the sharecroppers were compelled to endure this corruption and injustice.[57]

In an effort to remedy this violent system, the black farmers of Phillips County organized the Progressive Farmers and Household Union of America. The purpose of the union was to secure relief from debt servitude through legal redress and a more equitable settlement with the plantation owner.[58]

The challenge of the black union to the authority of the white power structure in Phillips County in 1919 prompted a violent response. The white community charged that the Progressive Union was an insurrectionary conspiracy to murder the white population and take over the county. Using this contrived defense, the white community determined to crush the union, punish the members, and restore the status quo. With the aid of mob rule, Governor Charles Brough, and the United States Army, the "uprising" was suppressed; an indeterminate number of blacks and five whites were killed and over 100 black men arrested. In the grand jury session that followed, 122 blacks were indicted. At the trials, with all-white juries, 12 blacks were sentenced to death and 67 sentenced to penitentiary terms ranging from 1 to 21 years.[59]

Through the legal efforts of the NAACP, working secretly for 6 years, the 12 men sentenced to death were released in 1923 and in 1925. The Elaine riots were important because the state was forced, by outside public pressure and by the federal courts, to curb its tendency to use its police powers in favor of one group against another.[60]

Within the hostile environment of Jim Crow, political reduction, and physical decimation, a philosophy of black solidarity and pride, economic development, and self-help pervaded the black community during the late nineteenth and early twentieth centuries. The coincidence of the materialism, imperialism, and Social Darwinist theories of the industrial age, and the ascendancy of Booker T.

Washington's gospel of wealth, culminated in a shift in black strategy from an emphasis on political and civil rights, immediate integration, and protest to racial self-help, economic independence, and accountability. The increased emphasis on material prosperity as a solution to the race problem rested on the assumption that by the accumulation of wealth and the demonstration of morality, blacks would earn the respect of whites and be granted their rights as citizens. This doctrine of economic independence conformed to the American promise of personal and ethnic success through the work ethic. The faith of the black community in the "promise of American life" through racial self-help and solidarity was embodied in the institutional life of the black community.[61]

By far the oldest and largest institution of social welfare, self-help, solidarity, and autonomy in the black community was the church. At the turn of the century, a larger proportion of the black population in Arkansas was affiliated with church organizations than the white population: 34 percent of the black population compared with 23 percent of the white population in 1890; 39 percent of blacks compared with 30 percent of whites in 1906; and 54 percent of blacks compared with 25 percent of whites in 1916.[62] Women dominated total membership, making up 62 percent of total black membership in 1916.[63] As Jim Crow became more firmly entrenched and institutionalized, black church membership increased correspondingly.

The National Baptist Convention (Colored), organized in 1895 and the largest black organization in the country, was also the largest denomination in the state. By 1916, the Baptist church accounted for 73 percent of total black membership in all churches. The second largest denomination, Methodism, was divided into four organizations. The African Methodist Episcopal Church (A.M.E.) was the largest with 13 percent of total black membership in 1916, followed by the Colored Methodist Episcopal Church (C.M.E.), the A.M.E. Zion Church, and the Methodist Episcopal Church.[64] Smaller black denominations included the Protestant Episcopal, Presbyterian, and Congregationalist churches. A profusion of black fundamentalist denominations included the Adventist Church, Church of Christ, Primitive Baptists, Church of God in Christ (Holiness), and Church of the Living God. Of 607 black churches organized between 1880 and 1920 and surveyed by the federal government between 1936 and 1942, 390, or 64 percent, were located in the Delta.[65]

Southland College in Helena, Phillips County, gave rise to a predominantly black Southland Monthly Meeting of Friends established in 1873. By 1890 the Meeting had established Preparative Meetings in the nearby communities of Hickory Ridge and Beaver Bayou. The total membership reached approximately four hundred, including four black ministers.[66] Meanwhile, by 1945, there were six black Roman Catholic parishes in the state, and four of them were located in the Delta. The oldest, St. Peter's in Pine Bluff, organized in 1894, was the only black parish established in the late nineteenth century.[67]

The black minister, who played an important role within the community, was expected to provide both spiritual and secular leadership. As a race leader, he acted as a liaison between the black and white communities and was held in high regard by both.[68] Reverend E. C. Morris of Helena epitomized the role of the black minister. He was the most prominent black Baptist minister in the Delta and in the state during the late nineteenth and early twentieth centuries. Morris was pastor of Centennial Baptist Church in Helena for forty-three years, president of the Arkansas Baptist Convention for forty years, and president of the National Baptist Convention (Colored) from its inception until his death in 1922. As president of the state convention, Morris inaugurated in 1882 the *Baptist Vanguard*, the weekly organ of the state convention, and established Arkansas Baptist College in Little Rock two years later.[69]

The activities of the State Baptist Convention reflected the centrality of the church in the lives of black Delta residents. The annual state meeting of the convention was an eagerly awaited and festive event.[70] District associations provided fellowship among groups of member churches. The associations held annual conventions to elect officers and to raise money for home and foreign mission work and educational institutions. The associations also held annual Sunday School Conventions. The Phillips, Lee, and Monroe (counties) District Sunday School Convention sponsored a choir competition among member churches during its two-day meeting in 1896. The District Convention, held later during the same week, was an occasion for "preaching, speechmaking, singing and resoluting."[71] The White River District Association was formed in Arkansas County in 1880 with fifteen organizing churches.[72]

The Women's Baptist Missionary Association devoted itself to charitable fund raising and promoting subscriptions to the *Baptist*

Vanguard. One of the charities of the association was the M. W. Gibbs Home for Elderly Women in Little Rock. The home was managed by a nine-member Board of Guardians that included the state president of the Association.[73]

Because of the inadequacy of black public school education, because education was usually part of the mission work of black churches, and because of the importance of education among all classes of blacks, church-supported, private schools filled an important gap in the black community. These schools trained teachers for the public schools and provided college preparation for the professions. In addition to education, they also taught habits of economy, hard work, and Christian morality, and provided social skills and middle-class values that in many instances were unavailable in the rural communities from which their students came.[74] By 1916, there were thirty black private schools in the state; nineteen were located in the Delta. Of the nineteen, four offered teaching degrees and maintained elementary and secondary departments.[75]

By the end of the nineteenth century, the church's dominance as the most visible symbol of black autonomy, as well as its monopoly of self-help and social welfare enterprises, was being challenged by secular fraternal and benevolent societies and by a growing entrepreneurial class. The most successful black business venture and secret fraternal organization in the Delta and in the state at the turn of the century was The Grand Mosaic Templars of America. In May 1882, John E. Bush, Chester W. Keatts, and twelve other men organized the Zephro Temple No. 1 at Little Rock. Incorporated in 1883, the order united in brotherhood men of good character regardless of class or occupation, encouraged members in business and helped them in finding work, maintained a benefit fund, and chartered subordinate Temples. By 1920, with national headquarters in Little Rock, the order had affiliates in twenty-one states, almost forty thousand members, and assets of nearly two hundred thousand dollars.[76] Other fraternal organizations in the Delta included the Knights of Tabor, the Colored Knights of Pythias, the Grand United Order of Oddfellows (Negro), and Prince Hall Masons.[77]

Bush's Mosaic Templars exemplified the changing black political emphasis from rights to duties. In describing why he and Keatts established the Order, Bush said: "I have so often been embarrassed while talking to some prominent white person when some old colored woman would come up and ask for a donation to bury some colored man who had been a citizen of the community all his life and had held good positions."[78] Bush was expressing the desire and belief that the black community should assume responsibility for the care of its members. Bush's perspective was also, undoubtedly, a partial result of his close association with Booker T. Washington. The National Negro Business League (NNBL), organized by Washington in 1900, was the expression of his philosophy of thrift, industry, and property ownership. Bush, a charter member of the League in 1900, became chairman of its Executive Committee in 1911. The Arkansas branch of the League was organized by Bush, Keatts, M. W. Gibbs, E. C. Morris, and Ferdinand Havis. The League was designed to encourage the development of black economic enterprise and to advertise the successes of black businessmen.[79] As white patronage of black businesses declined after 1890, the League made "buying black" a form of race protest and unity as well as a way of preserving one's dignity.

In Little Rock, J. E. Henderson became the only black jeweler in the Delta and in the state when he opened a jewelry store in 1896. A native of Little Rock, he studied for twelve years with a white jeweler in the city before becoming independent. In March 1906, W. O. Foster, a graduate of Howard University Pharmacy School, opened the Foster Drug Store in the city.[80] There were at least two black-operated grocery stores in Helena. Moses G. Turner was the owner and manager of one store; Rev. E. C. Morris operated and managed a cooperative store from 1901 to 1905.[81] The Colored State Fair was an annual event beginning in 1881 in Pine Bluff that became a showcase for black talent from around the state. Founded by a black dentist, inventor, and author in Little Rock, Dr. J. H. Smith, the annual affair attracted crowds from both races.[82]

Pine Bluff, a black majority city in Jefferson County, maintained a sizeable black business community. In 1903, four of the five barbers in town were black. There were also sixteen grocers, four blacksmiths, seven restauranteurs, five saloon keepers, and two dry goods merchants. The first beauty shop in the city was opened in 1906 by Mrs. Nettie Hollis Johnson whose husband, Dr. R. T. Johnson, was a dentist. The shop catered exclusively to white women.[83] Wiley Jones, also of Pine Bluff, was reputedly the wealthiest black man in the Delta and in the state. By 1890 he was the sole owner of the only streetcar line in the city and the proprietor of Wiley Jones Park, a racetrack and stables. In 1898 he organized the Southern Mercantile

Company, a wholesale supply house.[84] Jones's close associate and sometime political ally, Ferd Havis, was Pine Bluff's second wealthiest black man. Havis owned a home on Barraque Street, a fashionable Pine Bluff address, several tenements, and in 1884 built and opened a one-story wholesale and retail whiskey business on Main Street. In 1892, Havis added a second story to the Havis building. The first floor was rented to a white liquor dealer, and the second floor became a social hall for the black elite of Pine Bluff. By 1890 Havis also owned two thousand acres of farmland. In 1903 he was instrumental in organizing the local chapter of the NNBL and served as its first president.[85]

The efforts on the part of black Arkansans to establish and maintain banking institutions had auspicious beginnings, but each eventually failed. The Unity Bank and Trust Company in Pine Bluff was the first black-owned bank in the Delta and in the state. The company was organized in 1902 with Jacob Donohoo as president; it failed after six years. In 1903 the Capital City Savings Bank was established in Little Rock with M. W. Gibbs as president. By 1905 the bank had deposits of one hundred thousand dollars and during the same year organized a subsidiary, the People's Mutual Aid Association, a health insurance company. Unfortunately, mismanagement coupled with the Panic of 1907 forced the bank to close in 1908.[86]

Among women, who constituted the majority of church membership, the strongest competition to religious organizations was the national black women's club movement. The national black women's club movement, an aspect of the reform movement known as progressivism, was a response to the exclusion of black women from participation in the General Federation of Women's Clubs, organized in 1890. It was also a consequence of worsening racial tensions and the increase of discrimination in employment and education. Because of Jim Crow, black women felt a keen sense of race consciousness and a responsibility for the uplift and "progress of the race." In 1896, Ida Wells Barnett of Chicago, Mary Church Terrell of Washington, D.C., Josephine St. Pierre Ruffin of Boston, and Margaret Murray Washington of Tuskegee, and others formed the National Association of Colored Women (NACW). The federation's motto was "Lifting as We Climb."[87] Combining the themes of organized race protest, solidarity, and self-help, the NACW operated as a welfare agency and as a social uplift vehicle for middle-class black women. During the twenty years before the First World War, black women in the Delta worked toward improving conditions in their communities.[88]

The first NACW Federated club in the state was organized in Little Rock in February 1897. The City Federation of Little Rock was organized in June 1905. Some of the member clubs included the Rosa Morris Club, the Sunshine Charity Club, the Frances Harper Club, and the Provident Relief Club. Support for the M. W. Gibbs Home for Elderly Women was a primary charity of the Little Rock NACW City Federation. In 1909, the home had ten rooms and the property was valued at two thousand dollars. The City Federation underwrote the entire support for the home, including utilities, groceries, maintenance, insurance, and two full-time employees.[89] In Pine Bluff, the Social and Art Club (NACW) was organized in December 1911. The purpose of the club was "to improve the spiritual, educational and civic development of Negro Women."[90] Despite its limited resources, there was a concerted effort, through club work, "to zero in on the middle-class woman and motivate interest in her local community." These club women promoted the philosophy of self-help and solidarity and contributed significantly to the welfare of their communities. They also provided themselves with mutual moral support and social activity.

Other secular benevolent societies, literary clubs, and social clubs were also popular. There were two women's literary societies in Little Rock. Carrie Still Shepperson, the mother of the famous composer, William Grant Still, was a member of the Lotus Club. The Bay View Reading Club was organized by twelve Little Rock public schoolteachers.[91] The Ne Plus Ultra Club in Pine Bluff held cakewalks as fundraising events for the A.M.E. Church. On another occasion, the club held a grand moonlight picnic and ice cream supper at the home of one of the members.[92]

Economic conditions among blacks in the Delta during the institutionalization of Jim Crow were, to some degree, based on class. The black middle class, comprised of teachers, doctors, ministers, dentists, lawyers, businessmen, and railroad men, achieved a degree of financial security that tended to lessen the more onerous forms of the caste system. They were conservative and supported the conciliatory policies of Booker T. Washington; their defense of the status quo guaranteed their continued prosperity. The color line provided the black middle class with a closed market, and they took advantage of this aspect of segregation. But the black middle class represented less than 8 percent of all gainfully employed blacks in the state by 1920. The great majority of black residents of the Delta did not prosper behind the color line. The agricultural and working classes suffered most under segregation and disfranchisement. Overwhelmingly rural, the black working class in the Delta was isolated and subject to more severe and violent oppression. It was this group that participated most frequently in the back-to-Africa immigration movements of the 1890s and in the early decades of the twentieth century. During the first twenty years of the century, the average size of white farms was over three times the average size of black farms. The number of black share tenants increased and the number of black cash tenants decreased. The urban working class was economically exploited and had little opportunity for upward mobility. Consequently, for many blacks in the Delta, immigration, either to the North during the Great Migration, encouraged by the surplus of jobs created by the First World War and the cessation of European immigration, or to Africa, represented the only palatable alternative.

The impact of slavery and Jim Crow has been to imprint upon the region and the people a legacy of intemperate race relations. The legacy of slavery insured the continued concentration of black population in the Delta. From 1860 through 1910, an average of 64 percent of the black population of Arkansas lived in the twenty-seven Delta counties. From 1920 to 1980, the average was 71 percent. Arkansas was, and is, geographically, a border state rather than a member of the Deep South heartland, but the adoption of Jim Crow was a cultural phenomenon, and the Delta, in particular, did not offer an alternative.

By 1950 blacks in the Arkansas Delta made up three-fourths of the state's black population and 22 percent of the total population. The median income in 1950 for the black population in the state was $839 as compared to $1,987 for whites. The state average was $1,571. In the Delta region, the median income for blacks was $555.03 and $1,306.77 for whites. In the number of years of school completed in the state in 1950, over twice as many whites completed eight years of elementary school as blacks; and 11 percent of whites completed high school compared to less than 1 percent of blacks. The median number of years of school completed was 5.2 for blacks and 8.4 for whites. In occupational status, in the same year, agriculture remained the most important occupation for black men, and domestic service ranked first for black women.[93]

By 1980 the impact of the civil rights movement was diffuse. Blacks in Arkansas and especially in the Delta remained a largely economic underclass. While educational levels were more nearly comparable between blacks and whites, the median income remained relatively static, and occupational status degenerated. In 1980, 26.8 percent of blacks, age twenty-five and over, completed eight years of school compared with 19.8 percent of whites; 22 percent of blacks finished high school, 34 percent of whites; 6 percent of blacks were college graduates and 11 percent of whites. The median number of years of school completed for blacks was 10.1; 12.5 years for whites. In the same year, the median income for blacks in the state was $7,283; $13,169 for whites. Blacks' median income was 55 percent of the white median income. In occupational status, service occupations became the single largest category for blacks, both male and female.[94]

The inequities and disparities of black lives, legitimized and institutionalized by slavery and Jim Crow, continue to contribute to the paradox of poverty within a milieu of natural wealth and beauty. The Delta epitomizes an assessment made over a generation ago: "The mind of the section . . . is continuous with the past. And its primary form is determined not nearly so much by industry as by the purely agricultural conditions of that past. So far from being modernized, in many ways it has actually marched away, as to this day it continues to do, from the present toward the past."[95]

Blanche Hudson, a teacher at Southland College, around 1920.
Courtesy Southland College Papers, Special Collections Division, University of Arkansas Libraries, Fayetteville.

Sharecroppers evicted from a Parkin (Cross County) plantation, about 1936.
Courtesy Arkansas History Commission.

A fraternal group at Helena, around 1880, including former legislators A. H. Miller and J. T. White. *Courtesy Miller Collection/UALR Archives.*

Arnold's dry cleaners in
Blytheville (Mississippi
County), around 1920.
*Courtesy Era Floyd/Arkansas
History Commission.*

Phillips County black residents en route to Liberia. This group later
joined former legislator A. L. Stanford in New York.
From Frank Leslie's Illustrated Newspaper. *Courtesy Library of Congress.*

J. N. DONOHOO, PHILIP COLEMAN,
President. Treasurer.

UNITY BANK AND TRUST CO.

Capital $25,000.

Interest on Deposits

4%

We offer depositors every facility consistent with good banking principles.

316 State St. PINE BLUFF, ARK.
(Masonic Temple)

Mutual Indemnity Association

Incorporated under the laws of the State of Arkansas.

$20,000 Bond Filed with the Auditor of State

Home Office, Pine Bluff, Ark.

S. A. MOSELY, Pres. J. N. DONOHOO, Sec.

Pine Bluff, Arkansas.

A. W. SPEARS
Attorney-at-Law and Collections

Practice in all Courts both State and Federal—Special attention given to public and private land claims— Personal damage suits and all classes of criminal cases.

220½ State Street. **Pine Bluff, Ark.**

DR. G. W. BELL
Physician and Obstetrician

Diseases of women and children a specialty. Also skin diseases and chronic ulcers diagnosed and properly treated.

Rooms No. 3 and 4. 218½ State St. Old Phone.

PINE BLUFF, ARKANSAS.

WILEY JONES & CO.
223 MAIN STREET.
WHISKIES, WINES AND CIGARS.

James Jones solicits his own and the friends of the late Wiley Jones to call and see him at the above number. For 27 years I have handled the following brands of liquors to the satisfaction of my customers:

JOHN T. BARBEE, BELLE OF NELSON, KENTUCKY TAYLOR, CREAM OF KENTUCKY, MAYFLOWER. NEWSBOY, Etc.

Pine Bluff, Ark.

Black-owned businesses advertised in Polk's *Arkansas State Gazetteer and Business Directory, 1906–1907*, 538.
Courtesy Special Collections Division, University of Arkansas Libraries, Fayetteville.

Dr. Booker T. Washington with Scott Bond and family at their home
in 1911.   Dan. A. Rudd and Theo. Bond, *From Slavery to Wealth: The Life of
Scott Bond*, 39. *Courtesy Special Collections Division, University of Arkansas
Libraries, Fayetteville.*

"The Cedars," Scott Bond's Home at Madison, Arkansas.
Dan. A. Rudd and Theo. Bond, *From Slavery to Wealth: The Life of Scott Bond*, 287.
Courtesy Special Collections Division, University of Arkansas Libraries, Fayetteville.

"What Ain't I Been Doing?": Historical Reflections on Women and the Arkansas Delta

ELIZABETH ANNE PAYNE

Women in nineteenth-century America, especially in the Arkansas Delta, were uniquely situated to experience the juxtaposition of life and death in their daily lives. Witness the following entry in the diary of a Delta woman living near Helena: "June 24 1864 This day four years ago our darling little Sallie died, and our little Lou was born."[1] Mary Frances Sale Edmondson had been so transfixed by the day that had brought both birth and death into her household that she had been unable to celebrate Lou's birthday until the date of this journal entry. In that same paragraph, Mrs. Edmondson recalled a poignant scene with her father immediately following Lou's birth in which "little Lou was placed in her grandfather's arms—while our beautiful Sallie lay cold and white in her crib, waiting to be laid in her coffin . . ."[2]

Although the occasion for Mrs. Edmondson's reflection was, in fact, to record that she had finally decided to give "the one left" a birthday party, she never reconciled herself to the death of Sarah Susannah, or "Sallie," who had been born September 20, 1858. Indeed, baby Sallie's death seemed to have heralded an onslaught of trials: "Our family troubles then began. As the heavy cloud made itself darkly visible in our doomed country's horizon, sickness and death spread through our whole family, white and black. Out of a family of thirty, we lost six, all grown but two, and all between June and October."[3] In addition to baby Sallie, Mrs. Edmondson's father and stepdaughter Mollie, as well as three beloved slaves, had died during the summer months of the previous four years.[4]

Life and death as well as joy and dread were so emotionally connected in women's lives in large part because giving birth represented a serious threat to the life of a mother. In 1850, the Delta's maternal mortality was comparable to surrounding southern states; even so, it was twice as high as in northern states.[5] Virtually every nineteenth-century Delta cemetery held the graves of husbands buried between two wives, one who died in childbirth and the other who became the stepmother of his children.

Most women in the Delta relied on midwives, often black, who practiced a combination of common sense, herbal remedies, and at times even a benevolent witchcraft to ward evil spirits away from the delivering mother and her child. Although midwives doubtless were a rich source of practical wisdom on childbirth, their ignorance of germs guaranteed a high mortality rate from infections for both mothers and newborns. Midwives, for example, frequently went directly from the barnyard or field to attend a woman in labor without washing their hands.[6] Indeed, of those who died, relatively few— less than 10 percent—succumbed during or immediately after childbirth from hemorraging or complications from the mechanics of delivery. Most deaths for the mother resulted from infections within the first month after giving birth.[7] Delta newborns, especially blacks, not uncommonly died of "the nine day fits," or tetanus, caused by the use of contaminated instruments to sever the umbilical cord.[8] Because census records are not precise regarding the causes of childbirth-related deaths, one can only guess at the number of women who also died of tetanus. Home delivery by midwives was obviously full of hazards.

Mortality rates would likely have been higher as late as the 1930s if more Delta women had used doctors to deliver their babies. Women in labor who could afford a physician in the nineteenth century were often given treatments that included, for example, "letting" large amounts of blood or placing leeches on the vagina to lessen the bleeding.[9] Such practices, of course, left the woman weakened and incapable of rapid recovery. Furthermore, Delta doctors themselves often had limited training, sometimes a mere summer course in medicine, and were as ignorant as midwives of germs. Indeed, a trained nurse recalled her horror the first time in 1938 that she assisted a Delta physician with a home delivery: "I was young, just out of nursing school, and I very carefully went about doing everything I had been taught to do: sterilizing the instruments, baking the sheets and boiling the water. Then he [the doctor] came in and threw his dirty coat right down on top of my baked sheets."[10]

Puerperal fever, often called "childbed fever" or "milk fever," became the great tragedy of maternity in this country after the 1830s.[11] An epidemic that originated in hospitals in urban areas, the disease by the 1850s and sixties had spread into the Delta, carried from hospitals by doctors on their hands, clothes, and instruments to their patients. A wound infection of the birth passage caused by a deadly bacterium, the Puerperal fever raged in Delta counties until the 1920s. Even those in the most advanced scientific circles in the nation knew little of how to combat the infection until the 1880s, and ill-trained physicians in rural areas such as the Delta did not always take sanitary precautions until well into the twentieth century.[12]

As women from prosperous Delta families increasingly relied on physicians rather than on midwives (who, having never practiced in hospitals, did not carry the bacterium), they unwittingly exposed themselves to the single threat they most feared: the bacterium that caused widespread inflammation of the abdominal cavity, blood poisoning, and death within a few days. Ironically, inasmuch as it was physicians themselves who were spreading the bacterium, the Delta would have lost many more of its women if they had been able to afford doctors earlier. And the area was fortunate that virtually all of its hospitals were built after it became routine for surgeons and obstetricians to scrub and use an antiseptic before placing their hands inside a patient's body. In this case, at least, the area's isolation and poverty benefited the health of its citizens, especially its women.

Delta women, even when patients in hospitals, often continued to rely on folk practices. Julie Nixon of Gould recalled her difficult labor and delivery in 1952 at Dumas Hospital during which a female friend slipped a pair of scissors under her mattress to cut the pain.[13] Clearly, when it came to childbirth, Delta women mixed modern medicine and traditional folk cures, choosing without self-consciousness or apology those aspects from each that seemed to work.

Swamp-related diseases, epidemics, and infections combined with poor diet, forbidding conditions, and inadequate medical treatment to jeoparadize the health of all who lived in the Delta. They especially took their toll on married women of child-bearing age, most of whom were giving birth every two to two-and-a-half years.[14] Indeed, the pattern of settling in rich but swampy bottomland or in lowland areas that were frequently flooded meant that pregnant and postpartum women faced the threat of malaria, the Delta's most frequent killer, from late spring until early fall. Likewise, tainted water supplies, contaminated by frequent flooding and human waste, helped to spread typhoid fever, cholera, and dysentery. Winter, however, brought its own set of diseases, with respiratory infections like pneumonia, the leading cause of fatalities.[15] The quest for good bottomland and quick profits often put the family's economic interests at odds with the health of family members, creating a harsher environment in which to give birth safely and rear the young.

Few women spoke with enthusiasm for the Arkansas Delta in the nineteenth century, in large part because they understood the area's physical threats to themselves and to their families. Indeed, Mrs. Edmondson had begun her diary because she correctly assumed she would die an early death. "This old book," as she called her diary in her first entry in August 26, 1863, "I now devote as a sort of Journal, in my desolated Arkansas Home." She further explained, "I am now forty-seven years old. [My children's] ages are seven and three and in the present prospect of affairs, and event, it is quite probable they may know but little of their mother, and their own infancy and early youth, except what these pages may contain."[16] Written only a few days after a family council had determined that health considerations and nearby military conflicts necessitated the departure of her elderly parents, fourteen-year-old stepdaughter, and a beloved slave, these lines captured Mrs. Edmondson's experience of her new Delta home as forbidding, dangerous, and harsh.

Susan Cook, vivacious and twenty-one, was different in temperament and age from her neighbor Mrs. Edmondson, but both women railed against the diseases of the Delta that threatened the lives of people they loved. After nursing her father for several weeks in August of 1865 only to see her brother fall ill from the same disease, Susan exploded in her diary: "I am at last convinced Arkansas is not the country for white people to live in. I will leave it the First chance I get, certain. Will go to Brazil if the opportunity presents itself."[17]

In fact, frontier conditions made Delta counties even more forbidding to black women, for on their shoulders fell much of the labor for establishing new homes and farms in an area defined by swamps, floods, and mosquitoes. Black women as slaves were often in the advance guard of settlement, sent ahead before the white family and slave children to help bring order out of the swampy wilderness. Former slave Josephine Barnett, born in Germantown, Tennessee, vividly recalled her childhood on a De Valls Bluff plantation: "I muster been five or six years old when I come out here to Arkansas.

My grandma was a midwife. She was already out here. She had to come with the first crowd cause some women was expecting. I tell you it sho was squally times. This country was wild. It was different from Tennesse or close to Germantown where we come from. None of the slaves liked it but they was brought."[18] Even as an elderly woman, Mrs. Barnett would remember her Delta childhood as a period that was squally in a place that was wild.

Rosa Ingram, a former slave in her thirties, lived in Memphis when the yellow fever epidemic broke out in 1871. Nearly seventy years later, she described that summer's horror, with coffins piled as high as houses and "Women dead lying around and babies sucking their breasts."[19] After the epidemic, she moved permanently to higher ground in Conway, Arkansas. Hetty Haskell, also a former slave, listed the death of her mother and sister from an outbreak of cholera after the Civil War as another trial her people had to bear during that period.[20] In the 1880s, Fannie Cotten, a widow who owned a size-able plantation near Helena, permanently moved herself and her four children to Searcy because so many neighbors were dying of malaria.[21] For both black and white women, the Delta held its special threats, reminding them that life was precarious, that assumptions about the future must be tentatively held. Susan Cook, in 1864, wrote anxiously in her diary about a small child she loved: "Lela Dunn, my little pet, is much better. I am so glad. It would grieve me to the core for her to die; but I would not be surprised, for . . . 'All I love fade and die.'"[22] Women in the Delta shared with each other a sense of being on the edge of life, for they lived with the reality that life could become death, that even a birth could become a funeral.

It was not simply the threat to their own existence that gave women this special perspective. As the ones who nursed the sick and dying, women learned how quickly life could change because they observed at close range the vulnerability of others. Virtually every diary and collection of letters written by a Delta woman, whether of wealthy or of modest background, contains constant reference to "sitting up" with a very ill family member, neighbor, or friend. The ethos of Delta womanhood, black and white, demanded that no very sick person, and certainly no one dying, be left alone. This feminine imperative crossed racial lines, for women often kept sick watch over members of the other race. This meant, of course, that women were always on call to family, kinspeople, and neighbors when illness fell and that their heavy load of work was frequently interrupted to nurse the sick.

Women began assuming the responsibility of "sitting up" very young, as early as fifteen. Susan Cook, at age twenty, rarely went a week without spending the night, often with another woman, at the bedside of a sick person. The following entries from her journal indicate the sacrifice even young women made in caring for the sick: "January 27, 1864 I am sitting up with tonight at Mrs. Weatherly's with a sick lady, Miss Underwood. I do not think she will live twenty-four hours longer." "January 30, 1864 I am sitting up with Miss Underwood tonight. She is no better. . . . Mrs. Sam Weatherly and I are keeping watch alone." "January 31 Ma is sitting up tonight." "February 1 Ma is sitting up again tonight." "February 3 I am sitting up again tonight with Miss Underwood. She is still in a dying condition." In this case, Susan Cook barely knew Miss Underwood— she was a visitor in Mrs. Weatherly's home—yet Susan and her mother attended her because the feminine ethos demanded that even visitors be included in their circle.[23]

In January 1870, a prosperous Delta planter fell ill and was diagnosed as having pneumonia on Saturday, the twenty-second. The next few days followed a trajectory not only of the progress of pneumonia but, more crucially, of a growing recognition of his indebtness to the women of his family. By Sunday, the disease was fully developed and accompanied by a high fever, and he noted in his diary that "My wife and mother have been attentive to every want and are doing all they can to alleviate my sufferings." By Wednesday, he was restless with an unbroken fever and "spitting up large quantities of very ugly and offensive matter. I now require sitting up with as I have grown very weak and have to be helped up to take my medicine. My faithful precious wife and dear mother are constant in their ministrations and attentions." His fever remained unbroken on Thursday, but his diary now focused on his wife's ministrations more than his illness: "Lena will give place to no one, but watches me unceasingly by my bedside. God bless my darling wife. She is a treasure to me and there are few such women in the world. Not a murmur, not a complaint ever escapes her lips. Her patience and gentleness are remarkable. She bears with all my fretfulness and is always the same faithful kind and watchful nurse. Ma is also constant and kind and Sis Ann is come. How shall I thank and love them all enough."[24]

In fact, the Delta was full of women like Lena, women who created an emotional world through their tenderness, sacrifice, and strength that offered those who were physically weak and in pain a safe haven and the best chance for recovery. No wonder, then, that Delta women often went to extraordinary lengths to reach a relative who was stricken by illness or injury. One Delta woman recalled hearing a horse in full gallop approach her home and "immediately at the gate—I saw it was Mrs. Robinson! She had been told that her brother was desperately wounded. . . . I told her she couldn't go—it was full six miles from here and two days before she had fainted from being driven not so far in a buggy from [her] little Carrie's Burial!"[25] Of course, Mrs. Robinson went. Many women left their homes on long journeys to attend a relative; women routinely were called in the middle of the night to travel to a neighbor's bedside. In a world fraught with constant disease and sudden death, women created a social world that defied the swamps and infections and, most of all, the idea that death could take a relative or a neighbor without a woman's best fight through vigilance and tenderness.

Women lived so intimately with the juxtaposition of life and death not only because they ministered to the sick, but also because they cared for the dead. Death, like birth, was a social event in the Delta, and it was a violation of womanly honor, social responsibility, and community solidarity to allow an individual to die alone. And it was primarily women who presided over the rituals surrounding death that bonded families and neighbors into a community. When a death appeared imminent, especially of a woman, several women sat with her—day and night—ministered to her needs, and prayed with and for her. They remained with her and her family throughout the ordeal of dying.

After death, women washed the corpses, shrouded them, and prepared them for burial. As Mary Frances Edmondson watched the funeral procession of Betty Wilburn passing in front of her house, she recalled riding over "at 12 the night before last to help shroud her and sat with the corpse the rest of the night. . . . The Tuesday night that Miss Betty died and Jenny [the dead woman's sister] sent for me, it was dark and not having been out [on horseback] for more than seven years, and being a timid horsewoman, our faithful [slave] Davy led the old mare . . . for three quarters of a mile." Then she followed another slave "on the little foot path through weeds higher than my head over a large field until we reached the open field between the two plantations when we got on very well."[26] When a Delta neighbor in need—due to birth, sickness, or death—called for the help of a woman, she dropped her own responsibilities without hesitation and in so doing helped to carve a community out of the swampland.

When thirty-two-year-old Sam Hornbuckle died January 5, 1891, in Watson, Nannie Stillwell Jackson and her husband sat up with the corpse that night, offering comfort to his mother and sisters. The next day she and her best friend, Fannie, made a pillow and face cloth for his casket.[27] Throughout the Delta, women like Nannie presided over those rituals that assured individuals and families afflicted by death that they could rely on the compassion and responsibility of others during times of sorrow and pain. And it was women who continued caring for the dead by tending their loved ones' graves, for the graves of the beloved dead remained within that circle of a woman's care that honored bonds of tenderness, affection, and loyalty even in death.

That is why women especially wanted family members to be buried together. As Mary Frances Edmondson planted white lilies, tube roses, and shrubs at little Sallie's grave four years after her child's death, she surveyed her family's burial ground, mourning the fact that her daughter's grandfather and sister Mollie were not also buried there. "My dear father selected that place to bury my child—and expressed the wish to be laid by her but alas, both he and my poor Mollie lie hundreds of miles away in Louisiana." She was never reconciled to the faraway burial of her family: "They are all gone. Papa, Mollie, Diddy [a slave] buried in Louisiana. . . ."[28] To have her family lie together in death was a woman's cherished hope; it was a sure sorrow when it was not possible.

Giving birth, rearing the young, nursing the sick, caring for the dying, and tending the graves of the dead did give women a special perspective on life, creating its own points of reference as well as particular language. Women came to rely on one another, often making other women centers of emotional stability and vitality in their lives. When Lena's husband congratulated her on the care given him during his illness with pneumonia, not the least of her virtues in his eyes was that "Not a murmur, nor a complaint ever escapes her lips."[29] Indeed, at the center of their culture was the demand that a woman not complain of her sacrifices and not mention, for example, the toll that sitting up at night with the sick and running the household during the day took on her body and spirit. Indeed, women rarely complained. When they did, it was usually to express frustration with their own illnesses for interfering with their work. The code of honor of Delta women, the true meaning of the Delta lady, be she rich or poor, black or white, was that she should perform a staggering amount of work, give birth every two years, nurse the sick, care for the dying, make it look easy, and never complain.

It is therefore no wonder that women looked to each other for support, nurture, and intimacy. To begin with, social practices prohibited women from talking openly about changes in their bodies, leaving women officially veiled in silence regarding basic questions of menstruation, conception, birth, lactation, and menopause. One can read dozens of diaries before finding a single—and then always isolated—reference to "cramps," and only one letter was found mentioning "flooding." Women relied on each other in small circles of kinswomen and friends to offer comfort and practical help with "female complaints." Only within an enclosed and small community of other females could a woman voice those concerns and ask those questions that were essential to making sense out of the enormous changes often taking place in her body.

This group of kinswomen, neighbors, and friends encircled a woman in need. As an approaching birth drew near, for example, women became particularly solicitous of the expectant mother, as was the case with neighbors of Nannie Stillwell Jackson in Watson. As her delivery date approached in August of 1891, Mrs. Jackson's circle of female neighbors and friends became more attentive, dropped in on her more often, and took care to bring her treats, such as the okra and greens brought for her dinner the night before her son was born.[30] Women gave birth surrounded by kinswomen—if they lived close enough—neighbors, and friends who assisted the midwife or physician, encouraged the delivering mother in her efforts, and offered the mother comfort and reassurance as she moved through a threatening situation that they too had experienced.

Visiting defined the social world of women in the Delta and is the single activity about which they expressed the most pleasure. Nannie Jackson's circle of visiting friends included about twenty, five of whom she saw daily. She saw her best friend, Fannie Morgan, who lived three blocks away, several times a day. They constantly dropped in on each other, gave each other treats they had cooked, and shared each other's troubles. "I just talk to Fannie & tell her my troubles," Mrs. Jackson wrote in her diary, "because it seems to help me to bear it better when she knows about it."[31] They appeared more emotionally vital to each other than were their husbands, and they shared their work and pleasures as well as their troubles.

Constantly visiting one another's homes, sharing work as well as secrets, confiding in and finding comfort in one another created bonds of affection that nurtured women emotionally as well as practically and thereby strengthened them for their family responsibilities. Women, through nurturing other women, sustained themselves and were consequently able to cultivate a society that bonded women to men, parents to children, and neighbors to neighbors. Visiting was crucial to the experience of this community. Most nineteenth-century Delta women were newcomers to Arkansas and therefore had left their mothers, sisters, and aunts in another state. They often suffered agonizing homesickness and loneliness. Cordelia Hambleton of Phillips County wrote back home, "I do not like the wolves [because] they howl so lonely when I am lying awake studying about you all in Kentucky that I wish there was not one in the world."[32]

Women tried to keep alive relationships with kin and friends back in Kentucky, Mississippi, or Tennessee while they simultaneously sought to establish similar ties in their new Arkansas homes. Like visiting with neighbors, mail from kin or friends from her former homes was a high point in a woman's day. Nannie Jackson, for example, included daily information in her diary as to whether she received mail, and she considered a day with no mail virtually a lost one.[33] The one political issue she followed in her diary was the establishment of regular mail delivery to Watson as well as the appointment of the mail carrier.[34] Illiterate black women often exchanged services with other women, both black and white, offering to do others' wash, for example, in exchange for writing letters to their kin. Clearly, visiting with relatives and friends by mail kept alive ties with the past and helped sustain women in their new homes.

Where visiting left off and borrowing and trading goods began is impossible to define. Borrowing was a part of the daily rhythm of life among women throughout the Delta. In and out of one another's homes, women borrowed and swapped as an extension of being good neighbors and reliable women. Women borrowed sugar, flour, eggs, and thread when they were short of these supplies. They also provided fresh peaches for the pie a neighbor needed for company dinner, or peas when someone's garden failed. It would take a sophisticated economist to decipher the value of goods and services swapped by the community of women to which Nannie Stillwell Jackson belonged in Watson. Fannie Morgan and Nannie Jackson were especially close, but their pattern of visiting, helpfulness, and neighborliness extended into the neighborhood, incorporating black women as well as white. On Thursday, June 19, 1890, Nannie recorded that "I went up and washed the dishes for Fannie & helped her so as she could get an early start to washing for she had such a big washing Sue [Nannie's daughter] churned for her, Mrs. Nellie Smimthee helped her wash & they got done by 2 oclock. . . . Mrs. Cheatam [her mother-in-law] was here a few minutes at dinner time . . . Mrs. Gifford, Josie, & May all came to see me this evening. . . . I baked some chicken bread for Fannie & some for my self, & she gave me some dried apples & I baked 2 pies she gave me one & she took the other I made starch for her & me too." "Helping out" by making two pies and doubling the amount of starch increased efficiency, coordinated work, and allowed visiting at the same time.[35]

Weaving friendship with responsibility and integrating work with pleasure characterized the lives of Delta women, as the daily routine of the week following the above entry indicates. On Friday, June 20, Ella Chandler (who, with her physician-husband, would deliver Nannie's baby) visited, as did Fannie, who "paid back" some soap she had borrowed and brought along some artifical flowers for a hat Nannie was making. On Saturday, Nannie went to Mrs. Dyers, to get plums and apples for herself as well as enough to share with Fannie. Then, "I paid Mrs. Chandler the big dishpan of flour I owed her." On Sunday, Fannie brought Nannie a bowl of blackberries. On Monday, Frances Hines, a black woman, "was here a while to day I wrote a letter to Anna for her, I made a berry pie for Fannie & sent it up there for dinner. . . . Mrs. Smithee came & brought me a cup of good pot licker & some greens & a piece of corn bread. . . . I let Mrs. Chandler have 7 pounds of meat to day, she is to pay it back Wednesday." On Tuesday, Fannie helped Lizzie, Nannie's daughter, hang out the wash. In addition, Susan Watson, a black woman, "was here a while this morning & I gave her a pitcher of milk. . . . I lent Mrs. Chandler the quilting frames to day." The next day, she visited in Fannie's home and helped her patch and brought home additional fabric to patch. On Thursday, she gave Susan Watson more milk, and she provided Ella Chandler with more meat. This pattern of visiting, borrowing, trading, exchanging, and giving cemented women's friendships, made obvious their dependence on each other, and because they were in such close contact, alerted neighbors to those in need.[36]

Delta women took for granted an astounding and constant amount of work. When Matilda Fulton in 1832 wrote her husband about the birth of their son, she did so in a fashion that indicated the routine nature of arduous work in her life:

> I was in the midst of [slaughtering] my pork the day befor I was taken sick [A servant] and myself cut up nine hogs I spent the day in the smoke haus without seting down untill night the next morning I was very sick but thought I had fatigue myself and it would ware of . . . I found at night I was getting worse, and I did not think it prudent for me to stay a lone I sent for Mrs Field she came and staid all night with me the next morning I sent for Mrs Collins and Mrs Pope and Mrs Ellis the Child was born on Sunday.[37]

Race, status, and time separated the worlds of Matilda Fulton, a prosperous white woman, from those of Laura Abramson, a daughter of slaves who lived near Holly Grove. Nevertheless, work united them. Over one hundred years after Matilda wrote of her son's birth, Laura was asked about her work: "What is I been doing? Ast me is I been doing? What ain't I been doing be more like it. I raised fifteen of my own children. . . . I worked on the farm purty nigh all my life."[38] Then she went on to comment that even in 1938 she canned her own meat and dried her own beef. Mattie Aldridge from Hazen came immediately to the point when asked about her work: "I been raisin' up children . . . washin', ironin', scourin', hoein', gaterin' corn, pickin' cotton, patchin', cookin'. They ain't nothin' what I ain't done."[39]

Mattie Aldridge came close to defining the experience of Delta women and their work. Woman's work, in comparison to men's, was never done, in large part because it involved the basic maintenance of the family itself. Of course, financial position and social status influenced the particular shape of an individual woman's work, but virtually all women expected to perform a staggering amount of work, even as they bore their babies, nursed the sick, and tended the dying. To begin with, the demands of housework remained essentially unchanged well into the twentieth century. Electricity and indoor plumbing did not arrive in most middle-class homes until the 1940s, and only the most privileged enjoyed electrification and indoor plumbing before the 1920s. This meant, of course, that women performed most of their tasks in the same manner as had their grandmothers.

Men and women in the Delta, as elsewhere in this country, essentially divided their work into "his" and "hers." If he was a farmer—as most were in the Delta—"his" work involved clearing the land, constructing and maintaining buildings, plowing and cultivating the land, caring for the larger farm animals, and producing the family's cash crop. Her work encircled the house, expanded outwards to include the water pump, vegetable garden, and the orchards, and also took in the barn, where she milked her cows, and the barnyard, which included the chickens and pigs. Whereas men's work was centered away from the house, women's work involved constant traffic between the house, the vegetable garden, the barnyard, and the wellhouse.

In performing tasks much as their grandmothers had, women hauled fifty pounds of water to wash one load of clothes and then another fifty in which to rinse them. Their irons ranged in weight from one to ten pounds. They hauled all the water their families used inside from the well, and then they hauled every drop outside again. The only major technological breakthrough that aided women in the nineteenth century was the cast-iron stove, which burned evenly and used less wood, thereby reducing the hours needed to tend the fire. Until 1900, Delta women continued preserving their food much as had women when the Europeans settled this country. They dried fruit, stored turnips and potatoes in root cellars or banks, and smoked, pickled, or salted their meat. Home canning was not safe until after 1900, when machines were invented to produce uniform glass jars. After that time, home canning became central to the way Delta women preserved their food. One woman recalled that in the 1930s, her mother could not rest until she had canned 365 jars of vegetables and fruits, one for each day of the year.[41]

By 1900, virtually all Delta women bought rather than made their cloth, but they continued to make their own as well as their children's clothes. Even in towns, most women kept a cow as well as chickens and a pig. They furthermore churned their own butter, made their own pickles, and produced their own lye soap. And they followed rather elaborate procedures for accomplishing the best results. A 1904 cookbook circulated in the Delta contained a recipe on how to make the best lye soap:

6 pound fat (6¾ pints, melted)
1 13 ounce can lye
5 cups cold soft water
2 tablespoons borax.

Melt fat in a large iron or enamel kettle . . . and set aside to cool to 80 degrees F. then add gradually to lye, stirring until creamy, then add borax, mix well and pour into molds. Heavy cardboard boxes make good molds. Cool slowly without moving molds for 24 hours. When soap is firm, remove from molds and cut into bars with string. Stack in rows allowing space between cakes for air to circulate. Dry 2 weeks before using.

Making soap was a labor-intensive enterprise and indicates the extent to which Delta women, even in this century, were engaged in household manufacturing.

Farm women did all the work of the house as well as a substantial amount of agricultural labor. All but the most privileged farm women expected to contribute to the cultivation and harvesting of the family's cash crop. Therefore, chopping cotton, gathering corn, and picking cotton were part of the farm woman's yearly routine. And the Arkansas Delta had its fair share of women who plowed. During slavery, women who were considered barren were treated as males and consequently assigned to plowing. Other women, black and white, plowed when no husband nor son was available. In 1938 at age sixty-two, Liddie Aiken of Wheatley, for example, bragged, "We farm. I done everything could be thought of on a farm. I ploughed some less than 5 years ago."[43] If part of the nature of Delta womanhood was a commitment to a culture of caring, the complementary part was a firm belief in the efficacy and dignity of labor. Liddie Aiken summed up her vision of the role work should play in an individual's life: "I learnt to work. I learnt my boys to go with me to the field and not to be ashamed to sweat. It's healthy. They all works."[44]

An irony of the division of work between "his" and "hers" was that women were expected to step into a male's shoes if family needs dictated it or if emergencies occurred. Women routinely dropped what they considered their own work to assist their husbands in theirs, especially with the cultivation and harvesting of the cash crop. And women took over their husbands' business as a matter of course if he died. They moved between men's and women's work roles without threatening the deference they felt toward males as the heads of households. In 1871, Fannie Cotten was temporarily living in Tennessee while her husband rebuilt their devastated Arkansas house and farm. As she prepared to move back to Arkansas, she wrote her husband solicitously asking advice on how to dispose of their Tennessee property: "Write me exactly what to do in everything, what I must ask for the table, chairs, and bedsteads, and plows, hoe, and rake."[45] Two weeks later, her husband would be dead and within a matter of months, Fannie Cotten would take over and successfully manage the large plantation at Indian Bay on her own.[46] Men, however, did not reverse work roles with the same freedom as did women. If a woman became sick or died, another woman was secured to do her work.

Tommye Lindsey Satterfield's description of her grandmother, written in 1967 and based on her memories thirty years earlier, came close to capturing the image of true womanhood with a Delta accent. "She was present at the birth of the grandchildren, tended them in family emergencies," recalled Satterfield, "and gave not only her immediate family but other relatives and friends provisions from her smokehouse and canned goods pantry. She raised beautiful roses, seven children, flocks of turkeys and chickens, and gaggles of geese."[47]

Then the grandaughter recalled a ritual that showed how closely the web of caring and work were woven into a woman's life. It was her grandmother's tradition that each child at marriage be given a feather bed and two feather pillows, a total of seven mattresses and fourteen pillows made from feathers collected from her own geese. Then Satterfield described the art of goose picking that had been passed from mother to daughter over the generations, bemoaning the end of that tradition with her:

> The master goose picker knows . . . that if she pulls the feathers at too obtruse an angle against the way the feathers grow, there is greater chance of the goose bleeding. Grandmother never picked the large tail or wing feathers. . . . She picked the small sized feathers on the breast and underside, on the back and up the neck until she progressed to the very small feathers right below and on the head. . . . As she grasped the feathers between the out stretched thumb and bent forefinger her hand moved quickly and rhythemically [sic] back and forth from the goose to the thick sack in which she placed the feathers to later be sunned and aired before being placed in the ticks.[48]

This memory of a grandaughter of her grandmother embodies the core of women's experience and values in the Arkansas Delta. Such rituals of caring involved both love and labor, both expertise and relationship. As the grandmother lovingly, expertly, collected the feathers for the bed on which her grandchildren would be conceived, she stood at the center of a way of life that connected work to love and love to life. Women like Satterfield's grandmother performed such constant, arduous work without complaint because they tied that labor to relationships within the family and community.

Women, of course, did sometimes work for money. Within the home they made butter, sold milk and eggs, and sewed for others to provide additional cash for their families. Often women supplemented their family's budget by taking in boarders, as did Nannie Jackson when she opened her home to schoolteachers.[49] Poorer women, both black and white, "hired out" as day laborers when demand was heavy for agricultural labor, especially after the decline of sharecropping in the 1930s. In addition, black women routinely worked in white women's homes as domestic servants until other jobs were made available to them in the 1960s. Until World War II, however, comparatively few married white women with children worked outside the home for pay. Most white "working women" were young and unmarried and served in such positions as schoolteachers, secretaries, nurses, telephone operators, and sales clerks. Inasmuch as the Delta had little industry, few Delta women worked in factories until the 1940s.

Women's axis was certainly in the home, but many participated in a public culture that intersected without paralleling the men's public space. Women's sense of the civic was shaped by different concerns from those of men, and it was distinctly self-directed and, for the most part, voluntaristic. Women defined the public and civic differently than did men. The struggle to plant flowers wherever they moved, for example, should properly be seen as a public act, as an effort to enhance the visual environment, and to offer beauty to the family member as well as to the passerby. Women saved seeds and shared bulbs and cuttings with one another in order to beautify their yards, cemeteries, and other semi-public as well as entirely public spaces. In so doing, they signified that a potential world of order and beauty lay within reach of a seemingly chaotic, new society. Mary Edmondson summed up the esteem often evoked by women who paid attention to public space when she praised a neighbor who cared about her flowers: "She has plenty of all that is cultivated in [her] garden; what a wonderful woman she is—I like and respect her more and more, as I know her better."[50] In 1907, the Forrest City District meeting of the Arkansas Federation of Women's Clubs gave a civics lesson on the connection between the home and the civic:

"The center of civic activity lies in the home. As the circle formed by the pebble cast into the waters, multiplies and enlarges, until the borders of the shore are reached, so the efforts put into action to beautify our immediate surroundings, will extend from the home to the community and then to the uttermost confines of our State."[51]

Women's sense of the civic was most vigorously expressed in their clubs, organizations, and churches. In fact, women's associations contain the history of a female political culture in the Delta as compelling as the history of the area's electoral politics. No civic topic captured the attention of as many Delta women, both black and white, as did that of temperance. Founded in 1874, the National Women's Christian Temperance Union established its first branch in Arkansas in 1879.[52] By the early twentieth century, it claimed a substantial following in the Arkansas Delta. Its membership ranged from proper, upper-middle-class women from Helena to poor, black women who formed a branch in the Tiller Missionary Baptist Church.[53] In fact, the Delta's WCTU may be said to be one of the the area's most progressive movements in terms of its biracial emphasis. In 1942, for example, the *White Ribboner,* the state's WCTU publication, published an article describing a biracial community worship service sponsored by the WCTU and held at Stuttgart Presbyterian Church.[54]

The WCTU was able to draw such a diverse constituency because women shared a common concern for the threat alcohol represented to the family. Historians now agree that the single largest cause of poverty in the nineteenth century was the loss of the male's income, and drunkeness was not an infrequent cause of that loss. Furthermore, women and children were common victims of abuse resulting from drunken rages. No wonder, then, that the WCTU was the one women's organization that could most likely be found in a Delta town, and that its constituency was the most representative of any of the Delta's women's organizations.

The Delta branches of the Arkansas Federation of Women's Clubs ran a close second to the WCTU in membership.[55] Comprised of white, upper-middle-class women, the club movement represented the women's branch of reform that swept the nation during the early twentieth century. In 1912, the Forrest City District, "the sunrise section of our state," listed twenty-six clubs as branches, and its president, Mrs. H. C. Rightor of Helena, exhorted its members to "awaken, and, with fresh zeal, keep pace with the rising sun."[56]

She continued, "Eastern Arkansas constitutes the first congressional district of the state. Her sons have ever stood foremost in important legislation and patriotic prowess, and her daughters will not lag behind in any progressive movement that seeks to elevate humanity, and improve social conditions, the paramount object of our state federation."[57] By 1916, the number of clubs had doubled with a membership of 2,200.[58]

Elevating humanity and improving social conditions—albeit with the help of over two thousand women—was no small undertaking in the Arkansas Delta, but the women's organizations were bolstered by their visible achievements. Because virtually no public libraries existed in the area, several clubs had started traveling libraries, using trunks to ship books to remote places in the district and convincing railroads to ship the trunks free of charge.[59] Helena's hospital had its origins when a "group of interested citizens," all women, petitioned the Phillips County Circuit Court to establish the Helena Hospital Association.[60] Women's organizations had also been instrumental in starting schools, as the following case presented at the next meeting of the Forrest City District indicated:

> While we have accomplished great results, the greatest has been arousing the women to a sense of their opportunity, and the greatest good has been done in the towns in the state through this enthusiasm. One instance will prove this assertion. . . . One woman, the President of the [Crawfordsville] club, became fired with a desire to educate the children of Crittenden County in Arkansas instead of the nearby city of Memphis, Tenn. She called a meeting of the citizens, speeches were made by women and men, and the result is a new $40,000 high school in Crawfordsville, with . . . bonded drivers to carry the children from outlying villages to this well built, well equipped, modern high school.[61]

Whether in building schools or hospitals, or in founding libraries and child welfare associations, the progressive impulse of the women's club movement reshaped the institutional life of the Delta and left a legacy of benevolence.

Most, but certainly not all, women associated with the club movement supported suffrage. Indeed, the terms of debate on women's equality had been set early. In 1864, Susan Cook took note of the issue without taking sides: "Mr. Higgings is passing the night with us; had quite a debate upon 'Womans Rights', that never ending theme."[62] Whatever they thought of the proper role of the woman, it is clear that many Delta women supported her enfranchisement. Belle McKenzie of Helena wrote a friend in 1917 that around 1882 Susan B. Anthony visited Arkansas and "gave us 'A Womans Rights' speech, the most convincing discourse I ever heard, and I have been 'One of 'em' [ever since.]" But she also wrote, "A vote in the primaries doesn't suit me. I want a full grown, hardy vote that will oust some of these city officials who are draining all the water on me. Tonight as I write there is a sea of water all over my premises over two ft. deep."[63]

Other women, like those in the Southern Tenant Farmers' Union (STFU), would join with men to fight different political battles. When New Deal policies mandated crop reduction in the 1930s, sharecropper and tenant families suffered worst of all, and about a third of them were evicted from their homes. Women, both black and white, joined with men to demand rights for themselves as sharecroppers and to protect their homes. More literate than males in their families, women served as secretaries of their locals and kept members in touch with one another. For black women, the STFU would be a launching ground for work in the civil rights movement of the 1950s. Carrie Dilworth, for example, became secretary of her STFU local and then in the 1960s offered her home as a residence and center for young civil rights workers.[64] As one woman recalled, "The STFU was the first place anybody outside my church ever asked me to vote on anything."[65]

Black women's public activity, especially in the civil rights movement, was enhanced in the 1950s and 1960s. White women's role as influential volunteers diminished, however, and was ultimately replaced by the male professional. Helena's hospital, for example, had had a woman superintendent, a volunteer, from the founding of the hospital in 1909 until 1952, when a professional male administrator assumed that position.[66] Although women would begin to enter the professions in large numbers in the next decade, was questionable whether women would ever regain the degree of influence in public life through their professions that they had enjoyed in their voluntary organizations.

This sense of demise pervaded other aspects of women's lives. In 1938 Mattie Aldridge was questioned on whether she as a black woman had ever voted. Her response was telling, "No'm, I sure ain't voted. I don't believe in women votin'. They don't know who to vote for. The men don't know neither. If folks visited they would care more bout the other an wouldn't be so much devilment goin' on."[67] Mrs. Aldridge's comment should be taken less as a comment on voting and more as statement of loss in her life. Her words, in fact, hint that she found the political solutions of the twentieth century in some ways inferior to the communal responses of a previous era. In harkening back to a time when neighborliness meant knowledge of other people's needs and when women bartered, swapped, exchanged and borrowed as well as "sat up" and visited, Mattie Aldridge articulated the same loss that Tommye Satterfield felt when recalling the experiences of her grandmother. Sometime around the Second World War, the community-based way of caring for people to which women had been so central was being supplanted by new social relations defined by invisible, faraway forces. Whether modernity came to the Delta in the form of devilment, as Mattie Aldridge thought, is open for question. That women felt less powerful to create a sense of community and to rely on one another seemed clear. The bonds of tradition that had tied the experiences of mother and daughter for several generations in the Delta were severed, making Mattie Aldridge and Tommye Satterfield feel lesser for it.

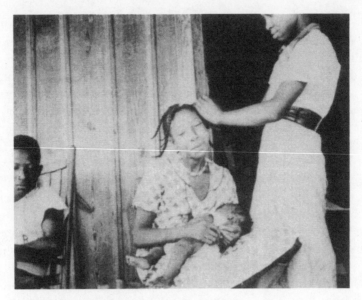

An Earle family at home, around 1936.
Courtesy Arkansas History Commission.

Members of the Pacaha Club (founders of Helena's public library), around 1893.   *Courtesy Phillips County Historical Museum.*

Members of the Southern Tenant Farmers' Union.
Courtesy of Louise Boyle and Elizabeth Payne/DCC Archives.

Myrtle Lawrence shelling peas with her family in St. Francis County,
around 1937.   *Courtesy of Louise Boyle and Elizabeth Payne/DCC Archives.*

Strangers in the Arkansas Delta: Ethnic Groups and Nationalities

BYRD GIBBENS

"The presence of [white] persons of other than English ancestry in the South," finds historian Jonathan Wolfe, "is unusual."[1] The South in general has prided itself on its Anglo-Saxon "purity." Arkansas, in particular, has been reputedly free of outsiders and distrustful of the foreign groups who did manage to settle within its boundaries. Census data confirm that foreign-born whites have never been a significant force in Arkansas.[2] From the time of statehood in 1836, Arkansas's heritage was homogeneously "American": diversity of origin corresponded to diversity of parent state (Tennessee, the Carolinas, Virginia, Mississippi, Alabama, Louisiana, Illinois, Kentucky); diversity of religion consisted only of Protestant sects. According to the United States census of 1890, only 1.26 percent of the Arkansas population was foreign born.[3] Even so, a number of Arkansas newspapers of the time cautioned against the "foreign threat."

While foreign settlers have, over the past two centuries, prospered in Arkansas, they have for various reasons maintained a low profile. Thus, even in the 1990s, people within and without the state continue to perceive Arkansas as one of the *least ethnic*, the *most homogeneous* in population of all the southern states and register surprise that scholarly attention should focus on an ethnic presence, especially in the Arkansas Delta.

Despite popular perception, Arkansas, particularly its Delta, has exhibited ethnic variety. From the late eighteenth century into the late twentieth century, people from different nations have settled in the Arkansas Delta; they have prospered and made major contributions to the state economically, intellectually, and socially. These "foreign" settlers have included individuals from France, Germany,

Switzerland, Italy, Czechoslovakia, Russia, Yugoslavia, China, and Ireland. They have been Protestant, Roman Catholic, Russian Orthodox, and Jewish. Each group has formed a significant part of the present configuration of Arkansas.

The stories of these people illustrate ingenuity, resilience, determination, anguish, hope, and humor. Their stories tell about people who have grown to define themselves by the Arkansas earth. The stories describe courageous people accommodating to strange government, geography, neighbors, language, and customs—people who have coped with the new environment and at the same time have kept in touch with the essentials of their cultures of origin—accommodating without assimilating. Within the dominant culture, most have retained distinctive identities, as well as intellectual and emotional bonds with their traditions.

Delta ethnic settlers came sporadically and in waves, prompted by different motives. Disturbances such as military takeover, economic depression, or restrictive land distribution impelled people to emigrate from the old world. Promotional advertisements from land agents, plantation owners, railroads, private immigration aid groups, and the state government conjured up images of a virtual paradise.[4]

By its "Donation Law" of 1840, the state of Arkansas offered tax-forfeited lands to settlers in return for the payment of taxes in the future. Ten years later the law was amended to permit a family as many 160-acre plots as there were family members, regardless of age or sex. By a federal act in 1850, Arkansas was allowed to open over seven-and-a-half million acres of swamp and overflow land for reclamation and farming. Many of these tracts made prize acquisitions because they were not actually swampy or subject to overflow. Prior to the Civil War, various legislative acts made Arkansas lands attractive and available. Many immigrants in the antebellum era simply became squatters, thus at least temporarily using public lands without the burden of rent or taxes.[5]

After 1865 Arkansas Delta immigrants envisioned not instant luxury, but gradual upward mobility and an increase of options won by hard, very hard, work. Although the descendants of these early settlers are thriving in the state today, many of them recount vivid stories of the obstacles confronting their ancestors. The language barrier, coupled with the cautious distance and downright distrust exhibited by the majority population, intensified their difficulties, which, together with the poverty that was the lot of most newcomers, made it especially difficult for the ethnic settlers to establish a solid foundation upon which to build their lives.

Despite an almost endemic distrust of "foreigners," certain factors conjoined in the late nineteenth century to compel white Arkansans to welcome foreign immigrants to the state. Repercussions of the Civil War pressured white citizens of Arkansas to organize campaigns to draw immigrants. Pressure came from the sudden labor shortage as the work system changed from slave to free labor. Pressure also came from the enfranchisement of blacks. Whites feared loss of their majority vote. Pressure further came from the very real need to develop state resources to make the economy recover after the impoverishment of the Civil War.[6]

In marked swings between zeal and apathy, a variety of groups set in motion actions that would bring immigrants to Arkansas. Factions in the state legislature spent decades voting in and then amending, ignoring, or voting out an official commission on immigration. Landowners and railroads collaborated on strategies for advertising the excellent lands available in the state. Several groups of Germans already settled in Little Rock devised plans for promoting Arkansas in Germany and for assisting immigrants once they arrived. State newspapers for the most part supported whatever effort espoused immigration, though they questioned some of the political appointees designated to lead the efforts. In marked swings, too, Arkansans in general alternately welcomed and antagonized foreign homeseekers.[7]

The larger social system in Arkansas, composed of white Anglo-Saxon Protestants, seemed, in most cases, to have been either a neutral or a negative factor in the immigrants' experience. The arrival of foreigners attracted minimal notice, especially since most of the foreigners stayed in tightknit, self-sufficient groups, setting up churches and schools in which their native tongues were spoken and taught. Outside interest in the new people seemed limited to discovering whether newcomers would support or threaten the lifestyles of the older and dominant culture.[8]

The newcomers often did skirt the established order. Many sanctioned dancing, card playing, and wine making, which were offensive to some Protestants. Certain groups, including Chinese, Syrians, and Italians, unsettled the already racially tense Delta whites by introducing, at least in complexion, almost a third "race," neither black nor white. The newcomers in general, if they won acceptance, had to win it not by simple acculturation but by gaining economic or political power.

Ethnic group arrivals came usually at a crest of prosperity or during a depression in the Arkansas economy. For example, the 1850 congressional decree, which allowed states to reclaim their swamplands for farming, opened lands for waves of immigrants. United States entrepreneurs (residents of other states as well as of Arkansas) invested in huge tracts of land, formed giant plantations, and then brought in slaves or immigrants to work the fields. Likewise, congressional land awards to veterans of several wars gave vast acreage to many who divided the land into small portions and sold them. The Slovakian community rode in on such a crest. On lesser crests, the emergence of small Delta settlements created the opportunities that enticed Jewish, Syrian, and Lebanese immigrants, many of whom began as peddlers and then with their meager profits set up dry goods stores. In the depressed economic environment following the Civil War, Delta plantation owners negotiated in Italy and China to hire seasonal workers to replace slave labor.[9]

The immigrants' relegation to the status of outsiders because of their language, religion, or "race" gave them a long-term advantage. Unable to lean on the larger community, they had to consolidate and to manage resources so as to squeeze maximum yield from every effort. In time such habits gained most of them marked success. Many of the Delta's flourishing banks, stores, medical centers, and farms are still owned and/or staffed by descendants of the early ethnic settlers.

In contrast to those groups in the Delta that did not or could not assimilate, there *were* ethnic groups that by the time of statehood in 1836 had, in great measure, already been assimilated into the dominant culture. French settlers, who came when Arkansas was still part of the Louisiana Territory, must today be traced through the Anglicized versions of their names. Imbeau became Imbo, Beaugis/Baugis became Bogy, Bonneau became Bono or Bone, Gravier became Greber. Some of the French who manned Arkansas Post married Indian or American women, and many in time became part of the political scene of the young state. Most of these were French Huguenots or their descendants, like Benjamin Desha after whom Desha County is named, and hence fitted easily into the predominantly Protestant settlements of early Arkansas. The French came mostly as loners, either as early political appointees to govern

Arkansas Post, as hunter/trappers from French Canada, or occasionally as "polished high-spirited French gentlemen" seeking in "free Arkansas" the liberal lifestyle curtailed in the France of the early eighteenth century. Frederick Notrebe, whose descendants continue to live in the area of Arkansas Post, came in 1813 and amassed a fortune through the fur trade, land acquisition, and cotton.[10]

The early American writer Washington Irving, on a trip into the Louisiana Territory, noted the "idyllic picture" of the French settlers at Arkansas Post. They were "kind and neighborly, more civil and courteous than Americans. They sing and dance and never quarrel except with their tongues. They are fond of holidays and when voting time comes they always vote for Col. Desha."[11]

Twentieth-century descendants of these early French do little more than note their French connection on a family tree. Because the early French had come in as authority figures and because of their Protestant religion, they did not feel the kind of cultural threat that might have pressured them to defend their individuality. Although some of these settlers, such as Frederick Notrebe, became extensive landholders, they did not harbor enclaves of relatives that might have nurtured a French tradition. Today the barest trace remains of this early French presence, the traces of names that few today would suspect of being French.

The Jews were an early ethnic group that have remained small yet distinct. The Jewish presence in Arkansas is pronounced, even though numerically Jews probably have never exceeded more than six thousand persons at a given time in the state. But Jewish people have lived in Arkansas from the early nineteenth century. Their paths in the state exactly follow the sequential developments of the state's history. The Jews in Arkansas exerted an influence disproportionate to their small number. They were a group that became linchpins of Arkansas economy, law, and art. And while most Jews in Arkansas thrived, they gave back to the state probably more than they had received.

Most of the Jews who came to Arkansas began by peddling wares and sometimes settling in towns along the rivers. They went first to the southeastern Delta to Helena and then branched inland from the Mississippi River to Camden and Pine Bluff, then to Little Rock and westward to Fort Smith. Later they settled on the upper Delta at Jonesboro and Blytheville. Carolyn Gray LeMaster, who has done extensive research on Jews in Arkansas, commented: "What's interesting about the Jewish history in this state is that it's like study-ing Arkansas history in a microcosm *because* the Jews went where there were people making a living. (Somebody once said that Jews are just like everybody else, only more so.) There were very few Jews settled up in the northwest part of the state. The people up there were just so scattered."[12]

The first Jews recorded in the state were Abraham and Frances (Fannie) Block, who were considered wealthy when they arrived in 1820 in Washington, in the Arkansas Territory. Abraham Block estab-lished a mercantile store that flourished and drew trade from Texas and Louisiana. The subsequent migration to Arkansas followed a variation on the Blocks' pattern.

Until the eighteenth century the Jews who came to Arkansas were single young men, usually from Germany, who sought greater opportunity in the United States. Generally poor but frequently well-educated, they began as "foot merchants," or peddlers, selling wares door-to-door, town-to-town. "Someone would just give them fifty dollars *or* someone would just give them the pack for their back. And they would start peddling and would make a little profit and then a little more."[13]

The Jewish peddlers wove in and out of the lives of the small Delta communities. Hutchins Landfair of Desha County recalled:

> Back in the days of the '80s and '90s, the peddlers with their pack on their back would walk through the country selling their mer-chandise; and in the evening as dark would be coming on, they would come to the nearest farmer and ask for lodging. To me, it seemed when they were in our neighborhood, they would make it to our house for the night.
>
> Mother never charged them, and after breakfast they would open their pack and spread their merchandise over the floor in the hall. It would be lace, silk, jewelry and items that the stores did not carry. I thought all these peddlers were Jews, and we children would get a kick out of hearing them talk; and whether mother bought anything or not, they would give her some lace or some-thing.
>
> One of the peddlers was Mr. Charles Dante, who later opened a general store in Dumas, and acquired a large estate.[14]

With the initial profit, the Jewish peddler bought a horse, then a wagon. And in a repeated pattern, he opened a small mercantile store in a Delta river town. Personal business success, however, was contingent on the success of the community. Carolyn LeMaster has pointed out that Jews brought a business acumen that early Arkansas farms and settlements seemed short on. In addition, Jews were disciplined, resilient workers bent on success. If bankruptcy folded a Jewish store in a bad crop year, the owner moved on and started again. Jewish merchants "bounced back."[15]

After they settled, the Jewish merchants started families. They became active in law, trade, finance, the arts, and civic concerns. They did not just make a living; they promoted the community and encouraged both business enterprises and the arts. Gus Waterman, for example, settled in Desha County in the mid-nineteenth century, arriving with literally what he had on his back, with no connections, and speaking only broken English. In the next century, one of Waterman's sons became dean of the Law School of the University of Arkansas. Abraham Dreidel, who served as mayor of Arkansas City from 1901 to 1911, was also the first Jewish state senator of Arkansas. Charles Dante, the early peddler, was selected "Dumas' Man of the Year" for the year of 1949 in recognition of his years of service in behalf of the civic improvements of Dumas.[16] And in many parts of the Delta, Jewish merchants and entrepreneurs stimulated the economy. Two Jewish businessmen promoted Arkansas cotton worldwide. Julius Lesser in Marianna and Jacob Goldman in Jacksonport founded the Lesser-Goldman Cotton Company. Their process of marketing changed the way cotton was bought and sold, much to the advantage of the cotton grower.

There seems not to have been notable anti-Semitism in Arkansas. In the 1920s, for example, the Arkansas Ku Klux Klan attacked Catholics and blacks, but not Jews. Still, there is evidence that the majority culture harbored *some* stereotypical views of Jews. LeMaster has found such evidence in the notations of nineteenth-century salesmen who supplied Jewish merchants. Typical comments were: "Very acculturated *for his race*" and "Does well *for his kind*."[17]

The Jews themselves have a record of supportive respect for and cooperation with the black community. They had few prejudices against blacks. Jewish bankers and storekeepers willingly extended credit to black customers. Such business respect was often denied blacks by most of the dominant culture. When in the late nineteenth century Pine Bluff Jews formed a cultural society to promote the arts, blacks were welcomed as members along with whites. Judge

Jacob Trieber, a Jew and federal district judge for eastern Arkansas in the early twentieth century, attracted considerable attention by convicting a white man who had killed a black man.

Jacob Trieber himself provides a remarkable study. His family had moved to Helena in 1868. His father opened a dry goods store, and young Jacob became its bookkeeper. The Jewish community in Helena was quite small. The Beth El Congregation of Helena, founded in 1867, still had only twelve pew owners and fourteen contributing members by 1900. Yet, the presence of this small but growing Jewish population was significant in attracting the Triebers to Helena.[18]

Trieber built an unusual reputation both for strict construction of the law *and* for humanity. Supposedly Trieber had said publicly: "Moonshiners as a rule are good citizens in every way except that they will break the law in making whiskey. In this they do not believe that they are committing any wrong and they are otherwise honest." Legend has it that one day, responding to the judge's tribute to them, over sixty moonshiners walked into his office and surrendered.[19]

Judge Trieber's consistent drive to effect legal justice for blacks was dramatic, especially because it appeared during an era of violent attempts to deny blacks basic civil rights. In 1898 Trieber, in open forum, attacked Arkansas election laws, accusing them in effect of disfranchising black voters. In 1903, in the celebrated federal case that tried "whitecappers" (*United States v. Morris*), Trieber ruled against the "whitecappers." Three years later this landmark decision was overturned by the Supreme Court (*Hodges v. United States*). Not until 1968 was Trieber's judgment vindicated by a decision of the same court. Jacob Trieber was a highly visible representative of the Jewish community in the Arkansas Delta.[20]

The Irish in the Arkansas Delta can be considered ethnically separate even though they in many respects possessed the characteristics of the dominant culture, especially in language and complexion. But many Irish were different in religion. Their Roman Catholicism stigmatized them in an area where Catholics were labeled devils by many evangelical Protestants. Of course, not all Irish were Catholics, but many were. The Roman Catholic church itself viewed Arkansas as a "mission country," and in the 1850s sent an Irish priest, Father Andrew Byrne, to minister to the Catholics of the state. Because of religious affiliation and because of the migrant lifestyle of some, Irish settlers in the Arkansas Delta were often identified as an unusual community.[21]

The Irish began to trickle in to Arkansas in the early nineteenth century. Terrance Farrelly and Thomas Curran, both from Ireland, formed a partnership for a hardware store at Arkansas Post in 1819. Farrelly, described emphatically in early records as an "Irishman," became an integral part of early Arkansas political and social life. Elected to the Arkansas territorial assembly in 1821, he was also closely linked to such notable Arkansans as Benjamin Desha, Francis Notrebe, and Albert Pike. Farrelly's large plantation near Arkansas Post hosted Albert Pike's wedding to Mary Ann Hamilton.[22]

Arkansas seems to have been a place of good fortune for the Irish. Large numbers of Irish emigrated to the United States not only because the potato famine in Ireland left thousands poverty-stricken and homeless, but also because of resentment of British rule and various economic and religious considerations. For many of these people, the Arkansas Delta marked a second or third relocation. Irish immigrants tended initially to seek employment in industrial cities in New York, Pennsylvania, and Illinois. Employment, when available there, usually meant low wages. For some, the Arkansas Delta, in desperate need of settlers and labor, offered an escape for them.[23]

The Irish came to the Arkansas Delta both as lone laborers for hire and as families. Some interesting 1870 diary entries from James Millinder Hanks, a wealthy landowner in Helena, Arkansas, probably expressed a common Arkansas perception of the incoming Irish. Hanks's references to his Irish workers showed an emphatic master/subject relationship. However, references to bargaining over wages and work schedules indicated the independent position of the Irish. Entries in Hanks' 1891 diary noted the migrant lifestyle of some Irish, a style so akin to that of gypsies that Hanks at first mistook Irish horse traders for gypsies.[24]

Though the Irish may have been designated "foreign" when they first came to Arkansas, the designation soon relaxed. More easily than other "alien" settlers, the Irish assimilated into the dominant culture. Census data suggest that many of the single Irish males who came to Arkansas found jobs, became tenant farmers, bought land, married Arkansas women from the dominant culture, and frequently became large landowners. The Britt family of Snow Lake, for example, grew to be one of the wealthiest families in the southeast Arkansas Delta. Michael Britt and his wife, Katherine Lambe, came to the small town of Laconia in Desha County in 1869. He began work as a tenant farmer for a Captain Rice who owned a large plantation. The 1870 census shows that Britt was renting fifteen acres of land valued at two hundred and fifty dollars. His livestock consisted of one mule and one milk cow. His production consisted of Indian corn, cotton, Irish potatoes, and sweet potatoes. By 1880 Britt had doubled the amount of farmland he was working and owned three horses, two mules, three milk cows, fifteen head of beef cattle, forty hogs, and fifty geese and chickens. Twenty years later Britt owned a thousand acres of land and was considered a wealthy man. The Britts, meanwhile, had assimilated into the dominant culture. While they began as Roman Catholics, having a visiting Catholic priest say mass regularly in their home, their children in great measure became members of the Baptist and Methodist churches in the area.

The Britts exemplify the Irish ethnic pattern in the Arkansas Delta. Irish-connected families thrived. Many of their surnames continue today: Cady, Furlong, McEvoy, O'Bannon, Heffron, Boggans, Lynch, Hollister, Burk, McCarty, McGrath, McPherson, O'Neal, McCoy, Holiman, McAdams, and Seaman are all common names. The family name, the historic memory, continues to mark these people as Irish, but more rapidly than other ethnic groups the Irish became "Americans."

In the 1890s several plantation owners in the Arkansas Delta tried to stem a labor crisis by contracting and importing people from Italy. Austin Corbin, a multimillionaire from New York City, who owned some eleven thousand acres of land (Sunnyside Plantation) in Chicot County, Arkansas, proposed bringing in one hundred Italian families per year for five years. These families from northern Italy were to provide a much-needed labor force for the Sunnyside Plantation cotton fields. The Italians themselves aspired to move from the status of farm/wage labor to that of farm owner. Italians were shipped in, arriving through the Port of New Orleans. For several years the plantation was farmed by Italians and blacks. As a whole, though, the "experiment," fared badly.[25]

Malaria epidemics, poor living conditions, and debt peonage compounded the difficulty of the Italians' adjustment to their new country. The immigrants tried to contact Italian consulates in New Orleans and New York to protest "unsanitary water, substandard housing, inadequate, expensive medical care, and rapacious prices and interest costs for goods at the company store."[26] The Italian cries for attention finally gained notice when they targeted the Crittenden Company with breach of the federal alien contract law, which forbade importation of immigrants to the United States to fill labor contracts signed in the country of origin. A federal investigation, however, though it exposed injustice, still failed to upset powerful state interests to help the Italians.[27]

Deliverance came to some of the Delta Italians at Sunnyside in the person of an Italian priest, Father Pietro Bandini, who had come to New York in 1891 to protect foreign immigrants from exploitation. Many Sunnyside Italians followed Bandini to the mountains of northwest Arkansas. There in a place they called Tontitown, they flourish to this day.[28] Meanwhile, after this depletion of labor the owners of the Sunnyside Plantation again negotiated to contract with families from Italy to replenish the work forces.[29] The public perceived these Italian farmers as careful tillers, attentive to agricultural details but suspected them to be people more loyal to Italy than to Arkansas.[30]

Early times were hard for Italians who remained in the Delta. Dan Fratesi tells a story from his childhood in Pine Bluff, a story in which his mother's good, hard traditional Italian bread saves him from antagonistic "Americans":

> Well, when we first came to this country, they weren't friendly at all. We'd go to school, and they'd call you Dago and they'd try to fight you and try to chunk a rock, try to throw a brick at you, and other things. . . . And even when we'd get out from school, we'd have to fight every day just about. . . . So one of the Italian boys one day they had a fight, you know, and they had the bread they cooked in the oven, used to cook—not in the pan but right on top of the brick in these ovens—and they'd keep the bread about, oh, they'd cook every week, you know, and bread'd get hard. And, you know the end of the bread, you know, it'd get just like a brick. So when he got angry, you know, with some boys, he got that piece of bread and it knocked the fool out of the other boy just like a rock.[31]

In addition to the emigrants from northern Italy, many came from southern Italy and Sicily, including those who fled the poverty and unrest of their island district of Palermo where the father of a growing family earned but a lira a day. But Arkansas had not been their original destination. After a twenty-one-day ocean crossing in which sometimes over a thousand people were packed in steerage, they landed in New Orleans in the middle of a yellow fever epidemic.

Penniless, they worked there unloading ship cargo, listening for talk of better places to settle before they sent for their families. After hearing promising things about the upriver city of Helena, Arkansas, they worked their way up the Mississippi on a lugger boat, a vessel manipulated by oars. Other Sicilians followed a similar pattern of brief work in New Orleans, on the docks or in the canefields, and then a move up the Mississippi either as part of a boat crew or as peddlers, selling items on the riverboats. Women, who waited in Sicily for their husbands' summons, supported themselves and their children by picking fruit and by weaving and sewing.[32]

When they first settled in Helena and lower towns of the Delta, many of the Sicilians made a living by peddling. Nunzio Messina, who came to Helena from Sicily in 1894, walked up and down the Helena area levee "carrying a large clothes-type basket over his shoulder, filled with fruit, nuts, and candies to sell. He would walk as far as Oneida, Lexa, and Old Town peddling his wares. After he sent for his wife and two boys, he still worked the country route while his wife ran the corner store."[33] Tony Saia of Helena remembered his own father "peddling, carrying the basket on his head. The children all along the route saved their nickels and pennies to spend with the peddlers. The farmers disliked the peddlers, because workers would leave their jobs to see what the peddlers had to offer and work was disrupted."[34]

Sicilians had strategies for running successful stores, despite the language barrier *and* despite the fact that Italians were accustomed to Roman rather than Arabic numerals. A piece of cardboard that hung from a store shelf, for example, kept credit records in a simple way. For each nickel's worth that a customer charged, a line was drawn; for each dime's worth, two lines were drawn, and so on.[35] The Sicilians were perceived as enterprising and industrious.[36]

The Sicilians found Helena a good place to live and encouraged others from their homeland to come. In time, between forty and fifty families arrived. Among Sicilian surnames still listed in Helena are Marzulo, St. Columbia, Messina, Policastro, Melio, Beveliaque, Provenza, Papa, Fazio, Coco, Danna, Tamburo, Lordi, Padula, Noto, Saia, Glorioso, Forte, Centenio, Madonia, Elardo, Brocato, Muffoletto, Cefalu, Depola, and Genusa.[37]

Ironically, while prejudice against Sicilian settlers seemed minimal in Helena, there was feeling against them from some of the other Italian communities in the Arkansas Delta. Apparently, there were few overt conflicts between groups of Italians, merely coldness and suspicion. Because southern Italians were reputedly connected with the Mafia and the "Black Hand," those from other sections of Italy sought to distance themselves from such association. But rather than admit this concern openly, the northern Italians gave rather euphemistic excuses for their criticism of Sicilians. Italian immigrant descendant Amalite Fratesi recalled that her parents pointed to Sicilians as bad examples because supposedly they never attended mass on Sunday.[38]

There was separation and isolation for both groups. Yet family ties provided strong communal support. Family unity still characterizes these people. Many live with an extended family in a given area, at times in the same house. Celebrations of religious and secular holidays, of baptisms, weddings, and even funerals continue to be marked by energetic community participation in large meals, music, dancing, and general festivity.

In his ethnographic survey of the Delta of the late 1930s, Edward Trice wrote about just such a people of celebration: "They [the Italians of Chicot County] are a fun-loving people, and when they hold a fiesta or celebrate a wedding there is usually quite a bit of wassail and jubilee. Invitations to these festivities are pretty general and townspeople are always glad to attend. Refreshments at an Italian wedding are always ample. Chicot County may well be proud of her Italian-Americans."[39]

Within the very real tragic struggles confronting their settlement in Arkansas, the Italian immigrants sustained themselves with deep community bonds. The glorious bursts of festivity as well as the onus of social discrimination were a coincidence of opposites that wove a richly textured community fabric. Amalite Fratesi summarized the world view sustaining the spontaneous spirit of fun:

> My parents, the Rocconis, and my husband's parents, the Fratesis, were natives in near-by towns in Italy. They knew hard work, hardships, disappointments in life. They were religious. They taught us to work and help carry family burdens from a very young age of 6 and 7. . . . We were taught to take disappointments in life because they said that was to be expected. . . .
>
> I try to tell my children that life isn't always a "bed of roses!" We do the best we can today, and ask God's help for the next: crop failures, low prices, sickness, droughts, wars; come and go by in through the years. We have survived! This has happened in past centuries. I'm sure it will happen in the future.[40]

As early as May 22, 1833, the Little Rock *Arkansas Gazette* welcomed German settlement in the territory.

> We are much gratified in being able to announce the arrival at this place, within the last week of about 140 Emigrants, direct from Germany, who purpose settling in this country, and most of them, probably in the vicinity of this town. . . . Those who are acquainted with the German character, will not require our recommendation, to encourage by every means in their power, the introduction of this class of emigrants into our country. To those who are not, we will merely say, they are hardy, industrious, honest, and peaceable people, and never fail to add greatly to the moral worth and respectability of every section of country they locate themselves in.[41]

To escape political problems in Germany, waves of immigrants fled to the United States between 1830 and 1860. A large number settled initially in the midwestern states and a few in central Arkansas. A substantial number pioneered in Nebraska. After the Civil War there was a notable out migration of Germans from the Midwest. From that relocation came many of the Germans who settled in and made a major impact on the Arkansas Delta. These Germans brought with them expertise in farming technology based upon their previous experience in the wheat-producing states.[42]

Early "American" settlers in the Arkansas Delta had avoided the vast section of virgin prairie land, known as the Grand Prairie, which stretches seventy miles in length and averages twenty miles in width, with a total area of over a half-million acres. The *Arkansas Gazette* of May 27, 1820, extolling the quality of Arkansas Territory land, made one qualification, "The Big Prairie is, probably, the greatest body of poor land in the Territory."[43] Explorer and scientist Thomas Nuttall had earlier described the same prairie as ". . . a vast plain like a shorn desert, but well covered with grass and herbaceous plants."[44]

The absence of trees gave the early "Arkansas" settlers from the lush woodlands of Tennessee, North Carolina, Mississippi, and Kentucky a foreboding of danger hovering over the prairie. Appalled by the scarcity of timber, they thought that it would be impossible to survive winters there. They saw the prairie as a picture of desolation. The saying was, "If it is too sorry to grow trees, it's too sorry to grow crops."[45] The "Americans," then, homesteaded along the rivers and bayous that provided abundant food and protection.

Prairie lands, however, were among the land grants awarded to veterans of the Civil War. According to one story, a German resident of Illinois who had fought in the Union army was deeded a tract of

Arkansas prairie. After inspecting the land, he "promptly traded it off for several gallons of whiskey and went back to Illinois."[46] But other Illinois Germans, particularly Charles Payer, looked at the prairie with different eyes. In fact, he was so impressed that he bought up thousands of acres of prairie land and advertised to the world that he had fine land to sell.

A German community near Highland, Illinois, responded to his claim. As much as anything else, the promise of a milder climate enticed them. Two of those who responded were Heinrich Kerksieck and his wife, Augusta Kreimeir Kerksieck, both originally from East Prussia. Heinrich, a Civil War veteran, had lost an arm from a gunshot wound. As a young cavalry scout, he had ridden over the Grand Prairie and thought it was beautiful land.

Because at the time there were no railroads in the Grand Prairie, the Germans from Illinois traveled by steamer from St. Louis, Missouri, to Helena, Arkansas, and then journeyed overland by wagon to the spot that was known first as "Payer," then as the "Illinois Settlement," and finally as "Ulm" after the immigrants' home in Germany. This name was pronounced "oolm" by the German settlers and "uh-lum" by their "American" neighbors. Other Germans, disheartened by the blizzards of Nebraska, joined the Ulm settlement.[47]

To the native southerners in 1880, the German settlers were at best foreigners and at worst "Yankees." Suspicious Arkansans allegedly tried to burn out the German newcomers by setting fires to the highly flammable prairie grass. But the Germans dug trenches around their houses and barns and refused to flee.[48]

The Germans in Ulm were Lutherans, and one of their first concerns was to build a church and a school and to import a minister. When she was in her late eighties, Mrs. Emilie Trede recalled, "I lived here [in Ulm] all my life. I speak German. I went to German school, in Ulm, the church school. We had German church all the time."[49] Ulm was a thoroughly German settlement. Most of the people who lived in Ulm in the early twentieth century, including the Kersiecks, Timmermans, Krismeiers, Payers, Scheiderers, Issinghoffs, and Driehauses, were related by blood or by marriage.[50]

Ulm's founding people were sturdy. Stories of their hardihood have waxed legendary. A favorite story recounts how an early woman settler served as her own midwife. Her husband was away buying lumber when her intense labor pains began. After quickly making a picnic lunch for her five young children, she sent them away to the woods with emphatic orders to stay there until they saw their father's wagon returning. Almost immediately after the children disappeared, the woman, crouching solitary in her birth pangs, delivered her baby, cut the umbilical cord, wrapped her newborn in a blanket, and collapsed exhausted onto the bed.[51]

Almost simultaneous with the settlement of Ulm was the even more ambitious settlement of what would become the rice capital of the United States, Stuttgart. In 1878 a German Lutheran minister, George Adam Buerkle of Woodville, Ohio, a native of Stuttgart, Germany, began the study of maps to find a place to relocate his congregation. He envisioned an area that would support a large number of Lutheran communities, not merely his single church.

When Buerkle scouted the Arkansas Prairie, he saw a possibility that had eluded the cautious southerners. He purchased the entire Mitchell or "Gum Pond" Plantation of approximately 7,747 acres. With his first group of 65 settlers, he also brought 17 Lutheran ministers who wanted to consider the prairie as a place to relocate their own congregations. These initial immigrants, laden with household goods, horses, and cattle, traveled by rail cars from Woodville, Ohio. In the next year more German settlers joined the community.[52]

An eyewitness account of the vitality of the German settlements was printed in *Westliche Post* in 1887 to encourage more German immigration to the Arkansas Delta.

> The most important place on this Grand Prairie of Arkansas is the German settlement of Stuttgart, where I spent some time. . . . Although the Lutheran minister, Reverend Buerkle, is looked upon as the actual founder of this colony, another German, a Mr. Zimmermacher, claims the distinction of being the first and oldest settler, since he located here fully a half year before the arrival of the Lutheran minister and his parishioners. Zimmermacher is an excellent example of industriousness, perseverance, and frugality, typical of so many Germans, and one can readily see what he has accomplished by these virtues.
>
> . . . Now he owns a fine piece of property, waving fields of grain and a wonderful orchard, a comfortable farm and a brick milk house, a wagon, and a fine herd of cattle. But with all this, he is not to be considered an exceptional farmer, rather, typical of all those in the area.

. . . I shall never forget the evening as I sat on the veranda with Reverend Buerkle, freely partaking of his various sorts of wine, while a choir of masculine voices, his nine sons and three nephews, entertained us with a group of German folksongs.[53]

The writer summarized his visits to other German settlements within a forty-five mile radius of Stuttgart, concluding: "The farms of these people are really model establishments, almost miraculous, when one considers that they wrested the fertile land from the virgin prairie earth in a period of so few years." His final reflections focused on the "contrasting southerners" who earlier scorned the virgin prairie and chose instead woods and fields near waters. Unlike the prairie lands, these areas bred mosquitoes and the deadly malaria.[54]

At the turn of the century the German Arkansas prairie became the center of the prosperous Arkansas rice industry. Since the evolution of a thriving rice culture, the once rather isolated traditional German communities of the prairie (Stuttgart, Ulm, Tull, Gillett, Hazen, and Carlisle) have abandoned many of their strong German customs and have merged with the economic power streams of twentieth-century Arkansas. Festive German foods continue, though, to mark calendar celebrations, and legendary tales of the challenging early days testify to a persistence of German pride.

The *Arkansas Gazette* of June 17, 1820, noted the arrival of "Mr. Samuel Reichenbach, a Swiss gentleman, . . . Agent for a Company in Switzerland . . . come with the intention of purchasing a large tract of land in Winter's Grant on the Arkansas river . . . he will bring on from 100 to 1000 families of his Swiss brethren."[55] Reichenbach's settlement failed to materialize, and not until the 1880s did Swiss immigrants break farm ground on the prairies of the Arkansas Delta.

The Swiss left their home country in the Swiss Alps because of a land shortage there. They settled initially in Kentucky in the 1880s. When they finally left Kentucky, they found the prairies of Arkansas to be vastly different from the Alps of Switzerland. Coming from a land where every square foot of tilled soil was precious, the Swiss brought a tradition of thrift and innovation. With their advanced farming methods, the Swiss could reputedly grow superior crops on low quality land. The Kentucky land, however, after having been cleared of trees and boulders, offered only inferior soil.[56]

In 1887 the Arkansas Midland Railroad (now the Missouri Pacific) advertised good farmland at low prices in Phillips County,

Arkansas. Many of the Kentucky Swiss were tempted by the offer. Initially, a few families tested the Arkansas possibility. After they had made a successful transition, there was a major exodus of Swiss settlers to the Barton and Hicks areas of Phillips County.[57]

In the summer of 1888, Rudolph Inebnit and his son Fred, along with Anton and Ernest Schaffhauser, moved from Kentucky to Arkansas by covered wagon. They began clearing the acreage they purchased and started construction of a log house, anticipating the arrival of their wives and other families in late fall. By November only the north side of the roof of their house had been finished. Mrs. Marie Inebnit Allen of Hicks, who was a young girl at the time, recalled that the newcomers "spread out bedding along the north wall and during the night a severe rainstorm soaked our feet along the whole row of beds."[58]

Initially, the Swiss chose "Waldheim" as the name of their colony. But when they discovered that Arkansas had another Waldheim, they changed the name to "Hicksville," after a Col. Bob Hicks, who operated a stave and heading mill nearby. Later the Missouri Pacific Railroad shortened the name of the town to Hicks.

Settlers in Hicks negotiated land purchases for other interested Swiss. In 1903 new Swiss families poured into Barton. Surnames of these people survive today: Von Kanel, Leifer, Lederman, Schmied, Raeber, Farner, Schubach, Hauselman, Bloesch, Bartchi, Ermer, Ruegsegger, Kummer, Steiner, Tschabold, Schaffhauser, Gschwend, Duboch, Weltis, and Heidleberger are still common.[59]

In the first years the people made a living by selling cords of wood to the railroad and also by making railroad crossties and heading bolts. In time the settlers planted and sold cotton and raised dairy cattle.[60] While many of the early settlers had been craftspersons by trade in Switzerland, in Arkansas they ultimately put their energy into farming. No one earned a living by a craft; yet, the community well knew whom to call on if a specific craft skill was needed. Ida Steiner's grandfather, for example, had been a cabinetmaker in Switzerland. In Hicks, his son, Steiner's father, made caskets, but only upon request, not as a livelihood.

Reverend Traugott Steiner recalled stories he had heard about the moves from Switzerland.

> Grandma Evert prepared barrels of food to come over. They had their own food on the boat. It sounded like a kind of cattle boat. Switzerland was overpopulated. It was so small and they had all

these children and they had to get out and do something. In Europe there was a lot of propaganda going on that America was the land of opportunity. It was anybody that didn't have any *real ties* just picked up and took a shot at it. That's what it amounted to. They had propaganda about Brazil, Brazilia. But they said they had snakes there. And my grandmamma was deadly afraid of snakes, so she wouldn't go there.

They got a contract with Mr. Owen who was contracting people in Helena. He told them about Barton, about they was two Swiss colonies. They kind of drifted together that way. They were writing, "Would it be better if we go here or if we go there?"

They had agents out there that could tell you what ship you had to take and what railroad you had to take. And so they got to New York and there they got the railroad to New Orleans. It was one day from New Orleans. It took a whole day to get from McGhee, Arkansas, and a half a day to get from McGhee to Barton.

When they got there [Barton] Mr. Buesh the station agent came to welcome them, a very hefty man and just had his sleeves rolled up (and in Switzerland, you know, nobody's without a *uniform*, I mean they got *buttons*) and they nearly passed out. They thought, "What have we gotten into!"[61]

The informal dress code was only one hurdle for the Swiss in Arkansas. But the land, stretches of land which they could own and farm, compelled them to stay. Having come from a country in which seven acres constituted a respectable farm, the Swiss were excited by the prospect of living in a land where four hundred acres was only a small-sized farm.

The Swiss succeeded in the Delta region; their success in agriculture and dairying marked them as competent and enterprising. Nevertheless, neighboring Southerners tagged the Swiss with the pejorative name "dutchmen," a slur the Swiss failed to perceive, interpreting the misnomer merely as an indication of American ignorance.

Money for early basics like seed had to be borrowed. But the Steiners recalled with obvious gratitude the support they felt from certain Jewish people in the area. In addition to a common concept of honesty in business transactions, they shared the German language. "This was a bond between the Swiss and the Jews."[62]

The Swiss in the Delta did not readily embrace certain practices common to agriculture in the region. They refused to engage in peonage, for example. The debt peonage system was, in a sense, a new form of slavery that kept agricultural labor entrapped in a web of debt. The practice ensured a permanent labor force after slavery was abolished. The Swiss farmers did have tenants. But Ida Steiner recalled:

> The [Swiss farmers] started having tenant houses. There were sharecroppers. The owner furnished everything and the share-cropper worked the field.
>
> But there was *no commissary* here. They [sharecroppers] bought their own things.
>
> But on the plantations there was commissaries and they [sharecroppers] was *made* to buy their things there. That was *not nice*. I don't know if the Swiss was too honest for that or what. If you had anybody working for you you gave *him* the money and he could go do with it anything he wanted. They [the Swiss] didn't give it to them and then say you still owe me so many hundred dollars. We never did that. But it was done. It was *definitely* done, in the South.[63]

The language that united the Swiss with the Jews separated them from their American neighbors. Church sermons and school classes in Swiss communities used German. But more than language distinguished the Swiss; certain accepted practices made them suspect. One such practice was wine making. Protestant-American farmers in the Delta judged the Swiss tradition of home wine making to be a marginal activity. To the Swiss, however, wine making was an art. They were adept at producing excellent wines from the apples, peaches, plums, cherries, and grapes they raised. Each family had a press and several prize barrels for aging the wines. The best vintages were given to the church for communion services.

The Steiners felt that, despite their religious and linguistic distinctiveness, the Swiss in no way clung to their Old World traditions. "We became Americans right away," they agreed.[64] The celebration of the Fourth of July illustrated the way the Swiss blended their new and old cultures: this holiday was an easy substitution for the Swiss Independence celebration traditionally held in August. On the Fourth of July, the new Independence Day, traditional Swiss games were played and "everyone reverted to his native tongue."[65] Ida Steiner remembered, "It was a big deal here. Mom would tell me that in the early days they would dance and they would wine and dine and dance. There was lotta musicians in this community."[66]

Musing over what sustained the Swiss in the Arkansas Delta so far from their native Alps, Ida Steiner reflected: "Our little community here was love, based on love. If you didn't have something you went to your neighbor and they would gladly share it with you. They all came here and they all knew how to work and they knew how to help each other out."[67]

Another and quite distinct Swiss group, the Mennonites, made a brief settlement in Yoder, a small town still on Arkansas maps named after Jacob Yoder, their leader. In 1881 one of the original settlers' daughters recorded in her diary that her father along with Jacob Yoder "repaired a mover wagon, hitched a good team to it, and went [from Missouri] to spy . . . the State of Arkansas." The men liked what they "spied," and in 1885 Jacob Yoder brought his church members from Missouri to settle in Arkansas. Many in the congregation joined Yoder directly from Switzerland; including the Sutters, Scheffels, and Norfzigers.

They traveled to an area near Stuttgart, Arkansas, by wagons, a twenty-two-day trip from Missouri. Settler Norfziger's daughter noted, "When we finally arrived the men threw their hats in the air and shouted, 'Hurray for Arkansas!' Those woods were paradise to us."[68] About seventeen years later, however, after they had settled, established productive farms, built a substantial church and school, the whole Mennonite community dismantled their school building board by board and moved it and themselves by train to Pryor, Oklahoma, where their descendants still use the building for education.

Between 1885 and 1914, a surge of immigrants from eastern and southern Europe came to the United States for a variety of reasons, including economic conditions, conscription, and conquests by foreign powers. Jacob Plafcan, a rice farmer in the Arkansas Delta, recalled: "I was born in Hungary. I left Europe in 1909, and I'll tell you why. I'm a Slovak—of Slovak nationality; they tried to make me a Hungarian when I was six years old. I don't know if I can explain what happened; but, anyway, King Joseph gave the Slovak nation to Hungary and tried to make a Hungarian out of a Slovak. That's why I'm here."[69]

Another Slovak rice farmer, Sam Koneceny, called to mind his family's slightly different perspective on their middle European homeland:

My people have always been rather touchy about "Czechoslo-vakia" cause when they were there one of the reasons why they left the country was because of the mandatory service. At that time the Czechs and the Slovaks were at war so one of the ways to offend *them* (the Konecenys) rather *strongly* was to call them Czechoslovakians. They were Slovakians; they'd tell you right away they didn't have anything to do with Czechs. They just con-sidered themselves Slovaks which is why they named this com-munity Slovak.[70]

Slovak, Arkansas, became an immigrant settlement of people from many different east European countries: Slovakia, Austria-Hungary, Poland, Moravia. But the founders of the settlement were Slovakian.

In 1894 several Arkansas landholders, in a search of labor for their fields, approached Slovakian immigrants who were working in the steel mills of Pennsylvania. The Arkansas landholders proposed a con-tract whereby the men would work the Arkansas fields and also have options to buy the land. One resident of Slovak explained: "most of the Slovaks were working in the coal mines and steel mills back there in the Northeast, you know. My uncle was a Slovak, and he was the one to homestead here [Slovak] the land. He was with the first group that came here and bought some land for five dollars an acre."[71]

The founding Slovaks, including those with the surnames of Krajniak, Brasko, Sandulak, Sekel, Moransky, Koneceny, Bornadek, Oleska, Janecko, Harnagy, and Plafcan, went to work immediately in the fields of the Grand Prairie. "When you say prairie, you say prairie. When they came here all this was just grass six or eight feet tall," Sam Koneceny emphasized. The men each cut twenty to thirty bales of hay a day. Sometimes when they came home in the ox-drawn wagons, they lost their way in the towering grasses through which there were no roads.[72]

More pressing to these men, though, than even their labor was the mapping out of a formal *town*. The layout was designed in the east European tradition that the men knew from their Slovakian homes. Following the old custom, the founders mapped out an entire town-scape and gave a free lot in the city limits to each man who purchased forty acres of surrounding farmland. Their vision was to establish a traditional Slovakian village on the Arkansas prairie. Yet there was one significant difference. In the Old Country the church had operated as landowner, leasing township property to the surrounding peasants, who became workers for the church. The men in Slovak, Arkansas, determined to shift from ecclesiastical to secular ownership. Hence, they allocated limited acreage to the church. The Arkansas Slovaks, despite this shift, nonetheless centered their lives around the church. Even before they were able to secure a priest, the men of the community presided over the ritual ceremonies.[73]

Life in the village of Slovak followed the liturgical calendar of the Roman Catholic ritual, which, along with a distinctive language and the settlers' self-sufficiency, kept the settlement a relatively self-contained community until the mid-twentieth century. "They worked together a whole lot in those days [at the turn of the century] in the thrashing and hauling and picking. It wouldn't have been profitable for each one of them to own their big thrasher and other things so they would work together."[74]

When the railroad came to Slovak, the people shipped hay and milk to Oklahoma to sell. Business went well. And by the first decades of the twentieth century, the community was thriving. When the Great Depression struck, the settlers' traditionally frugal ways served them well. An early settler later recalled that the people of Slovak were adept at saving money and living on the bare necessities. "It was kind of hard back then, but what they lived for was to leave their children something."[75] Since they were self-sufficient in many respects, the Slovaks were looked on with suspicion by their American neighbors. "They thought we were devils," one resident of Slovak observed. "But that was, I think, the result of the pressure from their ministers. Those ministers had worked hard to build their own [Protestant] congregations. They wanted to keep things real separate."

In 1909 the Arkansas Historical Society reported in regard to the Slavokian colony: "They have become prosperous farmers, and have attracted to that vicinity a small number of their countrymen."[76] In the latter decades of the twentieth century, the town of Slovak has diminished rather than grown in size. The young people have moved to the larger city of Stuttgart. However, the early settlers did leave a legacy of land, money, and tradition to their descendants. The family bonds were still strong in the traditional Slovak fashion. Weddings and funerals are occasions on which *at least* one representative member from every family is present, even if it requires traveling thousands of miles to Slovak.

Two scenes, perhaps, capture the Slovak spirit: a festival and a prairie bird nest. Each year for the past thirty-five years, an Oyster

Supper is held in Slovak. It was begun by a group of the older residents who got a sackful of oysters and a keg of beer and gathered around to have themselves a little midwinter party. Today the Slovak Oyster Supper is touted as the social and political event of the year, a widely publicized phenomenon that draws dignitaries such as the governor, congressmen, state legislators, and federal judges. The Slovak Knights of Columbus sponsor the festivity. The gathering echoes the Slovak Old World tradition of communitywide winter celebrations. The gathering also affirms the rootedness of *this* Slovak community in the state of Arkansas.[77]

Each year, also—but for how long no ones knows—a small flycatcher on its migratory route fifteen thousand miles between Canada and South America stops to build its nest in a rare species of hawthorne bush that seems to grow *only* on the Arkansas prairie at Slovak. Recently, the discovery was made, though, that the rare prairie hawthorne *does* grow in one, and *only one* other place—in the meadows of what was Slovakia in eastern Europe.[78]

Today in the 1990s, the few Chinese who reside in the Delta are widely scattered over the region. Overall, the educational achievements and financial success of the Chinese Arkansans ranks impressively high. Many of these Chinese Arkansans, who have become prominent businessmen, academics, and professionals in the fields of science and medicine, have left the Delta.

The Chinese who came to Arkansas during the past century and a quarter largely fall into three categories: unskilled laborers brought in during the 1870s and 1880s to labor in cotton fields, particularly in Lincoln, Jefferson, and Pulaski Counties;[79] small businessmen, who established themselves in the Delta between the turn of the century and World War II; and Chinese from Hong Kong and Taiwan, who settled in urban areas during the 1960s.[80]

In an effort to get more "working bodies for their fields" in the late nineteenth century, Delta plantation owners "established the Arkansas Valley Immigration Company which delegated Captain George Gift to go to China for the sole purpose of bringing Chinese to the Arkansas cotton fields."[81] Powell Clayton, Reconstruction governor of Arkansas, observed: "Undoubtedly the underlying motive of this effort to bring in Chinese laborers was to punish the negro for having abandoned the control of his old master."[82] No official record exists of how many Chinese actually contracted to work in Arkansas.

But there were enough to inspire an editorial in the *Pine Bluff Press* August 13, 1870: "A Chinaman has the same right to be born in the world as any other child of Adam. Having a right to live, he has right to earn his livelihood wherever he can best find work and wages. Knowing that of all countries on earth America offers the greatest advantages to working men, he has a right to come hither and take his chances with the rest. Being here, he has the right to be treated with the same justice and generosity as we show to other men. And that is the sum and substance of the Chinese question."

These workers from China contracted to work for at least five years, ostensibly to pay back the plantation owners' advance of ocean passage and several months' wages. As with the Italian labor "experiment," the effort to substitute Chinese for black labor failed. After working out their debt, the Chinese left the plantations and either returned to China or established themselves in other parts of the United States. The U.S. census shows only sixty-two Chinese residing in Arkansas in 1900.[83]

The Chinese who settled in Arkansas and other Mississippi River Delta states (Tennessee, Mississippi, Louisiana) after the First World War were merchants who ultimately became markedly successful because "they were willing to work long hours for small profit."[84] As an ethnic group, these Chinese were not true immigrants but what sociologists term "sojourners." Coming primarily from South China, the Kwangtung and Fukien provinces, and from families who were financially well-off, the Chinese "sojourners" came to the Arkansas Delta (and other parts of the United States) to add to the family fortune and success.[85] The sojourners were males, and after a time in the United States would return to China to take a bride. The young couple might return to the United States with a view toward setting up a successful business and acquiring wealth and eventually (even be it in their old age) returning to China.

Chinese families in the Arkansas Delta gave one another strong support. A breakthrough in the economic or social world for one often provided openings for others. Since few immigrant Chinese spoke fluent English, they depended on communal interpretation for understanding and communicating with the English-speaking community. In addition, the families shared and buffered the widespread stings of discrimination, "shivering memories."[86]

In southern states along the Delta, the temptation to settle permanently in the United States was minimized for Chinese because of the prejudice against any person of a race other than caucasian. To white southerners, Chinese were not black, but neither were they white. Discrimination was thus a social given. Churches, residential areas, recreation, and social and business organizations forbade Chinese membership. In some areas Chinese were actively harassed, and their businesses were vandalized. The state of Mississippi in 1925 officially ruled that Chinese children could only attend schools designated for blacks. (White schools were "preserved for the members of the Caucasian race alone.") The United States Supreme Court allowed the decision to stand. After this ruling several Chinese families left Mississippi and moved across the Mississippi River to Arkansas where they felt attitudes and opportunities were far better.[87] An elderly Chinese couple of Helena, Arkansas, noted that life for Chinese people was substantially better in Arkansas than in Mississippi. "We would *never* live in Mississippi!" they exclaimed.

Nevertheless, the reception of the Chinese in the Arkansas Delta could scarcely be characterized as cordial. The Chinese self-esteem had to draw from the affirmation of the family in China. This distancing actually worked for the benefit of Chinese immigrants, as it did for other ethnic groups, giving them an independence from the white community.

From the early twentieth century on, most Chinese immigrants to Arkansas engaged in small businesses. As one Chinese resident observed: "You know at that time [1920s] Chinese people didn't have too much choice or option, you know, about having their own business so consequently they had a laundry or restaurant or grocery. It wasn't too much *choice*."[88]

With steady economic improvement, though, and gradual social adaptation, the Chinese by the 1930s no longer considered themselves sojourners. They were in Arkansas to stay and to raise their children. Chinese groceries thrive today in the Delta towns of Helena, Blytheville, Pine Bluff, Turrell, Holly Grove, Dermott, and Round Pound.[89] The goal of the Chinese was business and financial success rather than social success. They achieved both.

Not only did these Chinese businesses flourish but also the children of these entrepreneurs acquired advanced university degrees, prestigious jobs, and high-ranking political positions. In West Helena, Mr. and Mrs. Willie Young exemplified this pattern of outstanding success achieved through concentrated industry and united family effort. Mr. Young's father, who was born in San Francisco, returned to China to marry. After a number of years, he left his wife and several young children in China and migrated to Memphis where he opened a laundry. When he had set aside sufficient money, he brought his family over from China. They lived in the back rooms of the laundry. Mr. Young vividly recalled:

> In those days you had to heat the pot belly stove and you had to steam your iron. There wasn't any modern conveniences. You just about neglected your family and it was seven boys and two girls and was really a big family and so when we lost my brother Harry my daddy thought that the laundry was just too rough so he decided to come to Arkansas. He had heard there was a grocery store for sale here in West Helena and he bought into it, never been in a grocery store in his life; didn't know a can of beans from a can a *corn*. But he felt like that was a easier life than the laundry which it turned out to be. But it was just cold turkey he took in and that's the store we been in since 1928.[90]

Young's mother spoke little English. When her husband died suddenly in 1933, she had to rely on relatives to arrange the burial. Determined to keep her family together, she refused offers of other Chinese to adopt her children, saying, "No, I can't do that. I got to keep my family. I don't care what it's going to take but I have to do it." She took over the store and also sent her children to school.

In the context of this ill-fated beginning, Young viewed with pride the achievements of his own five children: two were physicians, two were certified public accountants, and one was a corporation lawyer with the Bank of America in Los Angeles. Young commented:

> I've got a real nice family. I'm real proud of them scholastically. What makes me so proud of them is the fact that I grew up with adversity. You know back in those days Chinese people were not very well accepted. Now they were confined to certain places where you lived they were confined to certain things like they never went to church, never socialized. So really I had two strikes against me before I ever went to bat and I really had to do a lot of fighting to see that my kids would not have to suffer the same discrimination I did so it was really a big battle for me. But I'm real proud that I went through all that so my children wouldn't have to go through discrimination like that.[91]

The diligence and discipline that Chinese merchants applied to their stores was no less evident in the rearing of their children. Only the highest standards of scholastic work and social behavior were acceptable.

Mr. Young emphasized the key role traditional Chinese values have played in the remarkable achievements of his children. He felt his stress on the concept of *face* in Chinese culture imbued his children with the drive to preserve and add to the sterling reputation of their parents and grandparents. Young contrasted his long battle against discrimination with his children's acceptance socially. "They [Caucasians] were fighting to get 'em in the sororities and all that. Now that's the truth. And all my kids were on the honor roll. Like my son, he graduated in the upper 3 percent of his class when he graduated from med-school."[92]

Mrs. Young remembered her own timorous "birthing" of those now highly successful children. She was a young bride who only recently had come from China; she was educated in her own country but scarcely spoke the English language. She was a mother at sixteen who knew nothing of babies, and when the baby cried so did she. But she learned quickly and became knowledgeable in the ways of child rearing.

In Helena, where he began as a small grocery merchant who was excluded from the country club and even from churches, Young became a very wealthy man. He is now a sought-after member of social and business organizations and built his six-bedroom house in one of the finest residential sections of Helena.

Unique cycles of success typify the Chinese in the Arkansas Delta. From their initial immigration to the state into communities that admitted them only as marginal members to their impressive present-day positions of wealth, respect, and influence, the Delta Chinese dramatize the quintessential achievement of the "American dream."

Lebanese and Syrian merchants entered the Delta first in the late 1860s and brought their number to around a thousand by the early 1900s.[93] They became known in Arkansas as traders and merchants. Beginning as peddlers of goods, they soon settled and established stores in towns like Brinkley, Forrest City, Stuttgart, and Lake Village rather than in the country. In a 1909 report on immigration, the Arkansas Historical Association characterized the Syrian immigrants as not sturdy but leading honest lives.[94] Perhaps the "not sturdy" designation referred to Syrian gregariousness and their love of community celebration. Many filled a vacuum in the racially polarized Delta by setting up retail businesses that indiscriminately served white and black clienteles. Cultural values that sanctioned hard commercial work and a willingness to "serve former slaves" brought the Syrian merchants a good deal of success. Like Jewish merchants, Syrian merchants in the Arkansas Delta have positive civil rights' records.

The dominant culture categorized Syrians, along with Chinese and Italians, as a "third race," and as such they were deemed to be a threat to the established way of life.[95] The essentially biracial system of the Delta had no provision for a "third race" in its social hierarchy. The Delta caste system, which labeled Syrians "marginal," restricted their social mobility, yet was forced to permit Syrian children into the public schools. Since most of the Delta Syrians were Roman Catholics or Eastern Orthodox Catholics, acceptance into the Protestant churches was seldom tested.

While a number of Syrians and Lebanese traveled over the Delta as peddlers, many clustered in towns and formed small enclaves in Lake Village, Helena, Stuttgart, Forrest City, and Brinkley. The Syrians in Brinkley, for example, constituted a close-knit group.[96] Gregariousness was characteristic of Syrian culture; insularity was not. Traditionally, they were a sociable, community-oriented people. What appears to have been exclusivity of Syrians in the Arkansas Delta resulted in great measure from social barriers built by the dominant culture. As one Syrian in the Delta recalled: "In Brinkley I think there were times other people sort of looked down on us as outsiders that really shouldn't be there."

By the 1930s, for example, Victor Mahfouz, a Syrian, left Brinkley, where he had lived since the early 1900s and took a position as postmaster and opened a grocery store in Fargo, Arkansas. Fargo Agricultural School attracted black students from all over Arkansas and even surrounding states. Although the Mahfouz children had attended the white school in Brinkley, they had good, often close, relations with the black students at the Fargo school. One of Mahfouz's sons recalled a black family friend saying often about her relation with the Mahfouzes: "We integrated 'cause we *love* one another."

In the 1930s and 1940s in Fargo, the Mahfouzes were poor, but the parents, whatever their anguish, seem to have communicated to the children a sense of well-being, of security. Their small accommodations behind the family store housed eleven children. Challenged by poverty to improvise, the boys played basketball with Pet Milk cans and made baseballs by winding black tape around a rock.[97]

Like many other ethnic groups in Arkansas, the Syrians by the second generation had integrated into the surrounding culture, retaining few outward marks of Middle Eastern traditions. While the first generation Syrian immigrants continued to speak Syrian in prayer and intimate talk, children and grandchildren did not speak and could barely understand the Syrian language. Foodways, however, were the folk retention that connected multi-generations with the past. The young girls mastered preparation of dishes like Kibbeh [bulgur and lamb] and stuffed grape leaves by closely observing their mothers and grandmothers. One family matriarch sought to ensure tradition by ritually giving each of her children a cutting from the grapevine she nourished in her back yard. Each new family, then, could harvest, even in Arkansas, its own grape leaves essential to many Syrian foods.[98]

The Arkansas Mahfouz family demographics suggest the presence of a tension felt by many Syrian settlers in the Arkansas Delta. In the late 1940s the whole family transplanted itself to Alexandria, Louisiana. They moved because in southern Louisiana, in that enclave of "Cajun" culture, they found kindred spirits, a sense of open community, and a spontaneous *joie de vivre* that were lacking in the more conservative WASP traditions of Brinkley and Stuttgart. A significant number of Arkansas Syrians made the move to southern Louisiana to join a significant community of Syrians that had settled there directly when they emigrated from their homeland. The Syrian experience points to the conservative, cautious quality of the Delta's dominant culture, its wariness of the liberal, the nonconformist.

Still, Mahfouz's memories of Brinkley are good. "It was not bad. I really hated to leave. That first year, I remember at Christmas, right after midnight mass, my brothers and I got in a car and drove straight [from Alexandria, Louisiana] to Brinkley." Many Syrian ties remain in Arkansas. "My mother's father and my daddy's father and a couple of his brothers and others, they're buried in Brinkley, in a cemetery in Brinkley." And Syrian merchants remain in Stuttgart and Lake Village. "They're there today."[99]

In Arkansas, ethnic groups were not listed by the hundreds and thousands on ship manifests as they were at ports of entry like New

York and New Orleans. Ethnic groups did not pour into Helena and Osceola the way they poured into other upriver cities like Memphis, St. Louis, Louisville, and Cincinnati. Yet, ethnic groups came to the Delta of Arkansas in numbers significant enough to matter. If we accept anthropologist Joseph Guillotte's belief that the "immigrant is someone with more than the normal share of desperate courage" who breaks the somehow repressive bonds of the mother country, then Delta immigrants have contributed sturdy genes to Arkansas.[100]

The Chu family liquor business at Helena.
Courtesy Charley Chu/DCC Archives.

Prairie County land in the early 1900s. The owner offered ten thousand acres for sale.
Courtesy Arkansas History Commission.

Buerkle Brothers Band playing at the 1883 opening of the railroad in Stuttgart (Arkansas County). The Buerkle brothers were sons of Adam Buerkle, the Lutheran minister who founded Stuttgart in 1878. *Courtesy Amici Club Historical Collection/Stuttgart Public Library.*

Immigrant business establishment. *Courtesy of the University of Arkansas at Little Rock.*

Always a Simple Feast: Social Life in the Delta

KENNETH R. HUBBELL

Both abundance and limitation characterized life in the Arkansas Delta. Considered by many to be a "sportsman's paradise," the Delta supplemented the diets of those living there and provided wild game and fish to far-flung markets. But, at the same time, the very conditions that made wild game and fish so abundant also created certain serious hazards. The thick woods, the swamps, and the climate made a perfect breeding ground for disease-bearing insects that were produced almost as extravagantly as the wild hogs the Delta became famous for. Malaria, smallpox, and assorted "fevers" were not only troubling, they were often deadly. Yet people faced the specter of disease and death by creating a social environment that allowed them to do more than merely survive. They entertained themselves in a variety of traditional ways, and they created organizations that made their communities more viable. While some built churches and schools, others turned to gambling and drinking establishments. Whatever avenue they took, the people of the Arkansas Delta found ways to cope with an environment that was often both bounteous and harsh.

Two of the regions most venerable traditions—hunting and fishing—exemplified the excess of the Delta at the same time that they provided an escape from the limitations of life there. As early as 1809, the men stationed at Arkansas Post had but one amusement: hunting. A. Stewart wrote to a friend that no other place could offer more game for sportsmen: "We pursue bear, deer, panther, wild cat, foxes . . . with great success in Autumn, Winter and Spring. The River, prairie and lakes are filled with swan, geese, and ducks. On a hunting party we frequently kill sixty or seventy a day."[1]

In the late 1880s, local papers reported Delta hunting parties as "news." A Pine Bluff paper reported from Noble Lake in Jefferson County that squirrels were very plentiful and that "their slaughter is immense."[2] A railroad promotional booklet proclaimed the blessings of Clay County along the upper St. Francis River, referring to the Corning area as the "Sportman's Retreat." While describing the abundance of local game, the story claimed that "deer are slaughtered here every season without limit and shipped to Northern markets."[3]

Not far from the confluence of the L'Anguille and St. Francis rivers was a primeval forest in which wild game was abundant. According to one account, "it is the chosen haunt of the bear and deer, and panthers are occasionally encountered. Small game exists without limit."[4] In 1941, local wildlife was such an important aspect of life in Chicot County that the Lake Village Post Office commissioned a five-foot by ten-foot mural for the lobby wall that highlighted the area's diverse wildlife: deer, turkeys, squirrels, fish, and quail.[5]

The actual act of hunting was only one part of the experience; hunting clubs provided members with a sense of camaraderie and friendship. United States Senator Joe T. Robinson of Lonoke was an avid sportsman who frequented many Delta hunting and fishing clubs. During a 1933 hunting trip in the Delta, he wrote to a Washington colleague: "I have just returned from the hunt at Mr. Beck's place. . . . We killed ten deer. . . . There was the usual carousing, drinking, and playing poker, but I was provided with a comfortable bed in a large room with only Judge Hutchins as my roommate and I slept quite as well as though . . . at home."[6]

Local hunting grounds were legendary, and two towns in the prairie region close to the Delta, Stuttgart and Weiner, both claimed the title of "Duck Capital of the World." Weiner was featured in a Wide World of Sports TV special in December 1956, and the spectacular film footage showing thousands of ducks in flight drew attention to this tiny Poinsett County town.[7] Meanwhile, sportsmen from St. Louis, Dallas, Memphis, and other cities flocked to remote Delta fields each winter; often they paid local guides substantial sums of money to secure the best hunting. Novelist Richard Ford opened his novel entitled *Piece of My Heart* with a scene from a duck hunt in Hazen (Prairie County): "He had waited at the window until they came inside, old men in long wading boots and canvas coats . . . and herded the men across the field in the stillness toward the timber so that the cabin sank and became just a single light. . . . In the cold, the men grew silent and morose like lumps of soft coal, plodding into the trees, their boots squeezing together, until the ground gave way to water."[8]

Despite the weather and the dark hours that characterized the duck hunts, the most compelling part of the experience for many men was the sense of wonder: the cold country stillness, broken only by the awesome cacophony of flapping wings. In 1960, one young hunter testified to that wondrous feeling: "We stopped the jeep in the middle of the road because it was flooded anyway. We got out of the jeep and I have never heard so many ducks in all of my life. There must have been 10,000 ducks in two rice fields, and they were making so much noise that we could not even hear ourselves talk."[9] The whole experience was so much a part of local tradition that hunters coined an expression to describe a style of shooting ducks when they land in the water rather then when aloft. "Some men try to 'sky bust' them, which is shooting at them at tree tops," observed one hunter, "while others try to 'Arkansas' them, which is shooting them on the water and trying to get as many ducks as you can."[10]

The numerous oxbow lakes and winding streams that traversed the Delta's bottomland forests teemed with fish as well as game. The "sunken lands" along the upper St. Francis River in the northeast Delta and Big Lake in Mississippi County were famous at the turn of the century for bass fishing. Meanwhile, Chicot County, in southeast Arkansas, proudly sought the crown of Angler's Paradise in 1923 by promoting Lake Chicot as the "Home of the Big Black Bass."[11] But good fishing spots were abundant throughout the Delta; people fished from boats and on the banks of creeks and drainage canals. As with fishermen everywhere, Delta people enjoyed the relaxation of the sport as much as the actual prize. Fishing trips ranged from family outings to business affairs; both tapped the rich reservoir of "spirits" and tall tales that were a distinct part of fishing tradition. Earnest Best recalled a typical fishing weekend in the Arkansas County woods around 1930. "We caught a few fish," he wrote, "and as it was getting dark, we built a big camp fire. And of course, to celebrate we had a bottle of 'Benson Lake Tonic,' the kind that was manufactured right there at home. . . . We were cooking fish on an open fire, singing, and having a big time."[12]

Mixing talk and sport was the highlight of men's lives in the Delta. One journalist observed about Senator Robinson that his form of recreation was the great Arkansas recreation, "fishing and shooting and the talk and the food and the fun that go with fishing and shooting." Robinson once participated in a "fish story contest," while poling down the White River with a couple of tough "river rats." Defending the size of fish in Prairie County, he bragged:

> Up there the streams back up when it floods and when the water goes down again there'll be a pond out in cotton fields as big as a lake. And in these ponds there'll be fish. In one of these ponds last year there was something so big nobody could catch it. Broke their tackle and went away with their rods. So one day we took an anchor and baited it with a dead calf and tossed it in on the end of a two-inch rope tied to a grandpappy of all cottonwood trees in Prairie County. Pretty soon the cottonwood begins to buckle and we knew we had him. We hitched on six pair of oxen and we pulled him out. He was a catfish. And when we cut him open, what do you think we found? We found a pair of harnessed mules and a wagon and seven acres of burnt ground.

Even seven acres of burnt ground did not silence these contestants; one rugged boatmen ended the contest by chiding Senator Robinson: "Hell, I ought to have known a Senator would tell the biggest lie."[13]

But there was another side to the camaraderie and sport. Unlimited fishing and hunting, even in a region so conducive to wildlife, slowly pared down the supply of fish and game. The *Osceola Times* charted the decline of wild game in Mississippi County between 1885 and 1890. By 1885, small game hunting in the area was considered passé by some hunters. The *Times* reported that many avid sportsmen "have evidently become tired of shooting such small game and are now turning their attention to larger game. Mr. Goodman, last Monday, bagged a panther which measured nine feet in length."[14] But plentiful large game in the same area had also been considerably reduced by 1890. The paper reported: "The day of the hunter and trapper that used to be so prosperous and complete [is] now beginning to be a thing of the past."[15]

Such proclamations were not entirely true for the whole Arkansas Delta; along the region's key streams, wildlife prospered, and throughout the early twentieth century hunting clubs passed down memberships from father to son. In the Cache River bottomlands of Jackson County was a hunter's paradise called "Haw Thickets." One hunter claimed that "a traveler passing along this road could frequently see a wolf, a bear, a deer, a raccoon, a catamount, a polecat, a bobcat, or most any creature indigenous to our climate."[16]

While the threat of the depletion of the game and fish in the Delta stimulated locals to impose regulations, especially upon out-of-state hunting and fishing clubs, game and fish existed in sufficient abundance to augment the diets of Delta folk well into the twentieth century. Food, the catching or growing of it, the preparation of it, and especially the consuming of it, was a focal point in the Delta. And food was often another expression of the extravagance of life in the Delta.

Wild meats were staples of Delta diets for both black and white families. Though raccoon was commonly procured from hunting trips, sometimes it was bought from country stores. In the latter case, customers followed the traditional guideline: "Always check to see whether the one paw has been left on the coon to assure . . . they were getting the genuine article and not someone's dog." J. M. Taylor of Blytheville used this recipe for coon suppers in her Mississippi County home: "Wash it in cold water . . . then place it in a large pot and cover with water. Also into the kettle go generous portions, according to individual taste, of pepper, salt, garlic, sage, and bay leaves. Boil the coon in this for two hours (until tender). Then bake it with sweet potatoes until it browns, and serve with hot buttered corn bread."[17]

Wild greens picked along Delta streams, bayous, or ditches were favorite ingredients in "poke salad" (its botanical name is poke sallet). It was a hallmark of regional folklore too; many older subjects considered it a spring ritual to gather greens for meals that "cleaned out the system."[18] In this instance, a tasty meal also served a medicinal purpose.

Plentiful wild berries and fruits provided ingredients for pies, jams, and other desserts. In the 1930s, the Cooper family of Blytheville commonly picked dewberries for baked cobblers. For Beckie Cooper Taylor those hot summer outings were a highlight of her Delta childhood since they picked "in a secret place I liked to think was known only to us on the bluffs of the Mississippi River."[19] In fact, delicacies made from berries, honey, or fruit were prized offerings at social affairs. For example, entries in the Ladies' department at the annual Arkansas fair in 1860 included strawberry, muscadine, blackberry, scuppernong wines, grape, peach, and blackberry cordials, and one apple toddy.[20] Another favorite of that era, local beer, was made from persimmons. African-American slaves made special beer by a tried and true method of washing persimmons in a keg with meal and "let sour about three days."[21]

Game and fish, wild vegetables, and berries supplemented the diets of Delta people, and preparing the family's food—and the meals themselves—was equally important to rich and poor people. In a 1936 *Fortune* magazine article on Joe T. Robinson's childhood at Lonoke, Archibald MacLeish captured the essence of Delta life: "It was a hard life but it had its compensations. Food was one compensation. Meals at the Robinsons were always a simple feast."[22] This sense of security provided by ample food held true for poor farmers, too. One Phillips County resident, reflecting on his family's struggle during the crumbling economic conditions of the 1890s, noted that they always had enough to eat. "Money and fine clothes were both far from us," he wrote, "there were eleven of us in the family but we had a good garden, 150 sheep, 18 or 20 hogs, lots of chicken, turkeys, geese, and ducks so our table was always loaded."[23]

A diversity of livestock and garden crops was common, which helped families weather the lean years when cotton prices were depressed. Most families slaughtered hogs and canned vegetables, and little went to waste. Chittlins (the large intestines of hogs) were regional favorites, as was fried pork skin, which was added to corn meal to make "cracklin' bread." Chittlins were commonly served with greens, such as local wild turnip, mustard, or other green leafy vegetables. Bessie Driver of Marion (Crittenden County) described her favorite meal as "guts, greens, cornbread and molasses."[24]

Delta women translated the family vegetable patches into memorable meals. Most gardens yielded a colorful variety of produce: Irish and sweet potatoes, corn, English peas, squash, onions, tomatoes, okra, cabbages, greens, carrots, beets, and more. Stewed tomatoes mixed with bread ("tomato pudding") and sweet potatoes blended with bread, sugar, and butter ("sweet potato cobbler") provided tasty side dishes that were made from home-canned garden vegetables.[25]

Food was a central feature of family holidays in the Delta. Thanksgiving and Christmas dinners revolved around a lengthy meal with items made from traditional recipes passed down through generations. For one Marianna family, the special delight was ambrosia, made from a family recipe containing oranges, fresh coconut, pineapple, and whipped cream.[26] The presence or absence of traditional foods sometimes symbolized the holiday spirit. One Carlisle (Lonoke County) family regarded the Christmas meal itself as important to the celebration as gifts. "On Christmas morning," a family member explained, "toys were not the only proof of a visit by Santa Claus; he approved each child's dessert with the ultimate compliment: a missing slice."[27]

The food that people prepared and consumed revealed a simple "slice of life," one circumscribed by hard work and closely connected to the land. Dependence on the land, however, had some chilling side effects; the Delta's numerous bayous and swamps were breeding grounds for insects. Swarms of mosquitos living in the swamps and pockets of standing low water plagued early pioneers. Conditions at Arkansas Post, an early settlement on the lower Arkansas River, were so bad, according to one settler, that it took two people to write a letter—one to brush away the bugs while the other person completed the task at hand.[28] In 1869, a doctor en route to Jackson County ran into a swarm of bugs that drove him into the White River on horseback to seek relief: "The moment I pulled the rein, clouds of ravenous insects attacked both horse and rider."[29]

The sultry weather only compounded the insect nuisance. The mosquito situation was no better in McGehee (Desha County) where local folklorists ruefully joked that "all the cattle and horses of three counties used to come to town every night to escape the insects. . . . Everybody had a fence to keep the children in and the cows out."[30] Some people found the best method of dealing with the continuing nuisance: humor. Mosquito lore forms the basis of Delta anecdotes and tall tales. One "river rat" who lived in a Mississippi River houseboat colony near Horseshoe Lake described a particularly bad year, "Yesterday," he observed, "I seen a mule kick a stone to make a spark and start a smudge fire to keep 'em away."[31]

Perhaps the most famous Arkansas Delta mosquito story is entitled "Arkansas Snipe." The 1850 story described some local steamboat travelers leading a Northern visitor up the Arkansas River to hunt bear. In trying to fill the voyage's empty hours, the travelers took to drinking and conversing about their hunting exploits. One of the Arkansans bragged about a snipe-shooting excursion, "Cuss me," he declared, "if the man that shoots off them 'ar birds for me don't be my eternal friend—he will! Look hyar, the infernal things pitched into my youngest child arter it was born, so that its head swelled up as big as a punkin." Incredulous upon hearing this, the traveler from the North asked: "Did snipe do this?" "Wal, they did," confided one of the locals. "Leastwise, what you call snipe. We call 'em muskee-ters!"[32]

Humor could not defend Delta people against more severe epidemics like yellow fever and malaria, which killed hundreds of people in the late nineteenth century. Unsanitary drinking water, coupled with a vicious strain of malaria, devastated the Federal forces stationed at Helena during the Civil War. The atmosphere of stagnant water, summer heat, and humidity earned the town the reputation as "the most deadly place on the river."[33] Another common ailment was chronic chills. Most general merchandise establishments sold a variety of "chill tonics." Although most people were affected annually by the combination of chills and fever, the illness was not taken lightly. "I have been in bed all day, . . ." a Helena planter complained in his diary, "had a chill this morning and fever since . . . I am now trying the red puccoon root and whiskey . . . if that does not give me relief I shall feel discouraged."[34] Malaria symptoms and respiratory disease were ever-present. Delta blues singer Robert Johnson, who lived around Helena in the 1930s, compared the tenacious disease to the blues:

> Let the blues
> is a low-down achin' heart disease
> Like consumption
> killing me by degrees.[35]

From store-bought tonics to homemade whiskey, Delta people sought relief from the roughness of life. There were also numerous traditional cures and local remedies for life's ailments; many treatments were passed down from folk who sought, unsuccessfully, to transcend the region's climate, pests, and isolation.

Like other American pioneers, Delta people used local plants and foods to promote healing. Almost every family—or at least every community—had a "folk doctor" who provided the only available medical care for many poor, rural Delta people. Interestingly, this knowledge and the concomitant prescriptions included both magical and naturopathic properties. While many recorded Delta beliefs and remedies are similar to generalized folk medicine, there are clear instances that indicate specific regional differences, which were probably based upon the availability of local ingredients.[36] For example, a common treatment for mumps, widely used by black people living in Chicot County around 1930, incorporated sardine oil, occasionally mixed with turpentine. One elderly woman advanced a folk theory that the sardine grease must be rubbed "upwards on the jaw to affect the cure, then the sardines must be eaten."[37] The ever-popular turpentine (sometimes mixed with "blackened chicken") was also used in treating fresh wounds, snakebite, and common coughs. Lucy Sanders well remembered turpentine cures from her childhood in Phillips County around 1900. "In those days," she recalled, "a cut or mashed finger or toe, and there must have been many of them, was washed and turpentine and a rag put around it and we went happily off until it happened again."[38] And blends of local ingredients were highly regarded as tonics; whooping cough, a chronic illness among children, was among those diseases treated with indigenous plants. Bark from red oak trees was stripped for homemade cough elixirs. "Back then when I had the whooping cough," one Delta woman remembered, "my mother got some bark off a red oak tree, I believe, and boiled it down to a syrup down low."[39]

The mysterious ingredients in these folk medicines made scientific analysis risky business; however, most people believed in the power of such medicines, even if they could not identify every ingredient. One Chicot County hemorrhoid treatment required the healer to locate a strange local weed known only by its particular location in the woods, which was mixed with hog lard and boiled in a larger pot.[40] In Phillips County, people incorporated elm leaves into lineaments and salves. Judge James Hanks noted this type of treatment in his 1870 diary, "I procured some slippery elm this morning and have applied that to my toe. I believe that it has benefitted me considerably."[41] Leaves and roots were also cultivated for herbal teas. A Lee County farmer depended on Sassafras tea to "thin" his blood, claiming that this kept him cooler in the summer. Family tradition prescribed the digging of the roots "usually after Ground-Hog day."[42] Many Delta people collected herbs that played an important role in maintaining a person's health. "When the wild geese began to honk their way northward," noted a Jackson County woman, "it was time for her to begin making 'sassafrax tea' for the children in order to get them ready for the spring season."[43]

Women and children played an important role by collecting and preserving local herbs. Some farms had herb closets built into the kitchen wall near the chimney where the heat kept herbs, onions, and other foods dry. At one farmhouse, special hinges called "Holy Lord Hinges" were used on the cabinet door. The family believed they offered special blessings or protection for the healing herbs and foods.[44] But regardless of how herbs and roots were prepared, Delta people continued to rely upon their medicinal powers until well into the twentieth century.

The aggravation of insects and the threat of disease were ever-present realities in the Delta. And while hunting and fishing provided men with an enjoyable pastime at the same time that they supplemented the family diet, Delta people found other ways to cope with the sometimes harsh realities of life in or near the swamps. Because the Arkansas Delta was almost entirely rural, its social life and traditions were closely linked to the earth and landscape of the region. Farming issues—weather, crop prices, crop loans, labor, machinery, planting—were central to most families until the 1950s. An old Mississippi County saying reveals that sense of connectivity to the land: "[It is] time to plant cotton when the leaves on an oak tree are the size of a squirrel's ear."[45] When rural Delta people could put aside their concerns about earning a living from the land, they also looked to the land for relaxation and pleasure. Special events such as picnics and barbecues revolved around food and family. Even medicine and health cures were derived from locally grown items.

Yet not all forms of Delta social life were dependent on nature; people traveled to town for entertainment such as circuses, horse racing, gambling, motion pictures, dancing, and occasional lectures. Those who lived in the Delta towns had more entertainment avenues than those who lived in the country, but their traditions were similar; everybody cursed mosquitoes or the chills and everybody worked hard, usually in incredible heat, without air conditioning.

Some ways of entertaining oneself and coping with the environment were relatively simple. For example, visiting was a well-established pattern of life in the rural Delta. While women moved throughout their communities exchanging food, borrowing items, and performing services for one another, whole families also regularly visited each other. Nannie Jackson described a typical weekend in Desha County in 1890: "Mr. Jackson & I went up to see Mrs. Hornbuckle & stayed a while, Fannie & Nellie came a while this evening & Brother Charlie was here for dinner Lizzie & Sue fixed most of the dinner John Hornbuckle was here a while to day, Lizzie wrote to Mrs. Carrie Embree today Aunt Chaney & Emeline were here a while to night they brought me a loaf of light corn bread it is so good. Mr Jackson & I had a good nap to day."[46]

The exchange of news and occasional gossip was an essential part of the simple life. "We had to find our own amusements," recalled a Phillips County woman who grew up in the late 1890s. In another diary entry for 1891, Nannie Jackson described a Friday night when "Mr. Jackson got some sugar & invited a lot of the folks & they had a candy pulling & danced some but broke up at twelve o'clock."[47] Spontaneous gatherings like these were an invisible part of the social network throughout the Delta; this network was expanded and highly visible at holidays, especially July Fourth, since the cotton was "laid by." In some parts of Phillips County, entire communities celebrated the holiday with picnics, barbecues, or fish frys. Families gathered at Big Creek, and one participant recalled: "They used a seine as there was no law against it then, and it didn't take long to catch a croaker sack of fish. . . . Lemonade stands were set up, pavilions were built for dancing throughout the day to the lively tunes of string instruments, baseball games were started."[48] Men traditionally caught and cooked the game, and women baked and prepared the other foods. This was also true for Jackson County folks who annually held a community barbecue or "jamboree." Long pits were dug in the earth to roast the game, which was supplemented by eggs, sorghum molasses, egg custard, coffee, cakes, and pies, all prepared by community women.[49]

Many places in the Delta sponsored annual July Fourth picnics that provided opportunities for its residents to visit with neighbors and take a break from the daily manual work. The town of Weiner, located in the prairie close to the Delta in Poinsett County, celebrated the holiday from the 1890s until the 1930s with a complete picnic spread on a giant tablecloth on the school grounds.[50] Delta newspapers reported on the popularity of community feasts and political rhetoric. "Picnics and barbecues," noted the *Pine Bluff Weekly Press* in 1879, "are becoming every year more fashionable in our section of the country." Noting the appeal of such gatherings, the reporter observed that it was "proper for the people of their neighborhoods to assemble as often as they can mingle together and interchange opinions relative to the industrial, domestic and political condition."[51] Focusing more on feasting than speech making, Capt. Dewitt Anderson's annual barbecue at his Lee County plantation offered a bountiful variety of foods. In 1891 some participants boasted of "eating 2 or 3 pounds of barbecued pork, mutton, goat and bear."[52]

Because a vital part of life away from work incorporated visiting and getting together with neighbors, people in the Delta were accustomed to traveling. Not only did they have to travel to escape the isolation of rural life and seek entertainment through visiting friends and neighbors, but they were also accustomed to traveling great distances in order to get to market. Farm workers and laborers went to town on Saturdays for supplies, groceries, and entertainment. And even in the heyday of Delta town life, farmers who lived in town often traveled many miles back to the farm. "Ridin' around" became a popular form of social life; sometimes it was tied to "visiting," but often people took to the roads for pure enjoyment. Joy riding first became fashionable in Helena around 1890 when streetcars first appeared. The sudden cultural transformation shocked even progressive citizens. James M. Hanks noticed the tension caused by the town's progress when he observed that even local preachers approved of their brethren taking the new public transportation: "nor was it wrong to ride in them for recreation on Sunday. . . . And as all the other preachers favor it, street car riding on Sunday will be the thing after this."[53] Similar fanfare accompanied the arrival of Weiner's first automobile in 1907, and joy riding became the popular pastime. One local historian recalled that even though it took a small town like Weiner nearly forty years to pave every street, "going to Jonesboro is just about the favorite outdoor sport for people of all ages."[54]

The small size of Delta towns did not preclude the diversity of organized social events that were common activities for its residents. Outside of church or school functions, most rural people came to the towns for amenities and organized social networks. Newport, for example, offered residents and visitors recitals by the local cornet band in 1896. Women in the town joined together in temperance societies and secured notable temperance speakers. One was Frances Ellen Harper, a famous black poet and Women's Christian Temperance Union lecturer who spoke at the Newport courthouse to an "appreciative audience of both white and colored citizens."[55] Occasionally issues like temperance brought white and black people together in a mutual cause, though separate social spheres were more typical.

Organized social opportunities were perhaps more diverse for white people in the region, and a variety of organizations flourished throughout the Delta. Chicot County was probably typical of many other areas in the variety of clubs, coteries, and organized societies that bonded small town people together. For example, Dermott, Lake Village, and Eudora sponsored garden clubs in the 1930s. In addition to beautifying the highway along Lake Chicot, these clubs collaborated on a five-year plan to create a sunken garden. Local women's clubs joined a statewide federation; one of the earliest members was Lake Village's Delta Shakespeare Club, which was organized in 1905.[56] During the 1950s, Pine Bluff women established a Social and Art Club whose members sewed garments for the Red Cross and participated in buffet luncheons and "Silver Teas."[57]

Men participated in social, political, and fraternal clubs; like the women's clubs, these too were racially segregated. Black Democrats organized a club in Mississippi County as early as 1892,[58] and the Prince Hall Masons, a black fraternal order, had lodges in Helena, Brinkley, Marianna, and Pine Bluff.[59] White men in Chicot County joined the Blue Lodges, another Masonic organization. Throughout the region, sportsmen were loosely affiliated into hunting and fishing clubs, and Chicot County even had a Motorboat Racing Club.[60]

Although Delta people went visiting, held barbecues and picnics, or created clubs and associations in order to entertain themselves, sometimes entertainment came to them. As early as 1852, circuses attracted large crowds. That year, Dan Rice's Hippodrome brought over two hundred men and horses, a double brass band, and a cloud of dust to Helena. The *Southern Shield*, a Helena newspaper, announced the event and advertised that "the immense pavilion can hold comfortably 10,000 persons."[61] Whether there were that many interested souls even in the vicinity in 1852 may be open to question; yet, the hyperbole indicated the popularity of entertainment such as circuses. Troupes that came to Helena every autumn in the late nineteenth century set up camp under a big tent with two rings. Trick horses and clowns accompanied trained monkeys and dogs, and some large companies even brought elephants, lions, rare birds, and hypnotists.[62]

A twelve-day carnival was another type of special event likely to attract country people to neighboring towns. In 1910, Sulphur Rock in Independence County held such a program of lectures, political speeches, fireworks, and religious services that was held near an artesian spring. According to a local newspaper, these attractions were arranged to allow "baseball and basketball every day and merry-go-round shows." Barbecued meat, bread, and coffee were served, and the paper advised participants to "bring your hammock and sleep in the grove."[63]

By 1920, social life in the Delta had become more diverse. Aerial exhibitions were held at Walnut Ridge in Lawrence County and in

Chicot County, where Charles Lindbergh delighted residents with spectacular night landings in 1926.[64] "Modern picture shows" complete with live string bands became increasingly popular. McGehee's first picture facility was the "Airdome," an outdoor theater whose screen was the side of a local brick building. "Intermissions were frequent while the reel was being rewound," recalled one Desha County resident who attended the premiere screening. "The Keystone Cops, Fatty Arbuckle, Tom Mix, and others were the stars of that day."[65] In West Memphis, one early movie theater sponsored Bank Nights with cash giveaways and ushers outfitted in tuxedos.[66]

More than mere social gathering spots, Delta towns were centers for news about distant events. The musician Sonny Payne remembered lounging in front of Helena's Illinois Central Railroad ticket office to catch sports scores. "Most of us couldn't afford radios back in the thirties when I was growing up," he recalled, "so we'd sit there and wait for the telegraph operator in St. Louis to telegraph the innings in the baseball game. . . . This is how we used to listen to baseball, by Morse code."[67]

Radio dramatically altered the Delta's sources of information and entertainment; people stayed home and tuned into music and commentary on local stations that were sponsored by merchants and wholesalers. A few stations also broadcast national news and entertainment programs. Chicago's radio station WLS had a powerful signal that reached into the Arkansas Delta. "The Barn Dance, from Chicago, featured a pair of singers, a man and a woman, known as Lula Belle and Scott," according to Earnest Best, who remembered listening to the radio while traveling across the Delta in the 1930s. The songs tapped the feelings of unrest and frustration among poor people during the Depression and expanded their limited world of cotton farming, replacing it with a broader picture of life.[68]

Country music star Johnny Cash also depended on radio programs for entertainment as a youngster on his family's Mississippi County farm. "When we worked in the fields in the summertime," he observed, "we usually took an hour off from noon till 1:00 . . . listening to the High Noon Roundup over WMPS in Memphis." A half-hour variety show of songs, talk, and comedy, the show gave Cash "just what we needed to get us over the 'hump' of a long day in the fields."[69]

Churches across the region provided members with spiritual sustenance but also with social and educational opportunities. A Pine Bluff religious quintet advertised their services to other churches, schools, and public institutions: "The Famous Five Gospel Singers can help solve your financial problems with their concert programs."[70] Black Baptists throughout the Delta organized missionary associations and Sunday School boards. An announcement in the *Reporter*, an African-American paper published by the Baptists in the Delta, invited parents and church members to a conference at Helena in 1900 that called for a series of gatherings "until a general improvement is had and until our young people are inspired with a higher motive than many of them now exhibit."[71]

But churches were more than simply social institutions providing entertainment and education. The Delta was characterized by a strong spiritual pull that ran through most rural families. Frame churches dotted the countryside along the region's gravel roads. For many of the Delta's poorest sharecroppers or small farmers, their religious beliefs focused on a "better tomorrow" that contrasted sharply with their lives of seemingly endless toil and limited joy. People in the Arkansas Delta generally took their religion seriously; on an individual level, they embraced the concept of Christian love as the norm for human behavior.[72] Congregations often sought to clarify and enforce the larger community's morals.

Religious ceremonies often took the form of summer camp meetings. In the 1880s these events would often last for a week at a time, with whole families participating in successive day-long sessions.[73] In 1890 a reporter for a Lee County newspaper described the power of a revival held near the town of LaGrange, "Ringleaders who have hitherto served the devil with all their might and strength are now walking in the light."[74] Indeed, fighting the devil played a vital part in an individual's visceral act of faith. Family illness often brought personal fears and uncertainties into sharp focus and prompted many to employ religious faith against fevers and chills in the absence of decent medicine. Phillips County planter James Hanks remembered his own fight with terrible sickness in 1870 as a struggle between darkness and light: "I cannot drop off to sleep for a moment before I am troubled with the most horrid visions and filthy unclean thoughts. I imagine I am uttering the most shocking and obscene oaths and language. It seems as if the devil would have me. In my fright and disgust and misery I awake and cannot account for it, for I entertain no such and use no such words when awake."[75] This timeless struggle between good and evil also served as song lyrics in Delta blues music. In his composition "Me and the Devil

Blues," Robert Johnson testified to the power which he felt evil thoughts had over his actions:

Early this mornin'
    when you knocked upon my door
Early this mornin'
    when you knocked upon my door
And I said, "Hello, Satan,
    I believe it's time to go."[76]

Churches offered more than cures for evil spirits; there were other ceremonies and rituals that provided important opportunities for emotional release. Services in many denominations regularly used a "call and response" style to engage the worshipers. Pianists, organists, and choirs in both white and black churches involved entire congregations in a fulfilling musical experience that enhanced the individuals' feelings of belonging to a larger community. To extend the churches' broader mission, ministers rallied their congregations to support civic boosterism and education. Newspaper editors and civic leaders often joined the chorus; editorials frequently raised cultural and industrial progress to the realm of morality and righteousness. Typical was the advice of a Mississippi County editor, who urged his readers to "Stand Up For Your Town" in 1899. "You can stand up for your town," he enjoined, "by trying to keep down rowdyism, immorality and everything that offends the best people. You can stand up for it by trying to elevate the people intellectually and morally."[77]

In Delta communities even as large as Pine Bluff, weddings were important social events; they often incorporated both religious ceremonies and folk traditions. One city minister recalled that throughout his career people followed folklore and superstitions when approaching a wedding day. Tuesday and Thursday were considered good days of the week on which to be married, but Wednesday was the clear favorite according to local legend because: "You will get a good husband and you will both live a long time."[78] A common rhyme from southeast Arkansas provided insight for the bride's selection of wedding dresses:

Marry in green, your husband will be mean,
Marry in red, you'll wish yourself dead,
Marry in brown, you'll live in town,
Marry in blue, your husband will be true,

Marry in black, you'll wish yourself back,
Marry in gray, your love will stray,
Marry in pink, your love will sink,
Marry in white, you've chosen right.[79]

Funerals provided yet another glimpse into the Delta's social fabric. Even in death, white and black people were separated; morticians generally were of the same race as the deceased. Burial associations were common in the black community, and funeral services were often longer and more varied. Around 1900, night funerals were common. A key feature of African-American customs in that era called for all in attendance at funerals to prove that they had paid their last respects by bringing back a handful of dirt. There were multiple funerals for residents who had been especially active in their communities, because each organization or club in which the deceased held membership often showed its respects by holding an independent service. Probably the most common funeral style in the black community was the "emotion" funeral. According to Pine Bluff mortician T. Ralph Brown, mourners attended the service intent on expressing their grief through wailing, and an emotion funeral could last the entire day.[80]

Dependence on the Delta lands and rivers for sustenance sharpened people's appreciation of fate and chance. To a great degree, rural life was a gamble, one intricately tied to planting and harvesting cycles. Whether it was because of this prevailing uncertainty or something else, people in the Delta loved to gamble. This form of entertainment ranged from spontaneous family gatherings at home to backroom tables at "honky-tonks."

One particularly popular pastime in eastern Arkansas was horse racing; wagering on horses provided a welcome break from betting on the weather. Helena's Jockey Club at the Western Central Course advertised races as early as 1837.[81] By 1900, a half-mile track was constructed with a wooden grandstand that seated five thousand. Sunday races featured entries from most of the nineteen local saloons.[82] In Arkansas County, "progressive" farmers laid out Stuttgart's Fair Grounds in 1889 and later claimed it the "fastest track in the state."[83]

Gambling on riverboats was common in the early years of the nineteenth century, and the first settlements offered abundant gambling opportunities. Explorer Thomas Nuttall, who visited Arkansas Post in 1819, complained that the residents' "love of amusements . . . is carried to extravagance, particularly gambling and dancing parties or balls."[84] Open gambling arrived in Pine Bluff in 1876 when five saloons obtained licenses to operate "keno banks." (Keno was a game of chance played with numbered cards.)[85]

River towns like Helena were notorious for their "juke joints" and saloons. According to local folklore, Helena had at least forty saloons along the main commercial street as late as the 1940s. Most visibly displayed slot machines and served a predominantly white clientele. On nearby streets, other clubs catered to black patrons who engaged in dice games and listened to live music. Guitarist Johnny Shines recalled that beer was served in cups. "Whiskey you had to drink out of a bottle," he recalled, "See, they couldn't use mugs in there because the people would commit mayhem, tear people's head up with those mugs."[86] One visitor to a Helena gambling party reported losing his money during a game with a Chinese player who "knowed every card he [the storyteller] had the moment he picked 'em up, just like he was using X ray."[87]

In Crittenden County, gambling parties were often advertised on handbills using coded language to avoid police scrutiny. One such handbill read:

> Criminals at large—they'll be caught and held at the
> Big Apple for questioning.
> February 17 - 18 - 19 - 20.
> The Suspects Names are: Butler Boy, Soldier Boy,
> Cat Fish, Mr. Clean, Mack Gillim, Joe Simpkin,
> Roy Flowers, Thomas Dobbin, Buick Willie . . .
> They must be tried and sentenced before the judge,
> Mr. Pig Tail at Big Apple, Birdsong, Arkansas.[88]

"Crap" games were played by dropping dice through a "dice horn," a leather bottle with the large end removed and a series of strings stretched across to shake up the dice. It was typical for the owner of the store or house where the games were held to take 10 percent of the bets; in local folklore this was called "pinching the hit."[89] Casual gambling was popular in Lake Village and especially West Memphis, where a flourishing downtown nightlife centered around 7th and 8th streets in the late 1940s. The 7th Street Cafe was a popular eating, drinking, and dancing establishment along a strip separated by one block from gambling joints such as the Silver Moon, BeBop Hall, and the Brown Jug. The locus of the black entertainment district, this strip drew a large part of its clientele from

Memphis. It declined only when the state legislature legalized gambling on dog races at nearby Southland Park.[90]

Another component of Delta folk life that suggested the diverse character of social habits was the existence of whiskey stills, long after the passage of Prohibition. During the 1930s, whiskey making was probably at its peak. "[In] Arkansas County . . . practically every family out in the lake area was, in some way, involved in the moonshine business," recalled a former resident.[91] Small country stores stocked all the necessary supplies to produce sour mash: wooden barrels, kegs, corn chops, and wheat bran. According to one source, the actual process used in the Arkansas County backwoods near Bayou Meto was an informal cooperative: "One man might own a still, and he'd set it up in the deep woods near a little stream, where he would drop a piece of pipe in the water . . . and have all the water he needed. . . . Now maybe a couple of neighbors who want to make some liquor . . . they make a deal with the man who has the outfit set up. They may each set up two or more barrels of mash on their own. . . . The owner of the rig gets every fifth gallon of booze they make. Sorter like sharecroppin'."[92]

In Mississippi County, making whiskey was a wild business. On the isolated islands in the Mississippi River, rugged camps of moonshiners made brews featuring "brand names" of local places and animals. According to legend, a popular brand sold on Island 34 was: "Ike Williams, Pure Old Panther Piss—Distilled and Bottled in Marked Tree, Arkansas." The label featured a panther with its hind leg raised on a bush. Ike Williams, who ran his operation ruthlessly, packed his product in quantities as small as five-gallon milk containers and as large as fifty gallon kegs. But he obviously had a backwoods sense of humor. On one occasion, while showing off his distillery, he found a dead possum in a keg of his brew, and when one of his cohorts proclaimed that it was "too bad that possum ruined all of that whiskey," Ike "grabbed the possum by the tail and flung it out of the barrel and said, 'Auh, it didn't drink much.'"[93]

Whether Delta folks found their sustenance in one of Ike Williams' barrels or preferred the services that churches offered, they all coped, in one way or another, with an environment that could be both kind and cruel. The Arkansas Delta necessarily bred a hearty people whose lives were intimately linked to the region's landscape. If one survived insects, periodic floods, and disease and escaped the attention of a wild animal, then life in the Delta could be filled with wonder and plenty. From the simple pleasures of visiting with friends and neighbors to the more elaborate celebrations connected to national holidays and the appearance of carnivals, circuses, and other traveling troupes, the people of the Arkansas Delta found ways to amuse themselves and to endure.

Street music at West Memphis in Crittenden County, around 1972.
Photo by Eugene Richards from Few Comforts or Surprises. *Courtesy MIT Press.*

A Sunday school picnic at Walnut Ridge in Lawrence County, around 1908. *Courtesy Tom Moore/DCC Archives.*

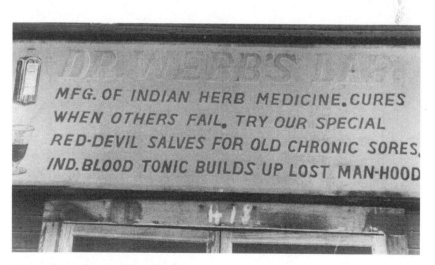

MFG. OF INDIAN HERB MEDICINE. CURES WHEN OTHERS FAIL. TRY OUR SPECIAL RED-DEVIL SALVES FOR OLD CHRONIC SORES. IND. BLOOD TONIC BUILDS UP LOST MAN-HOOD

An outdoor sign in Pine Bluff.
Courtesy Arkansas History Commission.

A baptism, around 1915.
Courtesy Mary Lue Hannon/UALR Archives.

Hauling in a giant White River catfish, around 1971.
Courtesy Boyd Smith/UALR Archives.

Delta Towns:
Their Rise and Decline

CARL H. MONEYHON

The history of the Arkansas Delta with few exceptions has been treated primarily in terms of a rural, agricultural people engaged in exploiting the rich natural resources of the region. Consideration of the area is more likely to prompt images of cotton fields and tenant farmers than towns. To a large degree, this view is an accurate one. Until 1970 the majority of people living in the Delta were rural, and as late as 1950 fewer than 30 percent of the people in the region lived in communities with more than a thousand inhabitants. In earlier years the total numbers and percentages of town dwellers were even smaller. Despite their size relative to the overall population of the Delta, the area's towns have exercised a major role in its history. These urban islands in the midst of a vast rural landscape dominated local economies. Their financial and marketing facilities tied farm and plantation with the outside markets. They were the centers of a thriving lumber industry, as well as numerous other economic enterprises. As a result, some residents amassed considerable wealth, especially relative to that of residents of the countryside, and that wealth allowed them to exert a powerful influence on the culture of their hinterlands. The towns provided the rural peoples of the Delta a window on the development of a more complex modern society.

In their earliest stages of development, the Delta's towns showed little promise of the economic and cultural domination that they would later exercise. The first towns were county court seats, post offices at country crossroads, or shipping points along the area's navigable streams. Of these, the towns along the rivers showed the earliest growth, tying the local economy to the major markets at St. Louis, Memphis, and New Orleans. A host of landings vied with one another to rise to the status of towns and become major shipping points. Along the Mississippi River, Columbia, Gaines Landing, Eunice, Arkansas City, and Helena at one time or another claimed to be a future center of commerce. Napoleon (along the Mississippi at the mouth of the Arkansas River), Arkansas Post, and Pine Bluff all attempted to capture the trade of their surrounding countryside. On the banks of White River, towns developed at St. Charles, Crockett's Bluff, Clarendon, De Valls Bluff, Des Arc, Augusta, and Jacksonport.[1]

A variety of problems restricted early urban growth. The marketing system for antebellum crops and difficulties in controlling the often unmanageable waterways of the region presented major obstacles to development. Of the two, the system of marketing the region's principal cash crop, cotton, probably was the more critical. Antebellum cotton crops were financed primarily through a credit system known as factorage. Large and small planters obtained advances of supplies from large merchants, known as factors, in the major market cities—principally St. Louis, Memphis, and New Orleans. When the crop was harvested, these farmers sold their crops directly through the business houses that had advanced them their supplies. Local merchants had little opportunity to participate in this trade except in providing goods for the small farmers, whose needs and crops did not warrant the attention of the outside houses or justify the services of the agents for the outside factors.[2]

Chronic flooding on the Delta's waterways was not, however, an insignificant problem. As early as the 1840s, town builders constructed levees, but early efforts were usually inadequate. In 1884, a resident of Helena described the levee being built in front of that town as about the size of a "small wagonload of hay." The town's residents dumped their ashes on the levee to increase its height. Such structures presented little resistance to floods, and, as a result, the river towns in the Delta suffered from repeated overflows, consequent destruction of property, and interruption of business activity. The scene described by Mark Twain on his visit to Helena after the 1882 flood could have been used interchangeably to portray any of the other Delta towns at high water. Twain wrote: "In its normal condition it is a pretty town; but the flood (or possibly the seepage) had lately been ravaging it; whole streets of houses had been invaded by the muddy water, and the outsides of the buildings were still belted with a broad stain extending upward from the foundations. Stranded and discarded scows lay all about; plank sidewalks on stilts four feet high were still standing; the broad sidewalks on the ground level were loose and ruinous . . . everywhere the mud was black and deep, and in most places malarious pools of stagnant water were standing."[3]

Movement of the riverbeds also destroyed river towns. Cave-ins along the Arkansas River washed away whole blocks of the original settlement of Pine Bluff in the 1880s. Helena lost its Front Street in the same floods. A slightly different fate befell Arkansas City and Osceola, left stranded when the Mississippi River moved its bed away from their town fronts. The greatest disasters took place when rivers washed away whole towns. Columbia, Eunice, and Napoleon all disappeared into the Mississippi. Mark Twain mourned Napoleon:

> Yes, it was an astonishing thing to see the Mississippi rolling between unpeopled shores and straight over the spot where I used to see a good big self-complacent town twenty years ago. Town that was county seat of a great and important county; town with a big United States Marine hospital; town of innumerable fights— an inquest every day; town where I had used to know the prettiest girl, and the most accomplished in the whole Mississippi Valley; town where we were handed the first printed news of the *Pennsylvania*'s mournful disaster a quarter of a century ago; town no more—swallowed up, vanished, gone to feed the fishes; nothing left but a fragment of a shanty and a crumbling brick chimney![4]

As a result of these economic and natural problems, most of the Delta towns prior to 1870 were little more than villages. The 1870 United States Census listed only one city and nine towns in all of the counties constituting the Delta region. Little Rock was the largest with 12,380 people. Helena was second with 2,249. Pine Bluff had 2,081. The rest were under 1,000. Napoleon, not even listed in the census as a town, was more typical of the ambitious riverside communities. Prior to being washed away, Napoleon never had more than several hundred inhabitants. Even at its height, its business district consisted of a few stores and offices. An Irish immigrant who settled there described it in 1851 as "but very small, containing about 100 inhabitants. It is not a pleasant place to live." It was, however, lively. Despite its ultimate failure, Napoleon would be remembered "as a city where a man inclined towards a game of draw could have his pile covered and raked in; and, if he was disposed to quarrel at the result, could easily find a gentleman who stood in solid with the coroner on whom he could rely as a corpse furnisher."[5]

After the Civil War new conditions removed many of the barriers to the growth of Delta towns and favored their development and expansion. From the 1870s until the 1950s, business opportunities increased, existing towns grew in size, and many new towns appeared. Both old and new imposed their economic and cultural domination on the surrounding countryside. Improvements in the region's transportation system, a change in how cotton planting was supported and marketed, and the development of new economic activities in the Delta fueled the new town life. The years 1870 to 1950 marked the heyday of the Delta town.

The improvement of transportation facilities provided a major boost for Delta towns. Better ties between regional towns and outside markets made it easier for local merchants to compete for the trade of the farmers in their immediate neighborhoods, and in the postwar years river towns tried to obtain expanded and regularized riverboat service with the major cotton markets and northern ports. By the 1870s Pine Bluff, Helena, and Arkansas City had regular passenger and freight service. In 1876 Pine Bluff had weekly service to Memphis on the *Belle of Texas* and biweekly service to Little Rock on the *Pine Bluff*. Later in the century the Arkansas River Packet Company offered Pine Bluff-to-Memphis connections. Helena and Arkansas City had regular service twice a week to Memphis on the boats of the Lee Line. The Anchor Line also provided regular service to the Arkansas ports along the Mississippi River.[6]

One of the best-known packets engaged in the new service to Arkansas towns was the *Kate Adams,* which ran nonstop from Memphis to Helena and then on to Arkansas City twice a week. Popularly known as "The Loving Kate," three different boats used the name. The 1882 vessel had a main cabin, described as one of the most elegant on the river, that was finished in ash, walnut, cherry, mahogany, and bird's eye maple with "appropriate genteel supporting furnishings of culture and refinement." The *Kate Adams* was not only luxurious, it was also speedy, setting the all-time record between Helena and Memphis—five hours, eighteen-and-a-half minutes.[7]

The riverboats improved transportation for the Delta, but the development of the railroads proved even more revolutionary for towns. Until the introduction of railroads, urban growth remained restricted largely to the river towns. Prior to 1889, the trade of Ashley County moved primarily through northern Louisiana river towns—Bastrop, Monroe, and Girard. Since they were unable to provide equally low prices for supplies or the best prices for cotton, the few merchants in Hamburg controlled less than one-third of the local cotton crop. For such merchants, growth required an easier access to goods and markets. The merchants of every crossroads vied with one another for a railroad line that would provide that access.[8]

The first main line through the Delta was completed in 1871 with the opening of the entire road between Memphis and Little Rock. Another main line, from St. Louis to Texarkana, skirted the Delta's northwestern counties by 1874. The 1880s saw a rapid expansion of roads in the Delta region. Ultimately, all of these lines would be consolidated into four principal routes by the 1950s. The Chicago, Rock Island & Pacific (Rock Island) ran on the line from Memphis to Little Rock, with several branches. The St. Louis and South West (Cotton Belt) ran from Clay County to Pine Bluff, with branches into Crittenden and Craighead counties and Little Rock. The St. Louis & San Francisco (Frisco) crossed from Mississippi County into Craighead and then Lawrence counties. The Missouri Pacific was the largest operation with two parallel main lines: one ran from Clay County directly to Little Rock; the other ran from the same county southward toward Helena, then along the western bank of the Mississippi River to the southern border of the state. The Missouri Pacific also developed major branches from Memphis to its main lines and also into the southeastern Delta counties.[9]

As each of these roads developed, the towns along the proposed roadways courted the builders to insure that they would have a station, and disaster awaited the slacker. What could happen to a town that did not secure a road was evident in the fate of Jacksonport in Jackson County. Asked by the builders of the road from St. Louis to Texarkana to provide support for their road, the merchants and political leaders of Jacksonport refused, believing that no road built on the proposed route could afford to go anywhere other than Jacksonport. When the road was built, it ran east of Jacksonport. The result was that Jacksonport quickly died. Its merchants moved to the point where the road crossed the White River and there developed a new town—Newport.[10]

Along the railroad, old towns grew and new towns emerged. Some had existed prior to the coming of the railroad but had not thrived. Jonesboro, in Craighead County, had a population of only about three hundred persons in 1880 with three or four small stores. Jonesboro fell along the routes of several lines completed in the

1880s and by 1889 had an estimated population of over two thousand. Harrisburg, in Poinsett County, was a post office with a general store in 1857. A branch of the Missouri Pacific reached it in 1882. A period of "slow but substantial growth" ended, and, as one observer noted, "its advance has been more rapid."[11]

Typical of the new towns was Brinkley in Woodruff County, which owed its existence almost entirely to the Memphis & Little Rock Railroad, which owned the land, laid it out in 1870, and sold the lots. By 1890 it was a thriving community with many facilities serving the railroads. Paragould was another railroad town, built on lands belonging to the Southwest Improvement Company, a subsidiary of the St. Louis & Southwest Railroad. Not even in existence until 1882, this community within seven years had a population of over a thousand with a bank and the other businesses that marked it as a major town. Cotton Plant and McCrory in eastern Arkansas; Piggott, Corning, and Rector in the northeast; and Dumas, McGehee, Dermott, and Eudora in the southeast were among the towns basically created by the railroads.[12]

The collapse of the antebellum cotton factorage system and its replacement by the crop lien system as the chief means of financing cotton, as well as experiments with the use of free labor, contributed to the development of conditions favoring town growth. By the 1870s, attempts by landowners to restore some sort of gang labor system to Delta cotton lands had been abandoned. Most landowners resorted to renting their land to tenants in return for a share of the crop. Renters were left on their own to secure the advances necessary for a farm year. The only thing the renter usually had to offer as collateral for such advances was another share of the crop, and thus a lien on the crop was offered in return for the advance. This was in a formal sense what antebellum planters had always done informally with their factors. The fragmentation of farm operations into smaller units, however, made the antebellum system of dealing with distant businessmen inefficient and difficult. As a result, "furnishing" merchants and banks emerged to connect tenant farmers and distant capital. The merchants or bankers acquired the goods to be advanced to farmers, then took a lien on the farmer's growing crop to secure payment. Entrepreneurs anxious to take advantage of the new economic opportunities presented by this change in the agricultural economy filled Delta towns.[13]

The development of the new system took place at the same time that cotton production began to recover from the setbacks caused by the Civil War. The amount of cotton produced annually in the Delta showed a steady increase after the mid-1870s. By 1880 the Delta counties harvested more cotton than they had before the war. The 342,124 bales produced that year constituted nearly a 64 percent increase over the 1860 crop. The production of more and more cotton in the Delta remained the basic agricultural trend until the late 1940s and early 1950s. The extent of this increase was evidenced in one of the peak years toward the end of the era when in 1949 the Delta counties produced a crop of 1,410,045 bales.[14]

The new system of supporting and marketing cotton and the steady increase in cotton production produced a parallel growth in the number of merchants and in the size of towns. In northeastern Arkansas by 1889, Blytheville in the center of a rich farm area, with a population of only two hundred, contained three general stores and one business specializing in groceries and provisions. Also in 1889, Harrisburg in Poinsett County, with seven hundred inhabitants, had five general stores. Arkansas City in Desha County, with fewer than seven hundred people, had over forty merchants trying to get a share of the some one hundred thousand bales of cotton passing through the town that year.[15]

The new merchants varied greatly in size and scope. Some concerns were very large and controlled trade over vast areas within the region. Wolff-Goldman of Newport, one of the largest, was described as being a "blend of commissary and supply base for the huge Wolff-Goldman land holdings." Farmers could buy dry goods, groceries, hardware, farm implements, and even "shiny new buggies." The firm also carried on an extensive wholesale trade with the smaller merchants up the White and Black rivers from Newport. McKenzie's General Store, later called Hornor's, at Helena was one of the largest along the Mississippi. It sent buyers to Cincinnati, Memphis, New Orleans, St. Louis, and even New York each year to obtain goods for sale. Farmers came to Helena from throughout eastern Arkansas and western Mississippi to deal with McKenzie's. On the other hand, Krow's General Store at Trenton, a small village of only two stores in Phillips County, carried fewer goods than its larger competitors and specialized primarily in selling to and buying from the farmers of the western part of that county.[16]

Cotton boosted town growth beginning in the 1870s, but new industries and the development of new agricultural products also contributed to this trend after 1870. Some of the new economic developments emerged from the already-existing cotton industry. One of these was the cotton compress industry, which was introduced in the region during the 1880s. Pine Bluff's Warehouse and Compress Company, organized in 1884, was one of the first. The compress reduced the size of ginned bales of cotton by one-half, thus saving space for shipping. These compresses were, however, expensive machines and required large amounts of capital to be constructed. As a result, there were relatively few of them, and they were located centrally in towns. Towns that secured compresses benefited from increased jobs (Pine Bluff's Standard Compress employed as many as forty men in 1897), better payrolls, and the tendency of businesses, gins, and machine shops to locate nearby.[17]

Another industry based upon cotton agriculture was the extraction of cottonseed oil. The process by which this was done had been developed in the 1830s, but a demand for the oil did not appear until the 1870s. The cost of equipment and the need for relatively skilled labor meant that most of the cottonseed mills also were built in towns. As with the compress industry, cottonseed oil plants brought new jobs and good wages to towns. In 1897 the Arkansas Cotton Oil Company at Pine Bluff employed fifty workers at what was then a munificent wage of ten dollars per week. The same year the Pine Bluff Cotton Oil Company was building a mill that promised to employ seventy-five men.[18]

Agricultural diversification in the 1880s and 1890s also affected Delta towns. Declining cotton prices through many of these years led some farmers to experiment with grains and grasses, fruit, and livestock in place of cotton in portions of the Delta. Wheat production led to the development of grist and rolling mills in northeastern Delta counties, although mills also operated at locations as far south as Pine Bluff and England, Arkansas. In 1896 the Jonesboro Roller Mills produced flour that was sold widely under various brand names—Jonesboro Lily, Lady of the Lake, White Wing, and Pride of Jonesboro. Rice cultivation, introduced after 1900, led to the emergence of mills at DeWitt, Lonoke, and Stuttgart. As with compresses and cottonseed mills, the plants to process grain products generally found their homes in towns.[19]

Next to the cotton industry, after the 1870s, the development of lumbering was the most important factor promoting economic expansion. The Delta region was blessed with what, at least in the 1870s, appeared to be unlimited forests. Extensive stands of ash, cypress, gum, oak, and pine existed along the numerous bayous, streams, and swamps of the Delta. The settlers saw the economic possibilities of exploiting this resource immediately. Beginning in the 1830s, they opened up logging operations and built sawmills. Full-scale use of this resource had to wait, however, until the development of better transportation. The railroads filled that need, and by the 1880s the lumber industry was a major part of the Delta economy.[20]

During the 1870s and 1880s, large lumber companies moved into the Delta's hardwood forests. John F. Rutherford's Pine Bluff–based Bluff City Lumber Company, one of the pioneering firms, acquired timberlands in Jefferson, Grant, and Cleveland counties. S. E. Howe, a pioneer in the industry at Helena, opened sawmills at Wabash and Helena and cut timber throughout the region. In the northeastern part of the Delta, Cornelius Dean purchased thousands of acres of timber land, cut the trees, and floated them down the White and Black rivers on rafts to sawmills at Newport. Virgin forests with trees as large as seven feet in diameter made the new lumbermen wealthy.[21]

Processing facilities followed the loggers. Most facilities were located in towns and became important in promoting their growth and prosperity. One of the earliest such plants was Bell & Bocage's Pine Bluff factory, which produced finished sashes, doors, and blinds in the 1860s. During the 1880s plants were built across the Delta. The new companies were large; they did volume business; they dominated some of the communities where they were located. Bluff City Lumber of Pine Bluff, with nearly 250 hands, was the city's second-largest employer. Howe Lumber became a major processor at Helena. Pond & Decker, Remmel & Empie, and C. B. Kelly were the largest employers at Newport. Jonesboro Stave and Jonesboro Wagon also offered a large number of jobs to that town's population. The Northern Ohio Company at Wynne, a major economic force in that community, combined its sawmill and stave plant operations with ginning and farming to control the majority of local jobs. At the height of the industry's development, the Delta's lumber mills produced a wide variety of products—furniture stock, hubs and spokes, veneer, floors, handles, cooperage, boxes, and shingles. Most of these mills produced only roughly finished products, although one firm at Pine Bluff produced fancy lumber, including scroll work and cornice brackets.[22]

The development of the railroads and mills spawned opportunities for machine shops and foundries in Delta towns. The Dilley Foundry Company at Pine Bluff specialized in manufacturing sawmill machinery, but also did general iron casting and foundry work for the community. The Cotton Belt Railroad developed its own shops for the construction and maintenance of engines and cars at Pine Bluff. The Frisco built shops at Brinkley. Acquiring these facilities was a major coup for any town because machine shops attracted other businesses. They also provided more jobs with relatively high wages. At the turn of the century the Cotton Belt's shops employed six hundred men, more than any other business in Pine Bluff. Its skilled laborers earned as much as seventeen dollars per week. The Cotton Belt's facility manufactured anything from flatcars to engines, and one observer promised these would be "in a style of workmanship that competes with the largest railway shops in the North and East." Operations of this magnitude added an important component to any community's economic base.[23]

Ultimately industrial growth between 1870 and 1950 in the Arkansas Delta was tied primarily to cotton culture, lumbering, and transportation. Despite efforts to diversify and especially to attract new industries, there were few changes in the basic components of the area's industrial mix. The emergence of small industries did encourage the expansion of particular towns. Clarendon, Corning, and Newport had pearl button factories that drew on the large supply of mussels in the White River. Helena, Monticello, Paragould, Pine Bluff, and Pocahontas had brick factories. Helena's Staub Pressed Brick Works produced bricks marketed throughout eastern Arkansas, western Mississippi, and northern Louisiana. Paragould had a facility to make clay tile. Though these industries were locally important, they remained only a small part of the total economic activity that infused life into the Delta communities and made possible the overnight transformation of a country crossroad or village into a town and then a city.[24]

As business expanded to support the developing agricultural, lumbering, and transportation components of the economy and as town populations grew, opportunities expanded within the towns, particularly for retail businessmen. A small town such as Jonesboro showed the diversification of business opportunity by 1889. In that year its business district contained a wide variety of retail enterprises—six general stores, ten groceries, eight drug stores, three dry goods stores, one clothing store, one undertaker, and a large number of blacksmiths. A larger town, such as Pine Bluff in 1901, was likely to include artists, cabinetmakers, cigar makers, confectioners, coppersmiths, decorators, dressmakers, florists, glaziers, jewelers, milliners, upholsterers, and watchmakers in addition to the usual businesses. The appearance of such concerns further accelerated the growth of town populations and economic opportunity for the residents.[25]

Opportunities also existed for the establishment of businesses that provided various services, particularly hotels and restaurants. At Pine Bluff, Joe Bone's log cabin with a sleeping room that served as Bone's Hotel in the 1840s had given way to the elegant Planters' House by the 1870s. Jonesboro's Electric Hotel promised its clientele an "elevator, water service, gas pipes, electric call bells, bathrooms, etc." The Hazel Hotel at Newport was a place with "a long front porch on Hazel Street, with rocking chairs and awnings." Its clientele included "permanent lady guests" who sat on the porch to keep "tab on town affairs," and a large number of "drummers." The Planters' in Newport had a less desirable trade. Its rooms were filled with "street carnival people, patent medicine men, second rate drummers, and persons of occupations less definite and decidedly less savory."[26]

Restaurants were generally for out-of-town visitors, but Riley Mahan's Cafe and Cooksey's Cafe in Newport intrigued one young man who remembered them as eating places "with a solid, enduring, and individual smell" coming out of their doors. Many restaurants were associated with hotels. The table at Newport's Hazel was especially popular with salesmen who took rooms there. The cuisine served at the restaurant at Forrest City's Avery Hotel was publicized as "all that can be desired."[27]

Opportunities also existed to make money providing entertainment. Virtually every town had a theater. Helena's Opera House, opened in 1887 and one of the best in the state, was fitted out with a dress circle and boxes. The Malone in Jonesboro claimed to attract "some of the best plays on the road." The Elks and the Orpheo were among the best places to get entertainment at Pine Bluff, offering legitimate theater and vaudeville. Even Newport had an Opera House, although one resident recalled that there were "no toilet facilities of any sort and no stove backstage. On a cold winter night when the curtain went up a heavy blanket of frigid air would roll out over the audience, and the actors would be blue under their grease paint."[28]

Saloons and bawdy houses provided other forms of entertainment in Delta towns. Drinking was a major activity among some inhabitants. In 1876, Pine Bluff's business directory listed fifteen retail liquor establishments for a town of three thousand. Five of the saloons also ran keno games. Perhaps an indication of the encroachment of a more civilized existence in the Delta was the fact that by 1901 Pine Bluff's population had tripled, but the number of saloons had only increased to sixteen. Prostitution was a more unseemly aspect of some towns' entertainment, and in the larger towns it did exist. One resident of Newport remembered "The Houses" located along the river across the railroad tracks from the business district that provided "entertainment" to the accompaniment of the "tinkle of the mechanical pianos."[29]

Newspapers also proliferated as towns grew. Every town worthy of the name had at least a weekly sheet. The number of newspapers appears particularly large given the size of the populations of towns. In 1892, the *Jonesboro Times* and the Craighead County *Sun* provided news to a town with only a little over two thousand people. Pine Bluff, with twenty thousand inhabitants, had two daily and five weekly papers. Papers owned and edited by blacks appeared throughout the Delta, including the *People's Friend* and the *Southern Review* in Helena, the *Enterprise* in Forrest City, the Wynne *Weekly Pilot,* and the *Hornet* in Pine Bluff.[30]

Professionals arrived to take advantage of opportunities presented by the new town frontier. Every community had its share of lawyers, doctors, and dentists. For example, Pine Bluff had thirty practicing attorneys and twenty-four physicians in a population of about nine thousand in 1901.[31]

Blacks had few opportunities as entrepreneurs in banking, the furnishing business, timber, or transportation. A major exception was Wiley Jones, who owned the Unity Bank & Trust Company and a streetcar company in Pine Bluff. There were greater possibilities, however, for black ownership of retail and service businesses. There were some black professionals as well. In Pine Bluff in 1901, four of the thirteen barbershops, nineteen of seventy-four groceries, four of fourteen butcher shops, three of eight boot and shoe shops, and one of sixteen saloons were owned by blacks. The greatest opportunity for blacks to own their own businesses in Pine Bluff appears to have been in the restaurant trade, where twelve of the twenty-three restaurants operating in the town were black-owned. At the same time, the town had three black attorneys and three black doctors.[32]

The growth of the local agricultural economy, new industries, and new opportunities for businessmen and professionals attracted more and more people to the towns and cities of the Delta after the

1870s and produced a transformation of the sleepy communities that had existed. The Delta, in fact, experienced a virtual urban explosion. While there had been only two towns in the region in 1870 with a population of over a thousand people, there were fourteen by 1890. Slow growth during the next decade meant that the number of such towns increased only to nineteen by 1900, but another spurt produced an additional fourteen during the next decade. Between 1910 and 1940 the number of towns with a population of over a thousand increased from thirty-three to fifty-three. Representing a little less than 2 percent of the population in the Delta counties in 1870, townspeople constituted over 20 percent of the population by 1940.[33]

Overall population figures showed a growth rate of 380 percent for towns between 1870 and 1940 compared to a growth rate of 233 percent for urban and rural areas combined. Statistics for individual towns showed even more remarkable increases. Pine Bluff, one of the two towns with more than 1,000 people in 1870, grew from 2,081 to 21,290, a rate of 923 percent. Blytheville, not even in existence in 1870, had become the second-largest town in the Delta by 1940 with a population of 10,652. Jonesboro, also not a town in 1870, had become the third-largest town with a total of 10,326 inhabitants in 1940.[34]

The Delta towns that mushroomed between 1870 and 1940 differed in many ways from the surrounding countryside. First of all, a remarkable homogeneity characterized town society. One Delta resident observed this phenomenon when he wrote of his hometown: "Brinkley had few extremes of riches and poverty." The writer suggested that he had grown up in what was practically a classless society.[35] Such an observation was obviously an exaggeration. There were poor people in every town. Race was one line that helped set apart the poor, but there were always white families and individuals living in poverty as well. On the other hand, the real lower class of the community often lived outside the town limits. Farmers and laborers in the countryside made up much of this class. The populations of towns were disproportionately white. The townspeople were bound together by occupation and ideas. There were internal differences, of course, but the most dramatic differences were between the people in the towns and those outside. Such conditions produced a community in which extremes of wealth did seem minimal.

The base upon which social homogeneity within the towns rested was the common economic interests of the majority of the population. Most businessmen were involved in some sort of commercial rather than industrial activity. Even workers were primarily part of the commercial world. Into the twentieth century such people were considered to be apprentice businessmen who were learning the practices and values that would ultimately allow them to go into business for themselves rather than remain members of a permanent wage-earning work force. The businessmen's statistical dominance of the population may be seen in Pine Bluff in 1901. Even though that city had a substantial industrial component in its economy that employed white workers, over 62 percent of all workers were white-collar components in the commercial class—bookkeepers, clerks, buyers, foremen, and managers. In towns without any industrial base the proportion of the population that could be considered part of the commercial business class probably would have been even larger.[36]

The only basis for this social homogeneity was work, because the populations of the towns came from a wide variety of regional, social, and economic backgrounds. Newport in 1895 attests to the diverse geographic origins that characterized the business community. Alongside many older merchants, there were also numerous recent arrivals. If there were southerners who had served with the Confederacy, there were also northerners who had fought for the Union. Capt. W. A. Joyce, in the drug business, was the dean of Newport's local merchants. A steamboat captain who had located in the town in its earliest stages, he was proclaimed "one of the 'oldest inhabitants.'" Such early settlers were the majority in the community and had owned businesses either in Jacksonport or Newport for many years. Newcomers, however, were readily accepted into the business community. Some could be accepted easily, such as the businessman-planter Capt. V. Y. Cook, "an officer in the Confederate army and . . . an ardent defender of his native State, Kentucky, and his adopted State, Arkansas." George W. Goddard, owner of the Planters' Hotel, however, had moved to the area from Kansas, where he had served in the quartermaster corps of the Union army.[37]

The members of the business class varied widely in their social and economic origins, and these differences were also apparent among the businessmen of Newport. John W. Wallace, a dry goods merchant who had been born and reared in Jackson County, was the son of a well-to-do slaveowning planter family. His qualifications for being a businessman, however, were that he had "gained his knowledge of business by years of service with the best firms in his native city. . . . He by hard work and honest methods has built up a fine trade." Adam Bach represented a completely different background. When he arrived at Jacksonport from Germany, via Indiana, he had been a "poor boy." Again, the proper behavior had gained success for him. "Today," an observer noted in 1895, "he owns one of the finest grocery stores in the State, and his success has been gained by years of hard work and perseverance." Despite such differences, townspeople were linked together, not by where they had come from, but by where they were going and by their belief that they could accomplish economic success.[38]

What the business class shared ultimately was an outlook born of their commercial interests—a business culture. They knew that they were different from the rural folks. They thought that they possessed modern ideas and believed that they were capable of making the Delta into a better place, not just for themselves but for others. Each town produced publications between 1890 and 1910 that extolled its particular virtues, but also implicit in these materials were the ideas and attitudes of its local business community—ideas that reflected local businesses' culture and that would presumably insure their success. The program of Pine Bluff's first annual fair in 1897 pointed to its businessmen who, while "unusually prosperous and enterprising," were "by no means satisfied with present conditions and are ever ready to lend a helping hand to any business enterprise . . . calculated to ultimately redound to the benefit of their city and section." The businessmen of Marvell made it "the hustlingest little town that ever started out to do business." Its "live people are not afraid to tackle any kind of proposition. They are noted, in fact, for their ability and disposition to do their own thinking along business, manufacturing, political and social lines." The message was simple—change and openness to change, plus modern business thought, insured prosperity for all.[39]

The description of such characteristics, provided by the booster literature, offered a catalogue of the ideas and behavior the business class considered essential for success. Business acumen and "modern" business attitudes were obviously important. R. J. Johnson, cashier at the Bank of Newport, was described as being young, but as one who enjoyed the reputation of being among the most "conservative, far-seeing and shrewd financiers of the age." Samuel L. Cooke, cashier of the Bank of Marvell, in Phillips County, was "level-headed and capable." J. W. Grubbs of the Newport Milling Company was a "young business man of energy and push."[40]

The businessmen's culture also idealized a sense of civic duty. Business people identified themselves with their town and its progress. A Newport booster pamphlet praised "Bunk" McCauly and Henry Bordwell, wholesale and retail liquor and cigar dealers, as being "identified with all the improvements of the city, contributing with a liberal hand to all public enterprises." The owner of the Remmel & Empie Lumber Works was a "progressive businessman," who possessed "an abiding faith in the continued prosperity of Newport."[41]

The business class not only transformed Delta communities economically but also constituted a major force in promoting modernization of the towns. Equating progress with modernization, members of the business class paid particular attention to public services that made their towns look up-to-date. Helena and Pine Bluff led the way with modern gas lighting in the 1870s. Helena won the race to acquire electric lighting when in 1888 the Van Depole Electric Manufacturing Company began producing power to light the business houses of the town. Other towns were not far behind. Helena and Pine Bluff also led the way with telephones. A company opened in Helena in 1880, and the first at Pine Bluff started operations three years later with forty subscribers. Improved water and sewer systems were seen as the mark of a "good" town, and in the 1880s most communities built them. Pine Bluff inaugurated its municipal water system in 1887, building water pressure with pumps run by a steam engine. Helena offered its residents municipal water in 1894, using a gravity system to maintain pressure in its lines. The larger towns began to operate professional fire departments by the 1890s, and most started professional police departments at the same time. Another critical improvement was some form of transportation. Both Helena and Pine Bluff inaugurated mule-drawn streetcar systems in the 1880s, then replaced them with electric trolleys in the 1900s. Pine Bluff's Citizens Light and Transit System started lines in that town in 1902 that continued to operate into the 1930s. In 1909 electric cars were placed in service in Helena along a line built to connect Helena with its suburb West Helena.[42]

Modern schools also reflected the character of a city and attracted the backing of the business class. A program printed for the 1897 Pine Bluff Fair asserted: "No city in the country has better public and private schools than Pine Bluff." Even boosters of the town of Marvell promised a public school that was "one of the best to be found in any community." Although schools were racially segregated, schools for blacks were generally considered to be important too. Pine Bluff businessmen proudly pointed out the educational opportunities for blacks in their town—Merrill Public School, the Colored Industrial Institute run by the Catholic Sisters of Charity, the Richard Allen Institute operated by Presbyterians, and the Branch Normal College, which was part of the Arkansas Industrial University.[43]

Beginning in the 1870s, public schools attracted increasing community support, even though private schools continued to flourish into the twentieth century. Much community support focused on improved facilities; substantial buildings were equated with good schooling. After opening a new brick schoolhouse, costing thirteen thousand dollars, at Newport, local boosters concluded that there could be no questions but that the town had lived up to the "motto of Arkansas that 'A well educated child is the best legacy possible to leave to the State.'" Notwithstanding their emphasis on bricks and mortar, community leaders supported and appreciated the academic work. The curriculum for most students was simple, but one considered essential to the operation of a "progressive" community. Mathematics, spelling, and English grammar filled the school day, and outstanding achievement in these areas was highly desired by businessmen who provided prize money for those who achieved the greatest success.[44]

Churches also figured in calculations about the progressiveness of a town. The Pine Bluff Fair program proclaimed: "Pine Bluff is a city of churches as well as schools, and her citizens are noted for the pride they take in their religious, as well as their educational, industrial, and financial institutions." The number of churches and the variety of religions were sources of particular pride. Methodist and Baptist churches were always more numerous, but town boosters pointed out the presence of Episcopal and Catholic churches as well. Three Delta communities also possessed Jewish congregations—Pine Bluff's Anshe Emeth, formed in 1858, Helena's Beth El, formed in 1867, and Jonesboro's Temple Israel, formed in 1898. Variety indicated modernity. Even the church buildings demonstrated a city's progress. Pine Bluff boasted of its First Presbyterian and Main Street Methodist churches as examples of "modern architectural design, . . . [that] would reflect credit upon much larger and wealthier cities."[45]

Secular architecture also mirrored a town's success. Businessmen proudly attached tin fronts to their wooden buildings to give them the appearance of multiple stories and to suggest that they were constructed of stone or other permanent materials. When a genuine stone or brick building was put up, it was greeted as the mark of real achievement. The pinnacle for any town was the construction of the first commercial building of more than two or three stories or, perhaps, the construction of the first elevator building.[46] In the same manner, homes demonstrated the prosperity of the town. Homes were a clear sign of accomplishment, and throughout the Delta businessmen engaged in an orgy of elaborate and ornate construction in the 1880s and 1890s that created neighborhoods, many still existing, that showed the aspirations of their residents. The display extended from the exterior to the interior. One such home at Newport, destroyed in a 1926 fire, showed the ostentatiousness of the business class. It was described as having "all the roominess and comfort of that generous period. The most notable feature of this old house, aside from the superb trees growing around it, was the oak woodwork. The parquet floor in the big entrance hall and the staircase with its elaborately turned balusters and newels and paneled sides were really fine." Such commodious homes were presumably tangible evidence of progress.[47]

The townspeople showed their achievements in other ways as well. Town-sponsored baseball teams were a particular point of pride for many residents. Brinkley's baseball team attracted large crowds and general interest, especially when a team from Clarendon was the opposition. The economic rivalry between Newport and Batesville was carried to the playing fields. One resident of Batesville remembered that local citizens considered Newport to be iniquitous, sunk in a swamp, and its people light-minded. The people of Newport thought those of Batesville purse-proud and stuffy, with "a touch of raw hillbilly." Every summer their hostilities were vented on the baseball field. Later some of this town spirit was redirected to school football, track, and even basketball. The ability of one town's team to beat that of another, however, remained an important part of civic pride.[48]

The presence of clubs, often with the purposes of providing entertainment, increasing public awareness of important issues, or aiding in civic development, was another important outgrowth of the culture of the business class. Every town had its local organizations. Osceola had a Literary and Dramatic Association that put on plays and sponsored debates. Jonesboro had its Twentieth Century Club, the Round Dozen, the Smart Set, and the Harmony Whist Club for Jews. In addition, almost every town possessed branches of the Catholic Knights, Elks, Knights of Honor, Knights of Pythias, Masons, Odd Fellows, Red Men, United Workmen, and Woodmen of the World as well as a host of local clubs and branches of national organizations for women.[49]

The businessmen who dominated the Delta's towns believed themselves not only able to control their own economic destinies, but also capable of directing those of their towns in every way. The town was their kingdom. Albert A. Hornor remembered that his father, S. H. Hornor, who was from an old planter family, had been a merchant and later president of the Bank of Helena, was interested in every industry that came to Helena and each Sunday took his children on walks through the town to see the community's progress. Horner also "had made it a rule to invest in every new industry that came to Helena." Bettering the community was a cardinal principle for Delta business people.[50]

Local businessmen considered themselves community leaders. Perhaps nothing revealed their self-appointed role more than their attire. Indisputably their dress set them apart from the rural folks who were their chief customers, and their clothes reflected their wealth and their urban station in life. More or less typical was a drugstore operator in Brinkley who always wore a suit to work, including a gold chain across his vest, even though he usually worked in his shirt-sleeves. The cashier at the Brinkley bank wore black, detachable sleeves at work. At Newport, businessmen usually had their suits made to order by a local tailor or in Little Rock or St. Louis. Regular business dress, even in the Delta heat, was a suit of thick, dark cloth, usually with a vest and white starched shirts with high collars. In the summer this might be changed a bit with a lighter alpaca coat, perhaps a suit of seersucker. By the 1920s linen suits had also become part of the summer uniform.[51]

The business class that emerged in Delta towns was much the same as that class elsewhere in the nation. In the Delta, however, some southern ideas persisted and made the town and its culture distinctly southern. This exceptionalism, evident in ideas about family, religion, and race, gave the Delta town a unique character.

Family life in many towns elsewhere in the nation was becoming increasingly defined in terms of the nuclear family. In the Delta towns the presence among the business leadership of many people who had emerged locally, often from agricultural interests, and who were likely to have family members present in the vicinity meant that the extended family continued to be important in these communities. One brother might work in town, but his other siblings might well remain on neighboring farms. Neill Phillips captured the continuity of an older lifestyle when he recalled of his youth in Newport: "Cousins, nephews and nieces of various degrees of relationship lived up and down the two streets, so that we were a sort of tribal encampment." Phillips' Aunt Jo was the *mater familias*, "a shuttle moving through the family and holding it together by her love and her absorbing interest in all of us. She counted that day wasted during which she had not visited the house of every relation, picking up and distributing all of the family news."[52]

Among the business class the role of women closely approximated that of middle-class women elsewhere in the nation. Their place was in the home where they were to be the ideal wife and mother. In this role they attended to household business, usually assisted, even in the less wealthy families, by cooks, washerwomen, and maids employed from the black population. The son of a druggist's family from Brinkley remembered that his mother subscribed to journals providing instructions on how to be a better housewife such as *The Ladies Home Journal* and *The Key to the Home*. Young women might work in local stores as clerks or as secretaries. Teaching was another possibility. Once married, however, the woman was expected to take over supervision of the household and rear the children. Reflecting the society's agrarian roots, a woman was also to perform the duty of Neill Phillips' Aunt Jo—to insure the continuity of the family's connections with all of its various parts.[53]

Religion also remained a more vital part of the life and culture of the Delta town's business class than it was among its counterparts elsewhere in the nation. Sidney H. Hornor of Helena was joined each Sunday at breakfast by other local businessmen before his men's Sunday School class—a class presided over by Judge James Hanks. At breakfast the men seriously discussed Biblical issues, along with cotton prices, high water, and levees. Hornor and his wife read a Bible chapter and prayed each morning after breakfast before he walked downtown to his bank. Religion did provide Delta women with one major means of acting in the community outside of the family. Through home missionary societies and the ladies' aide societies of various denominations, some women played central roles in the distribution of charities within the towns. While the urban setting produced greater religious diversity, the overwhelming predominance of evangelical Protestantism, especially Baptists and Methodists, in towns reflected their southern location.[54]

The South's basic view of blacks as unequal also survived among the business class. This meant that generally blacks were seldom considered when these people thought of community interests. Although blacks were a part of the consciousness of these people, nowhere in their memoirs or reminiscences do the great mass of black men and women appear. As a result, towns developed in which great disparities existed between the wealth and the living conditions of the two races. Whites, however, took this as the natural way of things.[55]

Despite the obliviousness of the white businessmen to the needs or even the presence of blacks or poor whites, both were there. A few blacks early appropriated the ethic and values of the dominant group, and within the various local black communities a "black bourgeoisie" developed, even though it was very small. In Pine Bluff in 1901 about 10 percent of the black population consisted of this class of independent businessmen or tradesmen and professionals. At the top were men such as Wiley Jones, who had risen from baker to saloon keeper to banker, real estate man, and owner of a streetcar company. The group also included young lawyers, doctors, and teachers. Despite the small size of this elite group, town life made possible a lifestyle different from that of the great mass of black urban and rural laborers.[56]

In many ways the lifestyle of the black bourgeoisie resembled that of their white counterparts. They supported community improvements, especially those that contributed to their own status and welfare. They backed elementary and secondary education and the few colleges available to them. They created their own churches and developed their own clubs, such as the Knights of Honor, Knights of Phythias, Daughters of Rebecca, and United Brothers of Tabor. They were not, however, ever accepted as equals by the white class whose lifestyle they attempted to emulate.[57]

Poor whites and the majority of blacks had little voice in the development of the towns in which they lived, although they were obviously essential to economic development. Without workers, especially black workers, the system run by the white business class would not have operated. The power of the white business class, however, was overwhelming. The lives of laborers, often recent immigrants from the surrounding farms, remain largely undocumented. Their attitudes and values probably had changed little from those they held in the countryside. Their lifestyles were probably little changed either. They now rented houses owned by a townsman rather than a rural landlord; they possessed few material goods and lived day-to-day often just a step from desperate circumstances.[58]

Towns had problems, but overall they were centers of prosperity, and their residents were well off compared to the people of the countryside. Prosperity produced in the town a cultural life quite different from that of the countryside. Between 1870 and 1940 the Delta's towns appeared to have been oases of pleasure and excitement in contrast to the drab existence in the surrounding agrarian world. The town was the theater of the business interests, a stage upon which to demonstrate the unique advantages of trading with Brinkley rather than Wynne, with Pine Bluff rather than Newport. For the country folk and for the townspeople alike, the Delta towns achieved a liveliness that today we associate primarily with only the largest of cities.

In part, the trinkets offered in drugstores and the bustle of the town itself were enough to set the town off from the countryside. The port towns had ready-made excitement each day with the arrival and departure of the boats from the landing. George John Ryan captured the excitement of the port at Pine Bluff in 1861, recalling "the levee and high bluffs were covered with people, black and white, all in Sabbath attire, and seeming quite interested in the boat's arrival. Quite a number of gentlemen came aboard and shook hands cordially with the officers of the vessel, and with many of the passengers, who proved to be Pine Bluffians returning from business and pleasure trips. After the friendly greetings, New Orleans and Memphis papers were inquired for, and eagerly taken. . . . In the meantime, hotel porters came aboard and took possession of the baggage that had to be left at port, and the boat's crew commenced discharging freight, from the hurricane deck." As long as the boats landed, the river towns could be assured of a crowd, even if only of children, to watch such exciting proceedings.[59]

The railroads added their own brand of excitement. For children and the country folks, a visit to the station or to the rail yards was an adventure. One man remembered the Pine Bluff of his youth: "My young life was a continuing experience of excitement as I listened to the engines blow their ear-splitting signals, and the 'chug-chug' of the steam locomotives seemed literally to come through the middle of the house." Brinkley was no less exciting. One resident recalled that "noise was an outstanding feature of life in Brinkley. There were three railroads, and bells clanged and whistles blew and freights banged through the town at all hours of the night."[60]

The din produced by the country trade that arrived on weekends added to the appearance that something was happening in town. Each weekend, especially after the crop was in or in the summer after the crop had been laid by, farmers and their families flocked to the towns. At Helena they camped in tents and in their wagons along the levee. One inhabitant of Newport recalled that in 1900 the town "was livelier . . . than it is now. The sidewalks were thronged not only with the townspeople but also with a sizeable transient population: gamblers, drummers, cotton buyers, and people brought in by trade and pearl fishing on the river, by traveling shows, and by the fact that the town was a railroad center in those days when freight did not whisk through by truck." The center of activity was in the business district where the "curb was blocked solidly with teams and wagons, the wagons packed with cotton bales if it were the fall of the year, the cotton buyers moving among them on foot, examining the length and quality of the staple and making their bids. . . . All the stores and sidewalks were jammed with country people, white and black, doing their marketing and enjoying a dash of town life."[61]

Such people found much to occupy them, for local merchants and traveling shows were ready to earn what change they might have. Vaudeville shows, such as Frank Davidson and His Famous Company, appeared at local theaters. Jewell Kelly and his company featured "singing comedians" Marvin and Rogus, the dancing of Miss Cressida Canada, and "illustrated songs and movies." Legitimate theater companies put on productions based upon popular stories and current novels. In 1907, productions at Jonesboro's Malone Theater included "Buster Brown" and "Sherlock Holmes." The Newport Opera House had "The Klansman," "Babes in Toyland," and "The Wizard of Oz."[62]

One form of entertainment, a peculiar product of southern culture, also made the rounds of the Delta towns, namely minstrel shows. Al G. Fields Minstrels, Richard & Pringle's Famous Georgia Minstrels, the Dandy Dixie Minstrels, and Cotton Pickers Band were typical of the touring companies. They either put on shows in theaters or threw up their own tents. A parade in the afternoon before the show was designed to drum up business, but it also added to the appeal of the town. One group that appeared at Newport saw "the performers dressed in top hats and red or green frock coats marching in smart military style down the middle of the street. . . . The resplendent brass band knocked out stirring tunes and the whole atmosphere was very cheery and lively." The evening show featured an interlocutor, blackfaced comedians, dancers, singers, a chorus, and the band with songs, dances, jokes, and acts. The jokes were always "immaculately clean, and ponderously and ceremoniously brought out by the interlocutor's courtly efforts."[63]

Some minstrel shows actually were staged by blacks, usually for predominantly black audiences. On such occasions, the town's black population turned out "one hundred per cent to see the parade and the strutting drum major." The show was similar to that of the white minstrels—songs, dances, jokes, and acts. The only difference was the tendency of many of these shows to rely on the tried and true, jokes everyone knew and songs that the audience could sing along with. The music, one white observer noted, was the "forerunner of the blues. . . . It had a haunting, atavistic quality that greatly appealed to the colored population."[64]

On the river, showboats added another variety of entertainment. Most of these operated out of Cincinnati. They announced their appearance with a calliope, which one river town resident remembered "sounded better a mile away than nearby." Tying up for several days or a week, the showboats brought minstrel shows, vaudeville, and even dancing and gambling to the inhabitants of the river towns and attracted customers from throughout the surrounding countryside.[65]

Circuses also made the rounds, and some of the best circuses in the country played in Delta towns. Newport had visits from Ringling Brothers, Sells-Floto, Barnum & Bailey, Hagenbeck-Wallace, and the 101 Ranch Wild West Show. The circuses often timed their visits to coincide with harvest time, when the farmers had money to spend. One resident of Helena recalled that the circus was the greatest fun his mother had each year; she took the children but enjoyed "every clown, lion, elephant and acrobat" herself. Rural folks could literally "see the elephant"—that is, encounter the unknown—in the Delta town.[66]

Entertainment did not have to be so professional. When the first automobiles were introduced at Brinkley, an enterprising showman erected a tent and placed a sign that said "See the Horseless Carriage" upon it. People lined up, paid a quarter, then entered the tent to find a buggy hitched to a team of mules. No one who had been gulled disclosed the joke, but left to stand around the rest of the day to watch others being taken in.[67]

At the end of each day, when the money in the hands of would-be purchasers was gone, the hustle and bustle of town life came to an end. Although most people went home, the saloons continued to sell their wares into the night. One resident of Newport remembered Saturday and Sunday afternoons when "long lines of wagons, their loads of corn and cotton converted into store-bought goods would begin streaming out of town, drivers soused with Bourbon whiskey bawling and swearing at their teams and at each other, while their women folk, jolting as usual on splint bottomed chairs set in the wagon beds, patiently accepted in a matter of fact way this normal ending to Saturday in town."[68]

All this came to an end in the 1940s. The continued growth of the Delta's towns was limited by the agricultural economy and the lumber industry. Both changed in the 1940s, leaving the towns without the economic base that had produced their expansion. Mechanization and the use of insecticides and fertilizers were central to agricultural change. For the landowner the results were startling. In 1928, farms in Phillips County produced 151 pounds of cotton per acre. The introduction of tractors, insecticides, fertilizers, and, in 1945, the first mechanical cotton picker caused a revolution in production. By 1955, the same Phillips County farms were growing 629 pounds of cotton per acre. At the same time, fewer agricultural workers were needed to produce the results. Tenants and laborers were displaced from the countryside, thereby removing the consumers who had contributed to the economic life of the towns. Many of these people moved first to a nearby town, but this was often only a first step in their journey out of the county and out of the Delta.[69]

The introduction of new crops that were more easily cultivated with machinery and which proved more profitable than cotton also revolutionized the economy of the Delta and undermined the towns. Rice culture, already in existence in Arkansas, Lonoke, and Prairie counties, spread elsewhere in the Delta, particularly in the northeastern section. Soybean farming became general through the region, and the price of this crop, especially resulting from the demand for oil during World War II, led many farmers to shift completely from cotton to soybeans. In some areas, a growing beef cattle industry, which required fewer hands per acre, displaced staple crops as a primary activity. This industry further accelerated the movement of the people who had been farming the staples as tenants and share-croppers from the Delta.[70]

The lumber industry did not change; it died. What originally appeared to be unlimited forests of hardwood trees proved illusionary. Mills closed and jobs disappeared. Leaders in the timber industry shifted to new products. Pine forests were planted to replace the hardwoods, but much of the wood was used in the production of paper or sawed into building materials. Highly specialized paper production was concentrated in only a few locations. Mills producing building products generally did not require the same number of hands that had been used in the more specialized earlier operations. The result was a reduction in jobs that further eroded the economic base of Delta towns.[71]

Improvement in transportation also undermined the economic role of these towns, especially in the 1950s, with the expansion and improvement of the state's highways. The state had begun to support road construction in the region in 1911, but no real progress was made on this system until after the beginning of the federally supported Interstate Highway System and renewed state efforts in the 1950s. These highways allowed many of the functions of the Delta's towns to be done elsewhere. Larger regional centers developed to provide services ranging from shipping to medical treatment. The small town was no longer needed.[72]

Changes in entertainment further threatened urban economies. Live theaters began to give way to motion pictures in the 1920s. Motion pictures still attracted people to towns, but their importance was relatively short lived. Radio was already shifting entertainment into the home. Television in the 1950s made that transition complete. Motion picture theaters had often gone the way of the live theaters by the 1950s. Accompanying their decline were the dwindling crowds in town seeking entertainment. In their absence, the restaurants, the soda fountains, and all of the other retail businesses that profited from the presence of town crowds gradually disappeared as well.[73]

As a whole, the changes that took place destroyed the economies that had made possible the rapid growth and prosperity of each of the Delta towns. From the 1940s to the present, some of the Delta towns continued to grow. In 1970, for the first time the town population of the Delta was larger than the rural population. But the growth was at a slower rate than in previous decades. During the 1970s overall county growth in the area was actually greater than that of the towns.[74]

To survive, most of the towns desperately sought new economic activities to sustain their existence. Retailing never fully recovered, but some of the larger towns were able to attract new industries, including some which employed skilled workers with good wages. Pine Bluff secured the National Cancer and Toxicological Research Center, the Pine Bluff Arsenal, and International Paper Plant. Jonesboro proved particularly successful, acquiring companies such as the American District Telegraph Company, Arkansas Glass Container, Colson, and a General Electric motor plant. Though less successful, Helena nonetheless attracted Bobbie Brooks, Allied Chemicals, and, for a time, Mohawk Rubber. Many of the smaller towns had to settle for clothing factories that employed minimally skilled laborers at low wages.[75]

Changes in the economic mix of the communities produced different societies. With the opportunities for retail profits reduced, many towns lost the wealthier commercial and professional components of their population. This loss left control of the towns, to some degree, in the hands of the landowners and larger farmers; some of the latter moved into town with the improvements in transportation. The majority of townspeople, however, were those displaced from the farm who for many different reasons chose not to leave the area and who sought whatever jobs were available in the towns. This change in population drastically diminished the wealth of the towns, and, consequently, much of the culture that had existed during their heyday. By the 1970s, most of the towns could have been easily mistaken for the same-sized town anywhere else in the nation. The business class, its culture, and the lifestyle that had made the towns unique, was gone.[76]

In the end, the Delta town and its culture reached their peak as the result of the peculiar relationship that existed between it and the countryside in the period of its greatest growth, from 1870 to 1940. One individual who grew up in Newport during the 1900s provides a metaphor that captures to some extent that relationship. Trying to describe what made that town so unique, he could find "no natural physical charms to make us love the place so much, except for a certain lushness of vegetation due to the rich swampy soil, and the fine trees." What he saw, however, was a town "as flat then as it is now and as constricted, with the countryside abruptly shut out by the surrounding swamps and levees; faintly like a medieval European town with the levee representing the outer wall, the swamps and river in place of a moat, and the courthouse the dominating castle." He could have taken the metaphor even further. The businessman of Delta towns, between 1870 and 1940, in a manner reminiscent of the medieval lord and merchant, extracted his living from that surrounding countryside. Like those medieval counterparts, the wealth received made possible a world that was prosperous and filled with a culture distinct from that of the rural world around it.[77]

Helena's Miller Hotel and Cafe, around 1909.
Courtesy Phillips County Historical Museum.

The *Kate Adams* riding near the top of the Mississippi River levee during high water.   *Courtesy Burt Jaeger and Loerena Connaway/UALR Archives.*

E. Ritter and Company mercantile establishment, Marked Tree (Poinsett County). E. Ritter is standing behind the counter with suit and tie and hat.   *Courtesy E. Ritter and Company, Marked Tree, Arkansas.*

Patterson mercantile establishment, Osceola (Mississippi County).
Courtesy City of Osceola, mayor's office, Osceola, Arkansas.

Horses pulling car out of the water.
From Elliott B. Sartain, It Didn't Just Happen *(Osceola, Ark: Drainage District No. 9, 1975), 24. Courtesy Grassy Lake and Tyronza Drainage District No. 9.*

The Plantation Heritage:
Agriculture in the Arkansas Delta

DONALD HOLLEY

In the early nineteenth century, pioneer farmers settled in the river bottoms of eastern Arkansas and carved out plantations and small farms, using slave labor to grow cotton. So began a long struggle to cultivate the Arkansas Delta—a struggle that required controlling floods, draining swamps, and clearing the land. Over the next 175 years, the Delta witnessed the rise and fall of plantation agriculture with its voracious need for cheap labor; the agonizingly slow emergence of mechanized agriculture; and, finally, the rise and fall of King Cotton, as rice and soybeans emerged as major crops.

Around the world, the plantation as a mode of agricultural production rose in undeveloped areas where a staple crop was grown on a large scale. A plantation economy was one in which farmers produced a crop for an external market, but large-scale production required the use of more workers—and cheaper workers—than were freely available. As a result, some nonmarket mechanism was used to secure a sufficient supply of workers, often a labor surplus.[1] This was exactly the situation in the Arkansas Delta throughout the nineteenth century and the first half of the twentieth century.

The central theme of Delta agriculture has been exploitation—master, landlord, and merchant exploited slave, sharecropper, and day laborer, and all exploited the land. The Delta has always meant rich land and poor people. Before the Civil War, black slaves were the source of the cheap, docile labor that plantation agriculture required. After the war, sharecropping replaced slavery, and in time more and more whites were drawn into tenancy. In a cashless economy, merchants furnished tenants with credit and took a lien on their share of the crop. The crop-lien system trapped many farmers in debt and kept them in a dependent position.

The plantation system emerged and prospered in the ante-bellum period, transformed itself in the aftermath of Civil War as it continued its hold on the region, but finally collapsed in the social and economic upheavals of the Great Depression and World War II. The contemporary Delta, still a contradiction between rich and poor, is a product of its plantation heritage.

Today we know the Arkansas Delta as an open, relatively flat region with a green blur of timber on the horizon—a sight totally different from what the Delta looked like in the early nineteenth century. When the first pioneer farmers entered the Mississippi River Valley, they found a formidable and forbidding world of dense forests and swamps that evoked a primeval quality. The original Delta was a land of enormous stands of oak, gum, cotton-wood, hickory, pecan, elm, pine, and cypress. Many of these trees had grown to enormous size, and some had stood for perhaps five hundred years. This wilderness contained large, impenetrable cane-brakes and areas of thick vines that made passage difficult. Large tracts of overflowed lands and permanent swamps also impeded cultivation. The long and arduous struggle to clear and drain the land for cultivation challenged even the strongest, and only a few achieved the promise of rich rewards.[2]

The Arkansas Delta consists of a series of river basins that empty into the Mississippi: the St. Francis, the White, and the Arkansas. Many smaller streams, bayous, and sloughs form their own rich bottomland. In annual floods, these streams have left behind a rich alluvial soil, running at places to a depth of a hundred feet. This soil-building process dates back thousands of years. The soil types range from a rich sandy loam to sticky buckshot.

The Louisiana Purchase of 1803 brought Arkansas into the United States. The westward movement of explorers, fur trappers, and pioneer farmers soon began, and their numbers increased as Arkansas gained territorial status in 1819 and statehood in 1836. This westward movement in the first half of the nineteenth century brought pioneer farmers from Tennessee, Mississippi, and other eastern states. More than 90 percent of the settlers came from the old slave states.[3]

The different social and economic traditions of the highlands and lowlands emerged early. The earliest stream of emigration favored the northern and western sections of Arkansas, shunning the bottomlands along the Mississippi River. Before 1830, the counties in northern Arkansas, despite their remote location, experienced the greatest population growth. The earliest pioneers moved into the Ozarks and Ouachitas, seeking familiar hill farms. Many people avoided bottomlands, which they associated with malaria and flooding.[4]

After 1830, the population movement increasingly focused on the Delta. In 1832 the Little Rock *Arkansas Gazette* observed:

> While the tide of emigration is setting so fast toward the newly-acquired country to the west, it is gratifying to be able to state, that almost every other section of our Territory is receiving a steady accession to its strength. . . . The counties bordering on the Mississippi are rapidly settling, as are those on the White River and its tributaries; and the southern counties are receiving their share from the emigrants daily passing through our town, and crossing the Arkansas at other points, as well as from great numbers who ascend Red River.[5]

As Arkansas's population grew, agriculture quickly assumed a familiar pattern. In antebellum Arkansas, the most valuable crops were cotton, corn, and wheat. Corn was grown everywhere for self-sufficiency. In the northwest, wheat was milled into flour and sold locally. But cotton was sold in national and international markets. Though grown widely over the state, cotton dominated the eastern and southern counties. The appearance of steamboats on the rivers of eastern Arkansas meant that it could be moved easily to out-of-state markets. As a cash crop, cotton began its reign as king.[6]

As early as 1808, the traveler Fortescue Cumings in his *Sketches of a Tour to the Western Country* reported seeing cotton fields north of Helena.[7] Farmers complained about not having a gin. When the botanist Thomas Nuttall traveled up the Arkansas River in 1819, he found cotton growing near Arkansas Post, and two gins were in operation. He also discovered cotton growing elsewhere along the Arkansas River. At Little Rock, Nuttall predicted: "The privations of an infant settlement are already beginning to disappear. . . . Those who have large and growing families can always find lucrative employment in a country which produces cotton."[8] The Arkansas Delta would clearly be cotton country. Table 1 shows the development of cotton production in Arkansas. By 1840 Arkansas had embarked on a period of dramatic growth. The young state's estimated per capita income was sixty-eight dollars, which placed Arkansas three dollars ahead of the national per capita income—an achievement not duplicated since the Civil War.[9]

TABLE 1

Arkansas Cotton Production, in Bales, by Decade, 1823–1908 (in thousands)

1823–1829	7
1830–1839	58
1840–1849	362
1850–1859	1,423
1860–1869	1,227
1870–1879	5,110
1880–1889	5,959
1890–1899	7,230
1900–1908	6,455

Source: James L. Watkins, *King Cotton: A Historical and Statistical Review, 1790–1908* (New York: Negro Universities Press, 1969), chapter XI.

Between 1850 and 1860, as seen in Table 2, the total number of acres of improved Delta land increased by 202.5 percent, while the overall production of cotton soared 423.5 percent.

The cotton boom increased the Delta's population as settlers dreamed of white gold. Table 3 compares population growth between 1850 and 1860. The growth of the white population was substantial in all Delta counties, ranging from 24.9 percent to 229.8 percent. But the black population exceeded the rate of growth of whites in every county. Overall, the white population increased 106.8 percent, while the black population increased 201.1 percent, more than double the white gain.

Like white pioneers, slaves arrived in Arkansas from the states east of the Mississippi River—Tennessee, Mississippi, Alabama, Georgia, and South Carolina. As the new cotton frontier pushed westward into Arkansas, the slave population supplied the ravenous demand for plantation labor in the bottomlands of eastern Arkansas. The hilly and mountainous regions developed small family farms, and the population was predominantly white.[10]

In the Arkansas Delta, slavery was similar to slavery in the rest of the South. Working as field hands, male slaves endured the heavy labor in the annual rhythm that cotton imposed—cultivating the land and planting in the spring, chopping out weeds in the summer, and picking cotton in the fall. When time allowed, they also built levees and dug drainage ditches. Many plantations also

TABLE 2

Improved Land in Acres and Cotton Production in Bales, Arkansas Delta Counties, 1850 and 1860

	Improved Land			Cotton Bales		
	1850	1860	Pct Chg	1850	1860	Pct Chg
Arkansas	12,193	45,493	273.1	3,769	20,178	435.4
Chicot	29,886	66,423	122.3	12,192	40,948	235.9
Crittenden	8,475	19,897	134.8	698	4,675	569.8
Desha	9,207	42,264	359.0	2,672	12,261	358.9
Greene	9,118	14,908	63.5	15	275	1733.3
Jackson	10,319	40,597	293.4	870	10,483	1104.9
Jefferson	22,245	65,387	193.9	4,273	28,586	569.0
Mississippi	8,711	17,584	101.9	455	1,244	173.4
Monroe	6,501	25,284	288.9	587	7,137	1115.8
Phillips	26,247	83,737	219.0	5,165	26,993	422.6
Poinsett	8,046	15,478	92.4	270	2,577	854.4
Prairie	6,615	35,704	439.7	246	6,495	2540.2
St Francis	14,442	38,730	168.2	1,540	9,275	502.3
Totals:	172,005	511,486	202.5	32,752	171,127	423.5

Source: U.S. Census Office, *Seventh Census of the United States: 1850* (Washington: Robert Armstrong, Public Printer, 1853), 556; U.S. Census Office, *Eighth Census of the United States: 1860* (Washington: Government Printing Office, 1864), vol. 2, 7.

raised hogs, and grew corn, hay, and other crops in an effort to achieve self-sufficiency. Larger plantations required the services of skilled artisans—blacksmiths, carpenters, and bricklayers. Slave women worked as cooks and maids; they also performed work in the fields when extra labor was needed. In towns, most slaves were women who cooked and washed for white families.[11]

Slavery was a profitable source of labor because slaves produced more than they consumed. According to general estimates, the average field hand on small plantations in the South, like most of those in Arkansas, produced $127.55 worth of cotton per year, while the average slaveowners probably spent $28.95 a year to feed, clothe, and house an adult slave. Capital costs—interest, depreciation, and management expenses—averaged another $65.09 a year. In other words, the planter expropriated at least $33.51 per slave or 53.7 percent of each slave's labor.[12] The return was greater if a planter cut costs and drove his slaves harder.

TABLE 3

Population Growth in Arkansas Delta Counties, 1850–1860

	1850		1860		Pct White Growth	Pct Black Growth
	White	Slave	White	Slave		
Arkansas	1,707	1,538	3,923	4,921	129.8	220.0
Chicot	1,131	3,984	1,722	7,512	52.3	88.6
Crittenden	847	801	2,573	2,347	39.3	193.0
Desha	1,742	1,169	2,655	3,784	52.4	223.7
Greene	2,540	53	5,654	189	122.6	256.6
Jackson	2,523	563	7,957	2,535	215.4	350.3
Jefferson	3,213	2,621	7,813	7,146	143.2	172.6
Mississippi	1,503	865	2,434	1,461	61.9	68.9
Monroe	1,654	395	3,431	2,226	107.4	463.5
Phillips	4,344	2,591	5,932	8,941	36.6	245.1
Poinsett	2,029	279	2,535	1,086	24.9	289.2
Prairie	1,824	273	6,015	2,839	229.8	939.9
St. Francis	3,772	707	6,051	2,621	60.4	270.7
Totals	29,829	12,861	61,673	47,608	106.8	201.1

Source: U.S. Census Office, *Seventh Census of the United States: 1850* (Washington: Robert Armstrong, Public Printer, 1853), 535; U.S. Census Office, *Eighth Census of the United States: 1860* (Washington: Government Printing Office, 1864), vol. 1, 18.

What did these figures mean for the Arkansas Delta? According to the 1860 census, the Delta produced 171,127 bales (weighing 400 pounds each) of cotton, which was worth 11.1 cents per pound on the New Orleans market.[13] Thus the Delta cotton crop that year brought in about $7,598,039. On average, Arkansas Delta slaves each produced $201.45, but they consumed only $36.22. Deducting capital and management costs, cotton planters expropriated from their slaves $1,992,809, or an average of $41.86 per slave.[14]

In Arkansas, large Delta plantations used a gang system in which an overseer supervised work gangs of 20 to 25 adult slaves. Since the overseer was paid for the size of the crop he brought in, he may have been more willing to abuse slaves to motivate greater production. On small farms, slaves worked in the fields beside their owners. They were probably driven harder because small farms were more tenuous operations than larger plantations.

Despite a rush of prosperity in the 1850s, the antebellum Arkansas Delta was too young to be considered a mature plantation society. By 1860, the region was still a raw, undeveloped frontier. Only a single generation had passed since Arkansas began as a territory.[15]

Phillips County illustrates the social and economic trends in the antebellum Arkansas Delta. Phillips County—one of the oldest counties in the state—was formed in 1823. Cotton was first planted north of Helena, the county seat, in the alluvial region along the Mississippi River and at the mouths of the L'Anguille and St. Francis rivers. Between 1850 and 1860 cotton production soared from 5,165 bales to 26,993 bales, while the value of the county's farms increased an amazing 691 percent. In the same decade, the black population shot up 245.1 percent, from 2,591 to 8,941 slaves.[16]

Unlike the Delta country lying across the river in Mississippi, wealth was not highly concentrated in Phillips County, and in fact it was less concentrated in 1860 than it had been in 1850. The county contained 88 large, elite planters, each of whom owned over 1,000 acres of land, but most farming was done by small-scale operators. There were also small, independent nonslaveholding yeoman farmers.[17]

Phillips County land was available at low prices in the 1850s—as low as $5 per acre for unimproved land. Surprisingly, however, over a fourth of the farms listed in the 1860 census were worked by someone other than an owner—by renters or tenants. They often worked farms on shares. Indeed, tenancy was not entirely new after the Civil War. But planters, large and small, were increasingly dominant, controlling 65 percent of all the land in the county, 40 percent of the improved acres, and 57 percent of the slaves. In other words, Phillips County offered more opportunity for small farmers than the more settled, eastern areas of the Cotton South.[18]

Of all Arkansas counties, Chicot came closest to matching the Old South plantation economy. According to county tradition, the Johnson family represented the high style of the antebellum South.[19] In the 1850s, Joel Johnson left Kentucky and moved to Lakeport plantation just south of Lake Village. His sons Lycurgus and Cyrus Johnson also established themselves as planters in Chicot County. Leona Sumner Brasher's reminiscence about the Johnsons drips with Old South style:

> In the lower end of this county about twelve miles below Lake
> Village lived one of the most noted families of pioneer times.
> They occupied a large tract of valuable land and were very

prosperous. This was the Johnson family, from Kentucky: Mr. Lycurgus Johnson, Mr. Cyrus Johnson and their widowed sister Julia J. Johnson. The sister married the governor of Louisiana, whose name was also Johnson. Their houses adjoined and they had the handsomest home[s] at that time in our county; very large houses, surrounded by highly cultivated grounds. They were prosperous in every sense of the word, lived like foreign nobility, highly cultivated, possessing noble traits of character and had friends in all classes of society.[20]

By 1860, Lycurgus Johnson owned Lakeport, and his plantation house still survives today, though in deteriorated condition.[21] According to the 1860 census, the Johnsons reported the figures seen in Table 4.

The Johnsons may have been the noblest scions of Chicot County, but Elisha Worthington was not only the largest planter in Chicot County, but also in Arkansas.[22] Worthington was born in Kentucky in 1805 and came to Chicot County in the 1840s. In 1850 he owned 5,000 acres of improved and unimproved land worth $24,000. He reported growing 510 bales of cotton and 6,000 bushels of corn, using 142 slaves. During the next ten years, he accumulated even greater wealth. By 1860, he owned 4 plantations and 529 slaves. Table 5 shows data for Worthington's plantations as reported in the 1860 census of agriculture.

The Civil War closed the first phase of plantation agriculture in the Arkansas Delta, just as it did across the South. Between 1860 and 1870, the amount of improved land dropped 19 percent, while cotton production fell from 171,445 bales in 1860 to 106,679 in 1870—a decline of 37.8 per cent.[23]

The emancipation of slaves destroyed the planters' source of cheap labor and shook the plantation system to its foundations.

TABLE 4

The Johnson Plantations, Chicot County, 1860

	No. of Slaves	Acreage	Corn (bu.)	Cotton (bales)
Lycurgus	155	2,700	10,000	1,380
Cyrus	57	1,800	30,000	545

Source: Manuscript Population Schedules, McConnell Township, Chicot County, 1860; Manuscript Slave and Agricultural Schedules, Louisiana Township, Chicot County, 1860.

TABLE 5

Elisha Worthington's Four Plantations in Chicot County, 1860

	No. of Slaves	Acreage	Corn (bu.)	Cotton (bales)
Sunnyside	234	1,300	12,000	1,700
Red Leaf	145	1,400	12,000	1,270
Meanie	56	400	1,500	
Eminence	94	500	6,000	

Source: Manuscript Slave Schedules, Old River Township, Chicot County, 1860; Manuscript Agricultural Schedules, Old River Township, Chicot County, 1860.

The question that hung over the plantation system at the end of the Civil War was survival itself. Yet recovery was surprisingly fast. By 1880, every Delta county but one (Arkansas County) had exceeded its cotton production levels of 1860.[24] Delta plantations had not only survived the war, but also had survived emancipation.

In the spring of 1862, Gen. Samuel R. Curtis's Army of the Southwest marched eastward along the White River toward Helena after the battle of Pea Ridge. When Curtis entered the Delta, thousands of slaves flocked to his army, giving Arkansas its first experience with emancipation.[25] By the end of the war, slavery had been swept away. The Delta, like the rest of the South, faced a momentous task of rebuilding economic institutions.

How would the plantation economy make the transition from chattel slavery to the new postwar world of free black labor? Most whites refused to believe that blacks would work without coercion.[26] Emancipation unquestionably created more opportunities for former slaves than for former slaveowners. While blacks emerged from slavery impoverished, they were in a position to take advantage of their freedom. At their first opportunity, many freedmen left their old plantations in search for separated relatives—often for children or spouses. Another widespread reaction to freedom was that black women and children no longer worked in the fields.[27]

Postbellum Arkansas, like the South as a whole, suffered a sharp drop in the number of black workers, creating a labor shortage that gave freedmen their first real power in the labor market. The *Arkansas Gazette* echoed complaints about the lack of labor, fields lying fallow, and small crops. In early 1867, the *Gazette* summed up the fears of all planters:

The question most seriously involving the prosperity of the people of this State at this time, is not negro suffrage, but negro *labor*. Not whether he shall vote, but whether he will work. The season is rapidly approaching when the necessary preparations should be made by the planter for the coming crop, and now is the time to make contracts with the freedmen for the coming year. For the present, they are our principle [*sic*] dependence, and we must do the best we can with them until such time as an increase of white laborers shall come into our state, and enable us to do without them. Then the high estimate which they now place upon themselves will, by competition, be brought down, and the question with them will not, as now, be, "who shall I work for?" but "who will employ me?"[28]

If it survived, the plantation system's need for cheap labor would somehow have to be met. The solution was sharecropping.

What was the origin of sharecropping? That is, who initially wanted the share system? The traditional explanation has been that mutual needs brought landlords and freedmen together.[29] Landlords needed labor, but did not have the cash to pay wages; freedmen needed land, but lacked capital to rent land or buy it outright. Nor did they have the capital to furnish their own livestock and tools. If this view is correct, poverty and desperation created a system that reduced the immediate need for cash by sharing the proceeds of the crop. Yet the payment of wages was fairly common even in the early postwar years.

One historian has argued that it was the former slaves who insisted on sharecropping and refused to work under any other arrangement. Planters wanted to restore the gang or "squad" system of labor that was associated with slavery and still practiced briefly after the war. The freedmen insisted on sharecropping. If freedmen could not secure land of their own, they were determined to rent land and work in family units without direct and constant supervision.[30]

In time planters accepted the share system because it gave labor a stake in the crop. Workers gained an incentive to see the crop through until harvest since they were not paid until the end of the year. Employers still controlled labor through the payment of wages, cash, or shares.

The role of the Freedmen's Bureau—the Bureau of Refugees, Freedmen, and Abandoned Lands, created by Congress in 1865— was crucial in the process of building new economic relationships.

Among the Bureau's functions was the supervision of written contracts between the former slaves and former slave owners, both of whom were forced to learn new roles as employees and employers respectively.

A systematic sample of Freedmen's Bureau contracts for 1866 and 1867 in eastern and southern Arkansas produced the results seen in Table 6.[31]

Most contracts were either for wages or for a share of the crop. A few were split—that is, included both wages and shares. These contracts confirmed that Arkansas, like other states, experimented with the payment of wages immediately after the war. In Arkansas, Bureau officials initially favored share contracts over wages, but many freedmen found at the end of 1866 that their share of the crop was insufficient to cover the cost of supplies furnished them on credit. As a result, the Bureau tried to guide freedmen toward wage contracts, but by 1868 agents were instructed "not to constrain the freedmen as to the form of labor contract they enter into, whether by the day, the month, upon shares, renting land, or upon any other condition. . . ."[32] The contracts showed that in both 1866 and 1867 freedmen apparently moved in the opposite direction from the recommendations of Bureau officials. The 1866 contracts favored wages when Bureau officials recommended shares. In 1867 the contracts showed a marked shift to shares despite the Bureau's recommendation of wages. Whether freedmen or landlords were behind this shift was not apparent in the contracts themselves, but Arkansas freedmen certainly made their preferences felt. Indeed, Bureau officials reported that Arkansas freedmen demonstrated considerable shrewdness in stipulating contract terms.[33]

TABLE 6

Number of Labor Contracts Made with Freedmen's Bureau,
by Type of Contract, Arkansas, 1866–1867

	1866	Percent	1867	Percent
Shares	85	38.5	66	63.5
Wages	113	51.1	28	26.9
Split	15	6.8	8	7.7
In-kind	8	3.6	2	1.9
	N= 221		N= 104	

These contracts represented an early battleground between the old economic structures and the new. What emerged clearly was the suspicion of black labor. Workers were required, in an often-used phrase, to perform "good and faithful labor." The contracts made it evident that workers were expected to work hard—with the work day spelled out as being from sunrise to sunset, including lunch hours as specified. Many contracts made a point of demanding respectful deportment. Some specifically ruled out drinking. The contracts also emphasized that the emerging labor system was a family system. Contracts were usually made with family groups. The duties of wives were specified along with those of children old enough to work.[34]

The uncertainties surrounding black labor generated a serious effort to increase immigration into Arkansas. In 1868, the Arkansas General Assembly created a Commission of Immigration and State Lands, charging it with the responsibility of advertising Arkansas and promoting immigration. The purpose of such efforts was not merely to promote the economic development of the state, but also to find a way to counter the sellers' labor market by, if possible, replacing black labor altogether. In late 1865, a group known as the Arkansas Immigrant Aid Society proclaimed: "The emancipation of the Slave has entirely changed the relations of labor to capital, and now the way is open and unobstructed for immigrants, whether from other states or foreign Nations."[35] Gov. Powell Clayton charged that immigration schemes were intended "to punish the negro for having abandoned the control of his old master, and to regulate the conditions of his employment and the scale of [his] wages. . . ."[36]

The desire for foreign labor focused initially on German immigrants. Little Rock's German population showed an interest in sponsoring immigrant aid societies, and several German communities, including Stuttgart, were indeed founded in the state.[37] The Chinese also attracted the attention of immigration promoters. Chinese workers allegedly possessed the qualities that planters most desired—they were docile and cheap. In fact, according to contemporary rumors, they worked so cheaply that they could grow rich on what whites and blacks wasted. In 1869, a group of southeast Arkansas promoters succeeded in bringing Chinese laborers to Chicot County.[38] In 1880, the census recorded several Chinese families still in the county, but they left soon for other areas.[39]

Plantation agriculture functioned through a system of social controls that kept labor dependent. Immediately after the war, Arkansas enacted laws that may be classified as Black Codes. Arkansas's codes did prohibit blacks from voting and attending schools with whites, but did not contain the most restrictive features found in such states as Mississippi or South Carolina. Under Arkansas law, blacks could make contracts and own real or personal property, and they faced no vagrancy provision. But the Democratic legislature clearly was concerned about stabilizing the labor system. In "An Act to Regulate the Labor System in this State," Arkansas legislators required written labor contracts and prohibited a laborer from breaking a contract by fining him the full amount that the employer would have paid him. The enticement of laborers was also made a crime.[40]

A year later, the legislature—now under Republican control—attempted to reverse the balance of power between employee and employer by enacting a laborer's lien law to protect the freedmen in their relations with landlords. The key issue was whose lien would have priority. Act 67 of 1868 gave a laborer's lien precedence over the landlords' liens in all cases. To the *Arkansas Gazette*, this "savage" law was proof that the Republican regime was "adverse to the interests of the property holders and white men of the state." With the defeat of Radical Republicanism and the election of a Democratic legislature in 1874, the lien law was repealed. Act 29 of 1874–75 made the lien of a landlord superior to a mortgage on the crop by the tenant. A large body of litigation in the decades ahead reinforced the landlord's position.[41]

In the courtroom, the law became a form of social control. Court cases reaffirmed the laborer's loss of status, as he dropped from a renter who paid rent in the form of a share of the crop to a wage laborer whose "share" of the crop was paid to him by the landlord. Though still commonly called a sharecropper, he did not own or control his share of the crop.[42] In time, slavery returned in the guise of sharecropping—a system that continued the exploitation of plantation labor.

New economic arrangements changed postbellum Delta agriculture. Cotton factors or brokers advanced money to planters, taking a mortgage on the expected crop. The planter, unless he paid wages, contracted with tenants to work on shares. The share varied, but usually one-third of the crop went for labor, one-third for land,

and one-third for seed and equipment. The average sharecropper farmed fifteen acres in the Arkansas Delta and received one-half of the crop if he could furnish any of his own equipment, or one-third of the crop receipts if he could not. The cropper charged his living expenses at the plantation store or at a local furnish merchant and paid his account in the fall with his share of the crop.

In *Life on the Mississippi*, published in 1883, Mark Twain related a planter's estimate of the average margin of profit on planting cotton. "One man and a mule will raise ten acres of cotton, giving ten bales cotton, worth, say, $500; cost of producing, say $350; net profit, $150, or $15 per acre. There is also a profit now from the cotton-seed, which formerly had little value—none where much transportation was necessary. In sixteen hundred pounds crude cotton, four hundred are lint, worth, say, ten cents a pound; and twelve hundred pounds of seed, worth $12 or $13 per ton."[43] Twain implied that the average farmer earned $150 per year, clearly an inflated estimate. Most farmers did not average a bale per acre. Twain also assumed 10 cent cotton, but in 1894 cotton hit bottom at 4 cents per pound.

The role of the merchant increased dramatically in the postwar Delta economy. Most farmers ran their farms on credit. Furnish merchants took mortgages directly on many small operators. To secure their investments, merchants demanded that farmers plant cotton, sometimes to the total exclusion of corn or food crops, which had to be purchased from outside sources. Thus the sharecropping system created the one-crop system, since credit arrangements forced farmers to devote more acreage to cotton. In time, the roles of landlord and merchant merged as merchants increasingly acquired land through mortgage foreclosures.

In 1880, the U.S. Census Office under the direction of Eugene W. Hilgard published a major study entitled *Report on Cotton Production in the United States*.[44] This report provided an assessment of how the new system of southern plantation agriculture stood fifteen years after the Civil War. In their work on Arkansas, Hilgard and his associates found that cotton production was a highly diversified system. Both whites and blacks were caught up in the production of cotton, and so were a few Chinese immigrants.

Cotton was still produced under two broad arrangements—wages and shares. Wages were paid weekly or monthly, with the intent of using wages to motivate workers to stay until the end of the season. But the share system had become the predominant labor arrangement.

There was no consensus about which system was best. Some observers argued that the share system deteriorated the soil. Nor was there agreement about which system—wages or shares—was better for the laborer; but the share system was definitely preferred in the Mississippi River alluvial region. The Crittenden County correspondent, for example, asserted that the share system was better for both owner and laborer. He described the situation as follows:

> The negro has his home, garden "patch," and fuel free of charge; has the loan of a cow, if he does not own one. He generally raises pigs (all his own), and his house is situated "away" from the "quarters." These conditions engender feelings of respectability and pride at home, a laudable ambition to excel in farming, and to a great extent obviates the necessity of overseeing on the part of the owner. The best class of colored citizens work this way, and prefer it.
>
> Only a portion of the land is able to be worked in this manner. When hired labor is employed, the hands are irresponsible, lazy, and vicious, and require wages every Saturday; when paid they leave for the city; when "broke" they return and work another week; are inveterate gamblers, and are called "roustabouts."[45]

Hilgard confirmed that in many Delta counties, supplies were often purchased, not grown, making farmers less self-sufficient and more dependent on merchants. In 1880, Lee County had purchased corn from Memphis because too much cotton had been planted. In fact, up and down the Delta, supplies were imported from as far away as St. Louis and New Orleans. Thus dependence on merchants increased.

After 1880, a new plantation economy of sharecropping had fully emerged—an economy that rested on force, intimidation, and racism.[46] In cooperation with all elements of white society, planters exercised every effort to maintain control of their cheap labor supply. In 1891, for example, when blacks in Lee County organized a cotton pickers' strike, a posse hunted down the strike leaders, and a mob of masked white men seized the prisoners and lynched them, crushing the strike totally.[47] The rise of lynchings across the South can be seen as the most extreme effort of labor intimidation. Arkansas experienced 313 lynchings between 1882 and 1927—many victims were Delta blacks.[48] The Elaine race riot of 1919 was an effort to repress the Progressive Farmers and Household Union, which had been formed to get higher prices for cotton grown by black tenant farmers.[49]

So Delta agriculture settled into a pattern that would last from 1865 until after World War II. The life of the Delta revolved around cotton and sharecropping. As the plantation system expanded, tenancy increased, and so did exploitation and violence. The region, along with the rest of the South, seemed to be locked in a changeless system.[50]

While Delta agriculture may have appeared to be unchanging on the surface, the region experienced significant progress in the period from 1890 to 1930. In the late nineteenth century, the plantation system underwent a dramatic period of expansion. Plantation interests combined with timber companies, railroads, and land speculators to promote land reclamation efforts. As a group, planters had the most to gain from flood control, land clearing, and drainage. Timbermen and others supported, but sometimes opposed, plantation interests in a fragile alliance that dramatically changed the physical landscape of the Arkansas Delta. One result of the development of the Delta was a further increase in tenancy and exploitation.

After the Civil War, timber emerged along with agriculture as a major Delta industry. Lumber companies began to harvest the virgin timber of the Delta as technological improvements and a growing market for lumber created attractive opportunities for large companies. The construction of shortline railroads that hauled logs to sawmills and to navigable streams facilitated the penetration of Delta forests. Loggers cut timber in a "big pickle" approach, taking out the largest and most valuable trees and leaving cutover land that held little if any value. While exploiting the land, lumber companies showed little or no concern for growing new stands of timber.[51] Many lumber companies of this period maintained real estate offices to capitalize on the agricultural potential of cutover land. This land could be sold to farmers after its timber value had been destroyed.

Consequently, diverse interests converged to promote land reclamation. When lumber companies began releasing cutover lands, they sponsored drainage projects that would make cutover land useable. Plantation interests and railroads also joined together to promote drainage. Land speculators obviously saw the potential in new, rich agricultural land that might be created by flood control and drainage projects.

Like lumbering, flood control efforts also began before the Civil War. The Swamp Lands Acts of 1849 and 1850 donated swamp and overflowed lands to the states, and encouraged drainage and levee projects. Under these acts, Arkansas received some 16.3 million acres, most of it in the Delta. Between 1850 and 1861, new levees were constructed, and scattered levees were joined together—projects consisting of 13 million cubic yards of material at a cost of over $2.5 million. Early levee projects unfortunately suffered from fraud and mismanagement. The original levees failed because they were low, poorly constructed, and improperly located.[52]

From 1879 to 1917, the Mississippi River Commission, a federal agency, coordinated river improvement and flood control through levee districts. These districts, managed by local boards, possessed the power of eminent domain and limited taxation. Like antebellum efforts, however, levee districts failed to control flooding. The work of the early levee districts has almost completely disappeared under modern levees. In 1917, local levee boards were turned over to the U.S. Army Corps of Engineers.

As noted earlier, Arkansas had promoted immigration in the late nineteenth century, hoping to attract settlers to undeveloped land. The drainage movement, too, sought to promote both immigration and land development. Similarly, lumber companies hoped that drainage projects would give them access to additional timberland or would extend the logging season; they also had logged out large areas and wanted to release their cutover land to avoid paying taxes.

After the turn of the century, a wave of drainage speculation projects swept eastern Arkansas. In a pamphlet entitled *The Dawn of a Greater State, Facts About Drainage, The Awakening of Arkansas* (1910), the inflated expectations of this time were evident:

> . . . In Arkansas there are six million acres of swamp land await-
> ing drainage, which, as shown by Government reports, will cost
> $6.88 per acre to prepare for cultivation. We all know that
> unproductive swamp lands held at from eight to ten dollars per
> acre after drainage will sell for from fifty to one hundred dollars
> per acre, depending on location, so it is safe to say that the
> swamp lands of Arkansas when drained would enhance in value

$35 per acre. This would add 210 million dollars to the value of farm land. Using the same basis as for the Mississippi Valley, of 80 acres to the farm, it would bring into cultivation 75 thousand additional farms from lands that are now producing nothing. With seven persons to the farm, it would mean an increase in the rural population of Arkansas of 525 thousand people in sections of the state that are now useless, then adding fifty per cent to the entire population of the state.

The annual production of these six million acres at twenty dollars per acre would mean an additional income to the farmers of Arkansas of 120 million dollars annually. Viewing it from another standpoint, an investment of 41 million dollars for the drainage of the swamp lands of Arkansas would increase the wealth of the state one-half billion dollars. To show the result in another way, the wealth of Arkansas would be increased $12 for each $1 invested in drainage.[53]

A flurry of pamphlets described the "ease" by which Delta land could be brought into cultivation.

S. E. Simonson, one of the pioneers in the drainage movement in northeast Arkansas, came to Mississippi County from Illinois in 1902. He had been involved with drainage projects in Illinois and recognized the potential in Mississippi County if the land were drained. He reported that about 5 percent of the county was in cultivation in 1905, and another 5 percent was susceptible to cultivation. Fully 90 percent of the county, he recalled, was "regarded as a hopeless permanent mosquito and malaria infested swamp." Many large landowners and lumber interests opposed drainage efforts because they did not want to pay additional taxes. Thus many powerful interests opposed drainage, and others simply doubted it could be done.[54]

As Simonson recalled, Mississippi County was one of the first to act under the old drainage laws, forming Drainage District No. 7 or Pemiscot Bayou Drainage District in 1905. The effort to sell bonds initially met with no success, because northern bankers knew that Arkansas had repudiated its debt in the 1880s. The drainage movement succeeded only because it had some of the most powerful leaders of Mississippi County behind it.

The leader of the drainage movement in southeast Arkansas was Henry Thane, a naturalized German who came to Arkansas from Chicago. According to Robert W. Harrison, the historian of Delta land development, "Thane envisioned an almost immediate translation of swamp, overflowed forest, and cutover land into an agricultural community capable of producing a surplus of truck crops and livestock products for northern markets."[55] Thus local land values would increase, enriching property owners. What Thane and other drainage promoters hoped to develop was a "corn belt" type of farming in the Delta bottoms. The crops most often mentioned were corn, barley, oats, alfalfa, and soybeans. Thane dreamed that the Delta would become a new food basket for the Midwest.[56]

In the case of Desha County drainage promoters, for example, such expectations were never realized. In time, crop selection did diversify, but agricultural development remained relatively low. Desha and Chicot counties were under water in the floods of 1912, 1913, 1916, and 1927. The Cypress Creek Drainage District was two million dollars in debt when it went bankrupt in 1930, but recovered to complete its work.[57]

In the early decades of the twentieth century, then, the Delta's physical landscape took on its present appearance. The virgin forests of oak, cypress, and other timber disappeared acre by acre. Similarly, drainage and flood control projects obliterated swamp and overflowed lands, and all of these efforts opened up vast new areas for agriculture.

In the 1930s, Arkansas pushed land clearing more vigorously than any other Mississippi Valley state. Clearing projects enlarged existing plantations and created new ones, and many small home-steaders cleared their own farms. The state government was particularly active in attempting to settle homesteaders on large alluvial tracts forfeited for flood control and drainage taxes.[58] By 1950, forests still covered about 37 percent of the Arkansas Delta. After World War II, the demand for rice land resulted in renewed efforts to clear land in northeast Arkansas. By the early 1960s, only about 25 percent of the Arkansas Delta remained forested.[59]

The expansion of Delta agriculture between the Civil War and World War II paralleled several important trends. The cotton market remained one of the most erratic of agricultural markets. After the Civil War, cotton fell into a downward spiral, hitting a low of five cents per pound in 1894. The market revived at the turn of the century, and cotton farmers again enjoyed prosperity. World War I increased the world demand for cotton and boosted prices, but after the war the demand fell off and farmers slid into a decade of depression. When the stock market crashed in 1929, many cotton farmers were already caught up in hard times. With their smaller profit margins, small farmers suffered more than large planters.[60] The life of small farmers in the Delta is chronicled in a diary left by Nannie Stillwell Jackson, who lived at Watson in Desha County. She was a widow with two daughters when she married William T. Jackson, a man ten years her junior. This marriage was one of economic necessity rather than of love. For part of 1890 and 1891, she kept a diary, recording her dreary and boring life in which the smallest event was important enough to write down.[61]

The Jacksons both owned small farms. Nannie owned 60 acres from her first marriage, and her husband owned 80 acres; but even with a combined 140 acres they were barely able to make enough to live on. The Jacksons had to count every penny if they were to survive.

The decline of cotton prices in the late nineteenth century pushed more and more small farmers into tenancy. After the Civil War, most sharecroppers were black; by the end of the century, an increasing number of white farmers also found themselves working someone else's land. Yet low cotton prices alone did not increase the tenant population. Tenancy was also a product of the expansion of Delta agriculture in the late nineteenth and early twentieth centuries. The development of new agricultural land expanded the plantation system, which increased the demand for cheap labor—that is, for tenant farmers and sharecroppers. Thus land clearing and drainage projects coincided with a spectacular increase in landless farmers.

Table 7 provides the growth of tenancy in Delta counties by percent of all farms for the fifty years from 1880 to 1930. In this period the percentage of tenant farmers in Arkansas doubled from 31 to 63 percent. Some Delta counties saw even more dramatic increases. Chicot County went from 19.2 to 87.7 percent, Poinsett County from 26.6 to 79.8. By 1930, 13 out of 21 Delta counties had tenancy rates of about 80 percent or above.

As prices declined, agriculturists warned about over reliance on cotton and urged southern farmers to diversify their crops. The cry for diversification rang in countless newspaper articles, but not in farmers' ears. The boll weevil, which began a march from Mexico in 1892 and by 1908 had reached the Mississippi River, finally forced

TABLE 7

Tenancy in Arkansas Delta Counties, by Percent, 1880–1930

	1880	1890	1900	1910	1920	1930
State	31.8	32.1	45.4	50.0	51.3	63.0
Arkansas	32.1	22.3	41.7	46.4	48.2	54.5
Chicot	19.2	57.0	78.2	84.5	83.9	87.7
Clay	34.9	32.6	40.8	51.3	51.7	63.5
Craighead	33.2	35.3	44.3	57.9	58.7	67.7
Crittenden	77.0	78.3	85.7	88.7	88.9	94.8
Cross	44.4	56.4	65.6	71.3	73.8	83.7
Desha	66.4	58.6	78.6	84.2	85.9	89.0
Greene	37.3	31.8	40.1	49.8	48.1	57.2
Jackson	60.1	62.7	66.2	74.1	75.8	80.3
Jefferson	60.7	51.5	77.5	82.0	79.9	86.3
Lawrence	45.1	41.1	49.8	58.9	58.1	65.0
Lee	48.9	68.5	72.1	74.7	75.0	81.2
Lincoln	30.6	36.1	62.5	67.8	72.8	83.2
Lonoke	52.0	45.2	56.8	68.4	67.5	77.2
Mississippi	57.2	58.4	70.0	81.6	82.9	90.3
Monroe	55.3	70.5	74.4	78.5	69.4	79.9
Phillips	61.0	66.4	77.7	81.2	80.7	86.0
Poinsett	26.6	15.7	59.1	62.6	73.2	79.8
Prairie	41.6	41.1	52.2	51.0	53.8	59.8
St. Francis	43.2	47.0	70.7	76.9	79.2	87.7
White	26.8	26.1	40.5	38.8	41.3	53.1
Woodruff	64.7	64.4	81.5	85.1	81.7	84.6

Source: U.S. Department of the Interior, Census Office, *Report on Cotton Production in the United States: Mississippi Valley and Southwestern States* (Washington: Government Printing Office, 1884); U.S. Bureau of the Census, *Tenth-Fifteenth Censuses of the United States: 1880–1930, Agriculture* (Washington: Government Printing Office, 1883–1932).

some farmers to diversify. For Arkansas Delta farmers, the first alternate crop was rice, which was grown on the Arkansas Grand Prairie. In 1897 William H. Fuller planted three acres of rice near Carlisle in Lonoke County. This experiment was so successful that rice production expanded rapidly. By 1910, farmers were clearing land between the St. Francis and Cache rivers to expand rice production.

The origins of rice farming in Arkansas closely paralleled the developments along the Louisiana Gulf Coast, which had emerged as the nation's leading rice-producing area. The Arkansas Grand

Prairie, which was similar in some ways to the Gulf Coast, was largely virgin land at the turn of the century. The pioneer Arkansas rice farmers, W. H. Fuller and John and Emma Morris, were from Midwestern states—a pattern that was also true of Louisiana and Texas. They acquired their knowledge of rice farming through direct contact with Louisiana rice farmers. What has always made rice farming unique in Arkansas and elsewhere was that rice farmers ran more mechanized operations and enjoyed greater affluence than did cotton farmers.[62]

Under the pressure of low cotton prices, the boll weevil, and racial discrimination, black farmers began a migration out of the Delta during the 1890s. Up to this time, blacks were virtually trapped in the South—trapped by intimidation, illiteracy, and debt. But better transportation and more knowledge of outside opportunities eventually had an impact. Breaking the ties of dependency, blacks sought industrial work during World War I. The black migration stalled during the depression of the 1930s, but resumed in earnest during World War II, threatening the existence of the plantation system's source of cheap labor.[63]

In the early 1930s, whites moved in the opposite direction from blacks. As the economy sank into depression, the improbable dream of back-to-the-land took hold in the minds of many unemployed families. Back-to-the-landers despaired of the city and talked in nostalgic and utopian terms of subsistence farming. For a brief time in the early 1930s, the tide of migration from farm to city reversed itself, giving the country a net gain.[64] The Delta benefited from this movement, since many hill people sought to escape their eroded farms and to find a new life in the bottomlands. White farm operators increased by 10 percent from 1930 to 1935, while black farm operators declined throughout the decade. The exodus of black farmers from the Delta continued without interruption.[65]

Beginning in the late 1920s, the plantation system faced a crisis even more critical than the end of slavery. A series of disasters, both natural and human, challenged planters for control over their labor supply. The result was the collapse of Delta agriculture as it had existed for over a hundred years.

Even nature swung capriciously from one extreme to another. In 1927, the Mississippi River overflowed its banks and backed up the Arkansas River and its tributaries, creating a sickening yellow tide from Cairo, Illinois, to the Gulf of Mexico. Arkansas experienced numerous breaks on the levee system of the Mississippi, White, St. Francis, and other rivers. Flood waters covered 4 million acres in eastern Arkansas, destroying millions of dollars of property and taking 127 lives.[66]

For many victims, the flood waters hit suddenly. One account described Arkansas City when the levee broke at Pendleton on the Arkansas River: "At noon, the streets of Arkansas City were dry and dusty. By 2 o'clock, mules were drowning in the main streets of that town faster than they could be unhitched from wagons. Before dark the homes and stores stood six feet deep in water."[67]

John H. Johnson, the founder of *Ebony* magazine, recalled the experience at Arkansas City in his autobiography.[68] He was nine years old when he and his mother received the message that the Pendleton levee had broken. They were told they should grab their pets and valuables and run to the Arkansas City levee. The next message came just minutes later: forget your pets and valuables and run for your lives! He recalled several hundred people huddled together on the levee in "muddy misery."

The federal government and the Red Cross provided aid, but agriculture suffered major losses. The extent of the 1927 flood was unexpected and demonstrated that previous flood-control efforts had failed. In addition, relief efforts exposed the poverty of the people in the Mississippi River Delta.

Next, in the summer of 1930, the worst drought in weather bureau records gripped the South and Southwest. Arkansas may have suffered more than any other state. Day after day the temperature hovered around 100 degrees, and farmers saw their crops wither and burn in the fields. During the winter of 1930–31, one-third of the entire population of Arkansas faced starvation. In the most severely affected areas, people rarely had meat on the table, except for wild game. They subsisted on a diet of turnips, herbs, roots, and nuts. A joke gave the recipe for a turnip sandwich: take three turnip slices and put one in the middle.[69] The only immediate source of help was private charity. By 1931, the Red Cross was feeding 519,000 Arkansans, almost one-third of the state's population.[70] The heaviest relief demands came from the Delta, and in some counties the majority of the population lived on Red Cross rations.[71]

During both the flood and the drought, planters worried about laborers leaving the region for better jobs elsewhere, and they sought to guarantee that their labor force would not escape their control. During the flood, Red Cross camps threatened plantation interests by feeding and housing plantation workers, possibly breaking their dependency on their landlords. But the planters' influence extended into the camps themselves. Some planters reportedly stocked their commissaries with Red Cross rations, which they in turn sold to their tenants. Under Red Cross rules, flood refugees could not leave refugee camps unless some person applied for their release and promised to give them jobs.[72]

The Red Cross always used local customs to measure the kind and amount of relief it provided. In the Arkansas Delta, this rule meant that Red Cross officials listened to local leaders, many of whom were connected with the plantation system. Most of all, planters were determined not only to retain control of their labor supply, but also to turn the relief effort to a profit if possible. What planters learned from both flood and drought relief was that outside forces could be co-opted and posed no real threat to their labor supply.[73] But the Great Depression posed the ultimate threat to planter hegemony.

The stock market crash of 1929 signaled the beginning of a decade of hard times. Arkansans, however, worried more about the cotton market than they did the about the stock market. The cotton market reached bottom in 1933 at five cents per pound, the lowest price since 1894. As a result, farm income plunged, while tax delinquency shot up to record levels.

By 1933, the cotton kingdom faced a crisis of multiple origins. The market for American cotton had declined in the face of growing competition from foreign cotton and from synthetic fabrics. As a nonperishable crop, the cotton carryover was so substantial that the cotton in storage could almost have supplied the world's demand without any additional production that year.[74] Cotton prices had declined to the point that growing cotton was no longer profitable. In this market situation, the over-population of the Delta was quite obvious. But still unknown was the fate of unneeded agricultural workers when cities already bulged with unemployed men and women. The depression brought conditions in the Cotton Belt to the point where planters could not continue to operate without federal intervention.[75]

The inauguration of Franklin D. Roosevelt as president in March 1933 raised expectations across the nation that his promised

New Deal would restore good times. The New Deal's solution for agricultural recovery was embodied in the Agricultural Adjustment Administration (AAA). The purpose of the AAA cotton program was to take cotton land out of production in the hope that lower production would raise prices. When the AAA became law in the spring of 1933, Delta farmers had already planted cotton; so a dramatic plow-up program was launched that destroyed about 26 percent of the cotton acreage.[76]

The cotton program favored large planters without regard for the Delta's landless farmers, and planters again co-opted a potential threat to their hegemony. Government payments for taking land out of production went to the landlord, and some landlords withheld their tenants' share, applying the amount to their tenants' debts. Other landlords evicted families no longer needed after acreage reductions. The AAA cotton program provoked a major reaction in northeast Arkansas at Tyronza, Poinsett County, and propelled the Delta's tenancy problem unexpectedly into the nation's headlines.

In July 1934, a small group of sharecroppers, black and white, met at the Sunnyside School near Tyronza and formed the Southern Tenant Farmers' Union (STFU). Two young Socialists, H. L. Mitchell, the owner of a local dry cleaning shop and a former cropper himself, and H. Clay East, a service station operator, supplied leadership for the group.[77] They faced squarely the problem of the racial composition of the union. A black man rose to make an eloquent plea: "We colored people can't organize without you, and you white folks can't organize without us. Aren't we all brothers and ain't God the Father of us all? We live under the same sun, eat the same food, wear the same kind of clothing, work on the same land, raise the same crop for the same landlord who oppresses and cheats us both."[78]

Most Arkansans viewed the union with horror—socialist led, biracial in organization, a brazen challenge to the plantation system. Planters used violence and intimidation against this threat to their labor supply.

Through the STFU, sharecroppers hoped to stop evictions, to receive their fair share of government benefits, and to gain a voice in bargaining with landlords. But the STFU never functioned as a real union. It conducted a cotton pickers' strike in 1935 and a choppers' strike in 1936. Neither strike was successful. The union membership totaled some thirty thousand scattered over several states, but the union's strength lay in its ability to attract national publicity.[79]

Delta visitors described the peasant-like existence of share-croppers. In the depression, tenants earned less than a hundred dollars a year. They lived a miserable existence, in the poorest housing, subsisting on a meager, starchy diet that promoted pella-gra. As the plantation system came under increasing scrutiny, crit-ics defined the sharecropping system as a social problem.[80]

Even before the STFU took shape, New Deal policy had already started moving in the opposite direction from the AAA with the rural resettlement program. The Federal Emergency Relief Administration (FERA) experimented with community projects as part of its rural rehabilitation work. More importantly, the Resettlement Administration (RA), created in 1935, not only absorbed the FERA rural rehabilitation projects, but also initiated a whole new series of communities, many located in the Delta. Two years later, operating under the Bankhead-Jones Farm Tenant Act, the Farm Security Administration (FSA) replaced the RA, inherited its organization and personnel, and completed the resettlement program.[81]

As head of the Arkansas FERA, William R. Dyess shared some of the agrarian fantasies of the early 1930s. He conceived the idea of building an agricultural community for Arkansas clients and providing them with an alternative form of aid. In May 1934, Dyess's FERA acquired 17,500 acres of cutover timber and swamp land near Wilson in Mississippi County and began dividing it into 500 farm units of 20 to 40 acres each. There, on the Tyronza River, Dyess built a new town complete with post office, cafe, stores, school, hospital, and cotton gin—at its peak a bustling com-munity of 2,000 people. After Dyess died in a plane crash in 1936, the community took the name Dyess Colony for its founder.[82]

The Farm Security Administration was the New Deal's answer to sharecropping as a social problem. The major thrust of the agency's rural poverty program was rural rehabilitation—a varied program of loans and grants to poor families in distress. But the community projects were better known and highly visible. In Arkansas the FSA was eventually responsible for sixteen resettle-ment projects. Some were complete communities formed by breaking up one or more large plantations; others consisted of single, isolated farms or clusters of farms scattered or "infiltrated" throughout several counties. Some were projects developed for black people, others were for whites only, and still others held both black and white families, although the races always lived separately. All projects functioned through a cooperative association that subleased the land to its members in family-sized units for individual operation. Despite the charge that these projects constituted socialistic farming, the resettlement program reflected the old American dream of the family farm.[83]

The community projects had both supporters and critics. At Pine Bluff, a friendly skeptic said:

> Well, it's this way. The government spends a million dollars or so to buy a forty-acre farm for a down-and-out sharecropper. They give him a mule, a bathtub, and an electric shoelacer. They lay a railroad track to his house to carry the tons of forms he has to fill in. A bunch of experts figure his milking I.Q. Lo and behold, they teach his wife how to hook rugs and can beef and spinach, and they show the feller how to plant soybeans and prune an orchard—and by darn, Luke, them government people can actually do it! After we poke fun at their red tape for a year or two, they ups and proves their experiment is self-liquidatin'— that the feller is makin' his payments and raisin' a family, too. And I don't know who's more surprised, me or the 'cropper.[84]

The New Deal invested $11,578,895 in Arkansas community projects—most of them located in the Delta. The program resettled 1,438 families on 98,670 acres.[85] Many of these families benefited enormously, and they repaid the government for their farms. But they were pitifully few among all the needy families in Arkansas. According to the 1930 census of agriculture, Arkansas contained 152,691 tenants.[86]

The New Deal's efforts to respond to agricultural distress contained more than one flaw. The AAA attempted to prop up the Delta plantation system that had collapsed under low cotton prices, competition from foreign countries, and the advent of synthetic fabrics. This effort was successful and enabled the plantation system to operate profitably for a few more years. But it was no more than a short-term solution. The resettlement program attacked the opposite end of the economic spectrum, but its flaw was that it tried to continue the small family farm economy of the past. Even in the mid-1930s, farm experts knew that the future belonged to large, more efficient farms. On every resettlement project, the small size of the family units condemned most client families to failure; few farmers could make a living on the thirty or forty acres they were allotted. If the projects had not been liquidated during World War II, they could not have survived in the new postwar world of large-scale, mechanized farming.

The New Deal agricultural programs inadvertently launched an era of change in southern agriculture.[87] The AAA cotton program bailed out southern planters at the expense of sharecroppers and tenants. Smaller cotton acreages reduced the need for tenants, thus freeing them to seek other employment or, indeed, pushing them into other employment. Between 1935 and 1940, the Delta had lost 13 percent of its farm operators.[88] Many agricultural experts predicted that the Delta plantation system with its reliance on cheap labor was doomed.[89]

World War II accelerated the out-migration of blacks and poor whites. While Arkansas's farm population declined 28 percent from 1940 to 1945, Delta farm operators dropped only 4 percent.[90] But the draft and defense jobs depleted traditional labor sources and actually forced landowners to compete for higher-priced labor. For the first time since the end of slavery, Delta agriculture confronted a labor crisis—a crisis of soaring labor costs and dwindling labor control. From 1940 to 1945, cotton prices doubled, while wage rates tripled.[91] Plantation interests fought to keep cotton prices high and wages low, but they had lost control of their cheap, dependent labor supply. In a sellers' market, workers gained real bargaining power, which destroyed the deference that the old system required.[92]

Table 8 shows that the number of white farm operators in the Delta remained virtually unchanged between 1940 and 1945, while the number of black farmers declined by 8 percent. Overall, the Delta lost 8 percent of all farm operators in the 1940s, but even greater change lay ahead. In the successive five-year periods beginning in 1945, Delta farm operators dropped by 10 percent, then by 20 percent, then by 40 percent, and so on.

After World War II, the Arkansas Delta experienced an agricultural *revolution*—no other word can adequately characterize the transformation from labor-intensive to capital-intensive agriculture. And after a century and a half, the plantation system itself crumbled, losing its hold on the lives of thousands of people; moreover,

Delta agriculture rushed to catch up with twentieth-century technology. Tractors had made some impact before the war. According to Table 9, Arkansas had almost ten thousand tractors by 1940; and many planters had replaced tenants with day laborers, who worked as tractor drivers. Many tenants complained of being "tractored off the land." After 1940, tractors appeared in large numbers. Even a two-row cultivator could plow ten times more in a day than a man and a mule. Experiments showed that herbicides could eliminate the need for cotton chopping in the summer. But these developments were relatively slow to come together.[93]

The mechanical production of cotton had to overcome several technical problems, from cultivation to chopping and picking, before planters could totally dispense with hand labor. Even after the advent of tractors, cotton still had to be chopped by hand until chemical methods of weed control were perfected. And the mechanical cotton picker remained the last technical hurdle in machine-harvested cotton.[94]

Cotton production had also been slow to attempt mechanization because of the availability of abundant, low-cost, and dependent labor. A subsidiary factor was the relative scarcity of capital for

TABLE 8

Farm Operators, Arkansas Delta, by Race, 1920–1974

	White	Pct Ch	Black	Pct Ch	Total	Pct Ch
1920	39,772		47,291		87,063	
1930	51,828	30.3	54,085	14.4	105,913	21.7
1935	57,298	10.6	48,640	-10.1	105,938	0.0
1940	52,472	-8.4	39,707	-18.4	92,179	-13.0
1945	51,877	-1.1	36,485	-8.1	88,362	-4.1
1950	50,136	-3.4	29,024	-20.4	79,160	-10.4
1954	40,447	-19.3	22,522	-22.4	62,969	-20.5
1959	27,071	-33.1	10,352	-54.0	37,423	-40.6
1964	21,202	-21.7	5,615	-45.8	26,817	-28.3
1969	19,398	-8.5	2,817	-49.8	22,215	-17.2
1974	15,299	-21.1	1,230	-56.3	16,529	-25.6

Source: U.S. Bureau of the Census, *Fourteenth Census of the United States: 1920, Agriculture*, vol. 5, pt 2, The Southern States (Washington: Government Printing Office, 1922); U.S. Bureau of the Census, *Census of Agriculture, 1925-1974* (Washington: Government Printing Office, 1927-1977).

TABLE 9

Tractors, Arkansas Delta, 1940–1964

		Pct Chg
1940	9,833	
1950	41,281	319.8
1959	52,314	26.7
1964	53,911	3.1

Source: U.S. Bureau of the Census, *Sixteenth Census of the United States: 1940. Agriculture* (Washington: Government Printing Office, 1942); U.S. Bureau of the Census, *Census of Agriculture, 1959*, vol. 1, Counties, Part 34, Arkansas (Washington: Government Printing Office, 1961); U.S. Bureau of the Census, *Census of Agriculture, 1964, Statistics for the State and Counties, Arkansas* (Washington: Government Printing Office, 1976).

investment. Before the 1930s conventional wisdom held that cotton would always be picked by hand. John D. Rust, a resident of Pine Bluff, Arkansas, was the inventor of the mechanical cotton picker.[95] The rumblings of mechanical cotton pickers in trial runs challenged this "wisdom" and set off alarms across the Cotton South.

Since 1850, inventors had filed hundreds of patents for mechanical cotton pickers. They relied on several methods ranging from pickers that stripped the lint from the plant to suction devices that operated like a vacuum cleaner. Rust designed the first practical spindle picker. It used spindles or metal fingers that passed through the plant and in a rotating action pulled the lint from the bolls. This method had the advantage that a cotton field could be picked more than once, collecting more lint as late ripening bolls matured. Rust discovered that wetting the spindles made the lint adhere to them better. He successfully tested his machine in the 1930s, and his tests received wide publicity. But he did not produce a cotton picker that could be commercially mass-produced. International Harvester and John Deere made the mechanical cotton picker a commercial success after World War II.[96] Starting in 1949, Ben Pearson, Inc., a Pine Bluff company best known for archery equipment, manufactured pickers using the Rust patents.

As mechanical cotton pickers emerged, states like Arkansas faced a dreadful question—what would be the human consequences of mechanized cotton farming? Some observers played down the prospect for change by arguing that mechanization would be a long, slow process.[97] Others reported that the entire political and social structure of the South—the world of hand labor and sharecropping—faced immediate upheaval.[98] Arkansas Gov. Carl Bailey was one of many who pondered the implications of agricultural mechanization. He told a visiting reporter in the late 1930s:

> I don't know what the mechanical cotton pickers are going to do. But they have already been built. They function now, it is true, with indifferent efficiency. But that they function at all is a warning that they will be perfected. And when that is done, they will displace thousands of individuals in the cotton belt, thus creating suddenly the most perplexing social and economic problem. I'm afraid of the meaning of the picker; but we might as well face it. . . . I'm scared of the human consequences.[99]

This agricultural revolution in the Delta left large numbers of people without jobs. Many former sharecroppers left to look for work elsewhere, heading for urban centers like Detroit, Chicago, and Los Angeles. Displaced Arkansans found work during World War II, but they populated urban ghettos in postwar America. Today Delta farmers quip that the impact of the mechanical cotton picker was to increase the population of Detroit. But most sharecroppers and farm workers who stayed behind also remained poor, keeping the Delta one of the poorest sections of the nation.

Before the mechanization of cotton fully evolved, planters attempted many experiments to satisfy labor requirements. In some cases planters employed relocated Japanese Americans in cotton production during World War II. German prisoners of war also worked Arkansas cotton fields, and some employers hoped to delay their release until the 1945 crop could be picked. The *bracero* program brought in Mexican workers in the 1950s.[100] In parts of the Delta, flocks of geese were released in the fields to eat weeds in an attempt to "chop" cotton without human labor. Finally, in the early 1960s, the Arkansas cotton crop was completely machine picked.[101]

Technological change created a new Delta, sweeping away the Delta as it had been known for a century and a half. The technological impact can be measured in changes in the number of farms, acres in farms, and the size of farms. Table 10 shows that the number of Delta farms declined by 85 percent in the past forty years, while the average size of farms increased almost sevenfold.

Still another dramatic change in the Delta was the dethroning of King Cotton. As seen in Table 11, today Delta farmers harvest more acres of rice and soybeans than acres of cotton. Cotton acreage has declined steadily since World War II, while the rice crop has increased. But the most dramatic increase has been in soybean acreage.

The Frizzell family of Lincoln County was a model of the postwar agricultural change in the Delta. In the late 1930s, the Frizzells moved to Crigler, located east of Star City along Bayou Bartholomew, where the Farm Security Administration had developed a resettlement project. After World War II, four Frizzell brothers bought land as the Crigler project was broken up. Eventually they farmed about 1,100 acres, half of it rented. Like other farmers, they faced a common problem: they could not hire enough labor, and the cost would have been exorbitant if they had.[102]

The Frizzells wanted to stay in cotton farming, however, and they decided the answer was mechanization. The four brothers formed a partnership so that they could have a farm large enough to justify the purchase of heavy equipment. In the early 1950s, they set out to mechanize cotton production completely—from land preparation through harvesting—with a goal of producing one-and-a-half bales of cotton per acre. They already owned two

TABLE 10

Number of Farms, Acres in Farms, and Average Size of Farms, Arkansas Delta, 1945–1987 (Acres in Farms in Thousands)

	Number of Farms	Acres in Farms	Average Size
1945	98,727	7,669	77.7
1950	88,709	8,451	95.3
1959	42,366	8,092	191.0
1964	31,090	8,305	267.1
1969	25,353	8,497	335.2
1978	18,401	8,427	457.9
1987	15,034	7,970	530.1

Source: U.S. Bureau of the Census, *United States Censuses of Agriculture: 1945–1987* (Washington: Government Printing Office, 1946–1990).

TABLE II

Cotton, Rice, Soybeans, Delta Counties, Acres Harvested, 1950–1989   (in Thousands)

	Cotton	Rice	Soybeans
1950	1,432	339	494
1955	1,300	428	1,142
1960	1,266	379	2,287
1965	1,168	429	3,068
1970	1,017	431	4,010
1975	662	860	4,357
1980	828	1,240	3,960
1985	427	1,020	3,413
1989	596	1,044	2,957

Source: Statistical Reporting Service, United States Department of Agriculture and Agricultural Extension Service, University of Arkansas, *1950–1989 Agricultural Statistics for Arkansas* (Fayetteville: Division of Agriculture, 1951–1990).

tractors, which they used to break up the ground and plant the high-yielding varieties of cotton seed. They also used fertilizer and relied on chemicals for weed control instead of hiring cotton choppers. They refused to worry about what cotton choppers would cost or even whether they would be available. They also dusted their cotton with pesticides to control insects. Finally they installed an irrigation system, pumping water from Bayou Bartholomew. In 1951, they picked their cotton crop with a one-row spindle picker, harvesting 972 pounds of lint per acre. The quality was not as clean as hand-picked cotton, but this quality loss was offset by the lower labor cost. In the late 1950s, they purchased two two-row John Deere cotton pickers.[103]

The Frizzell brothers also were quick to adopt other new agricultural technologies. Their weed control plan included both pre-emergence herbicides and flame control. They applied pesticides from the air. They bought airplanes and rented out a crop-dusting service to neighboring farmers. The Frizzells had to experiment to achieve the best results. They kept changing grass-control methods, used different irrigation systems, and tried various defoliants. They were among the first to try new technologies whose value was still subject to suspicion. According to Bernice Frizzell, the oldest of the brothers, "I call it 'keeping up.' . . . I don't know whether that's a good word for it. But you've seen folks sit down and let the world go off and leave them. I think you've got to try to keep informed on what other people are finding out. Then you've got to try new things—not to prove they won't work—but to try to prove they will work."[104] The Frizzells pioneered mechanized farming in Lincoln County. But the Frizzells also faced financial problems and, like other farmers in the 1970s, lost out in the continuing consolidation of Delta agriculture.

Over the past 175 years, the Delta has seen more change than any other part of Arkansas. It has been cleared, drained, even leveled, and extensively cultivated. The Delta remains a rich agricultural region, but it is no longer a region of planters, sharecroppers, and cotton; instead, it is a region of machines, chemicals, custom work, and diversified crops. Gone are the old plantations, and indeed even the word *plantation* is in disrepute, because it suggests exploitation. Today everyone who farms the Delta has a *farm* no matter how large the acreage.[105] Delta towns reflect the poverty of the region, with vacant stores along main streets staring back like empty sockets. Today's Delta is still the product of its past. Its agricultural legacy of wealth and poverty, of privilege and exploitation, still hangs over the region's future.[106]

A man on horseback and a horseless carriage on a Phillips County farm in 1914.
Courtesy Howe Collection/UALR Archives.

Large-scale cotton cultivation in Jefferson County, around 1935, before mechanization.
Courtesy Arkansas History Comission.

Field hands picking cotton, around 1930.
Courtesy Arkansas History Commission.

Mechanical cotton pickers.
Courtesy Diana Lee Wilson.

Sheeks-Stephens Cotton Gin, 1902, in Corning (Clay County). This cotton gin was owned and operated by the Sheeks-Stephens General Store. *Courtesy Special Collections Division, University of Arkansas Libraries, Fayetteville.*

Cotton choppers near Corning (Clay County) in 1906.
Courtesy Special Collections Division, University of Arkansas Libraries, Fayetteville.

Notes

The Arkansas Delta: The Deepest of the Deep South

1. Bob Lancaster, *The Jungles of Arkansas: A Personal History of the Wonder State* (Fayetteville: University of Arkansas Press, 1989), 178.

2. Gerald T. Hanson and Carl H. Moneyhon, *Historical Atlas of Arkansas* (Norman: University of Oklahoma Press, 1989), 2.

3. Dan F. Morse, "First Inhabitants," Tom Baskett, Jr., ed., *The Arkansas Delta: A Landscape of Change* (Little Rock: Delta Cultural Center, 1990), 31–35.

4. Morris S. Arnold, *Unequal Laws Unto a Savage Race: European Legal Traditions in Arkansas, 1686–1836* (Fayetteville: University of Arkansas Press, 1985), see especially 203, 208; for a full treatment of Arkansas under French and Spanish rule, see Morris S. Arnold, *Colonial Arkansas, 1686–1804: A Social and Cultural History* (Fayetteville: University of Arkansas Press, 1991).

5. See Willard B. Gatewood, "The American Experience: The Southern Variable," Diane D. Kinkaid and Nancy E. Talburt, eds., *The American Experience: A Series of Public Lectures in Honor of the Nation's Bicentennial* (Fayetteville: University of Arkansas, 1977), 26–42.

6. See Family Records and Journal of Dr. William Thomas Mebane, 1851–1857, 30–32, Special Collections Division, Mullins Library, University of Arkansas, Fayetteville; *Lee County Courier* (Marianna, Ark.), March 27, April 3, 10, 17, 1897; Pete Daniel, *Deep'n As It Come: The 1927 Mississippi River Flood* (New York: Oxford University Press, 1977); Elliott B. Sartain, *It Didn't Just Happen* (Osceola, Ark.: Drainage District no. 9, 1975), Jim Merritt and B. Gill Dishough, "The Levee System of Desha County, Arkansas," *Desha County Historical Society Program* 14 (Spring 1988): 7–25; Eugene Dobson and Jim Merritt, "Canal 81 of the Cypress Creek Drainage District," *Desha County Historical Society Program* 12 (Spring 1986): 34–37; S. E. Simonson, "Origins of Drainage Projects in Mississippi County," *Arkansas Historical Quarterly* 5 (Fall 1946): 262–73; S. E. Simonson, "The St. Francis Levee and High Waters on the Mississippi River," *Arkansas Historical Quarterly* 6 (Winter 1947): 419–29; no one chronicled the weather, climate, and floods more faithfully than James M. Hanks in his voluminous Diary, 1865–1905 (microfilm), Mullins Library, University of Arkansas, Fayetteville.

7. David Moyers, "Twin Sisters of Wretchedness: Rockefeller Philanthropy and Health Projects in Arkansas," unpublished manuscript in possession of the author, 90.

8. For examples of patent medicines for "chills, ague, and swamp fever" that regularly appeared in Delta newspapers, see *Pine Bluff Weekly Press*, September 11,

1879; *Osceola Times* (Osceola, Ark.), November 12, 1887; *Lee County Courier*, June 27, 1891; see also Moyers, "Twin Sisters of Wretchedness," 97–98.

9. See A. Cash Koeniger, "Climate and Southern Distinctiveness," *The Journal of Southern History* 54 (February 1988): 21–44.

10. Octave Thanet [Alice French], "Plantation Life in Arkansas," *Atlantic Monthly* 68 (July 1891): 48.

11. Diary of Mrs. Isaac Hilliard 1849–1850, entry for October 11, 1850 (microfiche), Mullins Library, University of Arkansas, Fayetteville.

12. French, "Plantation Life in Arkansas," 46; see also Margaret Jones Bolsterli, *Vinegar Pie and Chicken Bread: A Woman's Diary of Life in the Rural South, 1890–1891* (Fayetteville: University of Arkansas Press, 1982).

13. *Helena Weekly World* (Helena, Ark.), April 27, November 16, 1898; April 5, 12, 26, 1899, January 31, February 7, May 16, December 5, 1900, February 1, 1902; David Taylor, "Ladies of the Club: An Arkansas Story," *Phillips County Historical Quarterly* 23 (June–September 1985): 29–39; *Osceola Times*, October, 23 1882, November 7, 14, 1885; *Lee County Courier*, December 2, 1893, December 8, 1894; *Pine Bluff Weekly Press-Eagle* (Pine Bluff, Ark.), October 11, 1911.

14. On the STFU see Donald Grubbs, *Cry From Cotton: The Southern Tenant Farmers Union and the New Deal* (Chapel Hill: University of North Carolina Press, 1971).

15. *Osceola Times*, February 4, 1888.

16. *Pine Bluff Weekly Press*, July 6, 1877, August 31, 1880; *Pine Bluff Weekly Press-Eagle*, November 26, 1884; *Osceola Times*, February 11, March 24, 1888; see also Shannon Craig, "Arkansas and Foreign Immigration, 1890–1915," unpublished M.A. thesis, University of Arkansas, Fayetteville, 1979, 15–32.

17. *Arkansas City Journal* quoted in *Lee County Courier*, November 16, 1895.

18. *Osceola Times*, January 5, 1889.

19. See Walter P. Webb, *The Great Plains* (Boston: Ginn and Co., 1931).

20. The reference to the Arkansas Delta as "the paradise (terrestrial) of our territories" appeared in the report of Lt. James B. Wilkinson, who was a member of Zebulon M. Pike's expedition in 1807; see Owen Lyon, "The Quapaws and Little Rock," *Arkansas Historical Quarterly* 8 (Winter 1949): 340; for a description of the natural abundance of the early southeast Arkansas Delta, see Leona Brasher, "Chicot County, Arkansas—Pioneer to Present Times," an unpublished manuscript written about 1915 and located in Special Collections, Mullins Library, University of Arkansas, Fayetteville, 2–6.

21. Albert Pike, "Letter from Arkansas," *American Monthly* 7 (January 1836): 32; on Arkansas's reputation, see also *The Democratic Star* (Helena, Ark.), July 5, 1854; Frederic Trautmann, ed. *Travels on the Lower Mississippi, 1879–1880: A Memoir by Ernst von Hesse-Wartegg* (Columbia: University of Missouri Press, 1990), 95, 117; for Mark Twain's contribution to the state's reputation, see Arthur Pettit, *Mark Twain and the South* (Lexington: University Press of Kentucky, 1974), 86–88.

22. *Pine Bluff Weekly Press*, September 23, 1880; see also *Pine Bluff Weekly Press*, February 22, 1877, January 6, 1881; *Pine Bluff Weekly Press-Eagle* March 14, September 26, 1911; *Lee County Courier*, September 26, 1896.

23. Octave Thanet [Alice French], "Town Life in Arkansas," *Atlantic Monthly* 68 (September 1891): 336.

24. Ibid., 337, 339.

25. *Osceola Times*, August 9, 1890.

26. French, "Town Life in Arkansas," 338–339; French, "Plantation Life in Arkansas," 43.

27. See *Pine Bluff Weekly Press*, July 17, 1879; *Lee County Courier*, August 29, 1891, August 20, 26, 1898; *Helena Weekly World*, June 12, 1899.

28. *Pine Bluff Weekly Press*, February 28, 1878, November 27, 1879, February 12, 1880; *Osceola Times*, February 18, 1888, February 14, 1891, March 6, 1892, February 18, 1899.

29. T. B. Thorpe, *The Hive of "The Bee-Hunter": A Repository* (New York: D. Appleton and Co., 1854), 28–46, 72–94; Gustave Aimard, *The Trappers of Arkansas, or the Loyal Heart* (New York: T. R. Dawley and Co., 1867); *Osceola Times*, June 21, 1884, August 22, October 17, 1885, November 12, 1887, August 15, 1891, April 20, May 20, 1893; *Pine Bluff Weekly Press*, October 13, 1879, June 29, 1880; Albert Pike, "Life in Arkansas: The Philosophy of Deer Hunting," *American Monthly Magazine* I (February 1836): 154–59; George P. Kelley, "Hunting as a Youth in Desha County," *Desha County Historical Society Program* I (1974): 32–36; Wanda Moore, "Hunting and Fishing Clubs," *Greene County Historical Quarterly* 5 (Fourth Quarter, 1970): 18–19; Ted Ownby, *Subduing Satan: Religion, Recreation, and Manhood in the Rural South, 1865–1970* (Chapel Hill: University of North Carolina Press, 1990), 1–18, 21–37.

30. *Pine Bluff Weekly Press*, August 28, 1879.

31. Orville W. Taylor, "Arkansas," *Encyclopedia of Religion in the South*, Samuel Hill, ed. (Macon, Ga.: Mercer University Press, 1984), 50–69; *Census of Religious Bodies: 1936* (Washington: Government Printing Office, 1937), 724–25; *Churches and Church Membership in the United States* (New York: National Council of Churches, 1957), Series C, No. 49, tables 106–07; *Osceola Times*, May 15, 1886; *Lee County Courier*, November 4, 1893, September 25, 1897.

32. See Samuel S. Hill et al., *Religion and the Solid South* (Nashville: Abingdon Press, 1972); George L. Maddox and Joseph Fichter, "Religion and Social Change in the South," *Journal of Social Forces* 22 (January 1966): 44–57; Kenneth Bailey, *Southern White Protestantism in the Twentieth Century* (New York: Harper and Row, 1964).

33. Ted Ownby, *Subduing Satan*.

34. *Southern Shield* (Helena, Ark.), July 31, 1852; *Democratic Star*, March 5, May 3, September 30, 1855; *Osceola Times*, October 21, December 2, 1882, September 22, 1883, December 26, 1891, August 20, 1898; see also George M. Hunt, "A History of the Prohibition Movement in Arkansas," unpublished M.A. thesis, University of Arkansas, Fayetteville, 1933, 52–99; *Lee County Courier*, January 31, 1891; *Pine Bluff Weekly Press-Eagle*, May 17, 1887.

35. *Osceola Times*, October 24, 1885; on the "grog shops" in Osceola in 1881, see Edward Palmer, "Arkansas Mounds—Notes," *Publications of the Arkansas Historical Association*, IV (Little Rock: Arkansas Democrat Printing Co., 1917): 398.

36. Hunt, "A History of Prohibition in Arkansas," 130–52; Jeannie Whayne, "Progressivism in the Delta: the Ideology of Reaction and Repression," unpublished paper in possession of the author.

37. *Osceola Times*, October 24, 1883.

38. Ibid., November 16, 1889.

39. Computations based on data in the *Biennial Report of the Superintendent of Public Instruction, 1899–1900* (Little Rock: Arkansas Democrat Co., 1900).

40. "Delta" in *Arkansas Gazette*, December 31, 1886.

41. For an incomplete list of private schools in Arkansas at the turn of the century, see *Biennial Report of the State Superintendent of Public Instruction, 1899–1900*, Table A; see also *The Arkansas Star* (Little Rock), December 17, 1840; *Osceola Times*, August 19, 1893, March 4, 1899; *Pine Bluff Weekly Press*, January 6, 1881; *Pine Bluff Weekly Press Eagle*, January 13, 1881.

42. Margaret Jones Bolsterli, *Born in the Delta: Reflections on the Making of a Southern White Sensibility* (Knoxville: University of Tennessee Press, 1991), 65–78, 119–120.

43. Wilbur J. Cash, *The Mind of the South* (New York: Alfred A. Knopf, 1941), 49–50.

44. Joel Williamson, "Black Self-Assertion Before and After Emancipation," in *Key Issues in the Afro-American Experience*, Nathan Huggins, et al., eds. (New York: Harcourt, Brace, Jovanovich, 1971), I, 220.

45. See Lancaster, *Jungles of Arkansas*, 113; the most complete work on slavery in Arkansas is Orville Taylor, *Negro Slavery in Arkansas* (Durham, N.C.: Duke University Press, 1958).

46. This complaint by former masters appeared frequently in the Field Office Records of the Bureau of Refugees, Freedmen, and Abandoned Lands, Record Group 105, National Archives, Washington, D.C.; hereinafter cited as Bureau Records.

47. Mrs. Isaac H. Hilliard, Diary, entry June 19, 1850; Maude Carmichael, "The Plantation System in Arkansas, 1850–1876," unpublished Ph.D. diss., Radcliffe College, 1935; Patrick Dunnahoo, *Cotton, Cornbread and Cape Jasmine: Early Days Life on Plantations in the Arkansas River Delta* (Benton, Ark.: P. Dunnahoo, 1985).

48. James M. Woods, *Rebellion and Realignment: Arkansas's Road to Secession* (Fayetteville: University of Arkansas Press, 1987), see especially 144–145, 190, 196; Ralph Wooster, "The Arkansas Secession Convention," *Arkansas Historical Quarterly* 13 (Summer 1954): 172–95; C. Fred Williams et al., *A Documentary History of Arkansas* (Fayetteville: University of Arkansas Press, 1984), 98.

49. O. E. Moore to Joseph Medill, January 29, 1872, in *Arkansas Gazette*, February 4, 1872; see also Carl H. Moneyhon, "The Impact of the Civil War in Arkansas: The Mississippi River Plantation Counties," unpublished paper in possession of the author.

50. See C. Vann Woodward, *The Burden of Southern History* (Baton Rouge: Louisiana State University, 1968), 11–25.

51. See Sheldon Hackney, "The South as Counterculture," *American Scholar* 42 (September 1973): 283–93.

52. Quoted in French, "Town Life in Arkansas," 339.

53. See Ira Berlin et al., *Freedom: A Documentary History of Emancipation, 1861–1867, Series II. The Black Military Experience* (Cambridge: Cambridge University Press, 1982), 169, 631–32, 712, 763, 820.

54. For studies of Reconstruction in Arkansas, see Thomas Staples, *Reconstruction in Arkansas, 1862–1874* (New York: Columbia University Press, 1923); George H.

Thompson, *Arkansas and Reconstruction: The Influence of Geography, Economics and Personality* (Port Washington, N.Y.: Kennikat Press, 1976); Horace D. Nash, "Blacks in Arkansas During Reconstruction: The Ex-Slave Narratives," *Arkansas Historical Quarterly* 48 (Autumn 1989): 243–59; Tom W. Dillard, "'Golden Prospects and Fraternal Amenities': Mifflin W. Gibbs's Arkansas Years," *Arkansas Historical Quarterly* 35 (Winter 1976): 307–33.

55. "Delta" in *Arkansas Gazette*, December 31, 1886; see also *Osceola Times*, May 23, 1885, September 25, 1886, August 23, September 13, November 29, 1890; *Lee County Courier*, April 28, 1894.

56. Willard B. Gatewood, "Negro Legislators in Arkansas 1891: A Document," *Arkansas Historical Quarterly* 31 (Autumn 1972): 220–33.

57. On the cotton pickers' strike, see William F. Holmes, "The Arkansas Cotton Pickers Strike of 1891 and the Demise of the Colored Farmer's Alliance," *Arkansas Historical Quarterly* 32 (Summer 1973): 107–19; *Lee County Courier*, September 19, 26, October 3, 19, 1891; *Osceola Times*, October 10, 17, 1891; on the Elaine riot, see Richard C. Cortner, *A Mob Intent on Death: The NAACP and the Arkansas Riot Cases* (Middletown, Conn.: Wesleyan University Press, 1988).

58. See, for examples, J. T. Robinson to Captain Sweeney, March 4, 1866, Gen. J. W. Sprague to Gen. O. O. Howard, May 8, 1866, A. G. Cunningham to S. M. Mells, August ?, 1868, A. L. Cunningham to Lt. S. M. Mills, August 3, 1868, Bureau Records.

59. Cal Ledbetter, Jr., "The Constitution of 1836: A New Perspective," *Arkansas Historical Quarterly* 41 (Autumn 1982): 214–52; Jesse Turner, "The Constitution of 1836," *Publications of the Arkansas Historical Association*, III (Fayetteville: n.p., 1911): 116–17.

60. Richard L. Niswonger, *Arkansas Democratic Politics, 1896–1920* (Fayetteville: University of Arkansas Press, 1990), 1–30; Joe Franklin, *Arkansas Black Elected Officials Guide, 1990–1991* (Little Rock: Office of the Secretary of State, n.d.); see also Diane D. Blair, *Arkansas Politics and Government: Do the People Rule?* (Lincoln: University of Nebraska Press, 1988).

61. Y. W. Etheridge, *A History of Ashley County Arkansas* (Van Buren, Ark.: Press Argus, 1959), 46; see also on railroads, A. B. Armstrong, "Railway Systems in Arkansas," unpublished M.A. thesis, University of Arkansas, Fayetteville, 1923; Hesse-Wartegg, *Travels on the Lower Mississippi*, 117–18; *Pine Bluff Press-Eagle* published a column entitled "Railroad Rumbles" that chronicled railroad news in the Delta.

62. *Helena Weekly World*, May 17, 1899; see also *Pine Bluff Weekly Press*, May 6, November 18, December 2, 16, 1880; *Pine Bluff Daily Graphic*, November 26, December 8, 1899, April 18, 1911; *Osceola Times*, October 24, 1891, June 22, 29, July 13, August 3, 17, 1899; *Lee County Courier*, June 26, July 10, 1897; for a general treatment of the New South idea see Paul Gaston, *The New South Creed: A Study in Southern Mythmaking* (Baton Rouge: Louisiana State University Press, 1970).

63. *Helena Weekly World*, May 30, 1900, March 26, 1901.

64. Ibid., May 9, 1900, January 30, 1901.

65. Ibid., June 13, July 4, 1900; *Pine Bluff Daily Graphic*, November 26, 1899; Donald Holley, "The Rural Delta," *The Arkansas Delta: A Landscape of Change*, 54; see also Florence R. Beatty, "The Negro Under Reconstruction with Special

Reference to Arkansas," unpublished M.A. thesis, University of Illinois, 1936; Martha Ellenburg, "Reconstruction in Arkansas," unpublished Ph.D. diss., University of Missouri, 1967.

66. See Holley, "The Rural Delta," 55–56.

67. On the STFU, see H. L. Mitchell, *Mean Things Happening in This Land: The Life and Times of H. L. Mitchell, Co-Founder of the Southern Tenant Farmers Union* (Montclair, N.J.: Allanheld, Osmun and Co., 1979); Grubbs, *Cry From Cotton*; Anthony P. Dunbar, *Against the Grain: Southern Radicals and Prophets, 1929–1959* (Charlottesville: University Press of Virginia, 1981), 83–135.

68. On the transformation of agriculture in the Arkansas Delta, see Donald Holley, *Uncle Sam's Farmers: The New Deal Communities in the Lower Mississippi Valley* (Urbana: University of Illinois Press, 1975); Jeannie Whayne, "Planters and the Remaking of the Arkansas Delta," unpublished paper in possession of the author; Holley, "The Rural South," 56–58; for changes in Arkansas, including the Delta, see C. Calvin Smith, *War and Wartime Changes: The Transformation of Arkansas* (Fayetteville: University of Arkansas Press, 1986), especially chapters 5, 6, and 7; Williams, *A Documentary History of Arkansas*, 282–86; Glen T. Barton and J. G. McNealy, *Recent Changes in Farm Labor Organization in Three Arkansas Plantation Counties*, Fayetteville: University of Arkansas Agricultural Experiment Station, 1939, 1–49; the bulletins of the University of Arkansas Agricultural Experiment Station include a wealth of information on Delta agriculture, but see especially M. W. Shesher and Harold Scoggins, *Cotton Production Practices in Arkansas*, Bulletin 507, April 1951; Daniel Capstick, *Economics of Mechanical Cotton Harvesting*, Bulletin 622, March 1960; H. L. Parks, "Rice, Its History and Culture," *Craighead County Historical Quarterly* I (Summer 1963): 20–23; Jimmy Kemp, "Fifty Years of Agriculture in Desha County," *Delta County Historical Society* 2 (1975): 48–52; James H. Street, *The New Revolution in the Cotton Economy: Mechanization and Its Consequences* (Chapel Hill: University of North Carolina Press, 1957).

69. Interview with Robert Pugh of Portland, Arkansas, June 2, 1990; Alvin L. Bertrand et al., *Factors Associated with Agricultural Mechanization in the Southwest Region,* Fayetteville: University of Arkansas Agricultural Experiment Station, Bulletin 567, February, 1956.

70. Trusten H. Holder, *Disappearing Wetlands in Eastern Arkansas* (Little Rock: Arkansas Planning Commission, 1970); Gerald T. Hanson, "Arkansas' Environment: Inventory and Prospect," in John Schell, ed. *Agenda for the Eighties: Papers and Proceedings of the Arkansas Issues '82 Conference* (Little Rock: n.p., 1982), 138–47.

71. See Juanita D. Sandford, *Poverty in the Land of Opportunity* (Little Rock: Rose Publishing Co., 1978); Mary Jo Grinstead, Bernal L. Green, and J. Martin Redfern, *Social and Labor Adjustment of Rural Black Americans in the Mississippi Delta,* Economic Research Service, U.S. Department of Agriculture in cooperation with Arkansas Agricultural Experiment Station, University of Arkansas, Agricultural Economic Report, 274; Wendy Shaw, "Poverty in Arkansas Since World War II," M.A. thesis, University of Arkansas, Fayetteville, 1990; *Realizing the Dream, Fulfilling the Potential: A Report by the Lower Mississippi Delta Development Commission* (Memphis: Mercury Printing, 1990); *Arkansas Gazette,* January 27, 1991.

72. John Gould Fletcher, *Arkansas* (Fayetteville: University of Arkansas Press, 1989), 291–92.

73. See especially Bolsterli, *Born in the Delta*; interview with Robert Pugh, June 2, 1990.

74. John Shelton Reed, *The Enduring South: Subcultural Persistence in Mass Society* (Lexington, Mass.: D.C. Heath Co., 1972).

75. Robert Coles, *Farewell to the South* (Boston: Little, Brown, 1972), 48–51.

76. Quoted from *New York Times* (1979) in Willard Gatewood, "Keynote Address," *Agenda for the Eighties*, 19.

The River's Gifts and Curses

1. S. L. Clemens (Mark Twain), *Life on the Mississippi* (J. R. Osgood and Co., 1883), 120.

2. N. M. Fenneman, *Physiography of the Eastern United States* (New York: McGraw-Hill Book Company, 1938), 84.

3. H. N. Fisk, "Geological Investigation of the Alluvial Valley of the Lower Mississippi River," (Vicksburg: Mississippi River Commission, 1944); R. T. Saucier, "Quaternary geology of the lower Mississippi Valley," Fayetteville: Arkansas Archeological Survey Research Series No. 6., 1974.

4. Thomas Nuttall, *A Journal of Travels into the Arkansas Territory During the Year 1819* (Philadelphia: Thomas H. Palmer, 1821), 80–81. The species was actually misidentified by Nuttall and was formally described and named after Nuttall in 1927 in E. J. Palmer, "On Nuttal's Trail Through Arkansas," *Journal of the Arnold Arboretum* 8 (1927): 32–33.

5. Nuttall, *Journal*, 78.

6. Friedrich Gerstäcker, *Wild Sports in the Far West* (Durham: Facsimile reprint 1968 by Duke University Press of English translation of original German text, 1854), 183.

7. Ibid., 186–91.

8. E. G. Bourne, *Narratives of the Career of Hernando De Soto* (New York: A. S. Barnes and Co., 1904), 117.

9. B. Meanley, *Swamps, River Bottoms and Canebrakes* (Barre, Mass.: Barre Publishers, 1972), 99.

10. Pete Daniel, *Deep'n As It Come: The 1927 Mississippi River Flood* (New York: Oxford University Press, 1977), 4.

11. Nuttall, *Journal*, 81.

12. E. Rowland, *Life, Letters and Papers of William Dunbar* (Jackson: Mississippi Historical Society, 1930), 309.

13. W. A. Percy, *Lanterns on the Levee* (New York: Alfred A. Knopf, 1941), 3.

14. Le Page Du Pratz, *The History of Louisiana* (Baton Rouge: Facsimile reprint 1975 by Lousiana State University Press, English translation of original French text, 1774), 124.

15. Gerstäcker, *Wild Sports*, 134.

16. Percy provides a description of these people: "He is white, Anglo-Saxon. . . . Where he comes from no one knows or cares . . . his shanty boats, like Huck Finn's fathers, may be seen moored in the willows or against the sandbars as far up and down the river as I have ever traveled. . . . He seems to regard the White River as the Navajos regard the Canyon de Chelly—as a sort of sanctuary and homeland. . . ." (16–17). He also describes their role in rescue efforts during the flood of 1927, "No

one had sent for them, no one was paying them, no one had a good word for them—but they came. Competent, devil-may-care pariahs, they scoured the back areas . . . and never rested until there was no one left clinging to a roof or a raft or the crotch of a tree" *Lanterns on the Levee*, 251–52.

17. J. Treat, letter dated Nov. 15, 1805, in National Archives (Microfilm #M-142), Transcription at Delta Cultural Center, Helena, Arkansas.

18. Le Page Du Pratz, *History of Louisiana*, 134–35.

19. Percy, *Lanterns on the Levee*, 244.

20. J. M. Hanks, unpublished diary, 1867, transcription at Delta Cultural Center, Helena, Arkansas, 57.

21. Percy, *Lanterns on the Levee*, 249–50.

22. Ibid.

23. Ibid., 246–47.

24. Daniel, *Deep'n As It Come*, 9.

25. M. L. Fuller, *The New Madrid Earthquake* (Washington: Government Printing Office, 1912), 10.

26. *Lexington Reporter*, December 16, 1811, quoted in James Penick Jr., *The New Madrid Earthquakes of 1811–1812* (Columbia: University of Missouri Press, 1976), 33–35.

27. Fuller, *New Madrid Earthquake*, 11.

28. R. Jones and P. Jones, "Stephen F. Austin in Arkansas," *Arkansas Historical Quarterly* 25 (Winter 1966): 336–53.

The Delta's Colonial Heritage

1. For the official account of La Salle's activities in the Arkansas region in 1682, see Vol. 2, Pierre Margry, *Découvertes et établissements des Français dans l'ouest et dans le sud de l'Amérique septentrionale, 1614–1754* (Paris, 1881), 181.

2. For Tonty's outpost on the Arkansas, see Morris S. Arnold, *Unequal Laws Unto a Savage Race: European Legal Traditions in Arkansas, 1686–1836* (Fayetteville: University of Arkansas Press, 1985), 5–6, 15; Arnold, *Colonial Arkansas, 1686–1804: A Social and Cultural History* (Fayetteville: University of Arkansas Press, 1991), 5–7.

3. For Law's activities, see Morris S. Arnold, "The Myth of John Law's German Colony on the Arkansas," *Louisiana History* 31 (Winter 1990): 83–88.

4. The general outline of the events of the two Chickasaw Wars are traced in Patricia Woods, *French-Indian Relations on the Southern Frontier, 1699–1762* (Ann Arbor, Mich.: UMI Research Press, 1980).

5. This battle is discussed in Arnold, *Colonial Arkansas*, 17, 31–32, 105–07.

6. See, e.g., Dubruca, *L'Itinéraire des Français dans la Louisiane* (Paris, 1802), 78–79.

7. The peregrinations of the Post are documented in Arnold, *Unequal Laws*, 212–17; Morris S. Arnold, "The Relocation of Arkansas Post to Ecores Rouges in 1779," *Arkansas Historical Quarterly* 42 (Winter 1983): 317–31.

8. *Archivo General de Indias, Paples Procedentes de Cuba*, leg. 107: 221. Hereinafter cited as AGI, PC.

9. See the letter from Gov. Carondelet to Capt. Charles de Vilemont of the Arkansas dated 17 February 1797 in "Memorial of the Heirs of Carlos de Vilemont . . . ," *Documents of the 24th Congress, 2d Session*, No. 89 (1837).

10. Morris S. Arnold and Dorothy Core, eds. *Arkansas Colonials, 1686–1804* (De Witt, Arkansas, 1986), 50.

11. Ibid., 65.

12. Lawrence Kinnaird, ed. *Spain in the Mississippi Valley, 1765–1794*, 3, (Washington, D.C.: American Historical Association, 1946), 117.

13. Arnold and Core, 70.

14. AGI, PC, *leg.* 107: 463.

15. AGI, PC, *leg.* 107.

16. The architecture of the houses built in colonial Arkansas is discussed in Arnold, *Colonial Arkansas*, 25–52.

17. Arnold, *Unequal Laws*.

18. AGI, PC, *leg.* 107: 480.

19. AGI, PC, *leg.* 191 and de Vilemont to Gayoso, 15 November 1798, AGI, PC, *leg.* 215A: 281–82.

20. Arnold, *Colonial Arkansas*, 89.

21. Ibid., 90–93.

22. James Woods, "'To the Suburb of Hell': Catholic Missionaries in Arkansas, 1803–1843," *Arkansas Historical Quarterly* 48 (Autumn 1989): 217, 231, 233.

23. Thomas Nuttall, *Journal of Travels into the Arkansas Territory During the Year 1819* (Philadelphia: Thomas H. Palmer, 1821), 75.

24. Ibid., 77.

25. These matters are explored in some detail in Arnold, *Colonial Arkansas*, 112–124; Arnold, "The Significance of Arkansas's Colonial Experience," *Arkansas Historical Quarterly* 51 (Spring 1992): 69–82.

"Desolation Itself": The Impact of Civil War

1. *Arkansas Baptist*, February 13, 1861.

2. *Arkansas Gazette*, February 16, 1861.

3. U.S. Census Office, *Abstract of the Returns of the Fifth Census* (Washington: Duff Green, 1832), 43.

4. U.S. War Department, *The War of Rebellion: A Compilation of the Official Records of the Union and Confederate Armies* 70 vols. in 128 (Washington: Government Printing Office, 1885), ser. 1, vol. I, 690, hereafter cited as O.R.; all references are to series I.

5. Henry M. Stanley, *The Autobiography of Henry M. Stanley* (Boston: Houghton, Mifflin, Co., 1939), 171.

6. *Arkansas Gazette*, June 1, 1861.

7. U.S. National Archives, *Compiled Records of Confederate Soldiers who served in Organizations from the State of Arkansas, M317* (Sampling from microfilm M317, Arkansas History Commission).

8. O.R., vol. 13, 830.

9. Bobby Roberts, "Thomas C. Hindman, Jr.: Secessionist and Confederate General," M.A. thesis, University of Arkansas, Fayetteville, 1972, 82–86.

10. O.R., vol. 13, 30–37.

11. Charles Field, *Three Years in the Saddle from 1861–1865* (Goldfield, Iowa: n.p., 1898), 16–19.

12. William L. Shea, "A Semi-Savage State: The Image of Arkansas in the Civil War," *Arkansas Historical Quarterly* 38 (Winter 1989): 325–26.

13. Ibid., 325.

14. "Benjamin F. Pearson's War Diary," *Annals of Iowa*, 3d Series, vol.15 (October 1925): 102.

15. A. F. Sperry, *History of the 33rd Iowa Infantry Volunteer Regiment* (Des Moines: Mills & Co., 1866), 8, hereafter cited as Sperry, *33rd Iowa*.

16. Bobby Roberts and Carl Moneyhon, *Portraits of Conflict* (Fayetteville: University of Arkansas Press, 1987), 86–87.

17. William Forse Scott, *The Story of A Cavalry Regiment; the Career of the Fourth Iowa Veteran Volunteers* (New York: G. Putnam's Sons, 1893), 50–53.

18. Paul E. Steiner, *Disease in the Civil War* (Springfield, Ill.: Charles C. Thomas Publisher, 1968), 217–18.

19. T. J. Gaughan, ed., *Letters of a Confederate Surgeon, 1861–1865* (Camden, Ark.: Hurley, Co., 1960), 102, hereinafter cited as Gaughan, *Letters*.

20. Leander Stillwell, *The Story of a Common Soldier of Army Life in the Civil War* (Erie, Kans.: Press of the Erie Record, 1917), 84–85.

21. O.R., vol. 41, pt. 2, 715.

22. Ibid., 220.

23. Sperry, *33rd Iowa*, 41.

24. "The 28th Wisconsin Infantry Regiment at Helena: Part IV, Letters of Captain Edward S. Redington, Company D," *Phillips County Historical Quarterly* 13 (March 1975): 23, hereinafter cited as Redington Letters.

25. "Indiana Troops at Helena: Part IV, Letters of Sylvester Bishop, 11th Indiana Infantry," *Phillips County Historical Quarterly* 17 (June 1979): 37.

26. Jan Sarna, comp., "Letters of Joseph R. Edwards, Co. A., 12th Michigan Infantry," *Phillips County Historical Quarterly* 16 (June 1978): 6.

27. Sperry, *33rd Iowa*, 40.

28. Russell P. Baker, ed., "This Old Book: The Civil War Diary of Mrs. Mary Sale Edmondson," *Phillips County Historical Quarterly* 11 (March 1973): 8.

29. Redington Letters, Part V, *Phillips County Historical Quarterly* 13 (September 1975): 15.

30. O.R., vol. 13, 34.

31. Florence Marie Ankeny Cox, ed., *Kiss Josey for Me* (Santa Ana, Calif.: Friis-Pioneer Press, 1974), 86.

32. Edward Adolphus Davenport, ed., *History of the Ninth Regiment Illinois Cavalry Volunteers* (Chicago: Donahue & Henneberry, Printers, 1888), 49.

33. Dale P. Kirkman, "The Leased Plantations Below Helena," *Phillips County Historical Quarterly* 4 (September 1966): 8–14.

34. John N. Edwards, *Shelby and His Men: The War in the West* (Cincinnati: Miami Printing and Publishing Co., 1867), 105–06, hereafter cited as Edwards, *Shelby and His Men*.

35. O.R., vol. 17, pt. 1, 781; William Williston Heartsill, *Fourteen Hundred and 91 Days in the Confederate Army* (Marshall, Tex.: W. W. Heartsill, 1876; reprinted by Rare Book Publishers, Pine Bluff, Ark., 1982), 94.

36. Sperry, *33rd Iowa*, 22.

37. O.R., vol. 22, pt. 1, 407.

38. Edwin C. Bearss, "The Battle of Helena, July 4, 1863," *Arkansas Historical Quarterly* 20 (Autumn 1961): 260–65.

39. O.R., vol. 22, pt. 1, 409.

40. George M. Blackburn, ed., *"Dear Carrie . . . . ." The Civil War Letters of Thomas N. Stevens* (Mount Pleasant, Mich.: The Clarke Historical Library, Central Michigan University, 1984), 127.

41. Minos Miller to Dear Mother, July 6, 1863, Minos Miller Letters, Special Collections, University of Arkansas, Fayetteville.

42. O.R., vol. 22, pt. 1, 408.

43. Leo E. Huff, "The Union Expedition Against Little Rock, August–September, 1863," *Arkansas Historical Quarterly* 22 (Autumn 1963): 224–37.

44. Edwards, *Shelby and His Men*, 321–24.

45. John M. Harrell, "Arkansas," in *Confederate Military History*, vol. 14, extended edition (Wilmington, N.C.: Broadfoot Publishing, Co., 1988), 271–72.

46. Edwards, *Shelby and His Men*, 342–46.

47. O.R., vol. 34, pt. 4, 231.

48. Ibid., vol. 48, pt. 1, 237.

49. Eric Foner, *Reconstruction: America's Unfinished Revolution* (New York: Harper & Row, 1988), xxv, 128, 170.

50. C. Vann Woodward, *The Origins of the New South* (Baton Rouge: Louisiana State University Press, 1951), 215–21.

51. U.S. Census Office, Table XLIII, "General Statistics of Agriculture by States and Territory at the Censuses of 1880, 1870, 1860, and 1850," *Compendium of the Tenth Census* (Washington: Government Printing Office, 1883), 650–83.

52. John C. Wright, *Memoirs of Colonel John C. Wright* (Pine Bluff, Ark.: Rare Book Publishers, 1982), 257.

53. Daniel Harvey Reynolds Diary, April 20, 1865, Daniel Harvey Reynolds Papers, Special Collections, University of Arkansas, Fayetteville.

54. Charles Edward Nash, *Biographical Sketches of Gen. Pat Cleburne and Gen. T. C. Hindman* (Little Rock: Tunnah & Pittard Printers, 1898), 266–67.

55. Gaughan, *Letters*, 272.

56. Joe M. Scott, *Four Years' Service in the Southern Army* (Fayetteville, Ark.: Washington County Historical Society, 1958; reprint of 1897 volume published at Mulberry, Arkansas), 49.

57. "Civil War Reminiscences of L. A. Fitzpatrick, Sr.," *Phillips County Historical Quarterly* 15 (September 1967): 12.

58. Inscription of Lila Jabine in Samuel S. Greene's *Introduction to the Study of English Grammar*, in possession of the author.

59. "Camps Reported by Gen. W. E. Mickle," *Confederate Veteran* 12 (August 1904): 373.

60. *Report of the Fifth Annual Convention, Arkansas, State Division, U.D.C.*, 17.

61. Daryl T. Aikman, "The Confederate Memorial at Helena," *Phillips County Historical Quarterly* 17 (June 1979): 28–32.

62. Judge James M. Hanks Diaries, May 25, 1892; in the possession of Ms. Johnnie P. Schatz, Helena, Arkansas.

From Slavery to Uncertain Freedom: Blacks in the Delta

1. Indianapolis *Freeman*, January 5, 1889.

2. Vernon Lane Wharton, *The Negro in Mississippi 1865–1890* (Chapel Hill, N.C.: University of North Carolina Press, 1947; reprint ed., New York: Harper and Row, 1965), 108; George Brown Tindall, *South Carolina Negroes, 1877–1900* (Columbia, S.C.: University of South Carolina Press, 1952), 174–77; August Meier, *Negro Thought in America 1880–1915* (Ann Arbor: University of Michigan Press, 1964), 60.

3. *Eleventh Census of the United States, 1890: Population*, I: 400, 403, 451.

4. William Pickens, *Bursting Bonds* (Boston: The Jordan and More Press, 1923), 22.

5. For a discussion of the continuing disproportionate existence of poverty in the black community, see Jay R. Mandle, *The Roots of Black Poverty: The Southern Plantation Economy After the Civil War* (Durham, N.C.: Duke University Press, 1978), and Roger L. Ransom and Richard Sutch, *One Kind of Freedom: The Economic Consequences of Emancipation* (Cambridge, Eng.: Cambridge University Press, 1977).

6. Michael B. Dougan, "Slavery in Arkansas," in *Dictionary of Afro-American Slavery*, ed. Randall M. Miller and John David Smith (New York: Greenwood Press, 1988), 60.

7. Orville W. Taylor, *Negro Slavery in Arkansas* (Durham, N.C.: Duke University Press, 1958), 11–17.

8. J. Steele and J. M'Campbell, eds. *Laws of Arkansas Territory* (Little Rock: 1835), 20.

9. Ibid., 175, 268, 437–38, 520–26, 530–32; Taylor, *Negro Slavery in Arkansas*, 209.

10. William McK. Ball and Sam. C. Roane, eds., *Revised Statutes of the State of Arkansas* (Boston: 1838), 24, 37; Elbert H. English, ed., *A Digest of the Statutes of Arkansas* (Little Rock: 1848), 706; Taylor, *Negro Slavery in Arkansas*, 253–54.

11. English, ed., *A Digest of the Statutes of Arkansas*, 584–587; Joel Williamson, *The Crucible of Race: Black-White Relations in the American South Since Emancipation* (New York: Oxford University Press, 1984), 32, and *New People: Miscegenation and Mulattoes in the United States* (New York: The Free Press, 1980), 61–75; *Acts Passed at the Twelfth Session of the General Assembly of the State of Arkansas* (Little Rock: 1859), 69, 175–78; *Acts Passed at the Thirteenth Session of the General Assembly of the State of Arkansas* (Little Rock: 1861), 206; Taylor, *Negro Slavery in Arkansas*, 257–58.

12. *Third Census of the United States: 1810*, 84; *Fourth Census of the United States: 1820*, 41; *Seventh Census of the United States: 1850*, 548; *Eighth Census of the United States: 1860*, 18.

13. Taylor, *Negro Slavery in Arkansas*, 47–50.

14. U. S. Department of the Interior, Office of the Census, *Agriculture of the United States in 1860: 1860* (Washington, D. C.: 1864), 224.

15. Fay Hempstead, *Historical Review of Arkansas* (Chicago: Lewis Publishing Company, 1911), I, 209–14, 218, 253–54; Dallas T. Herndon, ed. *Centennial History of Arkansas* (Chicago: S. J. Clarke Publishing Co., 1922), I, 275–82; John William

Graves, "Town and Country: Race Relations and Urban Development in Arkansas 1865–1905," Ph.D. diss., University of Virginia, 1978, 13–14.

16. George P. Rawick, gen. ed., *The American Slave: A Composite Autobiography*, 19 vols. (Westport, Conn.: Greenwood Publishing Company, 1972), vol. 8: *Arkansas Narratives*, pt. 1, 33–39.

17. Ibid., 86–89.

18. Ibid., 168–69.

19. Leon F. Litwack, *Been in the Storm So Long: The Aftermath of Slavery* (New York: Alfred A. Knopf, 1979), 167–335; Rawick, *The American Slave*, vol. 8, pt. 2, 10.

20. David Yancey Thomas, *Arkansas in War and Reconstruction 1861–1874* (Little Rock: Arkansas Division, United Daughters of the Confederacy, 1926), 143, 389–90; Thomas S. Staples, *Reconstruction in Arkansas 1862–1874*, Studies in History, Economics, and Public Law, vol. CIX (New York: Columbia University Press, 1923; reprint ed., Gloucester, Mass.: Peter Smith, 1964), 53; John L. Ferguson, ed., *Arkansas and the Civil War* (Little Rock: Arkansas Civil War Centennial Commission, 1965), 322.

21. Staples, *Reconstruction in Arkansas 1862–1874*, 196–97, 202–03.

22. Ibid., 209–10.

23. U. S., Congress, Public Acts of the Thirty-ninth Congress of the United States, Chapter CLIII, 39th Congress, 2nd session, March 2, 1867, *Congressional Globe* 37: 197–98; U.S. Congress, Public Acts of the Fortieth Congress of the United States, Chapter VI, 40th Congress, 1st session, March 23, 1867, *Congressional Globe*, 38: 39–40; James Harris Fain, "Political Disfranchisement of the Negro in Arkansas," M.A. thesis, University of Arkansas, 1961, 4; *Debates and Proceedings of the Convention which assembled at Little Rock, January 7th 1868, under the Provisions of the Act of Congress March 2nd, 1867, and the Acts of March 23rd and July 19th, 1867, Supplementary thereto, to form a Constitution for the State of Arkansas* (Little Rock, 1868), 8; Joseph M. St. Hilaire, "The Negro Delegates in the Arkansas Constitutional Convention of 1868: A Group Profile," *Arkansas Historical Quarterly* 33 (Spring 1974): 38–69.

24. *The Constitution of the State of Arkansas* (Little Rock, 1891), 277–321; Graves, "Town and Country: Race Relations and Urban Development in Arkansas 1865–1905," 29; Fain, "Political Disfranchisement of the Negro in Arkansas," 8–9.

25. Harmon L. Remmel to Powell Clayton, October 18, 1899, Harmon Liveright Remmel Papers, Special Collections, University of Arkansas Libraries, Fayetteville, Arkansas; Marvin Franklin Russell, "The Republican Party of Arkansas, 1874–1913," Ph.D. diss., University of Arkansas, 1985, 125–27.

26. Mifflin W. Gibbs, *Shadow and Light: An Autobiography* (Washington, D. C.: 1902; reprint ed., New York: Arno Press and the New York Times, 1968), 159.

27. Joe Tolbert Segraves, "Arkansas Politics, 1874–1918," Ph.D. diss., University of Kentucky, 1973, 53.

28. *Arkansas Gazette*, August 30, 1882.

29. James W. Mason, of Sunnyside, Chicot County, was the illegitimate son of Elisha Worthington, the largest slaveowner in Chicot County in 1860. Mason served as state senator from 1868 to 1871 and as county sheriff from 1872 to 1874. See Willard B. Gatewood, Jr., "Sunnyside: The Evolution of an Arkansas Plantation, 1840–1945," *Arkansas Historical Quarterly* L (Spring 1991): 5–29; Gibbs, *Shadow and*

entary

ght,* 229; Jerome Riley, *The Philosophy of Negro Suffrage* (Hartford, Conn.: American Publishing Co., 1895), 19–21.

30. U.S. Department of the Interior, Bureau of the Census, *Eleventh Census of the United States, 1890: Population,* I: 400, 403.

31. Williamson, *The Crucible of Race,* 226–29.

32. Other Delta counties in which blacks retained offices after Redemption included Monroe, Crittenden, Mississippi, St. Francis, and Lee; Segraves, "Arkansas Politics, 1874–1918," 114–16.

33. William J. Simmons, *Men of Mark: Eminent, Progressive and Rising* (George M. Rewell and Co., 1887; reprint ed., Chicago: Johnson Publishing Co., 1970), 410; Tom W. Dillard, "The Black Moses of the West: A Biography of Mifflin Wistar Gibbs, 1823–1915," M.A. thesis, University of Arkansas, 1975, 78, 83, 90, 131.

34. C. Calvin Smith, "John E. Bush of Arkansas, 1890–1910," *Ozark Historical Review* 2 (Spring 1973): 50; Russell, "The Republican Party of Arkansas, 1874–1913," 205, 221.

35. *Indianapolis Freeman,* May 11, September 14, 1889; Russell, "The Republican Party of Arkansas," 179.

36. James W. Leslie, "Ferd Havis: Jefferson County's Black Republican Leader," *Arkansas Historical Quarterly* 37 (Autumn 1978): 240, 242, 244–47.

37. *Indianapolis Freeman,* April 4, 1891.

38. *Historical Report of the Secretary of State 1958,* 461–62; Fain, "Political Disfranchisement of the Negro in Arkansas," 18; Carl H. Moneyhon, "Black Politics in Arkansas During the Gilded Age, 1876–1900," *Arkansas Historical Quarterly* 44 (Autumn 1985): 233.

39. Willard B. Gatewood, Jr., "Negro Legislators in Arkansas, 1891: A Document," *Arkansas Historical Quarterly* 31 (Autumn 1972): 226.

40. W. Scott Morgan, *History of the Wheel and Alliance,* (1891, reprint ed., New York: Burt Franklin, 1968), 72–73; Francis Clark Elkins, "The Agricultural Wheel in Arkansas, 1882–1889," Ph.D. diss., Syracuse University, 1953, 108, 208; Garland Erastus Bayliss, "Public Affairs in Arkansas, 1874–1896," Ph.D. diss., University of Texas, 1972, 290–91, 311–12; James Edgar Howard, "Populism in Arkansas," M.A. thesis, George Peabody College for Teachers, 1931, 13.

41. Bayliss, "Public Affairs in Arkansas, 1874–1896," 297; Clifton Paisley, "The Political Wheelers and Arkansas' Election of 1888," *Arkansas Historical Quarterly* 25 (Spring 1966): 3–5, 7–8.

42. *Arkansas Gazette,* August 22, 1888.

43. *St. Louis Post-Dispatch,* n.d., quoted in the *Arkansas Gazette,* October 7, 1888.

44. Paisley, "The Political Wheelers and Arkansas' Election of 1888," 17–20; Bayliss, "Public Affairs in Arkansas, 1874–1896," 303–05; Moneyhon, "Black Politics in Arkansas During the Gilded Age, 1876–1900," 240; J. Morgan Kousser, *The Shaping of Southern Politics: Suffrage Restriction and the Establishment of the One-Party South, 1880–1910* (New Haven: Yale University Press, 1975), 123.

45. *Arkansas Democrat,* July 22, 1890.

46. *Arkansas Gazette,* January 6, 1889.

47. C. Vann Woodward, *Origins of the New South 1877–1913* (Baton Rouge: Louisiana State University Press, 1951), 347–48.

48. Williamson, *The Crucible of Race,* 111, 115–16.

49. *Biennial Report of the Secretary of State of the State of Arkansas* (Little Rock: 1891), 55; *Biennial Report of the Secretary of State of the State of Arkansas* (Little Rock: 1893), 56; *Biennial Report of the Secretary of State of the State of Arkansas* (Little Rock: 1896), 53; J. Morgan Kousser, *The Shaping of Southern Politics*, 127, 129.

50. Edward W. Gantt, ed., *A Digest of the Statutes of Arkansas* (Little Rock: 1874), 257–60.

51. Williamson, *The Crucible of Race*, 224–25, 254–55.

52. *Arkansas Gazette*, January 14, 20, 28, 1891; Graves, "Town and Country," 206.

53. John Gray Lucas, a graduate of Boston University Law School and a representative of Jefferson County in the Arkansas legislature in 1891, moved to Chicago in 1893. *Indianapolis Freeman*, April 4, 1891, July 30, 1892.

54. *Arkansas Gazette*, May 28, 1903; *Arkansas Democrat*, June 2, 1903; John William Graves, "The Arkansas Negro and Segregation, 1890–1903," M.A. thesis, University of Arkansas, 1967, 136.

55. *Thirty Years of Lynching in the United States 1889–1918* (New York: NAACP, 1919; reprint ed., New York: Arno Press and The New York Times, 1969), 32–33, 48–52, 104.

56. U.S. Department of Commerce, Bureau of the Census, *Fourteenth Census of the United States, 1920: Population*, 3: 96.

57. Walter F. White, "The Race Conflict in Arkansas," *Survey* 43 (December 13, 1919): 234.

58. For accounts of the Elaine riots, see Arthur I. Waskow, *From Race Riot to Sit-In: 1919 and the 1960s* (Garden City, New York: Doubleday and Company, Inc., 1966; Anchor Books, 1967), 121–74; O. A. Rogers, Jr., "The Elaine Race Riots of 1919," *Arkansas Historical Quarterly* 19 (Summer 1960):142–50; B. Boren McCool, *Union, Reaction and Riot* (Memphis: Memphis State University, 1970); Richard C. Cortner, *A Mob Intent on Death: The NAACP and the Arkansas Riot Cases* (Middletown, Conn.: Wesleyan University Press, 1988).

59. Waskow, *From Race Riot to Sit-In*, 122, 129; Rogers, "The Elaine Race Riots of 1919," 149–50; Cortner, *A Mob Intent on Death*, 2, 15, 18.

60. Waskow, *From Race Riot to Sit-In*, 173.

61. Meier, *Negro Thought in America 1880–1915*, 23–25, 42, 121.

62. U.S. Department of the Interior, Census Office, *Eleventh Census of the United States: 1890, Population*, I: 396–97; U.S. Department of Commerce and Labor, Bureau of the Census, *Twelfth Census of the United States: 1900, Population*, I: 483; U.S. Department of Commerce, Bureau of the Census, *Thirteenth Census of the United States: 1910, Population*, I: 141; U.S. Department of the Interior, Census Office, *Statistics of Churches in the United States at the Eleventh Census: 1890*, IX: 38, 49; U.S. Department of Commerce and Labor, Bureau of the Census, *Religious Bodies: 1906*, I: 160, 542; U.S. Department of Commerce, Bureau of the Census, *Religious Bodies: 1916*, I: 152, 558.

63. *Religious Bodies: 1906*, I: 542; *Religious Bodies: 1916*, I: 558.

64. *Religious Bodies: 1916*, I: 558; Clement Richardson, ed., *National Cyclopedia of the Colored Race* (Montgomery, Ala.: National Publishing Company, 1919), 575.

65. WPA Historical Records Survey, Arkansas, Records Inventory Files, 1936–1942 (MS H62), Special Collections, University Libraries, University of Arkansas, Fayetteville, Arkansas.

66. Thomas C. Kennedy, "Southland College: The Society of Friends and Black Education in Arkansas," *Arkansas Historical Quarterly* 42 (Autumn 1983): 215–16.

67. *City Directory of Pine Bluff, Arkansas, 1894* (Pine Bluff, Ark.: Wilson Publishing Co., 1894), 162; Box 450, Files 20–23, Roman Catholic, WPA Historical Records Survey.

68. Carter G. Woodson, *The History of the Negro Church*, 3d ed. (Washington, D.C.: The Associated Publishers, 1972), 257–59.

69. "Memorial Program in Honor of Rev. Elias Camp Morris, D.D. of Helena, Ark." (Nashville: National Baptist Convention, Inc., 1923), 2; E. C. Morris, *Sermons, Addresses, and Reminiscences and Important Correspondence* (Nashville: National Baptist Publishing Board, 1901), 174–79; Irvine Garland Penn, *The Afro-American Press and Its Editors* (Springfield, Mass.: Willey and Company, 1891; reprint ed., New York: Arno Press and The New York Times, 1969), 260–61; Richardson, *National Cyclopedia of the Colored Race*, 101.

70. *Baptist Vanguard*, February 16, 1894.

71. Ibid., August 6, 1896.

72. Thomas Phillips, Sr., S. V. Clemmons, and O. B. Elders, Sr., "Immanuel Community 1870–1980," *Grand Prairie Society Bulletin* 24 (October, 1981): 3–4.

73. *Baptist Vanguard*, March 2, 1894, May 28, 1896; *American Guide*, May 30, 1896.

74. August Meier and Elliott Rudwick, *From Plantation to Ghetto*, rev. ed. (New York: Hill and Wang, 1970), 157–65; See also Willard B. Gatewood, Jr., *Aristocrats of Color: The Black Elite, 1880–1920* (Bloomington: Indiana University Press, 1990).

75. Fon Louise Gordon, "The Black Experience in Arkansas, 1880–1920," Ph.D. diss., University of Arkansas, 1988, 248–52.

76. A. E. Bush and P. L. Dorman, eds., *History of the Mosaic Templars of America: Its Founders and Officials* (Little Rock: Central Printing Company, 1924), 13–18, 138–39, 158–59, 162, 174, 178.

77. *Arkansas Gazette*, July 15, 1903, July 26, August 4, 1911, August 4, 1915; *Indianapolis Freeman*, September 9, 1893.

78. Bush and Dorman, *History of the Mosaic Templars*, 132–33.

79. Smith, "John E. Bush of Arkansas, 1890–1910," 53; *Arkansas Gazette*, August 16, 1911; Booker T. Washington, *The Negro in Business* (Boston: Hertel and Jenkins and Company, 1907), 218; Louis R. Harlan, "Booker T. Washington and the National Negro Business League," William G. Shade and Roy C. Herrenkohl, eds., *Seven on Black* (Philadelphia: J. B. Lippincott Co., 1969), 76, 78, 81–82.

80. E. M. Woods, *Blue Book of Little Rock and Argenta Arkansas* (Little Rock: Central Printing Company, 1907), 104, 123.

81. *Indianapolis Freeman*, March 11, 1899; John Petty Moore Plantation and Business Records, 1897–1908, Thomas Hottel Gist Papers, Special Collections, University Libraries, University of Arkansas, Fayetteville, Arkansas.

82. Tom Baskett, Jr., ed., *Persistence of the Spirit* (Little Rock: Arkansas Endowment for the Humanities, 1986), 27.

83. *Pine Bluff City Directory 1903*, 292–303; Interview with Mrs. Sallye Alyeene Perry, Pine Bluff, Arkansas, July 16, 1987.

84. *Biographical and Historical Memoirs of Pulaski, Jefferson, Lonoke, Faulkner, Grant, Saline, Perry, Garland, and Hot Spring Counties, Arkansas* (Chicago:

Goodspeed Publishing Company, 1889; reprint ed., Easley, South Carolina: Southern Historical Press, 1978), 798–802; Leslie, "Ferd Havis: Jefferson County's Black Republican Leader," 240, 249–50; *Indianapolis Freeman*, March 18, 1899.

85. Leslie, "Ferd Havis," 246, 249–50; *Pine Bluff Weekly Commercial*, May 9, 1903; *Indianapolis Freeman*, January 31, 1891.

86. Dillard, "The Black Moses of the West: A Biography of Mifflin Wister Gibbs, 1823–1915," 104–10; John E. Bush, "Afro-American People of Little Rock," *Colored American Magazine* VIII (January 1905): 41.

87. Fon Louise Gordon, "Black Women in Arkansas," *Pulaski County Historical Review* 35 (Summer 1987): 26, 35.

88. Meier, *Negro Thought in America, 1880–1915*, 128–35.

89. Gordon, "Black Women in Arkansas," 26, 30, 34–35; W. E. B. Du Bois, ed., *Efforts for Social Betterment Among Negro Americans* (Atlanta: Atlanta University Press, 1909; reprint ed., New York: Arno Press and the New York Times, 1969), 29–30, 52; *Arkansas Gazette*, June 6, 1896.

90. "Social and Art Club 1987–1988 Year Book," (typewritten).

91. Gordon, "Black Women in Arkansas," 28.

92. *Indianapolis Freeman*, June 6, 1891.

93. U.S. Department of Commerce, Bureau of the Census, *United States Census of Population: 1950*, vol. 2, *Characteristics of the Population*, pt. 4, Arkansas, 37, 39, 42, 98–101.

94. U.S. Department of Commerce, Bureau of the Census, *United States Census of Population: 1980*, vol. 1, *Characteristics of the Population*, pt. 5, Arkansas, 39, 58, 62, 68.

95. Wilbur J. Cash, *The Mind of the South* (New York: Alfred A. Knopf, 1941), x.

"What Ain't I Been Doing?": Historical Reflections on Women and the Arkansas Delta

1. Russell P. Baker, ed., "Edmondson Diaries," pt. 7, *Phillips County Historical Quarterly*, 12 (December 1973): 4.

2. Ibid.

3. Ibid., 3.

4. Ibid.

5. J. E. B. DuBois, ed., *Mortality Statistics of the Seventh Census of the United States, 1850* (Washington: Government Printing Office, 1889).

6. Interview with Lindsey Cox, Memphis, Tennessee, August 14, 1989.

7. Sally G. McMillen, *Motherhood in the Old South* (Baton Rouge: Louisiana State University Press, 1990), 97–99.

8. Marian M. Davis, "Death and Nineteenth Century Arkansas: Frequencies in Causes of Death in Three Arkansas Counties During 1850 and 1880," honors thesis, University of Arkansas, Fayetteville, 1988, 15.

9. McMillen, *Motherhood*, 97–99.

10. Cox interview, August 14, 1989.

11. McMillen, *Motherhood*, 36.

12. Ibid., 95.

13. Interview with Julia Nixon, Gould, Arkansas, March 14, 1989.

14. Sally G. McMillen, "Obstetrics in Ante-bellum Arkansas," submitted to *The History of Medical Associates at the University of Arkansas*, Medical Sciences Library, Little Rock, 3, 19.

15. Davis, "Death and Nineteenth Century Arkansas," 14.

16. Baker, "Edmondson Diaries," pt. 7, 4.

17. "The Diary of Susan Cook," pt. 2, 4 (March 1966), 39; hereafter known as "Cook Diaries."

18. George P. Rawick, *The American Slave: A Composite Autobiography*, VIII, Arkansas Narratives, pt. 1 and 2 (Westport, Conn.: Greenwood Press, 1972), 111.

19. Ibid., 141.

20. Ibid., 193.

21. "The Cotton Correspondence," *Phillips County Historical Quarterly*, 7 (December 1968): 11.

22. "Cook Diaries," 31.

23. Ibid., 34.

24. James M. Hanks, Diary of J. M. Hanks, Mullins Library, University of Arkansas, Fayetteville, Arkansas, (Microfilm) Entries of January 22–27, 1870.

25. Baker, "Edmondson Diaries," pt. 8, *Phillips County Historical Quarterly*, 12 (March 1974): 5.

26. Ibid., pt. 3, *Phillips County Historical Quarterly* 11 (December 1972): 4.

27. Margaret J. Bolsterli, ed., *Vinegar Pie and Chicken Bread: A Woman's Diary of Life in the Rural South, 1890-1891* (Fayetteville: University of Arkansas Press, 1982), 66.

28. Baker, "Edmondson Diaries," pt. 4, *Phillips County Historical Quarterly*, 12 (March 1973): 4.

29. Hanks Diary, January 27, 1870.

30. Bolsterli, *Vinegar Pie*, 61.

31. Ibid., 16.

32. Conevery A. Bolton, "Health and Society in Early Arkansas: 1810-1860," submitted to Susie Pryor Award Committee, Arkansas Women's History Institute.

33. Bolsterli, *Vinegar Pie*.

34. Ibid., 38.

35. Ibid., 30.

36. Ibid., 31–33.

37. Bolton, "Health and Society in Early Arkansas," 72.

38. Rawick, *The American Slave*, VIII, 8.

39. Ibid., 22.

40. Susan Strasser, *Never Done: A History of American Housework* (New York: Pantheon Books, 1982), 104–07.

41. Interview with Anna Mae Nichols, Pine Bluff, Arkansas, March 20, 1989.

42. Rosalie Warren, "A Cookbook," *Phillips County Historical Quarterly* 10 (September 1972): 24.

43. Rawick, *The American Slave*, VIII, 19.

44. Ibid., 21.

45. "The Cotton Correspondence," 5.

46. Ibid., 10.

47. Tommy L. Satterfield, "The Art of Goose Picking Gives Way to Pate De Foie Gras," *Phillips County Historical Quarterly*, 5 (September 1967): 19.

48. Ibid., 20.

49. Bolsterli, *Vinegar Pie*, 17.

50. Baker, "Edmondson Diaries," pt. 1, *Phillips County Historical Quarterly* 10 (June 1972): 6.

51. *Arkansas Federation of Women's Clubs Yearbook 1906-1907* (Forrest City, Ark.: n.p., n.d.), 11; hereafter cited as *AFOWC Yearbook*, with appropriate dates.

52. Elizabeth Jacoway, ed., *Behold, Our Works Were Good* (Little Rock: August House, 1987), 16.

53. University of Arkansas Department of Agricultural Economics and Rural Sociology, Box 7, Series 4, Folder 7, Special Collections, Mullins Library, University of Arkansas, Fayetteville.

54. Mrs. J. A. Knoll, ed., *The White Ribboner* 37 (Stuttgart, Ark., 1942), 5.

55. *AFOWC Yearbook, 1910-1912*, 29.

56. Ibid., 30.

57. Ibid.

58. *AFOWC Yearbook, 1914-1916*.

59. *AFOWC Yearbook, 1906-1907*, 14.

60. Carlos J. R. Smith, "A History of Helena Hospital," *Phillips County Historical Quarterly*, 4 (March, 1966), 3.

61. *AFOWC Yearbook, 1912-1913*, 47.

62. "Cook Diaries," *Phillips County Historical Quarterly* 6 (March 1966), 35.

63. "The McKenzie Letters," *Phillips County Historical Quarterly* 8 (March 1970): 3.

64. Interview with Julia Nixon, March 20, 1989.

65. Interview with Fanny Booker, Lexington, Mississippi, July 18, 1989.

66. Smith, "Helena Hospital," 5.

67. Rawick, *The American Slave*, 8, 22.

Strangers in the Arkansas Delta: Ethnic Groups and Nationalities

1. Jonathan James Wolfe, "Background of German Immigration," *Arkansas Historical Quarterly* 25 (Winter 1966): 354-57.

2. John B. Mitchell, "An Analysis of Arkansas' Population by Race and Nativity and Residence," *Arkansas Historical Quarterly* 8 (Summer 1949): 115-32.

3. United States Census, 1890.

4. Beverly Watkins, "Efforts to Encourage Immigration to Arkansas, 1865-1874," *Arkansas Historical Quarterly* 38 (Spring 1979): 32-62.

5. Robert B. Walz, "Migration into Arkansas 1820-1880: Incentives and Means of Travel," *Arkansas Historical Quarterly* 17 (Winter 1958): 310, 312.

6. Watkins, "Efforts to Encourage Immigration," 32-33.

7. Ibid., 32-62.

8. Shannon Klug Craig, "Arkansas and Foreign Immigration: 1890-1915," M.A. thesis, University of Arkansas, Fayetteville, 1968.

9. Wolfe, "Background of German Immigration to Arkansas," 176-77; see also Robert W. Harrison and Walter M. Kollmorgen, "Land Reclamation in Arkansas

under the Swamp Land Grant of 1850," *Arkansas Historical Quarterly* 6 (Winter 1947): 369–409.

10. "American Take-Over in Arkansas," *Grand Prairie Historical Society Bulletin* 16 (March 1973): 3; see also Louis T. Bogy, "Some Notes on the Bogy Family," *Grand Prairie Historical Society Bulletin* 5 (January 1962): 19–22; Boyd W. Johnson, "Frederick Notrebe," *Grand Prairie Historical Society Bulletin* 5 (April 1962): 26; of interest, too, is the excerpt from Halli Burton's *History of Arkansas County,* reprinted in *Grand Prairie Historical Society Bulletin* 4 (July 1961): 12–18.

11. "Historic Arkansas Post," *Grand Prairie Historical Society Bulletin* 4 (January 1961): 17.

12. Carolyn Gray LeMaster, interview with author, Little Rock, Arkansas, January 8, 1990.

13. Ibid.

14. Hutchins Landfair, "Pack on the Back: Peddlers and the Old Country Store," *Programs of the Desha County Historical Society* (May 1973): 20.

15. LeMaster, interview.

16. E. M. Dreidel, "Temple Meir Chayim: A Century Old Need," *Programs of the 1977 Desha County, Arkansas Historical Society* (Spring 1978): 13–18.

17. Carolyn Gray LeMaster, "Jewish Immigration to Arkansas," *The Arkansas News,* 1987 (published by the Old State House, Little Rock, Ark.).

18. Gerald W. Heaney, "Jacob Trieber: Lawyer, Politician, Judge," *University of Arkansas at Little Rock Law Journal* 8 (1985–1986): 420.

19. Ibid., 432.

20. Ibid., 478.

21. Margaret Ross, "An Irish Catholic's Mission to Arkansas," *Phillips County Historical Quarterly* 4 (September 1966): 25.

22. "Historic Arkansas Post," 17.

23. James Michael Jones, "From Ireland to Snow Lake," *1983 Programs of Desha County Historical Society* 10 (Spring 1984): 2–6.

24. James Millinder Hanks, Diaries, 1870–1891, courtesy of Katherine Stephens Hill, Helena, Arkansas, entries from July 13, 1870, and February 25 and 26, 1891.

25. Jeffrey Lewellen, "'Sheep Amidst the Wolves': Father Bandini and the Colony at Tontitown, 1898–1917," *Arkansas Historical Quarterly* (Spring 1986): 19–40; see also Ed Trice, "Shadows Over Sunnyside," Little Rock, Ark.: Federal Writers' Project typescript, n.d., Arkansas History Commission, Little Rock.

26. Ernesto R. Milani, "Peonage at Sunnyside and the Reaction of the Italian Government," *Arkansas Historical Quarterly* 50 (Spring 1991): 37.

27. Randolph H. Boehm, "Mary Grace Quackenbos and the Federal Campaign Against Peonage: The Case of Sunnyside Plantation," *Arkansas Historical Quarterly* 50 (Spring 1991): 47.

28. Lewellen, "Father Bandini and Tontitown," 19–40.

29. J. M. Lucey, "History of Immigration to Arkansas," in *Publications of the Arkansas Historical Association,* vol. 3, John Hugh Reynolds, ed. (Little Rock, Ark.: Press of Central Printing Company, 1911), 216–18.

30. "U.S. Immigration Commission Report," *Arkansas Gazette,* February 20, 1902.

31. Deidre LaPin, Louis Guida, and Lois Patillo, *Hogs in the Bottom: Family Folklore in Arkansas* (Little Rock, Ark.: August House Publishing Company, 1982), 96.

32. Philip St. Columbia, "Sicilian Migration to Helena, Arkansas," *Phillips County Historical Quarterly* 4 (September 1966): 19–21.

33. Ibid.

34. Ibid.

35. Ibid., 29.

36. Lucey, "Immigration to Arkansas," 216–17.

37. St. Columbia, "Sicilian Migration," 29.

38. LaPin et al. *Hogs in the Bottom*, 94.

39. Trice, "Shadows Over Sunnyside."

40. LaPin et al.

41. "German Emigrants," *Arkansas Gazette*, May 22, 1833.

42. Watt McKinney, "An Interview with a Former Subject of Austro-Hungary," *Phillips County Historical Quarterly* 26 (March 1972): 27; see also "An Early Visit to Stuttgart," *Grand Prairie Historical Society Bulletin* 4 (January 1961): 13.

43. "Soil of Arkansas Territory," *Arkansas Gazette*, May 27, 1820; see also "Early Visit to Stuttgart."

44. Ralph Desmarais and Robert Irving, *The Arkansas Grand Prairie* (Eureka Springs, Ark.: The Ozark Institute, 1983), 33.

45. Bonnie Frownfelter Burkett, interview with author, Stuttgart, Ark., January 31, 1990.

46. Erwin Moehring, "History of Zion Lutheran Church, Ulm, Arkansas," *Grand Prairie Historical Society Bulletin* (January 1959): 1.

47. Ibid., 2.

48. Ibid.

49. Emilie Trede, taped interview with Steven Poyser, September, 1982.

50. Letter of Mrs. F. W. Kerksieck to family, 1969, Stuttgart Public Library Archives, Stuttgart, Ark.

51. Ibid.

52. "As It Was in the Beginning," *Grand Prairie Historical Society Bulletin* 7 (October 1964): 1–6.

53. Louis E. Brister, "The Image of Arkansas in the Early German Emigrant Guidebook: Notes on Immigration," *Arkansas Historical Quarterly* 34 (Winter 1977): 340.

54. Ibid., 343, 344.

55. "Swiss Gentleman Arrives," *Arkansas Gazette*, June 17, 1820.

56. Laura H. Von Kanel, "Swiss Settlers at Hicks and Barton," *Phillips County Historical Quarterly* 11 (December 1972): 9–15.

57. Ibid., 10, 11.

58. Ibid., 13.

59. Ibid., 12; see also McKinney, "Interview with Subject of Austro-Hungary."

60. Von Kanel, "Swiss Settlers," 9–15.

61. Traugott Steiner and Ida Steiner, taped interview with David Rottenstein, Hicks, Ark., Summer, 1987.

62. Ibid.

63. Ibid.

64. Ibid.

65. Von Kanel, "Swiss Settlers," 14.

66. Steiner, interview.

67. Ibid.

68. Clipping files in Stuttgart Public Library Archives.

69. Ibid.

70. Sam Koneceny, interview with author, Slovak, Ark., January 10, 1990.

71. Clipping files in Stuttgart Public Library Archives.

72. Koneceny, interview.

73. Ibid.

74. Ibid.

75. Ibid.

76. Lucey, "Immigration to Arkansas," 217–18.

77. Anthony Moser, "Oysters lure politicos to Slovak," *Arkansas Democrat,* January 28, 1990.

78. Koneceny, interview.

79. Lucey, "Immigration to Arkansas," 218.

80. Shih-Shan Henry Tsai, "The Chinese in Arkansas," *Amerasia* 8 (Summer 1981): 1–18.

81. Ibid., 4.

82. James W. Loewen, *The Mississippi Chinese: Between Black and White,* 2d ed. (Prospect Heights, Ill: Waveland Press, 1988), 23.

83. Tsai, "Chinese in Arkansas," 6.

84. Ibid., 7.

85. Loewen, *Mississippi Chinese,* 27.

86. Mr. and Mrs. Willie Young, interview with author, Helena, Ark., January 17, 1990.

87. Loewen, *Mississippi Chinese,* 67–68.

88. Young, interview.

89. Tsai, "Chinese in Arkansas," 8, 11.

90. Young, interview.

91. Ibid.

92. Ibid.

93. Nicholas R. Spitzer, ed., *Mississippi Delta Ethnographic Overview* (New Orleans, La.: National Park Service, 1979), 344–45.

94. Lucey, "Immigration to Arkansas," 218.

95. Loewen, *Mississippi Chinese,* 12.

96. H. A. Mahfouz, interview with author, Little Rock, Ark., March 5 and 12, 1990.

97. Ibid.

98. Ibid.

99. Ibid.

100. Joseph V. Guillotte III, "Creolization and Ethnicity," in *Louisiana Folklife,* ed. Nicholas R. Spitzer (Baton Rouge: Louisiana Folklife Program, Department of Culture, Recreation, and Tourism, 1985), 67.

Always a Simple Feast: Social Life in the Delta

1. A. Stewart, "An Early Letter from Arkansas Post," *Jefferson County Historical Quarterly* 4 (No. 2, 1976): 29–31.

2. *Pine Bluff Weekly Press,* June 29, 1880.

3. Missouri Pacific Railroad, *Arkansas* (n.p., 1888), 63.

4. Ibid., 64.

5. *Chicot County Spectator*, August 15, 1941.

6. Joe T. Robinson to J. F. McClerkin, November 19, 1933, Joe T. Robinson Papers, series I, subseries 9, Special Collections, University of Arkansas Libraries, Fayetteville.

7. Leila B. Lynch, "Thru the Years in Weiner, Arkansas," *Craighead County Historical Quarterly* 12 (Autumn 1974): 21.

8. Richard Ford, *Piece of My Heart* (New York: Vintage, 1976), 7.

9. John W. Adamson, "A Portrait of Duck Hunting," folklore collection, box 31, file 6.11, Special Collections, University of Arkansas Libraries, Fayetteville.

10. Ibid.

11. Untitled brochure, June 21, 1923, Federal Writers' Project, unprocessed Chicot County file, Arkansas History Commission (AHC).

12. Ernest L. Best, *The Hobo's Trail (Through the Depression)* (Little Rock: Heritage Press, 1988), 40.

13. Archibald MacLeish, "Robinson," Joe T. Robinson Papers, vol. 1, series 1, subseries 9. Special Collections, University of Arkansas, Fayetteville.

14. *Osceola Times*, October 17, 1885.

15. Ibid., August 9, 1890.

16. Jim Balch, "The Story of Richwood Township," *Arkansas Historical Quarterly* 16 (Winter 1957): 379.

17. Becki Taylor, "Sharecropper's Soul Food: A Collection of Recipes from Mississippi County, Arkansas," folklore collection, box 49, folder 6.8, Special Collections, University of Arkansas Libraries, Fayetteville, Arkansas.

18. Ibid., 17.

19. Ibid., 24.

20. *Pulaski County Historical Review* 8 (December 1960): 63.

21. Quoted in Bob Lancaster, *The Jungles of Arkansas: A Personal History of the Wonder State* (Fayetteville: The University of Arkansas Press, 1989), 123.

22. MacLeish, "Robinson," Robinson Papers.

23. James Belsha, "Early Settlers of Barton, Phillips County, Arkansas," *Phillips County Historical Quarterly* 11 (June 1973): 14.

24. Jeanie Hale, "The Negro of Crittenden County," folklore collection, box 34, fold 6.3, Special Collections, University of Arkansas Libraries, Fayetteville.

25. Deirdre LaPin, *Hogs in the Bottom* (Little Rock: August House, 1982), 58.

26. Ibid., 46.

27. Ibid., 56.

28. Lancaster, *Jungles of Arkansas*, 98.

29. Ibid., 99.

30. Luellen Jones, "McGehee in the Old Days," folklore collection, box 10, file 6.66, Special Collections, University of Arkansas Libraries, Fayetteville.

31. Ben Lucien Burnman, *Look Down That Winding River: An Informal Profile of the Mississippi* (New York: Taplinger, 1973), 83.

32. Benjamin A. Botkin, *A Treasury of Mississippi River Folklore* (New York: Crown Publishers, 1955), 457–58.

33. Bobby Roberts and Carl Moneyhon, *Portraits of Conflict* (Fayetteville: University of Arkansas Press, 1987), 147.

34. James M. Hanks diaries, Collection of Katherine Stephens Hill, August 20, 1867, (microfilm) University of Arkansas Libraries, Fayetteville.

35. Robert Johnson, "Preaching Blues," *Robert Johnson: The Complete Recordings* (New York: Columbia Records, 1990).

36. Donald Morson, Frank Reuter, and Wayne Viitanen, "Negro Folk Remedies Collected in Eudora, Arkansas, 1974–1975," *Mid South Folklore* 6 (Spring 1972): 13.

37. Ibid., 19.

38. Lucy Sanders, "Child Life in a Southern Town Eighty Years Ago," *Phillips County Historical Quarterly* 2 (February 1964): 3.

39. Morson, "Negro Folk Remedies," 22.

40. Ibid., 20.

41. Hanks diaries, July 11, 1870.

42. Larry McClendon, "Folk Medicine of Lee County," folklore collection, box 61, folder 6.4, Special Collections, University of Arkansas Libraries, Fayetteville.

43. Balch, "The Story of Richwood Township," 379.

44. Margaret Burnside, "Magnolia Farm," folklore collection, box 10, file 6.36, Special Collections, University of Arkansas Libraries, Fayetteville.

45. Richard Wilson, "Negroes in Mississippi County," folklore collection, box 15, folder 6, Special Collections, University of Arkansas Libraries, Fayetteville.

46. Margaret Jones Bolsterli, ed., *Vinegar Pie and Chicken Bread, A Woman's Diary of Life in the Rural South, 1890–1891* (Fayetteville: University of Arkansas Press, 1982), 51.

47. Ibid., 82.

48. Carolyn Robards Cunningham, "Phillips County Folklore," George E.N. deMan, ed., *Helena: The Ridge, The River, The Romance* (Little Rock: Pioneer Press, 1982), 53.

49. Balch, "The Story of Richwood Township," 380.

50. Lynch, "Thru the Years in Weiner, Arkansas," 22.

51. *Pine Bluff Weekly Press*, July 17, 1879.

52. *Lee County Courier*, May 16, 1891.

53. James M. Hanks diaries, January 28, 1890.

54. Lynch, "Thru the Years in Weiner, Arkansas," 22.

55. *American Guide*, May 30, 1896.

56. Field notes, March 5, 1936, Federal Writers' Project, unprocessed Chicot County file, Arkansas History Commission (AHC).

57. *The Negro Spokesman*, March 14, 1941, 3.

58. *Osceola Times*, August 6, 1892.

59. *Grand Masonic Temple, 112 Years of FreeMasonry, 1872–1984* (n.p., 1984), 10.

60. Federal Writers' Project, field notes, 2.

61. Dale Kirkman, "Early Helena Newspapers," *Phillips County Historical Quarterly* 4 (March 1966): 4.

62. Albert A. Hornor, "One Boys' Helena in the '90s," in *Helena: The Ridge, The River, The Romance*, George DeMan, ed. (Helena, Ark.: Pioneer Publishing Company, 1978), 33.

63. *Newark Journal*, September 1, 1910.

64. *Chicot County Spectator*, June 26, 1936.

65. Jones, "McGehee in the Old Days," 5.

66. *Way Back When*, slide program, Crittenden County Historical Society, 1980, slide 96.

67. Robert Palmer, *Deep Blues* (New York: Penguin, 1981), 175.

68. Best, *Hobo's Trail*, 20.

69. Johnny Cash, *The Man in Black* (Grand Rapids: Zondervan Press, 1975).

70. *The Negro Spokesman*, March 14, 1941, 2.

71. *The Reporter*, February 1, 1900.

72. Samuel Hill, Jr., *Religion and the Solid South* (Nashville: Abingdon Press, 1972).

73. Cunningham, "Phillips County Folklore," 53.

74. *Lee County Courier*, November 4, 1893.

75. Hanks diaries, January 28, 1870.

76. Robert Johnson, "Me and the Devil Blues," *Robert Johnson: The Complete Recordings*.

77. *Osceola Times*, April 29, 1899.

78. Linda L. Slocum, "Customs and Beliefs Surrounding Marriages and Funerals of Negroes in Pine Bluff, Arkansas," folklore collection, box 26, file 6.23, 8, Special Collections, University of Arkansas Libraries, Fayetteville.

79. Ibid., 9.

80. Ibid., 17.

81. Kirkman, "Early Helena Newspapers," 2.

82. Jack Young, "Sports: The Early Years," in *Helena: The Ridge, The River, The Romance*, 109.

83. "As It Was in the Beginning," *Grand Prarie Historical Bulletin* 7 (October 1964): 5.

84. C. Fred Williams et al., eds., *A Documentary History of Arkansas* (Fayetteville: University of Arkansas Press, 1984).

85. James Leslie, "Pine Bluff—1876," *Jefferson County Historical Quarterly* 7 (Number 2, 1977): 27.

86. Palmer, *Deep Blues*, 174.

87. Burman, *Look Down That Winding River*, 147.

88. Hale, "The Negro of Crittenden County," 26.

89. Ibid., 13.

90. Samuel Holbrook, personal interview by Ken Hubbell, July 1989.

91. Best, *The Hobo's Trail*, 33.

92. Ibid., 34.

93. Hi Cross, "Island Thirty-Four," folklore collection, box 10, file 6.41, Special Collections, University of Arkansas Libraries, Fayetteville.

Delta Towns: Their Rise and Decline

1. Dallas T. Herndon, ed., *Annals of Arkansas* (Hopkinsville, Ky.: The Historical Record Association, 1947), 379–80.

2. Mabel West, "Jacksonport, Arkansas: Its Rise and Decline," *Arkansas Historical Quarterly* 9 (Autumn 1950): 244.

3. *Helena World* quoted in Dale P. Kirkman, ed., "Helena in the 1880s," *Phillips County Historical Quarterly* 4 (September 1966): 42 (first quotation), Twain quoted in Ibid., 37; Mrs. J. E. Griner, "Recollections of Early Newport," *Stream of History* 3 (July 1965): 13.

4. Mark Twain, *Life on the Mississippi* (New York: Harper, 1917), 213; Faye Wallis, "I Remember Pine Bluff," *Jefferson County Historical Quarterly* 11 (1983): 11;

George DeMan, *Helena, The Ridge, The River, . . . the Romance* (Little Rock: Pioneer Press, 1978), 36; *Biographical and Historical Memoirs of Southern Arkansas* (Chicago: The Goodspeed Publishing Co., 1890), 1001, hereinafter cited as *Goodspeed's Southern Arkansas*.

5. John Kerr to Dear Uncle, May 25, 1851, Small Manuscripts Collection, Arkansas History Commission, Little Rock (first quotation); Twain, *Life on the Mississippi*, 213 (second quotation); *A Compendium of the Ninth Census (June 1, 1870)* (Washington, D.C.: Government Printing Office, 1872), Table IX.

6. James W. Leslie, "Pine Bluff—1876," *Jefferson County Historical Quarterly* 7 (1977): 21–22; Everett C. Evart, "My Steamboat Days—Circa 1909," *Phillips County Historical Quarterly* 10 (December, 1971): 1–7.

7. Albert A. Hornor, "Some Recollections of Mississippi River Steamboats," *Phillips County Historical Quarterly* 6 (March 1968): 1–6, quotation on 1.

8. *Goodspeed's Southern Arkansas*, 881.

9. Stephen E. Wood, "The Development of Arkansas Railroads," *Arkansas Historical Quarterly* 7 (Autumn 1948): 137–40, 156–93; Herndon, *Annals of Arkansas*, 384–91.

10. *Goodspeed's Southern Arkansas*, 883; *Biographical and Historical Memoirs of Northeast Arkansas* (Chicago: The Goodspeed Publishing Co., 1889), 839, hereinafter cited as *Goodspeed's Northeast Arkansas*.

11. *Goodspeed's Northeast Arkansas*, 315, 572 (quotation).

12. Herndon, *Annals of Arkansas*, 480, 482, 486, 487, 494, 495, 496, 500, 502.

13. For a discussion of changes in the postbellum economy, see Roger L. Ransom and Richard Sutch, *One Kind of Freedom: The Economic Consequence of Emancipation* (Cambridge: Cambridge University Press, 1977), 56–170.

14. *Compendium of the Tenth Census (June 1, 1880)* (Washington, D.C.: Government Printing Office, 1882), Table XLVII.

15. *Goodspeed's Northeast Arkansas*, 453, 572; *Goodspeed's Southern Arkansas*, 1003.

16. Neill Phillips, "What It Was Like: Newport, Arkansas—Not So Long Ago," *Stream of History* 10 (July 1972): 35; 11 (1973): 34; "A Pen and Pencil Sketch of Jackson County and the City of Newport To-day, 1895," *Stream of History*, 5 (October, 1967): 34; Albert A. Hornor, "One Boy's Helena in the Nineties," *Phillips County Historical Quarterly* 15 (December 1976): 16 and (March 1977): 9.

17. James W. Leslie, "Cotton Compresses of Pine Bluff," *Jefferson County Historical Quarterly* 8 (1980): 9–14; "City of Pine Bluff—Descriptive by Arthur A. Murray," *Jefferson County Historical Quarterly* 13 (1985): 17; Dallas T. Herndon, *Centennial History of Arkansas* (Chicago: S. J. Clarke Publishing Company, 1922), 870–908.

18. "City of Pine Bluff—Descriptive," 17; Herndon, *Centennial History of Arkansas*, 870–908.

19. "A Pen and Pencil Sketch of Jackson County and the City of Newport To-day, 1895," *Stream of History* 5 (October 1967): 31; see descriptions of town economies in Herndon, *Centennial History of Arkansas*.

20. Herndon, *Centennial History of Arkansas*, 468–69.

21. Mildred M. Minor, "Early Days of the Lumber Industry in the Jacksonport Area," *Stream of History* 5 (October 1967): 27–30; F. Brooks Henslee, "Harvest of Virgin Timber Brought Wealth," *Jefferson County Historical Quarterly* 9 (1981): 31–34.

22. "City of Pine Bluff—Descriptive by Arthur A. Murray," 6, 9; "A Pen and Pencil Sketch of Jackson County and the City of Newport To-day," 32, 34, 36; *Helena Centennial—1856–1956: Souvenir Program* (n.p., 1956), 56; "An Early History of Pine Bluff," *Jefferson County Historical Quarterly* 1 (1961): 20–21.

23. "City of Pine Bluff—Descriptive by Arthur A. Murray," 4–5; "An Early History of Pine Bluff," 21–23.

24. Phillips, "What It Was Like," *Stream of History* 11 (October 1973): 38; "Business in Helena in 1904," *Phillips County Historical Quarterly* 2 (June 1964): 20–25; see town descriptions in Herndon, *Annals of Arkansas, 1947.*

25. *Goodspeed's Northeast Arkansas*, 315; *Adams Printing Company's Pine Bluff Directory* (Pine Bluff: Adams Printing Co., 1901).

26. Phillips, "What It Was Like," *Stream of History* 11 (February 1973): 36; "An Early History of Pine Bluff," 20–21.

27. Phillips, "What It Was Like," *Stream of History* 11 (February 1973): 34 and 11 (May 1973): 33; *Biographical and Historical Memoirs of Eastern Arkansas* (Chicago: Goodspeed Publishing Company, 1890), 456, hereinafter cited as *Goodspeed's Eastern Arkansas.*

28. *Biographical and Historical Reminiscences of Pulaski, Jefferson, . . . and Hot Springs Counties, Arkansas* (Chicago: Goodspeed Publishing Company, 1889), 798–802, hereinafter cited as *Goodspeed's Central Arkansas; Adams Printing Company's Pine Bluff Directory.*

29. Cheryl Hinck, "Jonesboro Theaters: A Cultural Frontier," *Craighead County Historical Quarterly* 27 (Summer 1989): 10–13 (first quotation); Phillips, "What It Was Like, " *Stream of History* 10 (October 1972): 32 (second quotation); DeMan, *Helena*, 71; Faye Wallis, "I Remember Pine Bluff," 16.

30. "Pine Bluff—1876," 27; *Adams Printing Company's Pine Bluff Directory;* Phillips, "What It Was Like," *Stream of History* 11 (February 1973): 35 (quotation).

31. *Adams Printing Company's Pine Bluff Directory; Goodspeed's Northeast Arkansas,* 315; *Goodspeed's Eastern Arkansas,* 456, 747; *Goodspeed's Central Arkansas,* 137.

32. "An Early History of Pine Bluff," 23; *Adams Printing Company's Pine Bluff Directory.*

33. *A Message to the Homeseeker: Welcome Opportunity—Forrest City, Brinkley, Wynne, Parkin, and Earle, Arkansas* (Forrest City: W .J. Irie, 1939), 1 (quotation); Statistics based on figures in *A Compendium of the Ninth Census (June 1, 1870),* (Washington, D.C.: Government Printing Office, 1872), Table IX; *Compendium of the Tenth Census* (June 1, 1880) (Washington, D.C.: Government Printing Office, 1883), Table XIX; *Abstract of the Twelfth Census of the United States, 1900* (Washington, D.C.: Government Printing Office, 1904), Table 91; *Fifteenth Census of the United States: 1930, Population, Vol. I, Number and Distribution of Inhabitants* (Washington, D.C.: Government Printing Office, 1931), Table 4; *Census of Population: 1950, Vol. II, Characteristics of the Population. Part 4: Arkansas* (Washington, D.C.: Government Printing Office, 1952), Table 6.

34. Statistics based on census material cited above.

35. Boyce House, "A Small Arkansas Town 50 Years Ago," *Arkansas Historical Quarterly* 18 (Autumn 1959): 291 (first quotation); Phillips, "What It Was Like," *Stream of History* 10 (October 1972): 38 (second quotation).

36. Statistics based on data in *Adams Printing Company's Pine Bluff Directory*.

37. Based on biographies in "A Pen and Pencil Sketch of Jackson County and the City of Newport To-day, 1895," *Stream of History* 5 (October 1967): 31–36, 42.

38. Ibid.

39. "City of Pine Bluff—Descriptive," 15 (first quotation); "Marvell, The Best Town of Its Size in Arkansas," *Phillips County Historical Quarterly* 2 (June 1960): 26 (second quotation).

40. "A Pen and Pencil Sketch of Jackson County," 35; "Marvell," 27.

41. "A Pen and Pencil Sketch of Jackson County," 34, 36.

42. Leslie, "Pine Bluff in 1876," 30; see description of towns in the various Goodspeed histories; Ted R. Worley, "Early Days in Osceola," *Arkansas Historical Quarterly* 24 (Summer 1965): 125; DeMan, *Helena*, 115; "City of Pine Bluff—Descriptive by Arthur Murray," 6, 7–8, 14; *Goodspeed's Central Arkansas*, 135; *Goodspeed's Northeast Arkansas*, 315; Phillips, "What It Was Like," *Stream of History* 10 (July 1972): 38; 11 (February 1973), 32; Hornor, "One Boy's Helena in the Nineties," *Phillips County Historical Quarterly* 15 (March 1977): 4–6; Wallis, "I Remember Pine Bluff," 13.

43. "City of Pine Bluff—Descriptive by Arthur Murray," 10 (quotation), 10–11; "Marvell, the Best Town of Its Size in Arkansas," 29.

44. "A Pen and Pencil Sketch of Jackson County and the City of Newport To-Day," 32.

45. "City of Pine Bluff—Descriptive by Arthur Murray," 11 (quotation); "An Early History of Pine Bluff," 18; Charles A. Stuck, *The Story of Craighead County* (Jonesboro, Ark.: C.A. Stuck, 1960), 260; James W. Leslie, *Pine Bluff and Jefferson County, A Pictorial History* (Virginia Beach, Va.: Donning Co., 1981), 47; DeMan, *Helena*, 103–07.

46. For examples of the pride placed in brick and other permanent buildings, see "A Pen and Pencil Sketch of Jackson County and the City of Newport To-Day," 32; *Goodspeed's Northeast Arkansas*, 627–28; "An Early History of Pine Bluff," 20–21.

47. Phillips, "What It Was Like," *Stream of History* 11 (February 1973): 32 (quotation).

48. Phillips, "What It Was Like," *Stream of History* 12 (April 1974): 17; 12 (January 1974): 37; Worley, "Early Days in Osceola," 124; House, "In a Little Town Long Ago," 157; Donald Murray, "Recalling My Days in Jonesboro," *Craighead County Historical Quarterly* 9 (1971): 12.

49. Worley, "Early Days in Osceola," 123.

50. Hornor, "One Boy's Helena in the Nineties," *Phillips County Historical Quarterly* (December 1976): 17.

51. House, "In a Little Town Long Ago," 162; Phillips, "What It Was Like," *Stream of History* 11 (August 1973): 35.

52. Phillips, "What It Was Like," *Stream of History* 11 (February 1973): 30; House, "In a Little Town Long Ago," 161; Hornor, "One Boy's Helena in the Nineties," *Phillips County Historical Quarterly* 15 (December 1976): 20–21; 15 (March 1977): 3, 6–7, 15–17.

53. Phillips, "What It Was Like," *Stream of History* 12 (June 1974): 33; House, "A Small Arkansas Town 50 Years Ago," 291, 292; Hornor, "One Boy's Helena in the Nineties," *Phillips County Historical Quarterly* 15 (March 1977): 12–15.

54. Hornor, "One Boy's Helena in the Nineties," 12–20; Wallis, "I Remember Pine Bluff," 16; Phillips, "What It was Like," *Stream of History* 12 (January 1974): 35–36.

55. Phillips, "What It Was Like," *Stream of History* 11 (February 1973): 29, 35; 11 (May 1973): 31; Hornor, "One Boy's Helena in the Nineties," *Phillips County Historical Quarterly* 15 (March 1977): 7–8; amazingly few reminiscences refer at all to blacks.

56. See *Adams Printing Company's Pine Bluff Directory; Goodspeed's Central Arkansas*, 795–808, provides biographies of some of Pine Bluff's more successful blacks.

57. For examples of schools, clubs, and other connections maintained by blacks, see Pine Bluff biographies in *Goodspeed's Central Arkansas*, 795–808.

58. Almost no documentation exists for this class of people. Sam Boucher, "Memories of Pine Bluff, Arkansas 1913 to 1916," *Jefferson County Historical Quarterly* 13 (1985): 12–13, talks about lives of blue-collar railroad workers living near the tracks in Pine Bluff. Donald Murray, "Recalling My Days in Jonesboro," *Craighead County Historical Quarterly* 9 (Summer 1971): 9, is about the life of the family of a sheet-metal worker.

59. George Ryan, "Pine Bluff a Century Ago," *Jefferson County Historical Quarterly* 5 (1974): 39.

60. Boucher, "Memories of Pine Bluff, Arkansas 1913 to 1916," 14 (first quotation); House, "A Small Arkansas Town 50 Years Ago," 291 (second quotation).

61. Phillips, "What It Was Like," *Stream of History* 11 (February 1973): 34.

62. Hinck, "Jonesboro Theaters," 11; Phillips, "What It Was Like," *Stream of History* 10 (October 1972): 32; Wallis, "I Remember Pine Bluff," 16; DeMan, *Helena*, 71.

63. Phillips, "What It Was Like," *Stream of History* 10 (October 1972): 33.

64. Ibid., 33–34.

65. Hornor, "Recollections of Mississippi River Steamboats," 6.

66. Hornor, "One Boy's Helena in the Nineties," *Phillips County Historical Quarterly* 15 (March 1977): 16–17; Phillips, "What It Was Like," *Stream of History*, 10 (October 1972): 29; House, "In a Little Town Long Ago," 167.

67. House, "A Small Arkansas Town 50 Years Ago," 166.

68. Phillips, "What It Was Like," *Stream of History* 11 (February 1973): 35; DeMan, *Helena*, 122.

69. *Helena Centennial—1856–1956—Souvenir Program*, 45; DeMan, *Helena*, 86; John S. Ezell, *The South Since 1865* (Norman: University of Oklahoma Press, 1975), 438–40, for changes in cotton culture.

70. DeMan, *Helena*, 86, 87; Ezell, *The South Since 1865*, 441–43, for southwide agricultural diversification.

71. Ezell, *The South Since 1865*, 444, discusses changes in timber industry.

72. DeMan, *Helena*, 43.

73. Ibid., 73, 122.

74. Growth rates based upon statistics provided in the census.

75. DeMan, *Helena*, 115–23; Leslie, *Pine Bluff and Jefferson County, A Pictorial History*, 195–205; Stuck, *The Story of Craighead County*.

76. This conclusion is based on declining wealth in rural communities as well as what appears to be changes in the mix of jobs that were available during this period.

77. Phillips, "What It Was Like," *Stream of History* 10 (July 1972): 36.

The Plantation Heritage: Agriculture in the Arkansas Delta

1. See Jay Mandle, *The Roots of Black Poverty: The Southern Plantation Economy after the Civil War* (Durham, N.C.: Duke University Press, 1978).

2. Gerald T. Hanson and Carl H. Moneyhon, *Historical Atlas of Arkansas* (Norman: University of Oklahoma Press, 1989), maps 2–4; Charles Crow, *Arkansas Natural Area Plan* (Little Rock: Arkansas Department of Planning, 1974); Thomas Nelson and Walter Zillgit, *A Forest Atlas of the South* (New Orleans: United States Forest Service, 1969).

3. Hanson and Moneyhon, *Historical Atlas of Arkansas*, maps 32, 37; Robert Walz, "Migration into Arkansas, 1820–1880: Incentives and Means of Travel," *Arkansas Historical Quarterly* 17 (Winter 1959): 309–24.

4. Hanson and Moneyhon, *Historical Atlas of Arkansas*, map 37.

5. Little Rock *Arkansas Gazette*, February 2, 1832.

6. Hanson and Moneyhon, *Historical Atlas of Arkansas*, map 36.

7. Works Projects Administration, *Arkansas: A Guide to the State* (New York: Hastings House, 1941), 58.

8. Thomas Nuttall, *A Journal of Travels into the Arkansas Territory During the Year 1819* (Norman: University of Oklahoma Press, 1980), 79, 84, 103, 112.

9. National Bureau of Economic Research, *Trends in the American Economy in the Nineteenth Century* (Princeton: Princeton University Press, 1960), 97–104.

10. Robert Walz, "Arkansas Slaveholdings and Slaveholders in 1850," *Arkansas Historical Quarterly* 12 (Spring 1953): 38–73.

11. Orville W. Taylor, *Negro Slavery in Arkansas* (Durham, N.C.: Duke University Press, 1958), 92–117.

12. Roger L. Ransom and Richard Sutch, *One Kind of Freedom: The Economic Consequences of Emancipation* (Cambridge: Cambridge University Press, 1977), 2–3. See also Taylor, *Negro Slavery in Arkansas*, 118–30; Robert William Fogel and Stanley L. Engerman, *Time on the Cross: The Economics of American Negro Slavery*, 2 vols. (Boston: Little, Brown, 1974), I, 151–57.

13. Lewis C. Gray, *History of Agriculture in the Southern States to 1860*, 2 vols. (New York: Peter Smith, 1958), 1027.

14. These calculations, based on the data seen in Tables 2 and 3, assume a total production of 171,127 bales produced by 47,608 slaves.

15. Bob Lancaster, *The Jungles of Arkansas: A Personal History of the Wonder State* (Fayetteville: University of Arkansas Press, 1989), 131–40.

16. See Tables 2 and 3.

17. Carl H. Moneyhon, "Economic Democracy in Antebellum Arkansas, 1850–1860," *Arkansas Historical Quarterly* 40 (Summer 1981): 154–72. See also Moneyhon, "The Civil War in Phillips County, Arkansas," *Phillips County Historical Review* 19 (June and September 1981): 18–36.

18. Moneyhon, "Economic Democracy in Antebellum Arkansas, Phillips County, 1850–1860," 161.

19. *Biographical and Historical Memoirs of Southern Arkansas* (Chicago: Goodspeed Publishing Co., 1890), 1065, 1076, 1088; Maude Carmichael, "The Plantation System in Arkansas, 1850–1876," unpublished Ph.D. diss., Radcliffe College, 1935, 89.

20. Leona Sumner Brasher, "Chicot County, Arkansas: Pioneer and Present Times," 55–56, manuscript in Special Collections Department, University of Arkansas Libraries, Fayetteville, Arkansas.

21. Kenneth Story, "A Jewel of the Delta: Lakeport Plantation," *Arkansas Preservation* 9 (Winter 1990): 1, 3.

22. See Willard B. Gatewood, Jr., "Sunnyside: The Evolution of an Arkansas Plantation," *Arkansas Historical Quarterly* 50 (Spring 1991): 7–14.

23. U.S. Census Office, *Ninth Census of the United States: 1870* (Washington: Government Printing Office, 1872), vol. 3, 102.

24. U.S. Department of the Interior, Census Office, *Report on Cotton Production in the United States: Mississippi Valley and Southwestern States* (Washington: Government Printing Office, 1884), pt. 1, 3–4. Compare the figures in Table 2.

25. Ira Berlin, et al., eds., *Freedom: A Documentary History of Emancipation, 1861–1867*, series 1, *The Destruction of Slavery* (Cambridge: Cambridge University Press, 1985), vol. 1, 268, 285–87, 300–01, 308–10.

26. Many contemporary travel accounts described the attitudes of southerners toward freedmen: see Carl Schurz, *Report on the Condition of the South* (New York: Arno Press, 1969), 16–32; J. T. Trowbridge, *The South: A Tour of Its Battlefields and Ruined Cities* (New York: Arno Press, 1969), 362–68. Some Southerners, however, found that free labor was superior to slave labor. See Charles Nordhoff, *The Cotton States in the Spring and Summer of 1875* (New York: D. Appleton, 1876), 36–39.

27. Ransom and Sutch, *One Kind of Freedom*, 46–47.

28. *Arkansas Gazette*, January 15, 1867.

29. For the recent debate over the origins of sharecropping, see Jonathan M. Wiener, "Class Structure and Economic Development in the American South," *American Historical Review* 84 (October 1979): 970–1006; and Harold D. Woodman, "Sequel to Slavery: The New History Views the Postbellum South," *Journal of Southern History* 43 (November 1977): 523–54; Ronald L. F. Davis, *Good and Faithful Labor: From Slavery to Sharecropping in the Natchez District, 1860–1890* (Westport, Conn.: Greenwood Press, 1982); Joseph D. Reed, Jr., "Sharecropping as an Understandable Market Response: The Postbellum South," *Journal of Economic History* 33 (March 1973): 106–30; Ralph Shlomowitz, "The Origins of Southern Sharecropping," *Agricultural History* 53 (July 1979): 557–75; Jonathan M. Wiener, *Social Origins of the New South: Alabama, 1860–1885* (Baton Rouge: Louisiana State University Press, 1978); Michael Wayne, *The Reshaping of Plantation Society: The Natchez District, 1860–1880* (Baton Rouge: Louisiana State University Press, 1983).

30. Davis, *Good and Faithful Labor*, 6–12.

31. These contracts are found in Records of the Assistant Commissioner for the State of Arkansas, Bureau of Refugees, Freedmen, and Abandoned Lands, 1865–1869, Record Group (hereafter referred to as RG) 105, National Archives Microfilm Publication M-979, reels 35–43.

32. John Eaton, Circular to Superintendents and Provost Marshals of Freedmen, May 34, 1865, printed in *Arkansas Gazette*, June 10, 1865; Charles H. Smith Report, January 1868, Synopses of Letters and Reports Relating to Conditions of Freedmen and Bureau Activities in the States, vol. 136, RG 105, National Archives; James T. Watson to J. W. Sprague, September 30, 1866, Annual Reports of the Assistant Commissioners, box 1, RG 105.

33. Charles H. Smith Report, January 1868, Synopses of Letters and Reports Relating to Conditions of Freedmen and Bureau Activities in the States, vol. 136, RG 105.

34. Ransom and Sutch, *One Kind of Freedom*, 56–63; Davis, *Good and Faithful Labor*, 174–84.

35. "Arkansas! The Home for Immigrants," Little Rock, October 1865, pamphlet in Arkansas History Commission, Little Rock, Arkansas. See Beverly Watkins, "Efforts to Encourage Immigration to Arkansas, 1865–1874," *Arkansas Historical Quarterly* 38 (Spring 1979): 44–45.

36. Powell Clayton, *The Aftermath of the Civil War in Arkansas* (New York: Negro Universities Press, 1969), 208.

37. Jonathan James Wolfe, "Background of German Immigration," pt. 1–3, *Arkansas Historical Quarterly* 25 (Spring, Summer, Autumn, 1966): 151–82, 248–78, 354–86.

38. The possibility of importing Chinese labor can be followed in numerous issues of the *Arkansas Gazette*: June 16, 17, 30, July 7, 8, 14, 22, 1869. See also Shih-Shan Henry Tsai, "The Chinese in Arkansas," *Amerasia Journal* 8 (1981): 1–18.

39. Beverly Watkins, "The Chinese Labor Question, 1869–1870," *Pulaski County Historical Review* 30 (Fall 1982): 59–62; Manuscript Population Schedules, Chicot County, Arkansas, 1880.

40. Act 122, March 8, 1867, *Acts of the General Assembly of the State of Arkansas* (Little Rock: Woodruff and Blocker, 1867), 298–300. See also Act 13, December 20, 1866, 52, and Act 35, February 6, 1867, 98–100, in the same work.

41. Act 67, July 23, 1868, *Acts of the General Assembly of the State of Arkansas* (Little Rock: John G. Price, 1868), 245; *Arkansas Gazette*, August 4, 1868; Act 29, January 8, 1875, *Acts of the General Assembly of the State of Arkansas* (Little Rock: William E. Woodruff, Jr., 1875), 84–85. See also *Arkansas Statutes 1947* (Indianapolis: Bobbs-Merrill, 1971), vol. 5, section 51–201; Harold D. Woodman, "Post–Civil War Southern Agriculture and the Law," *Agricultural History* 53 (January 1979): 319–37; Robert A. Leflar, "Labor Legislation in Arkansas," in David Y. Thomas, ed., *Arkansas and Its People: A History, 1541–1930*, 4 vols. (New York: American Historical Society, 1930), vol. 1, 346–54; Allen Hughes, *Arkansas Mortgages* (St. Louis: Thomas Law Books, 1930).

42. Woodman, "Post–Civil War Southern Agriculture and the Law," 234–325.

43. Mark Twain, *Mississippi Writings* (New York: Literary Classics, 1982), 438.

44. U.S. Department of the Interior, Census Office, *Report on Cotton Production in the United States: Mississippi Valley and Southwestern States* (Washington: Government Printing Office, 1884).

45. Ibid., pt. 1, 105.

46. See William Cohen, *At Freedom's Edge: Black Mobility and the Southern White*

Quest for Racial Control, 1861–1915 (Baton Rouge: Louisiana State University Press, 1991); Pete Daniel, *The Shadow of Slavery: Peonage in the South, 1901–1960* (Lexington: University Press of Kentucky, 1978).

47. William F. Holmes, "The Arkansas Cotton Pickers Strike of 1891 and the Demise of the Colored Farmer's Alliance," *Arkansas Historical Quarterly* 32 (Summer 1973): 107–19.

48. Walter White, *Rope and Faggot: A Biography of Judge Lynch* (New York: Arno Press, 1969), 254; *World Almanac and Book of Facts for 1927* (New York: New York World, 1927), 322. A recent study that links racial violence and migration is Stewart E. Tolnay and E. M. Beck, "Racial Violence and Black Migration in the American South, 1910–1930," *American Sociological Review* 57 (February 1992): 103–16.

49. See Richard C. Cortner, *A Mob Intent on Death: The NAACP and the Arkansas Riot Cases* (Middletown, Conn.: Wesleyan University Press).

50. Gilbert C. Fite, "Southern Agriculture Since the Civil War: An Overview," *Agricultural History* 53 (January 1979): 3–21.

51. Hanson and Moneyhon, *Historical Atlas of Arkansas*, map 51.

52. Robert W. Harrison, *Alluvial Empire: A Study of State and Local Efforts Toward Land Development in the Alluvial Valley of the Lower Mississippi River*, vol. 1 (Little Rock: Pioneer Press, 1961), 71, 84.

53. Ibid., 192–193.

54. S. E. Simonson, "Origin of Drainage Projects in Mississippi County," *Arkansas Historical Quarterly* 5 (Fall 1946): 263–73; and "The St. Francis Levee and High Waters on the Mississippi River," *Arkansas Historical Quarterly* 6 (Winter 1947): 419–29.

55. Harrison, *Alluvial Empire*, 194–95.

56. Ibid.

57. Ibid.

58. Ibid., 305. See also Pamela Webb, "By the Sweat of the Brow: The Back-to-the-Land Movement in Depression Arkansas," *Arkansas Historical Quarterly* 42 (Winter 1983): 332–45. For contemporary views, see John Bird, "Delta Land Rush," *Country Gentlemen* (August 1941): 10–36; and Raymond C. Smith, "The Delta: A National Problem," *Land Policy Review* (March 1941): 22–25.

59. Harrison, *Alluvial Empire*, 307, 310–13.

60. Gavin Wright, *Old South, New South: Revolutions in the Southern Economy Since the Civil War* (New York: Basic Books, 1986), 115–23.

61. [Nannie Stillwell Jackson], *Vinegar Pie and Chicken Bread: A Woman's Diary of Life in the Rural South, 1890–1891*, ed. Margaret Jones Bolsterli (Fayetteville: University of Arkansas Press, 1982).

62. Henry C. Dethloff, *A History of the American Rice Industry, 1685–1985* (College Station: Texas A&M University Press, 1988), 83–87.

63. Simon Kuznets and Dorothy Swaine Thomas, *Population Redistribution and Economic Growth, United States, 1870–1950*, vol. 1, *Methodological Considerations and Reference Tables* (Philadelphia: American Philosophical Society, 1957), 86, 112–14; Cohen, *At Freedom's Edge*, 295–296.

64. See Table 8.

65. Pamela Webb, "By the Sweat of the Brow: The Back-to-the-Land Movement in Depression Arkansas," *Arkansas Historical Quarterly* 42 (Winter 1983): 332–45.

66. James W. Leslie, *Saracen's Country* (Little Rock: Rose Publishing Co., 1974), 30–38; Pete Daniel, *Deep'n As It Come: The 1927 Mississippi River Flood* (New York: Oxford University Press, 1977), 9–10.

67. Frederick Simpich, "The Great Mississippi Flood of 1927," *National Geographic Magazine* 52 (September 1927): 256.

68. John H. Johnson, *Succeeding Against the Odds* (New York: Warner Books, 1989), 27–28.

69. "Arkansas' Fight for Life," *Literary Digest* 108 (February 28, 1931): 5–6.

70. "Drought: Field Reports from Five of the States Most Seriously Affected," *New Republic* 66 (February 25, 1931): 40.

71. Nan Elizabeth Woodruff, *As Rare as Rain: Federal Relief in the Great Southern Drought of 1930–31* (Urbana: University of Illinois Press, 1985), 100–02. See *Arkansas Gazette*, January 31, 1931.

72. Daniel, *Deep'n As It Come*, 106–07.

73. Woodruff, *As Rare As Rain*, 112–16.

74. U.S. Bureau of the Census, *Historical Statistics of the United States: Colonial Times to 1970* (Washington: Government Printing Office, 1976), 517, reported a carry-over of 9.7 million bales in 1932 as opposed to the production of 13 million bales.

75. Charles S. Johnson, Edwin R. Embree, and W. W. Alexander, *The Collapse of Cotton Tenancy: Summary of Field Studies and Statistical Surveys, 1933–35* (Chapel Hill: University of North Carolina Press, 1935); Robert E. Snyder, *Cotton Crisis* (Chapel Hill: University of North Carolina Press, 1984).

76. Van L. Perkins, *Crisis in Agriculture: The Agricultural Adjustment Administration and the New Deal, 1933* (Berkeley and Los Angeles: University of California Press, 1969), 103–09; Lucy Wilmans, "The AAA and the Arkansas Cotton Farmer," unpublished seminar thesis, no. 25, University of Arkansas School of Business, 1935; *Arkansas Gazette*, July 28, 1933.

77. H. L. Mitchell, *Mean Things Happening in This Land: The Life and Times of H. L. Mitchell, Co-Founder of the Southern Tenant Farmer's Union* (Montclair, N.J.: Allanheld, Osmun, 1979).

78. Howard Kester, *Revolt among the Sharecroppers* (New York: Arno Press and the New York Times, 1969), 56.

79. The best history of the union is Donald H. Grubbs, *Cry from the Cotton: The Southern Tenant Farmers' Union and the New Deal* (Chapel Hill: University of North Carolina Press, 1971). See also George Brown Tindall, *The Emergence of the New South, 1913–1945* (Baton Rouge: Louisiana State University Press, 1967), 417–21.

80. T. J. Woofter, *Landlord and Tenant on the Cotton Plantation* (New York: Negro Universities Press, 1969). This study, originally published in 1936 by the WPA, illustrated the scholarly tone of the work on tenancy.

81. Donald Holley, *Uncle Sam's Farmers: The New Deal Communities in the Lower Mississippi Valley* (Urbana: University of Illinois Press, 1975).

82. Ibid., 34–51.

83. Ibid., 105–21.

84. Works Projects Administration, *Arkansas*, 65.

85. Holley, *Uncle Sam's Farmers*, 274–78, 284–85.

86. U.S. Bureau of the Census, *Fifteenth Census of the United States: 1930, Agriculture* (Washington: Government Printing Office, 1932), vol. 2, 1134.

87. Gilbert C. Fite, "Southern Agriculture Since the Civil War: An Overview," *Agricultural History,* 53 (January 1979): 15–16.

88. See Table 8.

89. Johnson, Embree, and Alexander, *The Collapse of Cotton Tenancy,* 2, 64. For another view, see Donald Crichton Alexander, *The Arkansas Plantation, 1920–1942* (New Haven: Yale University Press, 1943).

88. Ibid., 113–14.

89. See Table 8.

90. See Table 8. The change in the state's farm population was calculated from data in Bureau of the Census, *Historical Statistics of the United States,* 458.

91. U.S. Department of Agriculture, *Statistics on Cotton and Related Data, 1920–1956* (Washington: Agricultural Marketing Service, 1957), 68, 48.

92. Nan Elizabeth Woodruff, "Pick or Fight: The Emergency Farm Labor Program in the Arkansas and Mississippi Deltas During World War II," *Agricultural History* 64 (Spring 1990): 74–85.

93. See Robert C. Williams, *Fordson, Farmall, and Poppin' Johnny: A History of the Farm Tractor and Its Impact on America* (Urbana: University of Illinois Press, 1987).

94. James H. Street, *The New Revolution in the Cotton Economy: Mechanization and Its Consequences* (Chapel Hill: University of North Carolina Press, 1957) is the basic study of the mechanization of cotton. See also C. R. Hagan, "Twenty-five Years of Cotton Picker Development," *Agricultural Engineering* 32 (November 1951): 593–96, 599.

95. John Rust, "The Origin and Development of the Cotton Picker," *West Tennessee Historical Society Papers* 7 (1953): 38–56; Tom Honeycutt, "The Second Great Emancipator: Eccentric Inventor John Rust Changed the Face of Modern Agriculture," *Arkansas Times* 11 (February 1985): 76–82.

96. Wayne D. Rasmussen, "The Mechanization of Agriculture," *Scientific American* 247 (September 1982): 77–89; Hagen, "Twenty-five Years of Cotton Picker Development," 593–596, 599; R. Douglas Hurt, "Cotton Pickers and Strippers," *Journal of the West* 30 (April 1991): 30–42.

97. B. O. Williams, "The Impact of Mechanization on the Farm Population of the South," *Rural Sociology* 4 (September 1939): 300–14; C. Horace Hamilton, "The Social Effects of Recent Trends in the Mechanization of Agriculture," *Rural Sociology* 4 (March 1939): 3–25; Dero A. Saunders, "Revolution in the Deep South," *Nation* 145 (September 11, 1937): 264–66.

98. Oliver Carlson, "The Revolution in Cotton," *American Mercury* 34 (February 1935): 129–36. This article—reprinted in *Reader's Digest* 26 (March 1935): 13–16— first brought national attention to the Rust brothers.

99. Quoted in Jonathan Daniels, *A Southerner Discovers the South* (New York: Da Capo Press, 1970), 166–67.

100. Merrill R. Pritchett and William L. Shea, "The Afrika Korps in Arkansas, 1943–1946," *Arkansas Historical Quarterly* 37 (Spring 1978): 16–18; Wayne D. Rasmussen, *A History of the Farm Labor Supply Program, 1943–1947* (Washington: USDA Monograph No. 13, 1951).

101. Wright, *Old South, New South*, 241–49; U.S. Department of Agriculture, Economic Research Service, *Statistics on Cotton and Related Data, 1920–1973* (Washington: Government Printing Office, 1974), 218; *Arkansas Gazette*, May 19, 1977.

102. This information was provided by Steve Frizzell, Star City, Arkansas.

103. Noah D. Holmes, "No Help Needed," *Progressive Farmer* (October 1953): 21, 162; "'Keeping Up' is What It Takes to Keep Ahead," *Arkansas Union Farmer* (October 1960): 4, 5.

104. Noah D. Holmes, "'Keeping up' is What It Takes to Keep Ahead," *Arkansas Union Farmer* (October 1960): 4, 5.

105. Paul H. Williams, "The Rise and Fall of the Great Plantations," *Arkansas Times* 9 (July 1983): 87; *Arkansas Gazette*, April 23, 1990.

106. For overviews of post–World War II developments, see Gilbert C. Fite, *Cotton Fields No More: Southern Agriculture, 1865–1980* (Lexington: University of Kentucky Press, 1984); Pete Daniel, *Breaking the Land: The Transformation of Cotton, Tobacco, and Rice Cultures since 1880* (Urbana: University of Illinois Press, 1985); Jack Temple Kirby, *Rural Worlds Lost: The American South, 1920–1960* (Baton Rouge: Louisiana State University Press, 1987).

Index

Bordwell, Henry, 223
Bragg, Junius, 91
Brinkley, Ark., 177, 178, 179, 196, 213, 220, 226, 229, 230
Britt, Michael, 158
Brough, Charles, 113
Brown Decision, 13
Brown, T. Ralph, 200
Buerkle, George Adam, 165
Bush, John E., 116, 117
Byrne, Andrew, 157

Cabell, William, 87
Cache River, 34, 35, 43, 44, 187, 259
Caddo Indians, 63
Camden, Ark., 154
Capital Savings Bank, 118
Carlisle, Ark., 166, 190
Carlton, C. H., 72–73
Carette, Father, 66
Carondolet, Governor, 62
Cash, Johnny, 197–98
Catholics, 11, 66, 156, 157, 159, 172, 224
Cattle, 232–33
Centennial Baptist Church, 15
Chase, Lewis, 102
Chandler, Ella, 138
Chickasaw Indians, 58, 60
Chicot County, 13, 15, 17, 102, 104, 106, 107, 159, 162, 186, 192, 196, 197, 244–45, 249, 257, 259
Chinese: in the Arkansas Delta, 8, 152, 173–77, 249, 252
Civil Rights Act (1873), 110–11
Civil War: in the Arkansas Delta, 72–88; mentioned, 4, 9, 16, 245–46, 251
Clarendon, Ark., 78, 79, 217, 225
Class Structure, 10, 12, 14, 18, 22, 23, 71, 119, 120, 121, 144, 222–23, 228–29
Clay County, 185
Clayton, Powell, 104, 105, 107, 173–74, 249
Cleburne, Patrick R., 73
Cleveland, B. D., 108
Code Noir, 99–100
Coles, Robert, 25
Colored Industrial Institute, 224
Colored Knights of Pythias, 116
Colored Methodist Episcopal Church, 114
Colored State Fair, 117

Columbia, Ark., 209, 210
Commission on Immigration and State Lands, 249
Common School Law (1842), 13
The Confederate Veteran, 92
Conway, Ark., 132
Conway family, 19
Cook, Samuel, 222
Cook, Susan, 132, 133, 146
Cook, V. Y., 221
Coolidge, H. P., 76
Corbin, Austin, 159–60
Corbin, Joseph C., 103–04
Corning, Ark., 213, 217
Cotten, Fannie, 141–42
Cotton: cultivation of, 4, 14, 15, 20, 21, 22–24, 47, 71, 80, 81, 89, 154, 212, 213, 214–15, 238–71 *passim*
Cotton Belt Railroad, 212, 217
Cotton Plant, Ark., 212
Couture, Jean, 59
Craighead County, 212, 219
Crittenden County, 189, 252
Crossett, Ark., 20
Crowley's Ridge, 32, 33, 34, 40, 41–42, 43, 47
Cumings, Fortescue, 240
Curran, Thomas, 158
Curtis, Samuel R., 74, 75–76, 246

Daniel, Pete, 38–39, 49
Dante, Charles, 155, 156
Davidson, Frank, 230
Davis, C. W., 88
Davis, Jefferson, 72
Dawson, S. W., 107
Dean, Cornelius, 216
Democratic Party, 19, 90, 104, 105–06, 107, 108, 109, 110, 117, 250
Dermott, Ark., 175, 196, 213
Des Arc, Ark., 44, 79, 209
Desha, Benjamin, 153, 154, 158
Desha County, 107, 155, 156, 158, 190, 213, 256, 257
De Soto, Hernando, 37
De Valls Bluff, Ark., 75, 78, 86, 103, 131, 209
Dilworth, Carrie, 146
Disease, 6, 77–78, 129–31, 184, 191–93, 199
Dobbin, Archibald, 88
Donation Law (1840), 151

201, 209, 210, 211, 212, 216, 217, 223, 226, 230, 244
Helena Hospital Association, 145
Helena World, 20
Henderson, J. E., 117
Hicks, Ark., 167
Hilgard, Eugene W., 251–52
Hilliard, Mrs. Issac, 7
Hindman, Thomas C., 72, 73, 74
Hodges v. United States, 157
Holly Grove, Ark., 139, 175
Holmes, Theophilus, 82–83, 84, 85
Hookworm, 6
Hope, Ark., 92
Hornbuckle, John, 193
Hornbuckle, Sam, 135
Hornor, Albert A., 226
Hornor, S. H., 226, 227
Hotels, 218
Howe, S. E., 216
Hungarians, 170
Huntersville, Ark., 86
Hunting, 10–11

Independence County, 196
Indian Bay, Ark., 142
Indians, 4, 58, 60, 61, 63, 64
Industries: in the Arkansas Delta, 21, 22, 215–18, 234
Inebnit, Fred, 167
Inebnit, Rudolph, 167
Ingram, Rosa, 132
International Harvester Company, 267
Interstate Highway System, 233
Irish: in the Arkansas Delta, 157–58
Irving, Washington, 154
Italians: in the Arkansas Delta, 8, 152, 159–62

Jabine, Lila, 92
Jackson, Nannie Stillwell, 135, 136–37, 138, 193–94, 257
Jackson, William T., 257
Jackson County, 187, 192, 194, 221
Jacksonport, Ark., 84, 88, 156, 209, 212, 221, 222
Japanese Americans, 268
Jefferson County, 103, 106, 107, 112, 117, 185, 216. *See also* Pine Bluff, Ark.
Jews: in the Arkansas Delta, 153, 154–57, 168, 169, 224, 226

Jim Crow, 17, 99, 105, 114, 119–20. *See also* Segregation
Jockey Club, 200
John Deere Company, 267, 271
Johnson, Andrew, 91
Johnson, Cyrus, 244–45
Johnson, H. A., 107
Johnson, John H., 260
Johnson, Joel, 244
Johnson, Lycurgus, 244–45
Johnson, Nettie Hollis, 117
Johnson, R. T., 117, 222
Johnson, Robert, 191, 199
Johnson family, 19, 244–45
Johnston, Joseph E., 84
Jones, J. Pennoyer, 107
Jones, Wiley, 117–18, 219, 228
Jonesboro, Ark., 33, 43, 154, 195, 212–13, 216, 218, 219, 220, 225–26
Jonesboro Times, 219
Joyce, W. A., 221

Kate Adams (boat), 211
Keatts, Chester W., 116
Kelly, C. B., 216
Kelly, Jewel, 230
Kerksieck, Augusta K., 164
Kerksieck, Henrich, 164
Knights of Columbus, 173
Knights of Tabor, 116
Koneceny, Sam, 171
Krow's General Store, 214
Ku Klux Klan, 18, 156

La Grange, Ark., 198
La Salle, René-Robert Chavelier de, 58
Laconia, Ark., 158
Ladies' Aid Society, 7
Lake Chicot, 39, 87, 185
Lake Village, Ark., 73, 90, 177, 178, 179, 185, 196, 202, 244
Lakeport Plantation, 244–45
Lambe, Katherine, 158
Landfair, Hutchins, 155
L'Anguille River, 34, 44, 185, 244
Law, John, 59, 62
Lebanese: in the Arkansas Delta, 153, 177–78
Lee, Robert E., 82
Lee County, 115, 192, 194, 198, 252
LeMaster, Carolyn Gray, 154–55, 156

Slovaks: in the Arkansas Delta, 8, 170–73
Smith, E. Kirby, 84
Smith J. H., 117
Smithee, Nellie, 138
Snow Lake, Ark., 158–59
Social and Art Club, 119
Sons of the Agricultural Star, 107
Soto, Hernando de, 37
Southern Mercantile Company, 118
Southern Review, 219
Southern Shield, 196
Southern Tenant Farmers' Union, 7, 22, 46, 262–63
Southland College, 115
Southwest Improvement Company, 213
Sperry, A. F., 79
Soybeans: cultivation of, 4, 24, 232
Stanley, Henry M., 72
Steele, Frederick, 85
Steiner, Ida, 167, 169–70
Steiner, Traugott, 167–68
Stevens, Thomas N., 85
Still, William Grant, 119
Stillwell, Leander 77
Streeter, A. J., 108
Stuttgart, Ark., 144, 165, 166, 170, 177, 179, 185
Sulphur Rock, Ark., 196
Sunk lands, 42
Sunnyside Plantation, 159–60
Sunnyside School, 262
Sunshine Charity Club, 119
Swamp Lands Acts, 254
Swamps, 24, 151, 153, 255–56
Swiss: in the Arkansas Delta, 8, 152, 166–70
Syrians: in the Arkansas Delta, 152, 153, 177–79

Taylor, J. M., 188
Terrell, Mary Church, 118
Thane, Henry, 255–56
Thomas, Lorenzo, 81
Thompson, M. Jeff, 88
Tillar, Ark., 144
Timber, *See* Forests
Tonty, Henry de, 4, 58, 59
Totten, James, 70
Towns: in the Arkansas Delta, 5, 20, 43, 208–35
Tractors, 3, 266

Treat, John, 45
Trede, Mrs. Emilie, 164
Trenton, Ark., 214
Trice, Edward, 162
Trieber, Jacob, 157
Tull, Ark., 166
Turner, Moses G., 117
Turrell, Ark., 175
Tuscaloosa, Ala., 32
Twain, Mark, 31, 209, 210, 251
Tyler (gunboat), 85
Tyronza, Ark., 262

Ulm, Ark., 164–65
Union County, 89
Union Labor Party, 108, 109, 110
United Confederate Veterans, 92, 93
United Daughters of the Confederacy, 92, 93
United States Corps of Engineers, 254
United States v. Morris, 157
Unity Bank and Trust Company, 118, 219

Vaudeville, 230–31
Vicksburg, Miss., 33, 76, 82, 83, 85
Violence, 5, 9, 11, 112–13

Waldheim, Ark., 167
Wallace, John W., 221
Walnut Ridge, Ark., 197
Washington, Booker T., 114, 116, 119
Washington, Margaret M., 118
Waterman, Gus, 156
Watson, Susan, 138
"We Walk," 112
Weatherby, Mrs. Sam, 133
Weekly Pilot, 219
Weiner, Ark., 185, 194, 195
West Memphis, Ark., 60, 202
Westliche Post, 165
Wheatley, Ark., 141
White River, 3, 14, 30, 31, 34, 40, 44, 46, 64, 75, 78, 80, 84, 86, 212, 214, 216, 239, 246, 260
White River "Monster," 37
White Ribboner, 144
Whitecapping, 9
Wilburn, Betty, 134
Wildlife, 8, 34, 35, 36, 38, 39, 44, 184, 185, 186, 187–88
Williams, Ike, 202, 203

Wilson, Ark., 263
Wittsburg, Ark., 88
Wolfe, Jonathan, 150
Wolff-Goldman Company, 214
Women: in the Arkansas Delta, 6–8,
    128–47; organizations of, 7, 12,
    118–19, 144–46, 195, 196; and dis-
    ease, 6, 129–33; work of, 7, 139–43;
    and death, 134–35; and suffrage,
    145–46; mentioned, 227–28
Women's Christian Temperance Union,
    12, 144, 195

Woodruff County, 213
World War II, 22, 253, 256, 265, 266,
    268, 269
Worthington, Elisha, 245–46
Wright, John C., 89–90
Wynne, Ark., 13, 43, 229

Yazoo Pass Expedition, 83
Yazoo River, 30
Yoder, Jacob, 170
Young, Willie, 176–77